THE ROI
FIELDBOOK

IMPROVING HUMAN PERFORMANCE SERIES

Series Editor: Jack J. Phillips, PhD

LATEST BOOKS IN THE SERIES:
The ROI Fieldbook
Patricia Pulliam Phillips, Jack J. Phillips, Ron Drew Stone, and Holly Burkett
Coaching That Counts
Dianna Anderson and Merrill Anderson
Performance Through Learning
Carol Gorelick, Nick Milton, and Kurt April
The Leadership Scorecard
Jack J. Phillips and Lynn Schmidt
Bottom-Line Call Center Management
David L. Butler
Bottom-Line Organization Development
Merrill Anderson
The Diversity Scorecard
Edward E. Hubbard
Handbook of Training Evaluation and Measurement Methods, 3rd Edition
Jack J. Phillips
The Human Resources Scorecard
Jack J. Phillips, Patricia Pulliam Phillips, and Ron Drew Stone
Managing Employee Retention
Jack J. Phillips and Adele O. Connell
The Project Management Scorecard
Jack J. Phillips, G. Lynne Snead, and Timothy W. Bothell
Return on Investment in Training and Performance Improvement Programs, 2nd Edition
Jack J. Phillips

Visit http://books.elsevier.com/humanresources to see the full range of books available in the series.

THE ROI FIELDBOOK: STRATEGIES FOR IMPLEMENTING ROI IN HR AND TRAINING

Patricia Pulliam Phillips, PhD
Jack J. Phillips, PhD
Ron Drew Stone
Holly Burkett

AMSTERDAM • BOSTON • HEIDELBERG • LONDON
NEW YORK • OXFORD • PARIS • SAN DIEGO
SAN FRANCISCO • SINGAPORE • SYDNEY • TOKYO
Butterworth-Heinemann is an imprint of Elsevier

Butterworth-Heinemann is an imprint of Elsevier
30 Corporate Drive, Suite 400, Burlington, MA 01803, USA
Linacre House, Jordan Hill, Oxford OX2 8DP, UK

♾ Recognizing the importance of preserving what has been written, Elsevier prints its books on
acid-free paper whenever possible.

Library of Congress Cataloging-in-Publication Data
Application submitted

British Library Cataloguing-in-Publication Data
A catalogue record for this book is available from the British Library.

ISBN-13: 978-0-7506-7622-9
ISBN-10: 0-7506-7622-1

For information on all Elsevier Butterworth–Heinemann publications
visit our Web site at www.books.elsevier.com

Printed in the United States of America
06 07 08 09 10 11   10 9 8 7 6 5 4 3 2 1

CONTENTS

ACKNOWLEDGMENTS

From Ron Drew Stone

Thanks to the many people around the world who have participated in ROI workshops and certification programs and to the clients who have engaged our consulting services in needs assessment, measurement, and accountability practices. This fieldbook includes our latest refinements of the ROI Methodology, many of which reflect your challenges to us as well as your contributions. It represents our most comprehensive resource to help you to complete your measurement projects and to sustain momentum as you blend measurement practices into the processes of your organization. I encourage you to use it not only as a learning tool but also as a teaching tool for others. I wish you continued success as you champion assessment, measurement, and accountability initiatives in your organization.

From Holly Burkett

I can't describe the many ways in which learning and practicing the ROI Methodology has transformed my career path, electrified my commitment to the field, and enriched my network of professional support. Many thanks to my mentors, Jack, Patti, and Ron, for their enduring support and for the invaluable privilege of being able to contribute my experiences and lessons learned to this endeavor. Thanks to the diverse array of clients who have graciously allowed me to learn with them and from them. I also want to recognize friends, colleagues, and cheerleaders from the ASTD ROI Network, who continue to inspire, challenge, and humble me by modeling what it means to be "best in class." Implementing the ROI process has fueled my thirst for continual learning and development, has helped me show how my work matters, has inexplicably nurtured my spirit along the way, and has continued to leave me hungry for more. May it do the same for you in your own journey.

PREFACE

Current trends emphasizing the value and payoff of workplace learning efforts may lead one to ask, "Okay, there is a lot of interest in ROI. We're interested too. But how do we *do* ROI?" Good question. Few organizations go beyond the classroom to measure learning or use evaluation to assess how learning is applied back to the workplace. This *ROI Fieldbook* is designed to support the implementation of the ROI Methodology. Beginning with an overview of the ROI Methodology, this book will take you step by step through each phase of the ROI process. The exercises, case scenarios, case study, and tools and templates will help you apply the ROI Methodology to a case study of your own.

HOW THIS BOOK IS ORGANIZED

As shown in the chapter flow diagram, the book is organized into four primary parts, each representing a distinct phase of ROI implementation. For example, Part 1, "Getting Started," emphasizes organizational readiness issues, strategies, and tools, and shows fieldbook users how to get started with the process. Part 2, "Implementing the Process," emphasizes important areas of action around ROI implementation from start to finish. Part 3, "Implementation Issues," focuses on common implementation issues that can help or hurt your implementation efforts and provides strategies for building evaluation capability in your organization. Finally, Part 4, "Staying on Track," describes how to sustain commitment to the ROI Methodology after the momentum of your initial impact study has begun to wane.

Preface
Trends and Issues

PART ONE

Getting Started

Chapter 1	Chapter 2
Status of ROI: Trends and Issues	Planning Your Work

Chapter 1 — Tools, Job Aids
- ☐ ROI Model
- ☐ Five Level Framework
- ☐ ROI Best Practices
- ☐ Guiding Principles
- ☐ Example of Evaluation Targets

Chapter 2 — Tools, Job Aids
- ☐ Linking Needs to Objectives and Evaluation (Reliance Insurance example)
- ☐ Linking Needs to Objectives and Evaluation
- ☐ Data Collection Plan (blank)
- ☐ ROI Analysis Plan (blank)
- ☐ Communication Plan (blank)
- ☐ Project Plan (blank)
- ☐ Writing Objectives That Focus on Results
- ☐ Additional Data Collection and ROI Analysis Plans

PART TWO

Implementing the Process

Chapter 3 Collecting the Data You Need	Chapter 4 Giving Credit Where Credit Is Due	Chapter 5 Converting Benefits to Money	Chapter 6 Counting the Costs	Chapter 7 Calculating the Return on Investment	Chapter 8 Telling the Story	Chapter 9 Forecasting the ROI
Tools, Job Aids	Tools, Job Aids	Tools, Job Aids	Tools, Job Aids	Tools, Job Aids	Tools, Job Aids	Tools, Job Aids
☐ Sample L1 Questionnaire	☐ Techniques to Isolate the Effects	☐ Experts and Historical Costs	☐ Cost Estimating Worksheet	☐ Potential Magnitude of an ROI	☐ Format of Impact Study Report	☐ ROI at Different Time and Levels
☐ Action Plan Form	☐ Control Group Design	☐ Linking to Other Measures	☐ Table: Comparison of Cost Scenarios	☐ Table: Misuse of Financial Terms	☐ Feedback Action Plan	☐ Pre-Program ROI Forecast Model
☐ Questions When Developing Action Steps	☐ Plot of Reject Rate	☐ Table: Influences on Credibility of Outcome Data	☐ Table: Recommended Cost Categories	☐ Table: Chain of Impact Drives ROI	☐ Streamline the Communication with Executives	☐ Questions to Ask on Feedback Questionnaires
☐ Cyber International Follow-up Questionnaire	☐ Plot of Sexual Harassment Complaints	☐ Table: Methods of Converting Data	☐ Table: Calculating Overhead Costs— Example		☐ Sample Streamlined Report	☐ Forecast Versus Actual Data
☐ Sample Data Collection Plan— Performance Management	☐ Plot of Shipment Productivity	☐ Table: Supervisor Estimates	☐ Table: Executive Leadership Development Program Costs		☐ Table: Communication Plan for Program Results	☐ Relationships Between Test Scores and Performance
☐ Sample Completed Action Plans	☐ Daily Sales Versus Advertising ROI Analysis Plan Form	☐ Table: Turnover Cost Summary	☐ Table: Cost Classification Matrix		☐ Table: Common Target Audiences	
☐ Sample L1 Questionnaire	☐ Sample ROI Analysis Plan: Performance Management	☐ Job Aid: Five Steps to Convert Data			☐ Job Aid: ROI Conservative Approach	
☐ Sample L2 Performance Observation	☐ Template— Isolation Using Estimates	☐ Job Aid: To Convert or Not Convert				
☐ Sample Level 3 Before and After Questionnaire	☐ Sample Isolation: Adjusting Participants' Estimates from a Leadership Program	☐ Worksheet: To Convert or Not Convert				
☐ Template L2 Performance Observation	☐ Sample Isolation Impact Questions and Adjustments					
☐ Sample Size Table	☐ Estimates of Factors That Influenced Performance Improvement					
☐ Level 1 Utility Measures	☐ Steps to Determine Isolation					
☐ Table: Hard Data						
☐ Table: Soft Data						
☐ Level 2 CRT Reporting Format						
☐ Methods of Data Collection						
☐ Improving Response Rates						
☐ Job Aid: 7C Factors™ of Data Collection						

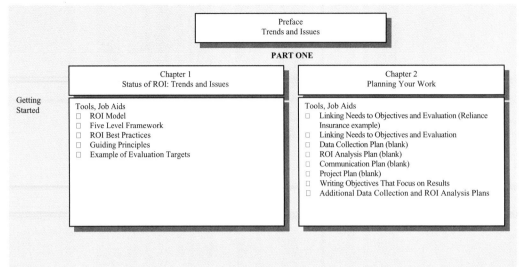

PART THREE

Chapter 10 Making the Transition	Chapter 11 Building Internal Capability and Management Support

Implementation Issues

Chapter 10 — Tools, Job Aids
- ☐ Transition Planning Steps
- ☐ Readiness Action Plan
- ☐ Sample Communication Plan
- ☐ Sample Policy Statement
- ☐ Policy Statement Checklist
- ☐ Sample Guidelines for Existing Training Programs
- ☐ Standardization Process
- ☐ Sample Project Plan
- ☐ Results-Based Transition Plan
- ☐ Cost-Savings Approaches for ROI
- ☐ Just-In-Time Gap Analysis
- ☐ Table: Myths, Fears, False Assumptions, and Reality-Based Countermeasures
- ☐ Table: Cost-Savings Flow Chart
- ☐ Job Aid: Roles and Responsibilities

Chapter 11 — Tools, Job Aids
- ☐ Stakeholder Engagement Tool
- ☐ Example of WLP Solution Adding Value to Performance
- ☐ Sample Business Case Outline
- ☐ Implementation Checklist for Planning and Managing Evaluation Projects
- ☐ Sample Individual Development Plan for ROI Leaders
- ☐ Table: AME Champion Profile
- ☐ Table: Management Plan for Evaluating Targets over Time
- ☐ Table: Management Involvement Checklist

PART FOUR

Chapter 12 Maintaining Momentum: Keeping the Process on Track

Staying on Track

Tools, Job Aids
- ☐ Stages of ROI Implementation
- ☐ WLP Roles During ROI Process Implementation
- ☐ Lessons Learned Report
- ☐ Individual Micro Level Data Is Integrated into Macro Level Scorecard
- ☐ Table: Reasons for Ineffective Implementation
- ☐ Table: Key Tasks for WLP at Stage One
- ☐ Table: Key Tasks for WLP at Stage Two
- ☐ Table: Key Tasks for WLP at Stage Three
- ☐ Table: Key Tasks for WLP at Stage Four

With the exception of the introduction, each chapter is divided into five core sections:

Fundamentals. The first section addresses the fundamental issues of the topic, giving the fieldbook user some knowledge of the purpose and importance of each step. This is meant to review and refresh your basic understanding of the ROI Methodology and to support the foundational concepts provided in the seven primary references cited later.

Potential Challenges. Next, potential implementation challenges are addressed, along with specific proven solutions for surmounting those challenges. This section will help fieldbook users anticipate challenges in their own application of the ROI Methodology and will provide tools and resources for proactively confronting such issues.

Action Steps. The third section offers action steps to assist fieldbook users in applying each step of the ROI model. Action steps are meant to be applied to individual case scenarios as well as to a specific program relevant to the reader's workplace.

Chapter Summary. The summary section reviews and reinforces key concepts of the chapter and provides a transition to the next chapter.

References and Resources. The final section includes supplemental tools, templates, case studies, and references to additional readings to assist with immediate and ongoing application of ROI implementation. Each tool, template, or case is available on the CD-ROM and organized by chapter. The last chapter in the book provides networking resources that offer fieldbook users the opportunity to connect with others addressing similar challenges in implementing ROI.

Primary recommended references for all chapters are listed in the following. These resources will provide a "soup-to-nuts" conceptual framework for the ROI Methodology and are useful supplements to this application-based fieldbook:

1. Phillips, Jack J. *Return on Investment in Training and Performance Improvement Programs,* 2nd ed. Woburn, MA: Butterworth-Heinemann, 2003.
2. Phillips, Jack J., and Patricia Pulliam Phillips. *Proving the Value of HR: How and Why to Measure ROI.* Alexandria, VA: Society for Human Resource Management, 2005.
3. Phillips, Patricia Pulliam, and Jack J. Phillips. *Return on Investments Basics.* Alexandria, VA: American Society for Training and Development, 2006.
4. Phillips, Jack J., and Patricia Pulliam Phillips. *ROI at Work.* Alexandria, VA: American Society for Training and Development, 2005.
5. Phillips, Jack J. *Handbook of Training Evaluation and Measurement Methods,* 3rd ed. Woburn, MA: Butterworth-Heinemann, 1997.
6. Phillips, Jack J., and Ron Drew Stone. *How to Measure Training Results.* New York: McGraw-Hill, 2002.
7. Phillips, Jack J., Ron D. Stone, and Patricia Pulliam Phillips. *The Human Resources Scorecard: Measuring the Return on Investment.* Woburn, MA: Butterworth-Heinemann, 2001.

HOW IS THIS BOOK DIFFERENT?

A wide range of books, articles, journals, conferences, and workshops help practitioners understand and gain knowledge and skills in implementing measurement and ROI evaluation for training and performance improvement, human resources, and other programs, processes, and initiatives.

This book is not meant to be a substitute for books highlighting the theories and premises behind ROI evaluation. It does, however, provide you with an ample "one-stop shop" of information, tools, and resources that can help you avoid the "reinventing the wheel" syndrome and can help move you forward in your own efforts to implement the ROI Methodology in your organization.

Specifically, this book will give you:

- A basic overview of the ROI Methodology.
- Case scenarios to enhance and synthesize learning.
- A six-part case study, Premier Motors International, which focuses on applying the ROI Methodology.
- Relevant, practical, and real-world tools and resources for your immediate use.
- Guidelines for applying learning, tools, and resources to your own specific project or program (see the following note).
- A CD-ROM with chapter-specific tools and resources from each phase of the ROI process.

Note: If you do not have a specific project, then you can follow the multi-part example case study provided throughout the fieldbook. The case study, Premier Motors International, is in six parts. Each part builds on each step of the ROI Methodology as it is presented chapter-by-chapter, beginning in Part 1, Chapter 2, and continuing throughout Part 2 of the fieldbook. This case presents a thorough treatment of how decisions are made to collect, analyze, and present data in a real-world situation in which things don't always go as you would like. Your learning experience will be greatly enhanced if you apply the methodology, tools, and processes to your own project as you proceed through the fieldbook chapter-by-chapter. Criteria to help you with selecting a project will be presented. In fact, by the end of Part 2, "Implementing the Process," you should be well on your way to completing the significant components of planning and executing an ROI impact study!

Case examples of other implementation efforts and their related tools can also be adapted to your own programs. We want to help build your skills in implementing the ROI Methodology so you can demonstrate not only program value to an organization but also your own value as a results-oriented workplace learning professional.

WHO SHOULD BE READING AND USING THIS FIELDBOOK?

Although interest in ROI comes from practitioners as well as from senior management and executives, choosing the right book for the right person is important. A number of books are available on the ROI Methodology, including books that present a high-level view of the process. These books are often more suitable for executives and senior management who are interested in the process but don't want the details. Other books are available that explain the theory behind the process. Many books span the multiple types of measurement and evaluation processes available and compare the ROI Methodology to those processes so practitioners can choose the most appropriate process. Other books are available that detail Phillips's ROI Methodology.

This fieldbook is designed for the practitioner who is conducting an ROI impact study or for the person who is trying to implement the ROI Methodology in an organization. It can be someone who is a novice at the process or someone who has had some experience but needs a little help with more advanced approaches. This book can be used by individuals in training and performance improvement, quality, technology, HR, public-sector, private-sector, and nonprofit organizations.

HOW CAN I GET THE MOST OUT OF THIS BOOK?

As you read, focus on the core concepts and tools presented in each of the four parts of the book. Challenge yourself by working through the situational exercises. Starting with Chapter 2, use your project as a point of reference and focus on each step in implementing the ROI Methodology by using the tools and templates provided. If you do not have a project in mind, the multi-part case study will illustrate how the process works. If you are not interested in completing an impact study but are more interested in specific, individual steps, each chapter will describe the underlying concepts behind each step as well as potential challenges and suggested solutions in implementing them.

Pay special attention to the tools, resources, and action items that can help you with project issues you're facing. And finally, use the References and Resources from each chapter as a source of additional guidance. Be sure to access the exercises, readings, tools, templates, and job aids available on the CD-ROM and use or replicate them freely (giving appropriate credit).

ABOUT THE AUTHORS

Patricia Pulliam Phillips, PhD, president and CEO of the ROI Institute, Inc., earned her PhD in International Development and her MA in Public and Private Management. Early in her professional career, she was a corporate manager who observed performance improvement initiatives from the client perspective and knew that results were imperative. As manager of a market planning and research organization for a large electric utility, she and her team were responsible for the development of electric utility rate programs for residential and commercial customers. In this role, she played an integral part in establishing Marketing University, a learning environment that supported the needs of new sales and marketing representatives. Internationally known as an accountability, measurement, and evaluation expert, Ms. Phillips facilitates workshops all over the world and consults with U.S. and international organizations—public, private, nonprofit, and educational—on implementing the ROI Methodology™. She is the author of *The Bottomline on ROI* (CEP Press, 2002), which won the 2003 ISPI Award of Excellence. She is editor or coauthor of *Return on Investment (ROI) Basics* (ASTD, 2006), *ROI at Work: Best-Practice Case Studies from the Real World* (ASTD Press, 2005), *Proving the Value of HR: How and Why to Measure ROI* (SHRM, 2005), *The Human Resources Scorecard: Measuring the Return on Investment* (Butterworth-Heinemann, 2001), and *Measuring ROI in the Public Sector* (ASTD 2002).

Jack J. Phillips, PhD, a world-renowned expert on measurement and evaluation, is chair of the ROI Institute, Inc., which provides consulting services, workshops, and keynote addresses for *Fortune 500* companies and major organizations around the world. His expertise in measurement and evaluation is based on more than 27 years of corporate experience in five industries. Jack has served as training and development manager at two *Fortune 500* firms, senior HR officer at two firms, president of a regional federal savings bank, and management professor at a major state university. Phillips developed the ROI Methodology™, a revolutionary process that provides bottom-line figures and accountability for all types of training, performance improvement, human resources, and technology programs and is used worldwide by corporations, governments, and nonprofit organizations. Phillips is the author or editor of more than 30 books and more than 100 articles. His most recent books are *Proving the Value of HR: How and Why to Measure ROI* (SHRM, 2005), *Investing in Your Company's Human Capital: Strategies to Avoid Spending Too Much or Too Little* (AMACOM, 2005), *ROI at Work: Best-Practice Case Studies from the Real World* (ASTD Press, 2005), *Return on Investment in Training and Performance Improvement Programs,* 2nd Edition (Butterworth-Heinemann, 2003), and *The Human Resources Scorecard: Measuring the Return on Investment* (Butterworth-Heinemann, 2001). Jack earned his PhD in Human Resource Management.

Ron Drew Stone is an author, international consultant and presenter, and one of the world's most recognized and accomplished authorities on improving and measuring training and performance improvement interventions. He provides consulting services in performance improvement, linking training to organization business measures, designing training for results and ROI, and measuring program results. Ron also certifies practitioners in the ROI process and conducts a full range of public and in-house performance improvement and measurement workshops. He also conducts a workshop on situational needs assessment. Ron has over 25 years of diverse experience in economic development, engineering, training, and human resources. He has coauthored *How to Measure Training Results: A Practical Guide to Tracking the Six Key Indicators* (McGraw-Hill, 2002) and *The Human Resources Scorecard: Measuring the Return on Investment* (Butterworth-Heinemann, 2001). He has contributed to numerous published case studies and resource books. He is a certified change consultant. He has a BBA from Georgia State University.

Holly Burkett, SPHR, CPT, Principal of Evaluation Works, has more than 20 years' experience assisting public- and private-sector organizations design and measure a wide range of performance improvement initiatives. As both an internal and external consultant, she has worked in the high-tech, petroleum, retail, and health care industries, as well as with government and nonprofit service agencies, to successfully create and implement results-based measurement systems, tools, and processes. Burkett is editor-in-chief of ISPI's *Performance Improvement Journal,* a select item writer for the Human Resource Certification Institute (HRCI), and an international conference presenter, workshop leader, and author on performance measurement. Her work has been featured in UK's *Industrial & Commercial Training Journal,* the *Istanbul HR Journal, T & D,* and Japan's *HRM* and *Training Magazine*(s). Publications include authoring the evaluation chapter in *HPI Essentials* and coauthoring ASTD's *Info-Line, Managing Evaluation Shortcuts,* numerous ROI case studies with ASTD's *In Action* series, and the third edition of Donald Kirkpatrick's *Evaluating Training Programs: The Four Levels.* Holly earned her MA in Human Resources and Organization Development from the University of San Francisco.

Part One
Getting Started

STATUS OF ROI: TRENDS AND ISSUES*

Measuring the return on investment (ROI) in learning, development, and performance improvement has earned a significant place among the critical issues in the workplace learning and performance (WLP) field. Today's workplace learning and performance professionals are being challenged to provide convincing data about the contribution of specific human resources programs and processes. The need for measuring the return on investment (ROI) of learning programs has never been greater. For almost a decade, ROI has been on conference agendas and at professional meetings. Journals and newsletters regularly embrace the concept with increasing print space. More than a dozen books provide significant coverage of the topic. Even top executives have enhanced their appetite for ROI information.

Measuring ROI is a topic of much debate. It is rare for any topic to stir up emotions to the degree the ROI issue does. Return on investment is characterized as flawed and inappropriate by some, while others describe it as the only answer to their accountability concerns. The truth probably lies somewhere between. Understanding the drivers for the ROI Methodology and the inherent weaknesses and advantages of ROI makes it possible to take a rational approach to the issue and implement an approximate mix of evaluation strategies that includes ROI.

Although interest in the topic has heightened and much progress has been made, it is still an issue that challenges even the most sophisticated and progressive WLP departments. While some professionals argue that it is not possible to calculate ROI, others quietly and deliberately proceed to develop measures and ROI calculations. The latter group is gaining tremendous support from senior management teams and is making much progress. Regardless of

*This is an updated, condensed, and modified version of the first two chapters of *Return on Investment in Training and Performance Improvement Programs,* 2nd ed., by Jack J. Phillips, Boston: Butterworth-Heinemann, 2003. All rights reserved.

the position taken on the issue, the reasons for measuring the return still exist. Today, most WLP professionals share a concern that they must eventually show a return on their learning investment. Otherwise, funds may be reduced or the WLP department may not be able to maintain or enhance its present status and influence in the organization.

The dilemma surrounding the ROI process is a source of frustration with many senior executives—even within the WLP field itself. Most executives realize that learning is a basic necessity when organizations experience significant growth or increased competition. They intuitively feel that there is value in providing learning opportunities, and logically they anticipate a payback in important bottom-line measures such as productivity improvements, quality enhancements, cost reductions, and time savings. Yet frustration comes from the lack of evidence to show that the process is really working. While payoffs are assumed to exist and learning programs appear to be necessary, more evidence is needed or future funding may be adjusted. The ROI Methodology represents the most promising way to show this accountability in a logical, rational approach.

In this chapter you will:

❑ Learn about the status and current trends of ROI.
❑ Learn the five levels of evaluation and how they are employed with the ROI Methodology.
❑ Learn the fundamentals of the ROI Methodology.
❑ Identify a specific workplace learning program or initiative with which to apply ROI principles and practices.

CURRENT STATUS

One thing is certain of the ROI debate—it is not a fad. As long as there is a need for accountability of learning expenditures and a desire for an investment payoff, ROI will be used to evaluate major investments in learning and performance improvement.

A fad is a new idea or approach or a new spin on an old approach. The concept of ROI is not a fad; it has been used for centuries. The 75th-anniversary issue of *Harvard Business Review (HBR)* traced the tools used to measure results in organizations (Sibbet, 1997). The early issues of *HBR*, published during the 1920s, credited ROI as the emerging tool to use to place a value on the payoff of investments. With increased adoption and use, ROI is here to stay. As highlighted in Table 1–1, today over 2,000 organizations are routinely developing ROI calculations for learning and performance improvement programs.

Specific applications of ROI began in the manufacturing sector, where it was easily developed. It migrated to the service sector, health care, the public sector, and now to the educational sector. Recent applications involve measuring the return on investment of a graduate degree program, in-service teacher training, and continuing education programs at universities. According to *Training*

TABLE 1–1

SUMMARY OF THE CURRENT STATUS OF ROI USE

ROI by the Numbers

- The ROI Methodology has been refined over a 25-year period.
- The ROI Methodology has been adopted by over 2,000 organizations in manufacturing, service, nonprofit, government, and educational settings.
- 5,000 studies are developed each year using the ROI Methodology.
- 100 case studies are published on the ROI Methodology.
- 3,500 individuals have been certified to implement the ROI Methodology in their organizations.
- Organizations in 40 countries have implemented the ROI Methodology.
- 15 books have been developed to support the process.
- A 500-member professional network has been formed to share information.

magazine, the use of ROI in training organizations continues to grow. Of those listed as the Top 100 Organizations in 2004, 75% are using the ROI Methodology (*Top 100*, 2004). A major study by the Corporate Executive Board indicated that ROI is the fastest growing metric in learning and development. It is also the metric with the widest gap between actual use and desired use, which underscores the many misconceptions about ROI (Drimmer, 2002).

It is estimated that 5,000 studies are conducted globally each year by organizations using the ROI Methodology. This number is based on the number of organizations that have participated directly in certification for the ROI Methodology. At least 100 of these studies have been published in various casebooks and reference books on ROI. Some of these are included in journals and trade magazines. Table 1–2 shows 15 studies in a variety of applications. This listing underscores the variety of applications, settings, and results that can be achieved. It should be noted that these studies represent a very high ROI, which is not always the case; these are more positive examples of the use of the methodology. Many of the published ROI studies have very high ROI values, representing some of the most successful programs. High ROI values are achieved only when the learning program is needed, addresses a specific performance gap, and is applied and supported in the workplace.

At least 3,500 individuals have attended a five-day workshop to learn how to implement the ROI Methodology. Most of the individuals who have followed through with projects have become certified in ROI implementation. These individuals develop a particular project as part of the weeklong workshop, plan the evaluation, and communicate it to team members. The certification focuses on building competencies in 10 skill areas, as shown in Table 1–3 (Phillips, 2004). These certification workshops have been conducted in most major cities in the United States and over a dozen countries outside the United States.

Measuring return on investment is becoming a global issue. To date, 40 countries have implemented the ROI Methodology, including Ireland, England, Holland, Italy, Germany, Denmark, South Africa, Chile, Peru, Australia, New Zealand, Singapore, Malaysia, Japan, China, India, and Canada, among others.

TABLE 1–2

PUBLISHED ROI STUDIES

Measuring the ROI	Key Impact Measures	ROI
Performance Management (restaurant chain)	A variety of measures, such as productivity, quality, time, costs, turnover, and absenteeism	298%[1]
Process Improvement Team (Apple Computer)	Productivity and labor efficiency	182%[1]
Skill-Based Pay (construction materials firm)	Labor costs, turnover, absenteeism	805%[2]
Sexual Harassment Prevention (health care chain)	Complaints, turnover, absenteeism, job satisfaction	1,052%[2]
Safety Incentive Plan (steel company)	Accident frequency rate, accident severity rates	379%[2]
Diversity (Nextel Communications)	Retention, employee satisfaction	163%[6]
Retention Improvement (financial services)	Turnover, staffing levels, employee satisfaction	258%[3]
Absenteeism Control/ Reduction Program (major city)	Absenteeism, customer satisfaction	882%[2]
Stress Management Program (electric utility)	Medical costs, turnover, absenteeism	320%[2]
Executive Leadership Development (financial)	Team projects, individual projects, retention	62%[2]
E-Learning (petroleum)	Sales	206%[2]
Internal Graduate Degree Program (federal agency)	Retention, individual graduate projects	153%[4]
Executive Coaching (Nortel Networks)	Several measures, including productivity, quality, cost control, and product development time	788%[5]
Competency Development (Veteran's Health Administration)	Time savings, work quality, faster response	159%[4]
First Level Leadership Development (auto rental company)	Various measures—at least two per manager	105%[7]

1. *In Action: Measuring Return on Investment*, Volume 3. Patricia P. Phillips, Editor; Jack J. Phillips, Series Editor. Alexandria, VA: American Society for Training and Development, 2001.
2. *The Human Resources Scorecard: Measuring the Return on Investment.* Jack Phillips, Ron D. Stone, Patricia P. Phillips. Woburn, MA: Butterworth-Heinemann, 2001.
3. *In Action: Retaining Your Best Employees.* Patricia P. Phillips, Editor; Jack J. Phillips, Series Editor. Alexandria, VA: American Society for Training and Development and the Society for Human Resource Management, 2002.
4. *In Action: Measuring ROI in the Public Sector.* Patricia P. Phillips, Editor. Alexandria, VA: American Society for Training and Development, 2002.
5. *In Action: Coaching for Extraordinary Results.* Darelyn J. Mitch, Editor; Jack J. Phillips, Series Editor. Alexandria, VA: American Society for Training and Development, 2002.
6. *In Action: Implementing Training Scorecards.* Lynn Schmidt, Editor; Jack J. Phillips, Series Editor. Alexandria, VA: American Society for Training and Development, 2003.
7. *The Leadership Scorecard,* Jack J. Phillips and Lynn Schmidt. Woburn, MA: Butterworth-Heinemann, 2004.

TABLE 1–3

TEN SKILL SETS FOR CERTIFICATION

Skill Areas for Certification

- Planning for ROI calculations
- Collecting evaluation data
- Isolating the effects of training
- Converting data to monetary values
- Monitoring program costs
- Analyzing data, including calculating the ROI
- Presenting evaluation data
- Implementing the ROI process
- Providing internal consulting on ROI
- Teaching others the ROI process

Implementation is defined as a particular organization establishing a consulting practice for the ROI Methodology in partnerships to present workshops and provide consulting services. As part of this implementation, an article on the ROI Methodology is usually featured in a prominent human resources and training and development publication in that country.

To date, 15 books have been developed to support the ROI Methodology; five complete casebooks are dedicated to the process—two of these have become the number 1 and number 2 all-time bestsellers for the ASTD. Special-interest ROI networks, such as the Public Sector ROI Network, housed at the Workforce Learning and Development Center at the University of Southern Mississippi, are also evolving.

Perhaps one of the most visible signs of acceptance of the ROI Methodology is the ASTD ROI Network, which now claims over 500 members. Founded in 1996, the ROI Network was formed by a group of practitioners involved in implementing the ROI Methodology. The purpose of the organization is to promote the application and use of ROI and exchange information on ROI tools, templates, practices, and applications. In 2002, the Network was acquired by ASTD and operates as the ASTD ROI Network. The Network shares information through newsletters, listserves, chat rooms, and conferences (www.ASTD.org).

The need for accountability and ROI is not limited to the private sector. Government leaders as well as taxpayers are concerned with government spending practices in all areas, including employee training and development. This concern is reflected in the United States by the Government Performance Results Act of 1993 (GPRA) and the President's Management Agenda of 2002 (PMA). The need for accountability within the government sector is reflected in governments around the world, including those of Canada, New Zealand, Australia, and the United Kingdom (Barzelay, 2001).

Without a doubt, the ROI Methodology is now becoming a mainstream tool to show the impact of human resources, learning and development, and performance improvement.

There are many measurement evaluation schemes, all aimed at reporting the success of training and performance improvement programs. Some of these methods focus on financial success; others on nonfinancial data; and still others offer a balanced approach to measuring program results. Table 1–4 lists the most common processes in use today.

The Kirkpatrick framework is by far the most widely recognized framework for categorizing training evaluation data. Initially cited as four steps, this approach provides a unique and practical method for categorizing training data (Kirkpatrick, 1975). In the 1980s, Phillips added ROI as the fifth level of evaluation and uses the levels as an important framework for his ROI Methodology. Also in the 1980s, Phillips created his systematic performance-based methodology with the tools to carry out evaluation at any or all of the five levels.

Why ROI?

Return on investment has gained acceptance for good reasons. Although the viewpoints and explanations may vary, some things are clear. The key issues are outlined here.

Increased Budgets

Most training and development budgets have continued to grow year after year. As expenditures grow, accountability becomes more critical. A growing budget creates a larger target for internal critics, often prompting the development of an ROI Methodology. The function, department, or process showing the most value will likely receive the largest budget increase.

The Ultimate Level of Evaluation

Phillips's ROI Methodology adds a fifth level to the four levels of evaluation, which were developed almost 40 years ago (Kirkpatrick, 1975). Table 1–5 shows the five-level framework. At Level 1, *Reaction and Planned Action,* satisfaction from program participants is measured, as well as a listing of how they planned to apply what they have learned. At Level 2, *Learning,* measurements focus on what participants learned during the program using tests, skill practices, role plays, simulations, group evaluations, and other assessment tools. At Level 3, *Application and Implementation,* a variety of follow-up methods are used to determine if participants applied what they learned on the job. At Level 4, *Business Impact,* the measurement focuses on the changes in the impact measures linked to the program. Typical Level 4 measures include output, quality, costs, time, and customer satisfaction. At Level 5, *Return on Investment* (the ultimate level of evaluation), the measurement compares the program's Level 4 monetary benefits with the program costs. For many, the evaluation cycle is not complete until the Level 5 evaluation is conducted.

TABLE 1-4
TRAINING MEASUREMENT AND EVALUATION SCHEMES

Benefit Cost Analysis	Probably the oldest process by which to evaluate feasibility of expenditures of all types of programs is benefit cost analysis. Based on theoretical frameworks of economics and finance, the original intent of Benefit Cost Analysis (BCA) was to ensure that society maintains optimum level of efficiency in allocating resources. Since its original use, it has been used to evaluate the success of many types of programs, including training and education.
Kirkpatrick's Four-Level Framework	The most commonly used training and evaluation framework is that developed by Kirkpatrick in the late 1950s. This framework describes four levels of evaluation: Level 1 reaction, Level 2 learning, Level 3 job behavior, Level 4 results. Many attempts have been made to successfully build on Kirkpatrick's concept of levels.
Phillips's Five-Level ROI Framework	Phillips's ROI Methodology and five-level framework is the most widely used process by which to evaluate training and performance improvement programs. Phillips added ROI as the fifth level of evaluation, recognizing that to move from Level 4 to Level 5, Level 4 measures must be converted to monetary value, fully loaded costs must be captured, intangible benefits identified, and the monetary benefits compared to the costs. Hence, combining the Kirkpatrick approach and Benefit Cost Analysis to ensure a balanced set of measures is reported. Phillips uses the five levels as a framework. Phillips also developed a systematic process that includes a performance-based methodology, strategies, approaches, and tools to implement evaluation at all five levels. The methodology also includes the critical step to isolate the effects of the program on key measures from other influences. In addition, the process identifies barriers and enablers to success and provides recommendations for continuous improvement.
Kaufman's Five Levels of Evaluation	Kaufman expands the Kirkpatrick four-level framework by defining Level 1 to include the concept of enabling, which addresses the availability of various resources and inputs necessary for successful intervention, and by adding a fifth level of evaluation concerned with societal and client responsiveness as well as the consequences and payoffs.
CIRO	Warr, Bird, and Rackham present another four-level framework in which four categories of evaluation make up the CIRO approach. CIRO stands for context, input, reaction, and outcome.
CIPP	Stufflebeam's CIPP model presents a framework around the program objectives, training content facilitation, program implementation, and program outcomes. CIPP stands for context, input, process, and product.
Marshall and Schriver's Model of Evaluation Knowledge and Skills	This five-step model evaluates knowledge and skills. The five-level model separates the evaluation of knowledge and skills. Level 1 measures participants' attitudes and feelings. Level 2 measures knowledge using paper-and-pencil tests. Level 3 measures skills and knowledge by requiring participants to demonstrate capability to perform the task's job standards. Level 4 measures skill transfer, and Level 5 measures organizational impact and ROI.

Continued

TABLE 1–4—*Continued*
TRAINING MEASUREMENT AND EVALUATION SCHEMES

Indiana University's Business Impact ISD Model	The evaluation process included in the Business Impact Instructional System's Design Model is based on six strata of impact beginning with Stratum 0, which accounts for activities such as the volume of training conducted or number of participants in the program. Stratum 1 measures participants' satisfaction with the program. Stratum 2 measures the extent to which participants exhibit knowledge and skills taught during the program. Stratum 3 measures transfer of the training, answering the question, "Are participants using what they learned?" Stratum 4 measures the extent to which employee performance has improved and whether this improvement affects profitability. Stratum 5 attempts to measure the effect changed performance in organizations has on society.
Success Case Evaluation	Brinkerhoff's success case evaluation uses purposive sampling rather than random sampling to gather data regarding program success. The process focuses on input from training participants who have been most successful as well as least successful in applying the knowledge and skills learned in the program. Through the process, stories of business value evolve as participants describe their success with application and elaborate on the barriers and enablers that either deterred or supported the use of skills and knowledge learned.
Utility Analysis	The work of Cascio brought utility analysis to the forefront. Utility analysis is a process by which the expected outcomes and the cost of decisions are taken into account. Specific outcomes are defined and the relative importance of the payoff is determined.
Brown and Reed's Integral Framework	This holistic approach to evaluation embraces both individual and organizational learning. Four key concepts to this approach include nested development, referring to the relationship of participant to the organization; interrelated realms, suggesting that development consider the interaction between the individual and larger groups; the integral framework, suggesting that there are multiple development pathways within each realm; and the link between development in one realm to the development taking place in another realm.
Balanced Scorecard	A common method used at the organization strategic reporting level, Kaplan and Norton's balanced scorecard presents a framework for an organization's vision from four perspectives (financial, customer, internal business processes, and learning and growth). The intent of the scorecard is to drive strategy for a business unit such as the training function.

TABLE 1–5
FIVE-LEVEL FRAMEWORK

Level	Brief Description
Level 1—Reaction and planned action	Measures participant's reaction to the program and outlines specific plans for implementation.
Level 2—Learning	Measures skills, knowledge, or attitude changes.
Level 3—Application and implementation	Measures changes in behavior on-the-job and specific application and implementation.
Level 4—Business impact	Measures business impact of the program.
Level 5—Return on investment	Compares the monetary value of the results with the costs for the program, usually expressed as a percentage.

These five levels of measurement provide a framework to categorize our types of data. The ROI Methodology addresses the planning, collection, analysis, and reporting of each level of data in the context of stakeholder requirements.

ROI Is a Familiar Term

The business management mind-set of many current learning and development managers causes them to place more emphasis on economic issues within the function. Today's chief learning officer (CLO) is more aware of bottom-line issues in the organization and more knowledgeable of operational and financial concerns. This new "enlightened" manager often takes a business approach to learning and development, with ROI as part of the strategy. ROI is a familiar concept for these managers, particularly those with business administration and management degrees. They have studied ROI in their academic preparation, in which ROI is used to evaluate the purchase of equipment, application of technology, building a new facility, or buying a new company. Consequently, they understand and appreciate ROI and are pleased to see the ROI Methodology applied to the evaluation of learning and performance improvement.

Accountability Trend

There has been a persistent trend of accountability in organizations all over the globe. Every support function attempts to show its worth by capturing the value it adds to the organization. From the accountability perspective, the learning and development function should be no different from other functions—it must show its contribution to the organization.

Top Executive Requirement

ROI is now generating increased interest in the executive suite. Top executives who watched training and learning budgets continue to grow without the appropriate accountability measures have become frustrated and, in an attempt to respond to the situation, have turned to ROI. Top executives are now demanding return on investment calculations from departments and functions in which they were not previously required. For years, training and development managers convinced top executives that the impact of training couldn't be measured, at least at the monetary level. Yet, many executives are now aware that it can and is being measured in many organizations. Top executives are subsequently demanding the same accountability from their training and development functions.

To date, the ROI Methodology you are about to embark on has been refined over a 25-year period. Consider the following facts:

ORIGIN/DEVELOPMENT

- The ROI Methodology™—developed by Dr. Jack J. Phillips in the 1970s, refined through application and use in the 1980s, and implemented globally during the 1990s
- First impact study—1973, Measuring the ROI in a Cooperative Education Program, for Lockheed-Martin
- First public presentation on the methodology—1978, ASTD Regional Conference
- First book published to include methodology—1983, *Handbook of Training Evaluation and Measurement Methods*, Gulf Publishing (now Butterworth-Heinemann)
- First one-day public workshop—1991, Birmingham, Alabama
- First two-day public workshop—1992, Johannesburg, South Africa
- First case study book published—1994, *Measuring Return on Investment*, ASTD
- First public certification workshop—1995, Nashville, Tennessee
- ROI Network organized—1996
- First ROI Network Conference—1997, New Orleans, Louisiana
- First ROI in Government Conference—2003, Gulfport, Mississippi, Cosponsored by the University of Southern Mississippi
- ROI Certification Online launched—2006, University Alliance (http://roiinstituteonline.com)

Applications

Typical applications of the ROI Methodology include:

- Apprenticeship programs
- Career development programs
- Competency systems
- Diversity programs
- E-learning
- Executive coaching
- Executive education
- Gain-sharing programs
- Leadership programs
- Organization development
- Performance improvement initiatives
- Recruiting strategies
- Self-directed teams
- Skill-based/ knowledge-based compensation
- Technology implementation
- Total quality management

- Reward and recognition programs
- Employee orientation
- Management development

- Training solutions
- HR programs
- Meetings and events
- Safety and health programs

- Business intelligence
- Wellness/fitness initiatives

The process has been challenged as well as supported by researchers, academics, professionals, and executives around the world. It is research-based with a strong theory serving as its foundation. The theoretical foundation serves to sustain the process in all types of organizations. By using this step-by-step process model, practitioners can easily complete an ROI study. Though there will be challenges along the way, if you use the guiding principles presented later in this book and select the appropriate methodologies for each step, you can be successful as an ROI practitioner.

ROI Best Practices

With the acceptance of ROI as a mainstream measurement tool for most learning and development functions, the debate has shifted from whether or not ROI should be conducted to *how* it should be conducted on a consistent, standardized basis. As a result, best practices for ROI have been developed. Table 1–6 shows the best practices collected from data involving several hundred organizations using the ROI process. These organizations have specifically decided to implement the ROI Methodology and have sent one or more individuals through ROI certification. The best practices reflect their use of the ROI Methodology and are explained in more detail later. These practices reveal

TABLE 1–6
ROI BEST PRACTICES

1. The ROI methodology is implemented as a process improvement tool and not a performance evaluation tool for the learning/development staff.
2. ROI impact studies are conducted very selectively, usually involving 5%–10% of programs.
3. A variety of data collection methods are used in ROI analysis.
4. For a specific ROI evaluation, the effects of learning/development are isolated from other influences.
5. Business impact data are converted to monetary values.
6. ROI evaluation targets are developed, showing the percent of programs evaluated at each level.
7. The ROI Methodology generates a microlevel scorecard.
8. ROI Methodology data are being integrated to create a macro scorecard for the learning/development function.
9. The ROI Methodology is being implemented for about 3%–5% of the learning/development budget.
10. ROI forecasting is being implemented routinely.
11. The ROI Methodology is used as a tool to strengthen/improve the learning/education process.

the comprehensive, integrated approach that is feasible, realistic, and achievable within most budget constraints.

Characteristics of Evaluation Levels

Although ROI is the ultimate level of accountability for training and performance improvement programs, not all programs should be evaluated with ROI. Different stakeholders need different information. If we categorize our stakeholders as consumers and clients, consumers represent those who are actively involved in the program or solution. This would include the training staff as well as the participants. Clients, on the other hand, are those people who fund, support, and approve the program. These are our line managers as well as senior management and executive staff. Although we evaluate training more frequently at Level 1 than at the ROI level, the value of the information for clients is higher at ROI than Level 1. The relative value of the five levels of evaluation is depicted in Table 1–7.

Determining whether to evaluate a program to ROI depends on stakeholder needs. Ask these questions: What does the consumer need? What does the client need? For instance, if key stakeholders are concerned with the cost of the program, then an ROI calculation may be necessary. However, if they're only concerned with how key business measures have changed because of a program or a solution implementation, then we may choose to stop an evaluation at Level 4. As you proceed through this fieldbook, you'll be better able to advise decisionmakers about which programs to take to which level of evaluation.

Even though a higher level of evaluation is conducted, we still evaluate at the lower levels. For example, if job behavior is the issue, we may choose to

TABLE 1–7
CHARACTERISTICS OF EVALUATION LEVELS

Chain of Impact	Value of Information	Customer Focus	Frequency of Use	Difficulty of Assessment
Reaction	Lowest	Participants (consumers)	Frequent	Easy
Learning				
Application				
Impact				
ROI	Highest	Executives/Sr. Management (clients)	Infrequent	Difficult

Customers: Consumers are customers who are actively involved in the program or solution (i.e., participants).
Clients are customers who fund, support, and approve the program or solution (i.e., executives/senior management).

evaluate only to Level 3. However, we do need to establish a chain of impact at the levels below Level 3. When a higher level evaluation is conducted, data must be collected at lower levels to establish this chain of impact. This reinforces the effort to report the complete story of program success.

Barriers to ROI Implementation

Although progress has been made, significant barriers inhibit the implementation of the ROI concept. Some of these barriers are realistic, while others are actually myths based on false perceptions. Each barrier is briefly described in the following subsections.

Costs and Time

The ROI Methodology adds additional costs and time to the evaluation process of programs, although the added amount is not excessive. A comprehensive ROI process can be implemented for 3% to 5% of the overall training budget. This barrier alone often stops many ROI implementations early in the process. The additional investment in ROI could perhaps be offset by the additional results achieved from these programs and the elimination of unproductive or unprofitable programs.

Lack of Skills and Orientation for WLP Staff

Many learning and performance improvement staff members neither understand ROI nor have the basic skills necessary to apply the process within their scope of responsibilities. Measurement and evaluation is not usually part of the preparation for the job. Also, the typical learning program focuses not on results but more on the learning process. Staff members attempt to measure results by measuring learning. Consequently, a tremendous barrier to implementation is the change needed for the overall orientation, attitude, and skills of the WLP staff.

Faulty Needs Assessment

Many of the current programs are not based on an adequate needs assessment. Some of these programs have been implemented for the wrong reasons based on management requests or efforts to chase a popular fad or trend in the industry. If the program is not needed, the benefits from the program will be minimal. An ROI calculation for an unnecessary program will likely yield a negative value. Lack of a needs assessment is a realistic barrier for many programs.

Fear

Some WLP departments do not pursue ROI because of fear of failure or fear of the unknown. Fear of failure appears in many ways. Designers, developers, facilitators, and program owners may be concerned about the consequence of a negative ROI. They fear that ROI will be a performance evaluation tool instead of a process improvement tool. Also, they worry that the ROI process will stir up the traditional fear of change. This fear, often based on unrealistic assumptions and a lack of knowledge of the process, becomes a realistic barrier to many ROI implementations.

Discipline and Planning

A successful ROI implementation requires much planning and a disciplined approach to keep the process on track. Implementation schedules, evaluation targets, ROI analysis plans, measurement and evaluation policies, and follow-up schedules are required. The learning team may not have enough discipline and determination to stay on course. This becomes a barrier, particularly when there are no immediate pressures to measure the return. If the current senior management group is not requiring ROI, the learning team may not allocate time for planning and coordination. Also, other pressures and priorities often eat into the time necessary for ROI implementation. Only carefully planned implementation will be successful.

False Assumptions

Many WLP staff members have false assumptions about the ROI process, which keep them from attempting ROI. Typical of these assumptions are the following:

- The impact of learning cannot be accurately calculated.
- Operating managers do not want to see the results of learning and development expressed in monetary values.
- If the CEO does not ask for the ROI, he or she is not expecting it.
- "I have a professional, competent staff. Therefore, I do not have to justify the effectiveness of our programs."
- Learning is a complex, but necessary activity. Therefore, it should not be subjected to an accountability process.

These false assumptions form realistic barriers that impede the progress of ROI implementation.

Benefits of ROI

Although the benefits of implementing the ROI Methodology may appear obvious, several distinct and important benefits can be realized.

Measure Contribution

The ROI Methodology is the most accurate, credible, and widely used process to show the impact of learning. The learning team will know the specific contribution from a select number of programs. An ROI study will determine if the benefits of the program, expressed in monetary values, have out-weighed the costs. It will determine if the program made a contribution to the organization.

Establish Priorities

Calculating ROI in different areas will determine which programs con-tribute the most to the organization and allow priorities to be established for high-impact learning. Successful programs can be expanded into other areas—if the same need is there—ahead of other programs. Inefficient programs can be designed and redeployed. Ineffective programs may be discontinued.

Focus on Results

The ROI Methodology is a results-based process that brings a focus on results with all programs, even for those not targeted for follow-up measure-ment or an ROI calculation. The process requires instructional designers, facilitators, participants, and support groups to concentrate on measurable objectives; that is, what the program is attempting to accomplish. Thus, this process has the added benefit of improving the effectiveness of all learning and development programs.

Earn Respect of Senior Executives and Sponsor

Developing ROI information is one of the best ways to earn the respect of the senior management team and the sponsor (the person who really cares about the program). Senior executives have a never-ending desire to see ROI. They will appreciate the efforts to connect training to business impact and show the actual monetary value. It makes them feel comfortable with the process and makes their decisions much easier. Sponsors who often support, approve, or initiate programs in training and development and performance improvement see ROI as a breath of fresh air. They actually see the value of the learning in terms they understand and appreciate.

Alter Management Perceptions of Learning and Development

The ROI Methodology, when applied consistently and comprehensively, can convince the management group that learning is an investment and not an expense. Managers will see WLP as making a viable contribution to their objec-tives, thus increasing the respect for the function. This is an important step in building a partnership with management and increasing management support for WLP.

These key benefits, inherent with almost any type of impact evalua-tion process, make the ROI process an attractive challenge for the WLP function.

When considering implementing measurement and evaluation as an ongoing process to bring results-based training to your organization, there are a number of important factors to consider. To help us understand these factors, imagine a puzzle in which the whole represents the sum of the component parts. This puzzle represents all the building blocks (the important factors) necessary to successfully implement measurement and evaluation in organizations. As shown in Figure 1–1, this puzzle has five pieces.

1. *Evaluation framework:* The first piece of the puzzle is the evaluation framework. The five-level framework represents a way in which data are categorized. Using defined categories (types of data) makes it is easy for us and our target audience to understand and communicate about the data. Table 1–5, presented earlier, illustrates the five-levels that serve as a framework for the ROI Methodology.

   Briefly, these five levels of evaluation represent the full extent of the results of the program. They represent what we call a chain of impact, suggesting that in order to achieve a positive ROI, this chain of impact is critical. Specifically, participants (1) have a positive reaction to the program; (2) acquire the knowledge, develop the skills, and/or change their attitudes and perceptions; (3) begin to use the new knowledge, skills, and attitudes on the job; (4) impact key business performance measures through the applied knowledge and skills; and (5) generate a return on investment based on the monetary value of business improvement measures compared to the cost of the solution.

   A positive result at one level does not guarantee positive results at the other levels. When we have less-than-desired results at any given

FIGURE 1–1

EVALUATION PUZZLE

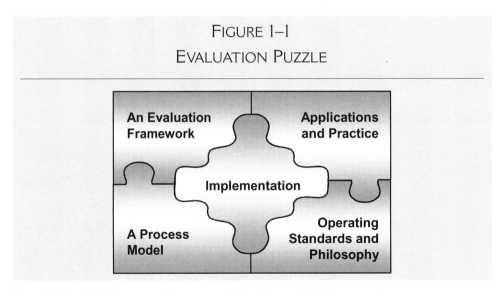

From Phillips, J. J. *Return on Investment in Training and Performance Improvement Programs,* 2nd ed. Woburn, MA: Butterworth-Heinemann, 2003. Used with permission.

level of evaluation, we can review this chain of impact to see what happened. It is necessary to look at the full picture, report complete results, and not limit findings exclusively to the financial success of the program.

2. *Evaluation process model:* The second piece of the puzzle is the evaluation process model. The model includes 10 steps and a systematic methodology that leads the way to a successful, comprehensive evaluation. This is the Phillips Methodology of planning the evaluation and collecting, analyzing, and reporting the data. This includes the use of a method to isolate the effects. The model is shown in Figure 1–2, and an overview of the process is provided.

3. *Operating standards and philosophy:* The third piece of the puzzle represents the operating standards and philosophy, which we call guiding principles. These standards, shown in Table 1–8, help guide our decisions in data collection, data analysis, and reporting of data as measurement and evaluation takes place.

   The standards allow for consistency and must be addressed as the ROI process is applied. The guiding principles serve as our decision-making tool. They provide a conservative approach to the analysis and keep the process credible in the eyes of stakeholders. For example, in the event a questionnaire is administered to 100 people and only 50 respond (a 50% response rate), what should be done with the missing data? Guiding Principle 6 clearly states that if no improvement data are available for a population or from a specific source, it is assumed that little or no improvement has occurred. On the other hand, when costs are tabulated, the cost for the entire 100 participants is considered, as noted in Guiding Principle 9, which says the cost of the solution should be fully loaded for ROI analysis. These standards help keep us consistent, keep us credible, and allow us to replicate the process.

4. *Implementation:* The fourth piece of the puzzle is implementation. Implementation holds the other four pieces together through integrating and sustaining the methodology over the long term. It is through implementation that organizations explore ways to ensure that the methodology becomes a routine part of the training activities and assignments. As part of this process, priority actions and evaluation targets are set, policies and procedures are developed, roles are assigned, and WLP staff are trained in the methodology. Training can be accomplished through books, certification, developing case studies, and participating in networks. Mechanisms are developed to provide technical support for questionnaire design and data analysis.

   Strategies must also be developed and continuously implemented to improve management commitment and support for the ROI process. The ROI process can fail or succeed based on these implementation issues. Part Three of this fieldbook is devoted to this important topic.

5. *Case Applications and Practice:* The final piece of the puzzle represents utilization to develop a history of application, build experience with ROI, and show how it works in the organization. This is accomplished through impact studies that capture the full scope of a program's success

and its value to stakeholders, participants, and the organization at large. The result is ROI experience and case studies that are used to demonstrate the contribution of WLP initiatives. Although case studies from other organizations are certainly beneficial, they will not be sufficient to convince your management of the payback of training in your organization. It is more important to obtain success with the ROI process within your organization and document and communicate the results as impact studies. In addition to showing the benefits from training expenditures, these studies form the basis of actions needed to improve training programs and processes. Your own organization will benefit from the studies you conduct on your training interventions.

Your management will embrace your efforts to show how training really contributes to the organization. We encourage you to begin with a very simple study—set yourself up for a win. While we are all often eager to go out and save the world with the new process that we have learned, we encourage you to quietly and methodically develop your first ROI study. Start small and move from simple to complex.

In addition to developing your own case studies and using them as learning tools, you can also learn from case studies developed by others. The American Society for Training and Development (ASTD) has published five casebooks edited by Jack Phillips. These case studies are used in conferences and workshops so that others can learn from the work of their peers. In Chapters 2 through 8 of this fieldbook, a case study will be presented to help you see how it is done. Case scenarios will also be used throughout this fieldbook to reinforce learning and challenge your thinking. The CD-ROM that accompanies this book makes additional case studies available for your use.

THE ROI MODEL

The ROI model, as shown in Figure 1–2, provides a systematic approach to ROI calculations. A step-by-step approach keeps the process manageable so users can tackle one issue at a time. The model provides a logical, systematic process that flows from one step to another. Applying the model provides consistency from one ROI calculation to another. Each step of the model is briefly described here.

Two specific elements are important to evaluation success and are outlined in this section.

Purpose

Although evaluation is usually undertaken to improve the WLP process, several distinct purposes can be identified. Evaluation is planned to:

- Improve the quality of learning and outcomes.
- Determine if a program is accomplishing its objectives.

FIGURE 1–2
THE ROI PROCESS MODEL

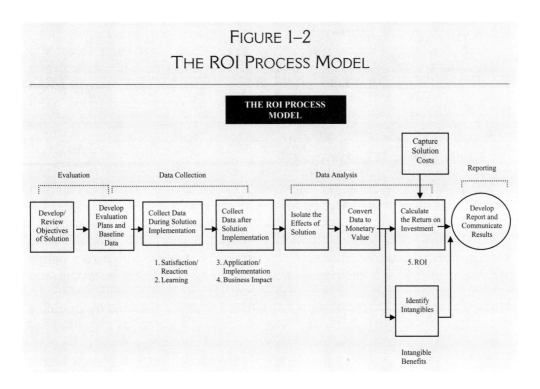

- Identify the strengths and weaknesses in the learning process.
- Determine the cost/benefit analysis of a WLP program.
- Assist in marketing WLP programs in the future.
- Determine if the program was appropriate for the target audience.
- Establish a database, which can assist in making decisions about the programs.
- Establish priorities for funding.

For most programs, multiple evaluation purposes are pursued.

Feasibility

During the planning stage, the feasibility for a business impact or ROI study should be examined. Relevant questions to address are:

- What specific measures have been influenced with this program?
- Are those measures readily available?
- Can the effect of the program on those measures be isolated?
- Are the costs of the program readily available?
- Will it be practical and feasible to discuss costs?
- Can the impact data be converted to monetary value?
- Is the actual ROI needed or necessary?

These and other questions are important to examine during the planning process to ensure that the evaluation is appropriate for the program.

Objectives of Programs

Learning and development programs are evaluated at different levels as briefly described earlier. Corresponding to the levels of evaluation are levels of objectives:

- Reaction and satisfaction objectives (Level 1)
- Learning objectives (Level 2)
- Application/implementation objectives (Level 3)
- Impact objectives (Level 4)
- ROI objectives (Level 5)

Before the ROI evaluation begins, the program objectives must be identified or developed. Developing/reviewing objectives is the first step in the model because objectives are frequently insufficient. Program objectives link directly to the front-end analysis. The objectives form the basis for determining the depth and the level of evaluation. Historically, learning objectives are routinely developed. Application and impact objectives are not always in place, but are necessary for the proper focus on results.

Tied closely to setting objectives is the timing of the data collection. In some cases, preprogram measurements are taken to compare with postprogram measures, and sometimes multiple measures are taken. In other situations, preprogram measurements are not available and specific follow-ups are still taken after the program. The important issue is to determine the timing for the follow-up evaluation. Chapter 2 will address *objectives* and *timing* in more detail.

Evaluation Plans

To complete the planning process, three simple planning documents are developed—the Data Collection Plan, the ROI Analysis Plan, and the Project Plan. These documents should be completed before the evaluation project is implemented—ideally, before the program is designed or developed. Appropriate upfront attention will save much time later when data are actually collected. The documents are usually included in the impact study reports and published case studies. Chapter 2 will address *planning* in more detail.

Collecting Data

As with any measurement process, data collection is central to the ROI Methodology. Both hard data (e.g., output, quality, cost, time) and soft data (e.g., job satisfaction, customer satisfaction) are collected. Data are collected using a variety of methods, including the following:

- **Surveys** determine the extent to which participants are satisfied with the program, have learned skills and knowledge, and have used various aspects of the program.

- **Questionnaires** are usually more detailed than surveys and can be used to uncover a wide variety of data. Participants provide responses to several types of open-ended and forced response questions.
- **Tests** measure changes in knowledge and skills (Level 2). Tests come in a wide variety of formal (criterion-referenced tests, performance tests and simulations, and skill practices) and informal (facilitator assessment, self assessment, and team assessment) methods.
- On-the-job **observation** captures actual skill application and use. Observations are particularly useful in customer service training and are more effective when the observer is either invisible or transparent.
- **Interviews** conducted with participants determine the extent to which learning has been used on the job.
- **Focus groups** determine the degree to which a group of participants has applied the training to job situations.
- **Action plans and program assignments** are developed by participants during the program and are implemented on the job after the program is completed. Follow-ups provide evidence of program success.
- **Performance contracts** are developed by the participant, the participant's supervisor, and the facilitator, who all agree on job performance outcomes.
- **Business performance monitoring** is useful where various performance records and operational data are examined for improvement.

The important challenge in data collection is to select the method or methods appropriate for the setting and the specific program within the constraints of the organization.

Isolating the Effects of Learning and Development

An often-overlooked issue in most evaluations is the process of isolating the effects of learning and development. In this step of the process, specific strategies are explored that determine the amount of output performance directly related to the program. This step is essential because many factors will usually influence performance data after a learning and development program is conducted. Specific strategies taken in this step will pinpoint the amount of improvement directly related to the program and will result in increased accuracy and credibility of ROI calculations. Organizations have used the following techniques to tackle this important issue:

- A **control group** arrangement is used to isolate the impact of learning. With this strategy, one group participates in a program while another, similar group does not. The difference in the performance of the two groups is attributed to the program. When properly set up and implemented, the control group arrangement is the most effective way to isolate the effects of learning and development.
- **Trend lines** are used to project the values of specific output variables as if the learning program had not been undertaken. The projection is compared to the actual data after the program is conducted. The difference represents

the estimate of the impact of learning. Under certain conditions, this strategy can accurately isolate the impact of learning.

- When mathematical relationships between input and output variables are known, a **forecasting model** is used to isolate the effects of learning. With this approach, the output variable is predicted using the forecasting model with the assumption that no learning program is conducted. The actual performance of the variable after the program is conducted is compared with the forecasted value, which results in an estimate of the impact of learning.
- **Participants** estimate the amount of improvement related to the learning and development program. With this approach, participants are provided with the total amount of improvement, on a pre- and postprogram basis, and are asked to indicate the percent of the improvement that is actually related to the program.
- **Supervisors or managers** estimate the impact of learning on the output variables. With this approach, supervisors or managers are presented with the total amount of improvement and are asked to indicate the percent related to learning. The estimates are adjusted for the error of the estimates.
- **Experts** provide estimates of the impact of learning on the performance variable. Because the estimates are based on previous experience, the experts must be familiar with the type of program and the specific situation.
- When feasible, **other influencing factors** are identified and the impact estimated or calculated, leaving the remaining unexplained improvement attributed to learning.
- In some situations, **customers** provide input on the extent to which training or learning has influenced their decision to use a product or service. Although this strategy has limited applications, it can be quite useful in customer service and sales training.

Collectively, these techniques provide a comprehensive set of tools to tackle this important issue.

Converting Data to Monetary Values

To calculate the return on investment, business impact data collected in the evaluation are converted to monetary values and compared to program costs. This requires a value to be placed on each unit of data connected with the program. Several techniques are available to convert data to monetary values:

- **Output data** are converted to profit contribution or cost savings based on their unit contribution to profit or their unit contribution to cost reduction. Standard values for these items are readily available in most organizations.
- The **cost of quality** is calculated and quality improvements are directly converted to cost savings. Standard values for these items are available in many organizations.
- For programs where employee time is saved, the **participants' wages and employee benefits** are used to develop the value for time. This is a standard formula in most organizations.

- **Historical costs,** developed from cost statements, are used when they are available for a specific variable. In this case, organizational cost data establishes the specific monetary cost savings of an improvement.
- When available, **internal and external experts** may be used to estimate a value for an improvement.
- **External databases** are sometimes available to estimate the value or cost of data items. Research, government, and industry databases—usually available on the Internet—can provide important information for these values.
- **Participants** estimate the value of the data item. For this approach to be effective, participants must be capable of providing a value for the improvement.
- **Supervisors and managers** provide estimates when they are both willing and able to assign values to the improvement.
- **Soft measures are linked mathematically to other measures** that are easier to measure and value. This approach is particularly helpful when establishing values for measures that are difficult to convert to monetary values but have linkages to other measures.
- **WLP staff** estimates may be used to determine a value of an output data item.

This step in the ROI model is necessary for determining the monetary benefits from a learning program. The process is challenging, particularly with soft data, but it can be methodically accomplished using one or more of these strategies.

Tabulating Cost of the Program

The other part of the equation on a cost/benefit analysis is the program cost. Tabulating the costs involves monitoring or developing all the related costs of the program targeted for the ROI calculation. Among the cost components that should be included are:

- the cost to design and develop the program, possibly prorated over the expected life of the program;
- the cost of all program materials provided to each participant;
- the cost for the instructor/facilitator, including preparation time as well as delivery time;
- the cost of the facilities for the learning program;
- travel, lodging, and meal costs for the participants, if applicable;
- salaries plus employee benefits of those who participated in the learning program; and
- administrative and overhead costs of the WLP function, allocated in some convenient way.

In addition, specific costs related to the needs assessment and evaluation should be included, if appropriate. The conservative approach is to include all of these costs so that the total is fully loaded.

Calculating the Return on Investment

The return on investment is calculated using the program benefits and costs. The benefits/cost ratio (BCR) is the program benefits divided by cost. In formula form the BCR is:

$$BCR = \frac{Program\ Benefits}{Program\ Costs}$$

The return on investment uses the net benefits divided by program costs. The net benefits are the program benefits minus the costs. In formula form, the ROI becomes:

$$ROI(\%) = \frac{Net\ Program\ Benefits}{Program\ Costs} \times 100$$

This is the same basic formula used in evaluating other investments in which the ROI is traditionally reported as earnings divided by investment.

Because ROI is always expressed as a percentage, the formula component of ×100 is necessary to convert the answer to a percentage. An example of the ROI calculation is as follows. Innovative Computer Company conducted a one-week pilot of a continuous improvement training program for entry-level manufacturing assemblers and line supervisors. The results of the program, based on measures of improved labor efficiency and improved quality, yielded an annual value of $221,500. The total fully loaded costs for the program were $150,500. Before there can possibly be a return on investment, we must first recover our cost of $150,500. This is why the program cost is subtracted from the benefits in the numerator of the formula. Thus, the return on investment is:

$$ROI(\%) = \frac{\$221,500 - \$150,500}{\$150,500} = 0.47 \times 100 = 47\%$$

The same results from the above example can also be reported as a benefit-cost ratio (BCR). The benefit-cost ratio is developed from cost-benefit analysis, which compares the annual economic benefits of the program with the cost of the program. Originating in London and dating back to the 1600s, it has been used for centuries to determine the feasibility of programs. In the early 1900s BCR became prominently used in the United States, where it was first used to determine the feasibility of major public projects and later used to evaluate the effectiveness of education and training programs. The equation for the benefits-cost ratio is as follows:

$$BCR = \frac{Program\ Benefits}{Program\ Costs}$$

Using the previous example, then, the BCR calculation is as follows:

$$BCR = \frac{\$221,500}{\$150,500} = 1.47:1$$

A BCR of 1.47:1 indicates that for every $1 spent in training, $1.47 is returned. However, this representation does not illustrate the recovery of the program cost. So the actual gain after recovering the cost is only 47 cents on each dollar spent. The ROI formula takes this cost recovery into account by using "net benefits" in the numerator. In reporting the ROI, the *net* monetary benefits of the program are reported as a percentage gained. For instance, a 100% ROI tells us that for every $1 invested, $1 is returned *after* the cost is recovered. ROI communicates the net gain. This 100% ROI would be expressed in the BCR formula as a BCR of 2:1.

Although accounting and economic practitioners tell us that the ROI and cost-benefit ratio are the ultimate level of measure of profitability of our investments, they also acknowledge that they are only one measure of success and are an incomplete measure unless supplemented with additional measures of performance. By incorporating ROI as the fifth level of the framework, the additional four levels of measures can be reported along with intangibles.

Identifying Intangible Benefits

In addition to tangible, monetary benefits, most learning programs have intangible, nonmonetary benefits. The ROI calculation is based on converting both hard and soft data to monetary values. Intangible benefits may include items such as:

- increased job satisfaction,
- increased organizational commitment,
- improved teamwork,
- improved customer service,
- reduced complaints, and
- reduced conflicts.

During data analysis, every attempt is made to convert all data to monetary values. All hard data such as output, quality, and time are converted to monetary values. The conversion of soft data is attempted for each data item. However, if the process used for conversion is too subjective or inaccurate and the resulting values lose credibility in the process, then the data are listed as an intangible benefit with the appropriate explanation. For some programs, intangible, nonmonetary benefits are extremely valuable, often carrying as much influence as the hard data items.

Reporting Data

The final step in the ROI model is reporting. This critical step often lacks the proper attention and planning to ensure that it is successful. This step involves developing appropriate information in impact studies and other brief reports. The heart of the step includes the various techniques used to communicate to a wide variety of target audiences. In most ROI studies, several audiences are interested in and need the information. Careful planning to match the communication method with the audience is essential to ensure that the message is understood and appropriate actions follow.

POTENTIAL CHALLENGES

To ensure consistency and replication of impact studies, operating standards must be developed and applied as the process model is used to develop ROI studies. It is extremely important for the results of a study to stand alone and not vary depending on the individual conducting the study. The operating standards, called guiding principles, detail how to address each step and issue of the process. Table 1–8 shows the 12 guiding principles that form the basis for the operating standards.

These guiding principles serve not only as a way to consistently address each step but also provide a much needed conservative approach to the analysis. A conservative approach may lower the actual ROI calculation, but it will build credibility with the target audience.

Evaluation Targets

As mentioned earlier when addressing ROI best practices, evaluation targets should be developed on an ongoing basis to determine the percentage of programs to be evaluated at each level. Table 1–9 illustrates evaluation targets by percentage that one organization established for measuring workplace learning programs across multiple levels. These targets are only an example based on one organization's situation and requirements. Your targets may look considerably different as you assess your own situation. For example, your stake-

TABLE 1–8

THE GUIDING PRINCIPLES

1. When a higher-level evaluation is conducted, data must be collected at lower levels.
2. When an evaluation is planned for a higher level, the previous level of evaluation does not have to be comprehensive.
3. When collecting and analyzing data, use only the most credible source.
4. When analyzing data, choose the most conservative among the alternatives.
5. At least one method must be used to isolate the effects of the solution.
6. If no improvement data are available for a population or from a specific source, it is assumed that little or no improvement has occurred.
7. Estimates of improvements should be adjusted (discounted) for the potential error of the estimate.
8. Extreme data items and unsupported claims should not be used in ROI calculations.
9. Only the first year of benefits (annual) should be used in the ROI analysis of short-term solutions.
10. Costs of the solution should be fully loaded for ROI analysis.
11. Intangible measures are defined as measures that are purposely not converted to monetary values.
12. The results from the ROI methodology must be communicated to all key stakeholders.

TABLE 1–9

Evaluation Levels	Measures	Percent
Level 1	Reaction, satisfaction	100%
Level 2	Learning	60%
Level 3	On-the-job application	30%
Level 4	Business impact	20%
Level 5	Return-on-investment	5%–10%

holders may require a much higher evaluation target at Level 3 and a much lower target at Level 2. The challenge is to balance the number of programs you evaluate at each level with the expectations of your stakeholders. It is wise to seek stakeholder input as you begin to set priorities on which programs to evaluate each year.

If a higher level of evaluation is conducted, we still evaluate at the lower levels. Therefore, if changed job behavior is the primary need (Level 3), we may target only evaluation of a skills training program at Level 3. However, as our Guiding Principle 1 in Table 1–8 tells us, when a higher level evaluation is conducted, data must be collected at lower levels. This reinforces the effort to report the complete story of program success. Guiding Principle 2, however, tells us that when an evaluation is planned for a higher level, the previous level of evaluation does not have to be comprehensive. So, when we evaluate a Level 3, our evaluation at Levels 1 and 2 do not necessarily have to be as comprehensive as they would be if we only evaluated at those lower levels.

Hurdle Rate

Hurdle rate is the ROI you and your stakeholders hope to meet or exceed in order to be satisfied with the payback of the program. An ROI that is too low might be unacceptable and the need for the program may be questioned. An ROI with an extremely high value (i.e., 1,000%) may be achievable but may also raise serious questions about credibility. But it is what it is, and we must be able to explain how we arrive at the value when we complete an impact study. We suggest that you consider four options for targeting the hurdle rate of your ROI measurement efforts.

1. Option One: Set the value as you would with other investments. For instance, if the typical investment in technology or a new operating facility is expected to bring an ROI of 12–15%, you may want to use the same expectation for the ROI of your training.
2. Option Two: Set your ROI target slightly above other investments. One philosophy suggests that much is expected from training and performance improvement programs; therefore, the ROI should have a higher expectation. For instance, if your operating plants or technology show

a return of 12 to 15%, perhaps your ROI should be at least 25%. We often use 25% as a rule of thumb for the ROI studies we conduct.

3. Option Three: Set your ROI target at break even, which is 0%. We often find this to be acceptable for those programs offered through the public sector, education, and nonprofits. Programs are often intended to improve critical measures and at least recover the cost. If yours is one of those programs, perhaps your stakeholders will agree that an ROI of 0% or break even is appropriate.

4. Option Four: Set your ROI target at client expectation. When a client asks you to conduct an ROI study or suggests they want to see the return they get from investing in your program, discuss it with them and decide together what an appropriate ROI would be for the program. Be sure the client is aware of the strict conservative standards we use before arriving at a hurdle rate.

Criteria for Levels 4 and 5 Evaluation

It would be expensive and unnecessary to evaluate all programs at Levels 4 and 5. Seven criteria have been identified that help us make the decision whether or not to evaluate at Level 4 and Level 5. A program/project is a candidate for Levels 4 and 5 evaluation if it:

- has a long life cycle (generally 18 months or longer).
- is deemed important in meeting the organization's operating goals.
- is closely linked to the organization's strategic initiatives.
- is very expensive to implement (i.e., more than 20% of the training budget).
- is highly visible and sometimes controversial.
- has a large target audience (i.e., 20% of the organization's population, or a high percentage of a specific job classification).
- commands the interest of a top executive group.

By following these seven criteria, we can help decide which programs are candidates for evaluation at Level 4 and 5. We encourage you to use these criteria as a guideline for discussion with stakeholders when considering which programs are most appropriate for comprehensive measurement and ROI evaluation. You may want to refine the criteria somewhat for use in your organization.

ACTION STEPS

A variety of environmental issues and events influence the successful implementation of the ROI process. These issues must be addressed early to ensure that the ROI process is successful. Specific topics or actions include:

- establish a policy statement concerning results-based training and development;

- set up procedures and guidelines for different elements and techniques of the evaluation process;
- conduct meetings and formal sessions to develop staff skills with the ROI process;
- establish strategies to improve management commitment and support for the ROI process;
- provide mechanisms for technical support for questionnaire design, data analysis, and evaluation strategy; and
- establish specific techniques to place more attention on results.

The ROI process can fail or succeed based on these implementation issues.

Implementation begins by understanding your readiness for a comprehensive methodology such as ROI. Exercise 1–1, "Is Your Organization a Candidate for ROI Implementation?," will help you assess your organizational readiness. Complete it now and keep it handy as a reference. Chapter 10 will give you more detailed information about implementation.

As you proceed through this fieldbook, the next step in implementation is determining which of your programs to use when developing your first impact study. We encourage you to begin with a simple study with a high potential for a quick win. Think about the programs in your organization and, using Job Aid 1–1, "The Selection Matrix," as a guideline, rank your programs according to the seven criteria described earlier. The criteria are summarized in the matrix of Job Aid 1–1. List several programs across the top of the matrix and rank them according to the one-to-five point scale shown below the Selection Matrix.

Those programs that result in the highest scores are the best candidates for conducting an impact study encompassing Levels 4 and 5 evaluation. If you are just beginning to pursue ROI evaluation, it is suggested you select the simplest program in the list of programs with the high ranking. If you are more advanced, select a more important program for the evaluation. If you are not currently in an organization with a set of programs to consider, then rank the most recent three or four training programs you've attended as a participant. Imagine the business objectives and management interest associated with those programs, with your most recent employer as a frame of reference.

For instance, if you recently attended a one-day program on negotiation skills, how might the knowledge and skills gained from that workshop be of benefit to your last organization's business goals? What interest would managers have in an employee coming back to the job with improved negotiating skills/knowledge? How would you implement these skills to get your job accomplished, and what would be the benefit to the organization?

The program you select now will be the program that you'll use as a reference when applying methods and tools throughout the remainder of the fieldbook. In Chapter 2, we'll pick up this program again and begin to apply the evaluation planning steps and guidelines.

EXERCISE 1–1. IS YOUR ORGANIZATION A CANDIDATE FOR ROI IMPLEMENTATION?

Check the most appropriate level of agreement for each statement:
1 = Strongly Disagree; 5 = Strongly Agree

	Disagree				Agree
	1	2	3	4	5
1. My organization is considered a large organization with a wide variety of programs.	☐	☐	☐	☐	☐
2. We have a large budget that attracts the interest of senior management.	☐	☐	☐	☐	☐
3. Our organization has a culture of measurement and is focused on establishing a variety of measures in all functions and departments.	☐	☐	☐	☐	☐
4. My organization is undergoing significant change.	☐	☐	☐	☐	☐
5. There is pressure from senior management to measure results of our programs.	☐	☐	☐	☐	☐
6. My function currently has a very low investment in measurement and evaluation.	☐	☐	☐	☐	☐
7. My organization has experienced more than one program disaster in the past.	☐	☐	☐	☐	☐
8. My department has a new leader.	☐	☐	☐	☐	☐
9. My team would like to be the leaders in our field.	☐	☐	☐	☐	☐
10. The image of our department is less than satisfactory.	☐	☐	☐	☐	☐
11. My clients are demanding that our processes show bottom-line results.	☐	☐	☐	☐	☐
12. My function compete with other functions with our organization for resources.	☐	☐	☐	☐	☐
13. There is increased focus on linking our process to the strategic direction of the organization.	☐	☐	☐	☐	☐
14. My function is a key player in change initiatives currently taking place in the organization.	☐	☐	☐	☐	☐
15. Our overall budget is growing and we are required to prove the bottom line of value of our processes.	☐	☐	☐	☐	☐

Scoring

If you scored:

15–30   You are not yet a candidate for ROI. Reading this fieldbook will help prepare you.

31–45   You are not a strong candidate for ROI; however, it is time to start pursuing some type of measurement process.

46–60   You are a candidate for building skills to implement the ROI process. At this point there is no real pressure to show the ROI, which is the perfect opportunity to perfect the process within the organization.

61–75   You should already be implementing a comprehensive measurement and evaluation process, including ROI.

Are you a candidate? _____

The Selection Matrix

Selecting Programs/Interventions for Levels 4 and 5 Evaluation										
Please rate 1, 2, 3, 4, or 5 in each block below for each program you are considering evaluating.										
Programs/Interventions										
Criteria	**1**	**2**	**3**	**4**	**5**	**6**	**7**	**8**	**9**	**10**
1. Life cycle										
2. Importance to company operating goals										
3. Linked to organization's strategic initiatives										
4. Cost is very expensive to implement										
5. Highly visible										
6. Large target audience										
7. Interest of top executives										
Total										

Rating Scales	
1. Life cycle	5 = Long life cycle 1 = Very short life cycle
2. Importance to company operating goals	5 = Closely related to company operating goals 1 = Not directly related to company operating goals
3. Linked to strategic initiatives	5 = Closely linked to strategic initiatives 1 = Not closely linked to strategic initiatives
4. Cost	5 = Very expensive 1 = Very inexpensive
5. Visibility	5 = High visibility 1 = Low visibility
6. Audience size	5 = Very large audience 1 = Very small audience
7. Interest of top executives	5 = High level of executive interest in evaluation 1 = Low level of executive interest in evaluation

CHAPTER SUMMARY

While there is almost universal agreement that ROI needs more attention, it is promising to note the tremendous success of ROI. Its use is expanding. Its payoff is huge. The process is not difficult or impossible. The approaches, strategies, and techniques can be useful in a variety of settings and are not overly complex. The combined and persistent efforts of practitioners and researchers will continue to refine the techniques and create successful applications.

The first step in implementing ROI is understanding what it's all about. To date, the ROI Methodology you are about to embark on has been refined over a 25-year period. The ROI Methodology has a significant history of use worldwide in both the government and the private sector. It has been refined after years of practical application. By using this research-based, systematic, step-by-step methodology, workplace learning practitioners can easily complete an ROI study. Although there will be challenges along the way, if you use the tools and resources provided in this fieldbook, adopt the guiding principles for ROI practice, and select the appropriate methods for each step, you can successfully initiate an ROI endeavor.

The ROI process provides multiple ways to collect data, isolate the effects, and convert data to monetary values, with choices being made to fit the situation, environment, and constraints. The process is systematic and accompanied by a set of 12 operating standards (guiding principles). At the end of the day, an ROI evaluation is not about the ROI value you achieve. It's about the process; that is, the improvements you can make to your programs by evaluating at such a comprehensive level. The data you find through the evaluation process not only improves the specific program being evaluated but can lead to improving the processes in your training function.

The next chapter addresses planning your evaluation impact study. This is where you have to sharpen your pencil and get to work. Your learning will be enhanced by seeing examples and by doing. So get ready for a challenging and instructive experience. The fun is about to begin.

REFERENCES

Barzelay, M. *The New Public Management: Improving Research and Policy Dialogue.* Berkeley, CA: University of California Press, 2001.

Drimmer, Alan. *Reframing the Measurement Debate: Moving Beyond Program Analysis in the Learning Function.* Washington D.C.: Corporate Executive Board, 2002.

Kirkpatrick, D. L., "Techniques for Evaluating Training Programs," in *Evaluating Training Programs.* Alexandria, VA: American Society for Training and Development, 1975, pp. 1–17.

Phillips, Jack J., "The ROI Certification Process," www.roiinstitute.net, 2004.

Sibbet, D. "75 Years of Management Ideas and Practice: 1922–1997: A Supplement to the *Harvard Business Review.*" *Harvard Business Review,* September–October 1997.

"Top 100 Training Organizations," *Training,* March 2004.

FURTHER READING

Government Performance Results Act of 1993, Office of Management and Budget, Washington, DC (www.whitehouse.gov/omb/mgmt-gpra/gplaw2m.html), 1993.

Phillips, Jack J. *Handbook of Training Evaluation and Measurement Methods,* 3rd ed. Woburn, MA: Butterworth-Heinemann, 1997.

Phillips, Jack J. *Return on Investment in Training and Performance Improvement Programs,* 2nd ed. Woburn, MA: Butterworth-Heinemann, 2003.

Phillips, Jack J., and Ron Drew Stone. *How to Measure Training Results.* New York: McGraw-Hill, 2002.

The President's Management Agenda, Executive Office of the President Office of Management and Budget, Washington, DC (www.whitehouse.gov/omb/budget), 2002 fiscal year.

Reframing the Measurement Debate. Washington, D.C.: Corporate Executive Board, 2002.

Van Buren, M. E., and W. Erskine. *State of the Industry Report 2002.* Alexandria, VA: American Society for Training and Development, 2002.

CD ☉

Exercises and Case Studies	Tools, Templates, and Job Aids
Exercise 1–1. Is Your Organization a Candidate for ROI Implementation?	Figure 1–1. Evaluation Puzzle
	Figure 1–2. ROI Model
	Job Aid 1–1. Selection Matrix
	Table 1–1. Summary of the Current Status of ROI Use
	Table 1–2. Published ROI Studies
	Table 1–3. Ten Skill Sets for Certification
	Table 1–4. Training Measurement and Evaluation Schemes
	Table 1–5. Five-Level Framework
	Table 1–6. ROI Best Practices
	Table 1–7. Characteristics of Evaluation Levels
	Table 1–8. Guiding Principles
	Table 1–9. Example of Evaluation Targets

PLANNING YOUR WORK

Planning is one of the most critical steps in developing an ROI impact study. It is also one of the most neglected steps. This is due in part to the time necessary to develop a solid, comprehensive plan. Planning the evaluation answers the questions why, what, how, who, and when—why evaluate the program, what is evaluated, how to go about doing it, whom to get data from and whom to tell, and when to collect the data. Four documents are developed when planning an ROI impact study: (1) data collection plan; (2) ROI analysis plan; (3) communication plan; and (4) project plan.

In this chapter you will

- ❑ Define the purpose of your evaluation.
- ❑ Identify key stakeholders.
- ❑ Link program objectives to the evaluation.
- ❑ Begin the initial planning for your ROI impact study.

THE FUNDAMENTALS

Planning your ROI evaluation can accomplish four objectives: (1) save money and time; (2) improve the quality and quantity of data collected; (3) ensure stakeholders' needs are met; and (4) prioritize budgeting. Making final decisions up front about data collection methods, sources of data, timing of data collection, and data analysis procedures can save time, cost, and frustration. Conferring with the client and other key stakeholders and gaining upfront agreement on the type of data to be collected is a key component of a successful evaluation. Making upfront decisions also enables you to implement the evaluation process smoothly, without having to think of next steps along the way. A comprehensive evaluation plan eliminates unnecessary, inappropriate data from creeping into the process, resulting in the garbage-in-garbage-out syndrome. Planning allows the evaluation to be played out with the appropriate end in mind. Finally, evaluation planning can help streamline the project budget by identifying specific steps and resources necessary to implement the process.

Planning an evaluation begins with identifying and communicating with the key stakeholders, identifying the purposes for the evaluation (which includes meeting stakeholder expectations), and linking the evaluation to the program objectives. Once these three steps take place, data collection, ROI analysis, and communication plans as well as the project plan can be developed. To set the stage for this step in the ROI Methodology, read and complete Exercise 2–1.

Marge's situation is not unusual. Marge went to a workshop that her friend was teaching. She got excited about the Myers-Briggs process and decided that it would be the right program for her organization. She received favorable reactions and so decided to try it on top executives. They too reacted positively. Then she launched it for the entire staff, and they reacted positively. Based on Frank's comments, however, positive reaction is not enough; he wants to see results. He further pinned Marge down to find out if she had any idea of the cost of the program. Marge is now in a hurry to conduct a quick evaluation to try to resolve these questions for Frank. In her situation, the purpose of her evaluation is to get out of hot water, which is not a very enviable position to be in. Perhaps if she had begun by identifying her key stakeholders and their expectations, she would be in a better position now. Perhaps this would have led to a lot of things being done differently.

Purposes of Evaluation

Purposes of evaluation vary. In Marge's case, now that Frank has expressed his expectation, the purpose of the evaluation of the MBTI is to show how the program adds to the Reliance bottom line (bottom line usually means something like ROI). The evaluation purpose is typically reflective of the intent of the program. Unfortunately for Marge, however, her intent behind the MBTI had more to do with sharing an interesting process with her colleagues than with the impact the program's results would have on the organization. It would have been a great start if Marge had identified her key stakeholders and done some research to identify the Level 3 and Level 4 objectives and measures for MTBI. The objectives were unclear when Marge rolled out this program.

Program evaluation is intended to provide useful information. Evaluation data can be used to answer questions, make decisions, and take action. Unnecessary or unused evaluation data are useless. Therefore, the purpose of evaluation drives the type of data to be collected and reported. The purpose of the evaluation clearly tells us how we will use the data. In Marge's case, participant reaction data would have met her initial purpose. She clearly hoped her colleagues would be as excited about the program as was she. Her use of these positive data would generate interest in the program from others. However, participant reaction data is insufficient in meeting Frank's purpose.

At the end of a monthly staff meeting, Frank Thomas, CEO of Reliance Insurance Company, asked Marge Thompson, manager of training and development, about the communications workshops that had been conducted with all supervisors and managers throughout the company. The workshop featured the Myers-Briggs Type Indicator (MBTI) and showed participants how to interact with, and understand, each other in their routine activities. The MBTI classifies people into one of 16 personality types.

Frank said, "I found the workshop very interesting and intriguing. I can certainly identify with my particular personality type, but I'm curious what specific value these workshops have brought to the company. Do you have any way of showing the results of all 25 workshops?"

Marge replied, "We certainly have improved teamwork and communications throughout the company. I hear people make comments about how useful the process has been to them personally."

Frank added, "Do we have anything more precise? Also, do you know how much we spent on these workshops?"

Marge quickly responded by saying, "I'm not sure that we have any precise data and I'm not sure exactly how much money we spent, but I can certainly find out."

Frank concluded with some encouragement, "Any specifics would be helpful. Please understand that I am not opposing this learning effort. However, when we initiate these types of programs, we need to make sure that they are adding value to the company's bottom line. Let me know your thoughts on this issue in about two weeks."

Marge was a little concerned about the CEO's comments, particularly because he had enjoyed the workshop and had made several positive comments about it. Why was he questioning the effectiveness of it? Why was he concerned about the costs?

These questions began to frustrate Marge as she reflected over the year-and-a-half period in which every manager and supervisor had attended the workshop. She recalled how she was first introduced to the MBTI. She attended a workshop conducted by a friend, was impressed with the instrument, and found it to be helpful as she learned more about her own personality type.

Marge thought the process would be useful to Reliance managers and asked the consultant to conduct a session internally. With favorable reaction, she decided to try it with the top executives, including Frank Thomas. Their reaction was favorable. Then she launched it with the entire staff, and the feedback had been excellent.

She realized that the workshops had been expensive because over 600 managers had attended. However, she thought that teamwork had improved, but there was no way of knowing for sure. With some types of learning you never know if it works, she thought. Still, Marge was facing a dilemma. Should she respond to the CEO or just ignore the issue?

Continued

Consider these four questions and answer them as best you can.

What is the purpose of Marge's evaluation?

_____

_____

_____

Who are the key stakeholders?

_____

_____

_____

What are the objectives of the MBTI program?

_____

_____

_____

Is this situation typical?

_____

_____

_____

Based on Frank's reaction, the purpose of evaluating the MBTI should have been to:

- Demonstrate the contribution and value of the program, or
- Help make investment decisions.

Frank's viewpoint certainly differed from that of some of the other stakeholders. However, a little research with department heads (clients) might reveal viewpoints similar to Frank's. Additionally, department heads may be able to help identify how MBTI could best be applied (if at all) to help address their operational problems.

Other typical purposes for evaluation include:

- Identify strengths and weaknesses in the training process.
- Determine if the skills learned are being applied on the job.
- Improve training processes to track participant progression with skills.
- Boost credibility of training practices.
- Gain stronger commitment from key stakeholders.
- Determine which employees would benefit most from participating in a training program.
- Supply data for training researchers.
- Increase knowledge and expertise in *developing* and *delivering* results-based training programs.

- Determine if participants like a program and consider it relevant to their job.
- Determine if learning has occurred.

It is rare to find an evaluation project that has only one purpose. Evaluation often has multiple purposes. Defining these purposes determines the scope and expectations of the evaluation, types of instruments used, types of data collected, whom data is collected from, and when it is collected.

Stakeholder Groups

What is meant by *stakeholder*? Stakeholders are individuals or groups who have a vested interest in a project, program, or intervention, who have something to gain or lose by successful implementation of a program; they are the decision makers at every aspect of the training process. Participants are stakeholders as well. Stakeholders are the key audience in identifying expectations for the evaluation project and for communication of the evaluation results. In thinking back to Marge, who are the stakeholders?

Who are the stakeholders of the MBTI?

_____

_____

_____

_____

_____

_____

_____

If we begin from a fundamental viewpoint, one stakeholder is certainly Marge. The feedback she receives from participants satisfies her need. Positive feedback satisfies her realization that her colleagues feel the same about the program as she does. But what if Marge has a full-scale evaluation plan in mind? Her purpose for evaluating the MBTI program is to increase interest. Who would be the stakeholders? One group may be employees at large. By creating demand based on positive feedback (Level 1), interest in a program grows. To whom can Marge go to build credibility for the program? One group may be participant supervisors. If she can show how implementation of the MBTI is improving communication and building teamwork (Level 3), supervisors may recognize its importance. Another stakeholder is executive management, including Frank. Credibility to them means measures such as productivity increase and other business outcomes (Level 4) outweigh the cost of the program.

Just as there is rarely only one purpose for an evaluation, there is no single key stakeholder group. Multiple stakeholders have varying perspectives. In evaluating programs, these perspectives should be considered. The key is knowing who these stakeholders are at the outset, seeking out their expectations, and then focusing the evaluation on their needs. To help you identify your key stakeholders, complete Exercise 2–2.

Who are your key stakeholders and what evaluation purposes and results interest them regarding your program/project?

Defining key stakeholders is important in determining the scope of your evaluation project, the type of data you will collect, the type of instruments to use, and your communication strategy. In Column I identify your key stakeholders by name or job title. Then identify the evaluation purposes from Column III (these are typical purposes) that match the needs of each stakeholder you identify. Just as your purposes may differ slightly, all of the stakeholders shown below may not be interested in your situation. Place the appropriate letter designation(s) in Column II (A through M) adjacent to the stakeholders you identified. Multiple purposes may apply to one stakeholder. There is space for you to add stakeholders or purposes not listed.

Column I Key Stakeholders	Column II	Column III Evaluation Purpose
1. Executive management	_____	A. Demonstrate contribution and value of training including ROI
2. Middle management	_____	B. Help make training investment decisions
3. Front-line management	_____	C. Identify strengths and weaknesses in the training process
4. General employee population	_____	D. Determine if the skills learned are being applied on the job
5. Training program participants	_____	E. Improve training processes to track participant progression with skills
6. Training director/managers	_____	F. Boost credibility of training practices
7. Training program designers and developers	_____	G. Gain stronger commitment from key stakeholders
8. Training program facilitators and instructors	_____	H. Determine which employees would benefit most from participating in a training program
9. Other _____	_____	I. Supply data for training researchers
10. Other _____	_____	J. Identify knowledge and expertise in *developing* and *delivering* results-based training programs
11. Other _____	_____	K. Determine if participants like a program and consider it relevant to their job
12. Other _____	_____	L. Determine if learning has occurred
13. Other _____	_____	M. Other _____

After completing Exercise 2–2, document your key stakeholders below who are interested in the results of your program. While many of your stakeholders may be interested in your evaluation project, identify which stakeholder needs you are really trying to satisfy with this project.

_____

_____

_____

_____

Now that you have identified your key stakeholders, think about the program that you have selected to evaluate. What is the purpose of the evaluation? What type of data did you identify in Exercise 2–2 that your key stakeholders are interested in? Are you seeking approval for funding? Are you trying to show value? Are you conducting the evaluation for research purposes? Do you want to understand how to improve your training process? Perhaps this is your first ROI study and you are just testing the waters. Whatever the purpose of your evaluation, define it and let the purpose(s) drive your remaining evaluation decisions.

In Chapter 1, you were asked to select a program/project that met the criteria for Levels 4 and 5 evaluation. Since this is a fieldbook on ROI, your selected program should be at the ROI level in order to advance your learning. Document the purposes of your evaluation project below.

_____

_____

_____

_____

_____

_____

_____

Evaluation Linked to Program Objectives

Program objectives form the basis of the depth of the evaluation, which means they determine at what level the evaluation will take place because they define the desired results. Ideally, this comes from the needs assessment process. It is the business need, such as the potential payoff of reducing excessive turnover, that drives the need for a training solution (or other solution) and the ROI evaluation process. Had Marge conducted a thorough needs assessment and identified her key stakeholders, she may have found a deficiency in productivity at Reliance Insurance. She would have also known that Frank would be looking for a financial payoff of the investment in whatever program she offered to solve the productivity problem. These form the Level 5 (ROI) and Level 4 (business impact) needs.

Through her needs assessment process, Marge may have found that productivity (Level 4) is lacking because teams are dysfunctional (Level 3). The teams lack cohesion. Team members have limited and poor-quality communication with each other and their supervisors. This represents a Level 3 need, inadequate job performance. A critical factor Marge may find during her needs assessment process is that there are a variety of personalities in each team. As such, when a supervisor offers feedback to one employee, she may receive positive reaction, but in offering feedback to another, the reaction is defensive. The same is true among the teams. Team members often offend each other because they lack understanding in how best to communicate to others who are different from themselves, hence, a Level 2 need, learning.

Finally, Marge may find that employees respond positively to facilitator-led programs. Facilitator-led sessions allow for interaction among participants. This represents the Level 1 need, preferences.

These needs drive the objectives for the program. Objectives then drive the program as well as the evaluation. This connection is shown in Figure 2–1.

An explanation of the linkage is on the CD-ROM (Figure 2–1 explanation) to help you think through the linkage of the needs of your program, the objectives, and the levels of evaluation. Practice your ability to recognize the levels of objectives by completing Exercise 2–3. The answers to the exercise are found on the CD-ROM, along with explanations by the authors.

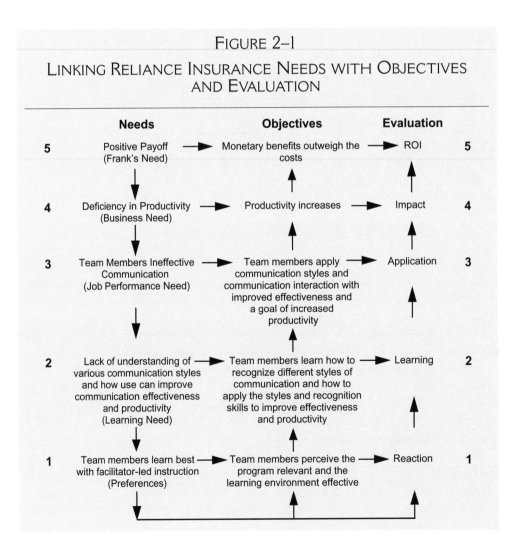

FIGURE 2–1

LINKING RELIANCE INSURANCE NEEDS WITH OBJECTIVES AND EVALUATION

	Needs	Objectives	Evaluation	
5	Positive Payoff (Frank's Need)	Monetary benefits outweigh the costs	ROI	5
4	Deficiency in Productivity (Business Need)	Productivity increases	Impact	4
3	Team Members Ineffective Communication (Job Performance Need)	Team members apply communication styles and communication interaction with improved effectiveness and a goal of increased productivity	Application	3
2	Lack of understanding of various communication styles and how use can improve communication effectiveness and productivity (Learning Need)	Team members learn how to recognize different styles of communication and how to apply the styles and recognition skills to improve effectiveness and productivity	Learning	2
1	Team members learn best with facilitator-led instruction (Preferences)	Team members perceive the program relevant and the learning environment effective	Reaction	1

EXERCISE 2–3. MATCHING EVALUATION LEVELS WITH OBJECTIVES

Instructions: For each objective listed below, indicate the level of evaluation at which the objective is aimed.

- Level 1—Participant Reaction
- Level 2—Learning
- Level 3—Application
- Level 4—Impact
- Level 5—Return on Investment

Objective	Evaluation Level
1. Decrease error rates on reports by 20%	_____
2. Increase the use of disciplinary discussion skills in 90% of discussions	_____
3. Achieve a posttest score increase of 30% over pretest	_____
4. Initiate at least three cost reduction projects	_____
5. Decrease the amount of time required to complete a project	_____
6. Achieve a 2:1 benefit-to-cost ratio one year after program implementation	_____
7. Receive an instructor rating from participants of at least 4.5	_____
8. Increase the external customer satisfaction index by 25% in 3 months	_____
9. Handle customer complaints with the 5-step process in 95% of complaint situations	_____
10. Achieve a work simulation test score average of 75	_____
11. Conduct a meeting with direct reports to set improvement goals	_____
12. Use customer interaction skills with every customer (50% target)	_____

If the objectives already exist for the program you selected for evaluation, review them and decide whether they meet the guidelines for acceptable objectives. It is extremely important to have clear and specific program objectives at each level. If the objectives are not clear and specific, you will likely have a difficult time developing an evaluation strategy and evaluation instruments.

It is also worth noting that without clear and specific program objectives, we will remain uncertain regarding what participants must know and do to meet expectations. It is bewildering that professionals in the training profession often develop and deliver content without really identifying the objectives. Yet we continue to wonder why we do not get results. To use a cliché, something is certainly wrong with this picture.

If your program objectives are unacceptable, see Job Aid 2–1 on the CD for additional help in identifying acceptable objectives. The Job Aid includes guidelines and examples for writing Level 2, Level 3, and Level 4 objectives and it includes space for you to capture your objectives.

Evaluation Planning Documents

Up to this point, we've identified our key stakeholders and we have identified the purposes of our evaluation. We've also practiced matching evaluation levels with program objectives and we have reviewed the program objectives. We can now begin thinking about how to link our evaluation to these objectives as we begin the planning process. As we begin the planning process for the evaluation, we will work with four planning documents: the data collection plan, the ROI analysis plan, the communication plan, and the evaluation project plan. All four plans are on the CD-ROM for you to print and work with as we move along through the book. We will begin, however, by introducing you to each plan, starting with the Data Collection Plan.

Data Collection Plan

Figure 2–2 presents the Data Collection Plan. As shown, six items are developed in planning data collection for each evaluation. First we identify the broad program objectives for the program/project we are evaluating. You may have developed these objectives in the previous section using Job Aid 2–1 provided on the CD. Objectives are measurable targets that describe the end result of a program, process, or initiative to be expected over a period of time. They are

FIGURE 2–2
DATA COLLECTION PLAN

Level	Broad Program Objective(s)	Measures	Data Collection Method/Instruments	Data Sources	Timing	Responsibilities
1	SATISFACTION/PLANNED ACTION					
2	LEARNING					
3	APPLICATION/ IMPLEMENTATION					
4	BUSINESS IMPACT					
5	ROI	COMMENTS:				

DATA COLLECTION PLAN: _____

Program/Project: _____

Date: _____

Responsibility: _____

Client signature _____ Date: _____

to follow the SMART requirements; they should be specific, measurable, achievable, realistic, and time-based.

The next item on the Data Collection Plan is our measures. Measures determine whether or not the objectives are being met. But they should be directly related to the SMART objective that specifies a single result. *Performance Measurement Concepts and Techniques,* 3rd edition, published by ASPA's Center for Accountability and Performance, offers 11 criteria for developing ideal measures. Exercise 2–4 reflects these criteria. If your objectives meet the SMART criteria, then your measures may already be included in the objective statements provided to you or that you have created. Whether you chose to visit Job Aid 2–1 or not, complete Exercise 2–4 to capture your objectives at each level. Capturing your measures in the adjacent column of Exercise 2–4 will allow you to more clearly judge the quality of the measures. This is also why the Data Collection Plan includes measures in a separate column.

To reinforce your understanding of what constitutes an objective and a measure, please complete Exercise 2–4. The exercise is also found on the CD-ROM to be used by you and your team.

After you have identified your objectives and measures as you proceed through the next chapter, you will complete the Data Collection Plan by identifying your data collection method, data sources, timing of data collection, and the person (or persons) responsible for collecting the data. These components of the Data Collection Plan are discussed in detail in the next chapter.

ROI Analysis Plan

The next planning document you will complete is the ROI Analysis Plan. This document is critical when evaluating a program to Levels 4 and 5. As shown in Figure 2–3, there are eight columns to be completed. The first column represents your Level 4 measures. These are the impact measures that are targeted for improvement by the training program you are evaluating.

The next column represents the method(s) you plan to use to isolate the effects of the program on the Level 4 measures. This step is critical because it gives credit to the training program only for the improvement that is actually influenced by the training process. Chapter 4 addresses isolation in detail. Even if a program is only evaluated to Level 4, this step must be taken.

The next column identifies the methods to convert data to monetary value. Here is where we begin moving toward Level 5, ROI. You will only complete this column if you decide to convert the Level 4 measure to a monetary value. In Chapter 5, a four-part test is described that will help you decide whether or not to convert the data to a monetary value. If you do not, you will mark out the box next to the measure and move the measure to the column marked Intangible Benefits. Again, data conversion is described in detail in Chapter 5.

Cost categories, intangible benefits, communication targets, other influences, and comments complete the ROI analysis planning step. Here you identify in general terms these additional areas. Each of these is addressed in detail throughout the book. Along with summarizing the communication targets on the ROI analysis plan, you will develop a communication plan to help you stay

EXERCISE 2–4. OBJECTIVES AND MEASURES

Measures determine whether objectives have been met. They should be:

- Relevant
- Results Oriented
- Responsive
- Valid
- Reliable
- Economic (where practical)
- Useful
- Accessible
- Comparable
- Compatible
- Clear

Objective	Measure
1. Receive positive feedback from 95% of the participants.	1. Score an average of 4.5 out of 5 on relevance, importance, and new amount of information.
2. 90% of all participants score a passing grade on first attempt.	2. Minimum score of 80% correct on a 30 item objective test.
3. Participants apply 60% of the new skills taught during first three months.	3. Six out of ten skills are applied 100% of the time during the first three months.
4. Increase sales of TCG telephone systems.	4. Monthly sales increased by 25%.
5. Reduce the number of client documentation errors.	5. Monthly errors in documenting client contact information, client "trouble requests," and "response time commitment codes" reduced by 15%.

Insert your objectives here	Insert your measures here
1. _____	1. _____
2. _____	2. _____
3. _____	3. _____
4. _____	4. _____
5. _____	5. _____
6. _____	6. _____

focused on the target audience and the type of communication your audience will receive. This is discussed below.

At the bottom of the Data Collection Plan and the ROI Analysis Plan, you see a space for the client signature. It is highly recommended that you have your client sign off on these evaluation plans. This ensures that when the results are reported, the client accepts the steps taken to evaluate the program.

48   THE ROI FIELDBOOK

FIGURE 2–3
ROI ANALYSIS PLAN

| ROI ANALYSIS PLAN: | | | | | | Date: | |

Program/Project: Responsibility:

Data Items (Usually Level 4)	Methods for Isolating the Effects of the Program/ Process	Methods of Converting Data to Monetary Values	Cost Categories	Intangible Benefits	Communication Targets for Final Report	Other Influences/ Issues During Application	Comments

Client signature _____ Date: _____

Communication Plan

Communicating the results of an evaluation is often the most neglected step. However, it is the most important. Why evaluate a program if you're not going to do something with what you find? A golden rule of evaluation: If you ask for the data—do something with it.

In order to do something constructive, you must tell the right people. As you will read in Chapter 8, the first step in communicating results is to define the audience with whom you will communicate in order to get what you want. Sound familiar? You got it: It's the stakeholders—those people or groups who are interested in the results. These are the individuals from whom you can get what you need.

The next step is to identify the purpose of communicating to each audience. Is your purpose to build credibility, gain funding, demonstrate accountability for an existing budget, or demonstrate the extent to which posttraining execution has occurred? This sounds much like defining your evaluation purpose, right? Well, it is. Your audience and their communication needs often reflect the purpose of the evaluation.

The third step is to define the communication timeline to each audience. When is the best time to present the results? The timing of communication can be a crucial factor in the receptivity of your audience, getting the response you want, and getting the evaluation results acted upon.

The fourth step in planning your communication is deciding the best medium by which to communicate the results to each target audience. Is a detailed report necessary? How about an executive summary? Is it better to present the results in a special meeting, or will a routine staff meeting do? Will e-mail or a Website be an appropriate channel? What about the organization's communication media, such as the monthly house organ publication or video communication channels?

Next we identify responsibilities for the communication. Who is best positioned to communicate to each respective audience? The communication objectives for each target audience will be key factors in determining responsibilities. Then we provide a column to capture the status of each communication component.

Then, when it's all said and done, we conduct a debriefing with our evaluation team to evaluate the effectiveness of our communication. Did the communication meet the stated objectives? Did stakeholders get what they needed? Did we get the results we needed? All of these issues will be discussed in detail in Chapter 8. For now, Figure 2–4 presents the Communication Plan. This plan, along with the Data Collection Plan and the ROI Analysis Plan, is on the CD so you can complete the plan as you move through the book.

FIGURE 2–4
COMMUNICATION PLAN

Evaluation Project: _____   Date: _____

Target Audience	Purpose/Objective of Communication	Communication Timeline	Distribution Channel	Responsibility	Status

Project Plan

The final planning document is the Project Plan. The Project Plan maps each step of the evaluation process. This plan is a culmination of the previously described plans, plus the detailed steps. The Project Plan begins with developing the evaluation team and ends with communication and follow-up activities. As you complete each chapter in the book, the steps in the Project Plan will become clear. The first step is to describe the program to be evaluated, followed by the development of the evaluation team. From there you begin with the data-collection-planning process. The Project Plan includes these steps as well as steps to design the data collection instrument and to administer the data collection process. Then the ROI Analysis Plan and the Communication Plans are also included. The final section of the Project Plan includes any follow-up activity after you have communicated results.

The Project Plan helps track resources. As you will see in Chapter 6, everything you spend on the evaluation is included in the cost calculation. Accounting for resources expended while implementing the Project Plan is a plus. It will save you time as you go. Microsoft Project is a useful tool when planning a comprehensive evaluation project. It allows you automatically to account for the costs of people involved in the evaluation as well as the cost of other resources. However, spreadsheet tools such as Microsoft Excel work just fine, or your organization may have an in-house project-planning tool. Microsoft Word is even a sufficient tool to develop a Project Plan, although it does lack some of the calculation capabilities. Nevertheless, the Project Plan should represent an operational tool you can use. Develop it by using the best tool for you and your team. Figure 2–5 presents the Project Plan found on the CD. Use it as is or as a template to develop your own, but be sure to plan the project in detail. It will save you time, money, and frustration!

In this section we addressed the fundamental issues of planning your ROI evaluation. Although we have tried to make the process as simple as possible, we recognize that the best-laid plans are sometimes derailed. The next section addresses potential challenges you may face as you begin planning your evaluation.

POTENTIAL CHALLENGES

There are four primary challenges you may face when planning your evaluation: (1) time, (2) no needs assessment, (3) unclear objectives or intent of the program, and (4) no help. All we can say is—PLAN ANYWAY.

Time

Think about Marge in Exercise 2–1. How much time does she have? Frank is ready for additional information about the MBTI, so time is certainly a challenge. There is no better time to plan than when time is of the essence. Developing a detailed plan about the data needed, the method used to collect the

FIGURE 2–5
PROJECT PLAN

Program: _____

Description: _____

Duration: _____   No. Participants: _____   Begin Date: _____   End Date: _____

	J	F	M	A	M	J	J	A	S	O	N	D
Form the Evaluation Team												
Team Member 1												
Team Member 2												
Data Collection												
Develop Data Collection Plan												
Develop Data Collection Instruments												
Design												
Test												
Redesign												
Data Collection Administration Plan												
Begin Data Collection												
Receive Responses												
*Distribute Incentives *see DC Admin Plan*												
Data Analysis												
Develop ROI Analysis Plan												
Develop Cost Profile												
Analyze Data												
Communication Plan												
Develop Communication Plan												
Results Stakeholder Group 1												
Results Stakeholder Group 2												
Results Stakeholder Group 4												
Evaluation Follow-up												
Steps to be taken to improve program												
Respond to questions from stakeholders												

data, and the sources of the data will serve as a checklist for Marge. Also, she needs a plan detailing what to do with the data once she has it—her ROI Analysis Plan. She also needs to be able to develop a report that will provide Frank the information he needs to make a decision about the future of the MBTI program—the Communication Plan. Finally, a Project Plan will serve as her map to get from where she is to where she wants to go.

No Needs—No Objectives

This is often a deterrent to evaluating programs. "We can't evaluate a program that has already been conducted because there was no needs assessment; therefore, we have no clear objectives" is often a cry from those who just don't want to go there. Fear not; the planning stage is the point in time when you will take up arms and go to battle with this frequently occurring practice.

Again, think about Marge. Was a needs assessment conducted? No. Did she have clear objectives? No. Did Frank set an objective for her? Yes. See, it's simple. You can work backwards to develop your objectives when necessary.

If there was no needs assessment and there are either no objectives or poorly written objectives, work through the linking process depicted in Figure 2–1. Answer these five questions:

1. Is there a concern about the costs of the program? This is sometimes driven by executive management. If there are concerns about program costs, then how much more than the cost do you hope the program brings in monetary benefit? Setting your target ROI is discussed later in the book, but for now a good hurdle rate is about 25%. So if the fully loaded cost of your program is $100,000, you would need benefits of $125,000 to achieve the 25% ROI. By definition, an ROI cannot be achieved without first recovering the costs, so you must recoup the cost of $100,000. The additional $25,000 is the net gain resulting in the 25% ROI.
2. What impact has the program had on key business measures? Here you will need to get together with some of the participants. Interview some of them or take them to lunch and ask them to give you feedback on the results they have seen.
3. What skills are being applied or what behavior has changed as the result of participants attending the program? While you are having lunch with the participants, ask them to identify the skills they applied from the program. This will give you some data; however, even though you may not have developed appropriate objectives, you should already have some indication of the skills they should apply as a result of the program.
4. What skills and knowledge did they learn in the program? This is where your program developer comes into the picture. If the program is designed in house, what skills was the program designed to develop? If it was a packaged program, purchased from your favorite training supplier, why was it purchased?

5. Was the program relevant and important, and did it provide new information? Was it facilitated in such a manner that participants responded positively? These are questions you probably asked in your basic Level 1 end-of-course questionnaire. However, if you did not, then ask participants in the follow-up. This will give you Level 1 data on a post-program basis, but will still provide important information you can use to improve the program.

Intent of the Program

Is the MBTI really intended to drive business measures? Perhaps not, although there are cases in which it is used strategically to build teams and yield a great payoff. But many times a program such as the MBTI is intended to build awareness (Level 2) and hopefully change some behavior (Level 3). If we can change Level 3 behavior, then there may be a possible link to one or more business measures. Nevertheless, many times an evaluation is conducted on programs that have not identified an intended business measure improvement. When this is the case, you have to dig to develop the higher level objectives. Using the steps above, work with participants to see the consequences of their applying the knowledge gained from a program. It's a challenge, but not impossible. The planning process is when these issues should be addressed. If Level 4 objectives cannot be identified, then this raises serious questions about the program's priority and even the need to implement it at all.

No Help

So you are the sole person responsible for evaluation. There is no team to work with to develop a plan. PLAN ANYWAY. We plan every day when working alone. Just because you're it does not justify working without a plan. You need it now more than ever. As in Marge's case, with time—it's you and the evaluation—plan the process.

CASE STUDY INTRODUCTION

The CD includes the case study Premier Motors International to help you visualize and learn how to plan and execute an ROI Impact Study. This case study represents a real situation in which an ROI Impact Study was completed. The names and certain proprietary information have been changed and a few of the issues and events have been slightly modified at the request of the organization in which the study was conducted.

The case study builds progressively with Part A (Chapter 2) through Part F (Chapter 8), so the illustrations are relevant to the information being covered in each respective fieldbook chapter. It is strongly recommended that you review each part of the case study as you proceed through each chapter (either before, during, or after you review the chapter). Before proceeding with the Action Steps of Chapter 2, review Part A of the case study to see how the Data Collection Plan is initially developed. Part A also includes other important information that will help you see the nature of the information needed in order to embark on an evaluation of this magnitude.

ACTION STEPS

- Okay, now it is time to take action. You are about to embark on the first step toward evaluating your program. Print the Data Collection Plan from the CD, or if you work better from a computer monitor, use that.
- In the first column of the Data Collection Plan, list your program objectives. If necessary and if you have not already done so, go to Job Aid 2–1 on the CD to review how to develop objectives.
- Develop your measures. How will you know if you achieve your objectives?
- For your Level 5 ROI objective, put in 25% for now. As you will read later, the target ROI can depend on a number of issues; 25% is above the minimum your organization expects on many other investments. Because training is often held to a higher standard, we want to shoot for a higher return. But it may be that your client expects more, or if you break even (0% ROI) on your program, management will be happy. Nevertheless, use 25%.

We will complete the remaining columns of the Data Collection Plan in the next chapter. Your ROI Analysis Plan will be addressed beginning with Chapter 4.

CHAPTER SUMMARY

In this chapter we focused on planning your evaluation. As we hope you learned, planning is one of the most crucial steps in the evaluation process. The chapter helped you

- Define the purpose of your evaluation.
- Identify key stakeholders.
- Link program objectives to the evaluation.
- Begin the initial planning for your ROI Impact Study.

Now that you have the preliminary details, move on to designing the data collection process. The next chapter focuses on selecting a data collection method, identifying data sources, determining the timing for the data collection, and assigning responsibilities to your evaluation team.

Books

Broom, C., M. Jackson, J. Harris, and V. Vogelsang-Coombs. *Performance Measurement: Concepts and Techniques,* 3rd ed. Washington, DC: American Society for Public Administration, 2000.

Chatfield, C., and T. Johnson, T. *Microsoft® Office Project 2003 Step by Step.* Redmond, WA: Microsoft Press, 2004.

Phillips, J. J. *Return on Investment in Training and Performance Improvement Programs,* 2nd ed. Boston: Butterworth-Heinemann, 2003.

Phillips, P. P., and H. Burkett. *Managing Evaluation Shortcuts.* Alexandria, VA: ASTD, 2001.

Phillips, P. P., J. J. Phillips, and C. Gaudet. *Evaluation Data: Planning and Use.* Alexandria, VA: ASTD, 2003.

Young, M. J., and M. Halvorson, M. *Microsoft® Office System 2003 Edition.* Redmond, WA: Microsoft Press, 2004.

Software

Microsoft® Excel 2003
Microsoft® Project 2003
Microsoft® Word 2003

CD

Exercises and Case Study	Tools, Templates, and Job Aids
■ Exercise 2–1. Reliance Insurance	■ Figure 2–1. Linking Needs to Objectives and Evaluation (Reliance Insurance example)
■ Exercise 2–2. Stakeholder Interest In Evaluation	■ Figure 2–1A. Linking Needs to Objectives and Evaluation (explanation)
■ Exercise 2–3. Matching Evaluation Levels with Objectives (blank)	■ Figure 2–2. Data Collection Plan (blank)
■ Exercise 2–3A. Matching Evaluation Levels with Objectives (with answers and author comments)	■ Figure 2–3. ROI Analysis Plan (blank)
■ Exercise 2–4. Objectives and Measures	■ Figure 2–4. Communication Plan (blank)
■ Case Study—Part A, Premier Motors International (PMI)	■ Figure 2–5. Project Plan (blank)
	■ Job Aid 2–1. Writing Objectives that Focus on Results
	■ Additional examples of Data Collection and ROI Analysis Plans

Part Two
Implementing the Process

COLLECTING THE DATA YOU NEED

To this point you have defined the purpose of your evaluation, identified key stakeholders, refined your program objectives, and developed measures that will tell you if objectives are met. Now you must decide whom you will collect data from, and how and when you will collect it. This step in the process is data collection.

Collecting data requires that you plan your questions and present them in such a way that you can collect the most credible and reliable data possible. You should address four questions when collecting the data you need for your evaluation: (1) What do I ask? (2) How do I ask? (3) Whom do I ask? (4) When do I ask?

In this chapter you will:

❑ Develop the questions you plan to answer through your evaluation.
❑ Identify the appropriate data collection instruments for evaluating your program.
❑ Identify the sources of your data.
❑ Determine the timing of data collection.

THE FUNDAMENTALS

Developing the questions you plan to ask is actually quite simple—especially now that you've worked through the previous chapter. The measures defined to meet your objectives become the basis for the questions you ask; then, you decide the sources and the methods you can best use to ask those questions. There are a number of data collection methods. The answer to the question as to which method to choose is, "It's situational." It depends on the type of data you need—quantitative, qualitative, or some combination of the two. Do you need to probe, or will a numeric indicator suffice? Do you need to collect the input in a group setting, or is confidential dialogue needed to get the full scoop? The scope and methods of data collection depend on the resources you plan to invest in the process. Are you willing to spend the time it takes to interview the appropriate number of people? Will a brief survey e-mailed to participants do the job? Is the data you need already being collected? Is it available through organizational records? Data collection also depends on the credibility of the source—who knows best about the success of the program and the improvement in the measures?

To get started, read and complete Exercise 3–1. Take your time. The exercise assesses your recognition of data as they relate to the five levels of evaluation. It gives you a first opportunity to match a data collection instrument to a typical scenario. The answers to the exercise are found on the CD in the Chapter 3 folder. This exercise should help provide you with a better understanding of how to make decisions about data collection.

You should also review Job Aid 3–1. The job-aid presents seven steps that include questions you should answer and gives a perspective about seven important factors for collecting Level 3 and Level 4 data. These 7Cfactors™ represent the major constraints and opportunities of data collection. As you design your follow-up data collection strategy, reflect on and apply these 7Cfactors to improve cooperation and credibility in your data collection efforts. Always pay particular attention to how a specific data collection method, the timing, and the sources affect all of your stakeholders (those providing the data, those supporting the data collection, and those the data will be presented to).

What Do I Ask?

For the most part, you have answered this question in the previous chapter. The questions that should be asked in evaluating the program are represented by the measures that indicate successful achievement of your objectives. If a measure of success is to achieve a 4.5 out of 5 from 90% of participants on relevance of content to the job, the question morphs into:

	Not At All			Extremely	
	1	2	3	4	5
To what extent was the course content relevant to your job?	❏	❏	❏	❏	❏

Easy, right?

As mentioned earlier, most programs have multiple measures of success at each level of evaluation (with exception of Level 5—the ROI is what the ROI is—or is it?). For instance, at Level 1, relevance is important, but so is the extent to which the program is important, as well as the participants'

EXERCISE 3–1. APPLICATIONS OF DATA COLLECTION INSTRUMENTS

For each of the following situations, please indicate the most appropriate type of instrument for collecting data needed to assist in the program's evaluation. Select from these types:

(a) Survey   (e) Focus Groups
(b) Test   (f) Observation
(c) Questionnaire (g) Performance Records
(d) Interview

Write the instrument's letter in the box to the right of each question. Also, indicate the level of evaluation pursued.

                                                                 Instrument   Level

1. Customer service representatives have learned to resolve   ❑   ❑
   customer complaints in the most effective manner. An
   integral part of the program required customer service
   representatives to follow a series of planned steps to resolve
   the complaint, using empathy and listening skills. As part
   of the evaluation, the training staff must determine the
   extent to which participants are actually using the newly
   acquired skills.

2. Intact team members attended a conflict resolution program   ❑   ❑
   where they acquired skills to resolve conflicts and disputes
   among themselves. Team members in this work group have
   a high degree of interaction, and some responsibilities
   include checking the work of others. There had been an
   unusually high level of friction with displays of open
   conflicts in the group. In the program, participants learned
   how to deal with these issues and work together as a
   smooth operating team. The training staff needs to collect
   information about the group's progress, ideally in an
   environment where there is an opportunity for group
   members to listen to comments from others.

3. Technicians plan to attend a course on basic mathematics   ❑   ❑
   and are required to have a predetermined level of
   competency in mathematics before entering the program.
   The training staff measures the level of mathematical ability
   before and after the training program.

4. The front desk staff at a major hotel has attended a   ❑   ❑
   training program to learn to use a new reservation system
   that is being installed. As part of the evaluation, it is
   important to obtain reactions to the training and capture
   planned action.

Continued

5. A company has implemented a new compensation plan in   ❑   ❑
   which the employees share in the overall profits of the
   company. Employees have attended a briefing at which they
   had the opportunity to learn how the program works and
   what is required of them to make it successful. As part of
   the evaluation, management is interested in finding out
   what the employees think about the new plan after
   attending the briefing.
6. Sales representatives attended a training program designed   ❑   ❑
   to improve sales skills. One objective of the program is to
   improve sales volume, and the training staff must
   determine exactly what increase was achieved by each
   individual since the program was conducted.
7. Supervisors attended a problem-solving program at which   ❑   ❑
   they learned a logical approach to solving significant
   problems facing their work units. As a part of the
   program's evaluation, the training staff needs feedback
   from participants concerning their use of the acquired
   skills. The staff thinks there is a possibility of a success
   story.

interaction with each other and the facilitator's success in communicating the content. Given this, a question is developed for each key measure of success within each level of evaluation. When evaluating to Level 5, ROI, you will always collect data at each level so that the chain of impact can be reported in its entirety—Guiding Principle 1. But keep in mind Guiding Principle 2; when an evaluation is planned for a higher level, the previous levels of evaluation do not have to be as comprehensive. This means if you are going to expend resources on an ROI impact study, you want to expend the resources at the higher levels but also have acceptable evidence at the lower levels while containing the cost and effort at these levels.

Level 1: Reaction and Planned Action

A typical Level 1 evaluation focuses on the content of the materials, the facilitator's skills, and the environment in which the training was presented. A typical Level 1 evaluation is often a measure of overall satisfaction that answers the question, "Did the participants like the program?" While participants liking the program may provide you some satisfaction in your work as a trainer, it provides little data about how the learning will be used once participants leave the classroom. However, at Level 1 there are other measures that provide valuable information that you can immediately use, including utility measures

7CFACTORS™ of DATA COLLECTION

While considering the objectives of your data collection and reporting strategy, consider all possible sources and methods. Because *cost, time, and disruption* are issues when collecting data, you may be unable to collect the exact data you prefer, or collect it in exactly the way you prefer. Selecting data collection methods is a matter of making choices and trade-offs. You should determine upfront what data your stakeholders will accept.

Follow the seven Steps listed below and review the 7Cfactors™ to help make decisions about the data you need, the timing, the methods, and the possible sources. Each Cfactor™ potentially affects the other 7Cfactors and your ability to collect, analyze, and report the data you need. The 7Cfactors present questions that, when addressed, will aid in making acceptable choices for you and your stakeholders.

Step 1. What are the objectives for data collection?

Step 2. What do my client and other stakeholders need to know?

Step 3. What are the best timing and methods for data collection to achieve the coverage I need?

Step 4. Who is best positioned to provide the data? Who should know best about the data you are collecting?

Step 5. Are these sources credible in my client's eyes?

Step 6. Will these sources cooperate?

Step 7. How will I partner with these sources to influence cooperation?

How can I get people to cooperate with me to collect credible data in a timely fashion at a reasonable cost?

Job Aid 3-1—*Continued*
7Cfactors™ of Data Collection

7Cfactors™ of Data Collection

7Cfactors	Definition of Factors	What Issues/Questions Should Be Considered?
Comprehensive	Completeness in meeting the approved objectives of the data collection effort.	Is the data collection as inclusive as it needs to be? Is the data credible enough to develop conclusions and satisfy stakeholders? Is the timing of data collection suitable relative to organizational climate and performance opportunity?
Convenience	The ready availability of data because it is already being collected and/or a situation exists where people are easily positioned to provide data.	How can I make my data collection effort easier and more expedient? If credible data is already available and it serves my purposes, can I use it? If data is available even though the timing is not exactly as I would prefer, will the data still be credible if I change my original timeline? When people must provide data and there is a place, situation, or time frame that is more convenient for them, how will I make adjustments in my methods to accommodate this convenience?
Consideration	Respect for others' time and priorities when data is being collected.	How will I minimize the disruption and distractions of data collection? How will I collect the data without being too invasive regarding people's feelings and the work processes? Will a different method, source, or time frame work better?
Cost	The economic impact of time away from task and any additional expense in collecting data.	Does my budget allow for travel and other expenses? How do supervisors and team members feel about taking time away from task to respond to data collection needs? How will I overcome resistance? How will I communicate what's in it for them?
Confidentiality	Certainty that the data and/or the sources will be properly safeguarded now and in the	Are there sensitive or privacy issues that may require anonymity for respondents (even if not, is it politically wise to provide anonymity)? Will anonymity (or lack of it) affect response bias? Is the

	future.	organization/company data considered proprietary or sensitive? Is anyone vulnerable or at risk if the data is made public or if sources are revealed?
Credibility	Data is accepted as being useful, reliable, and legitimate as others view the source and nature of the data.	Which data are important to which stakeholders? Have I identified business impact and job application measures/outcomes? Are those providing the data positioned to know? Are they close to the situation? Is their input objective and unbiased? How accurate and reliable is the data? Is the data collected at the right time? Is there a baseline comparison? Is the data from business records stable (rather than being erratic and unpredictable, etc.)? During collection, analysis, and reporting, what adjustments should I make to the data and what standards will I apply to do it. How will I isolate the effects and convert data to a monetary value when reporting business impact?
Cooperation	The willingness of others to provide the time to engage in the data collection process.	What strategies will I employ to seek cooperation? How will I inform my sources of the benefits of the data collection? How will I discover and ease their concerns about the data collection? Can I commit to them that they will see the consolidated results?

that have been shown to predict use of learning. This is covered in more detail later in this chapter.

Program Content

Participant reaction to program content is important. When participants are queried about this at the end of a course, they are often asked, "To what extent were you satisfied with the program content?"

As in the case of asking participants if they like the program, knowing the level of participant satisfaction with program content lends nothing to the effort to improve it. More information is needed in order to continuously improve program content. Questions about program content should address issues such as:

- The scope of the material.
- The organization of the materials.
- The relationship between examples and activities and their usefulness to participants' understanding of the content.
- The usefulness of materials back on the job.

Answers to these questions provide some value to the designers and developers of the program so that the need for improvements can be determined.

Facilitator Skills

Understanding participant reaction to facilitator skills is important to improving the overall training process (ratings on these questions should not be used as performance appraisal for facilitators but only for process improvement). However, asking a question such as "To what extent was the facilitator effective?" gives you no basis for making change. Allowing participants to react to specific skills important to knowledge transfer allows facilitators to improve, thereby improving the workforce learning and performance process. Questions regarding facilitator skills may cover issues such as:

- Knowledge about the subject.
- Preparedness for the class.
- Effort to encourage class participation.
- Responsiveness to participant needs and questions.
- Energy and enthusiasm.

Questions should be asked that provide information from which facilitators can glean their own developmental opportunities.

Learning Environment

How many end-of-course evaluations have you completed that have a question similar to "To what extent do you agree that the facilities were conducive to learning?"

Some designers probably include a similar question on the end-of-course questionnaire, right? Our questions about this question are:

- What if the facilities are not conducive to learning?
- What will be done to change it?
- If you can change the learning environment, how do you know what to change?

All too often we ask a question from which we can glean nothing to help improve the training process. If a measure of training success is that participants view the environment as conducive to learning, then we need to define "conducive." What does that mean and how can we improve it? Specific questions or a comment section that allow the opportunity to address how to fix the problem provide more insightful data to those who need it.

Planned Action

During the early 1990s, Jack Phillips modified the definition of Level 1 as originated by Donald Kirkpatrick. Phillips's modification included addressing "planned action." By asking participants "what they plan to do differently," Level 1 ventures into the work setting. It's a Level 3 question being asked with Level 1 timing. Participants must think about how they will apply what they learned and respond accordingly. This does not mean they will actually do it, but it greatly increases the possibilities as well as providing important data that can be used in many ways. Responses to "what do you plan to do differently" can be used beneficially to:

- Conduct a follow-up evaluation at Level 3 to determine if the participants applied the behavior/skills as planned.
- Confirm needs that were addressed during the course.
- Identify new needs.
- Identify relevant examples that can be used when teaching the course.
- Aid in identifying how specific populations are benefiting from the course.
- Communicate with line managers in their language.

Utility Measures

Research has shown that positive responses to five specific Level 1 measures (referred to as utility measures) have a strong correlation to results. These measures are shown in Table 3–1.

Keep in mind a program may be relevant but may not be important, or on the participant's—or organization's—radar screen at the time. These five types of questions should be asked when appropriate and tracked to make changes in program design or content and eligible population.

TABLE 3–1

1. To what extent is the program relevant to your job?
2. To what extent is the program important to your job?
3. To what extent did the program provide you new information?
4. Would you recommend this course to others?
5. How will you apply what you learned (planned action)?

Level 2: Learning

Evaluating learning is a crucial step in verifying the extent to which participants can apply new skills and knowledge when they return to the job. If participants don't know what to do (or how to do it) when they complete the learning engagement, how can you assume they will make any contributions they are supposed to make? On the other hand, if participants are not increasing their knowledge and skills, then they could be the wrong participants for the course, the information could be dated, or the facilitator (or e-learning methods) simply may not have done the job.

When participants complete your training courses, you should have a very high confidence level that they can apply the required new knowledge and skills. More importantly, participants should feel confident to go out and apply what they learned when returning to the work setting. Therefore, Level 2 evaluation answers three critical questions:

1. Are they making progress?
2. Did they get it?
3. Are they confident in using it?

By keeping these three simple questions in mind, you can offset any scares or trepidation you might feel in the thought of testing learning and knowledge. These are the three primary reasons we test for knowledge and skill. There are other reasons, but most of them are secondary. If participants are not confident in applying a skill or using a new process, they will often find a way to avoid it, especially when one or more of the following conditions are present:

- Use of the skill or process might reveal a personal weakness.
- Use of a skill or process might result in embarrassment in front of others.
- A different but familiar approach can be substituted (even if it is known to yield less results).
- Other people are avoiding using the skill/approach.

By testing at Level 2, you can determine the extent of participants' confidence and address this with content and repetitions of skill practice. If the training design (including the amount of time allowed) does not accommodate sufficient skill practice, this should be communicated to key stakeholders.

If key stakeholders are aware of this deficiency, sound decisions can then be made to address the need for continuing on-the-job training, coaching, or implementation of other approaches to enable participants to grow in confidence.

Level 3: Application and Implementation

As one senior executive put it, "It's not what they learn, it's what they do with what they learn." Hence, there is the need for evaluating at Level 3 application and implementation. When behavior change is needed, evaluating at Level 1 and Level 2 provides you with lead indicators of possible success at Level 3, but it does not tell you about actual application/implementation. You want to evaluate the actual behavior on the job. Also, when you are conducting an ROI Impact Study and you observe low Level 4 business impact, you want to take a close look at your Level 3 measures to see what barriers may have prevented the use of the skills and knowledge. You can then recommend action to marginalize or remove these barriers. Conversely, when you observe high Level 4 business impact measures, you want to look at Level 3 data to see what enablers supported the use of skills so that those enablers can be replicated for other initiatives or in other parts of the organization. Therefore, at a minimum, at least four types of questions are asked when evaluating at Level 3:

1. To what extent is the range of the new skills and knowledge being applied?
2. How frequently are the new skills and knowledge being applied?
3. What barriers have prevented the use of the new knowledge and skills?
4. What enablers have supported the use of knowledge and skills?

These four types of questions provide you with evidence of actual use of skills. They also help you to take a deeper look at the work setting in which the skills must be applied. By evaluating the system itself—meaning the organization, management support, peer support, and the availability of technology and other work processes within the organization—you can help recommend adjustments not only to the program but to the work system as a whole. And by combining your Level 3 data with the Level 2 and Level 1 data, you can get a pretty good idea of how the training process has worked. By analyzing responses to the four types of questions at Level 3, you begin a systemic approach to evaluating and improving your program's design and the performance support in the work setting.

Additional questions can also be asked at Level 3 to address other data needs. For example, you may want to collect data on the quality and effectiveness of the skills applied, which skills are most beneficial in achieving the intended result, which skills are most difficult to apply, which skills need more development attention, and so on. The types of questions you ask are a function of what your purposes are in collecting the data. What do your stakeholders want to know? This should be determined during the evaluation planning phase (covered in Chapter 2).

Level 4: Impact

Level 4 measures are defined as the consequence of doing something different as a result of the program. When you break this definition down, you look first at the consequence, which is your Level 4 measure. This consequence is also defined as your program benefit or your business impact measure. The second part of the definition, doing something different, refers to the Level 3 application that influenced the Level 4 outcome. What are the participants doing differently? Are they doing anything differently? The third part of the definition—as a result of the program—lends itself to the concept of isolating the effects of the program. How do you know it was the learning program that resulted in the consequences of the new behavior? This step in the process will be addressed in more detail in Chapter 4, but it is important to recognize its place in the process of data collection. You must isolate the effects for your program when you address your Level 4 data.

Level 4 improvement data can represent any type of outcome data that results from applying new skills and knowledge—outcomes such as job satisfaction, increased revenue, reduction in absenteeism, reduction in employee turnover, the number of applications processed, productivity, improved quality, reduced complaints, reduced litigation, customer retention, customer loyalty, and so on. As you can see in Tables 3–2 and 3–3, these examples illustrate the variety of data that are usually referred to as hard data and soft data.

Hard data are typically categorized into four categories: output, quality, cost, and time. So when you are thinking of consequences from your programs, you can simply think of one or more of these four categories that your program is likely to influence. Your programs may also influence the soft data categories.

Soft data are represented by categories such as work habits, work climate, customer service, employee development or advancement, job attitude, and initiative. Soft measures are also very important outcomes or consequences of applying new skills and knowledge. They can be equally as important as the hard measures, but more difficult to quantify. The major distinction between hard and soft measures is the relative ease with which hard data can be converted to a monetary value. So in answering the question "What data do I need?", you first have to look back at the intent of the program, which comes from your client or your needs assessment. As you saw in the previous chapter, the needs assessment process should identify the Level 3 job performance needs and the Level 4 business needs. What is the original intent of the program? What are you trying to do? Level 3 answers what participants should do to achieve the intended result. Level 4 data answers the question "So what?" So, you send someone to a leadership program and their behavior changes on the job—so what? Or you send someone to a creative thinking class and they come back to the office and they become more creative—so what? Or you send someone to a problem-solving workshop and he solves problems more quickly and effectively—so what? What does that do for your organization?

Level 4 measures are imperative if you want to determine the ROI. But it's important to realize that you do not have to be a revenue-generating organization to influence important Level 4 measures. About 85% of training pro-

TABLE 3–2
CATEGORIES OF HARD DATA

Output	Time
Units produced	Equipment downtime
Tons manufactured	Overtime
Items assembled	On time shipments
Money collected	Time to project completion
Items sold	Processing time
Forms processed	Supervisory time
Loans approved	Break-in time for new employees
Inventory turnover	Learning time
Patients visited	Meeting schedules
Applications processed	Repair time
Students graduated	Efficiency
Tasks completed	Work stoppages
Output per hour	Order response
Productivity	Late reporting
Work backlog	Lost time days
Incentive bonus	
Shipments	
New accounts generated	

Cost	Quality
Budget variances	Percent of tasks completed properly
Unit costs	Number of accidents
Cost by account	Scrap
Variable costs	Waste
Fixed costs	Rejects
Overhead costs	Error rates
Operating costs	Rework
Number of cost reductions	Shortages
Project cost savings	Product defects
Accident costs	Deviation from standard
Program costs	Product failures
Sales expense	Inventory adjustments
	Time card corrections

grams drive measures other than revenue. Most programs in all types of organizations (profit and nonprofit) drive one or more of the following type measures: some level of output, quality, cost, and time, or work habits, work climate, customer service, employee development or advancement, job attitude, and initiative. For example, a government agency wants to reduce the recruiting cost of new hires, so they develop an incentive to promote from within. This incentive is to invest $100,000 per managerial candidate to participate in a leadership development program so that these high potential employees will (1) stay within the agency and (2) have the skills to lead the agency in the future. Why would a government agency want to spend that kind of money on leadership development? Well, in considering the cost to recruit, screen, and hire externally as well as the cost of training newly hired managers, one can see how the ROI could be quite positive by developing talent for promotion from within.

TABLE 3–3

CATEGORIES OF SOFT DATA

Work Habits	Customer Service
Absenteeism	Churn rate
Tardiness	Number of satisfied customers
Visits to the dispensary	Customer satisfaction index
First-aid treatments	Customer loyalty
Violations of safety rules	Customer complaints
Excessive breaks	Product or service turnaround
Communication breakdowns	

Work Climate	Development/Advancement
Number of grievances	Number of promotions
Number of discrimination charges	Number of pay increases
Employee complaints	Number of training programs attended
Job satisfaction	Requests for transfer
Employee turnover	Performance appraisal ratings
Litigation	Increases in job effectiveness
Workplace conflict	

Job Attitude	Initiative
Organizational commitment	Implementation of new ideas
Perceptions of job responsibilities	Successful completion of projects
Employee loyalty	Number of suggestions implemented
Increased confidence	Number of goals

In another example, a government agency with highly skilled technical staff begins losing its technology expertise to the high-tech industry. To retain its high-tech staff, it implements a master's degree program. The program is a three-year opportunity for employees to obtain their master's degree at no personal cost. Their only commitment is to sign an agreement to stay with the agency for three years after the master's degree. So in essence, the agency is holding on to employees six years. This is plenty of time for the agency to see a monetary benefit from their investment in the master's degree program. Here, the Level 4 measure is increased retention or, in other words, reduced employee turnover. An innovation company uses the concept of empathy to develop a better understanding of customer needs and desires. It sends their employees to a course on developing empathy. Employees come back from the course and can better empathize with their customers. What is the consequence of this new behavior? A consequence is more ideas that turn into new or refined products used by their clients. Hence, by developing the skill of empathy in generating more ideas, the organization ultimately generates revenue through the products because these ideas are then implemented by their clients. Their clients continue to pay for their ideas by buying the products that better suit their needs. Without the ideas, new and innovative products would not be developed and the increase in revenue would not be generated.

So this issue of defining Level 4 measures is not as difficult as we are sometimes led to believe. We often keep ourselves from thinking outside the box because we gravitate to revenue as the only way to calculate an ROI. The consequences of new behavior and skills can be virtually anything that benefits the organization. The question isn't "Is there any hard data or soft data?"; the question then is "Do we convert it to monetary value or not?" The answer is "yes" if we need to calculate ROI, and "no" if our stakeholders are not interested in ROI. This issue will be discussed later in Chapter 5.

Level 5: ROI

To move from Level 4 to Level 5, we follow five simple steps representative of those steps in cost-benefit analysis. The first step is to identify the program benefit—the Level 4 business impact. The second step is to convert the benefits—which could be more than one measure—to a monetary value. Third is to tabulate the fully loaded cost. Fourth is to identify the intangible benefits or the benefits we choose not to convert to a monetary value. Fifth, we compare the monetary benefits to the fully loaded cost to calculate the ROI. In Step 1, the program benefits that are identified are the Level 4 measures that have been isolated as improvements resulting from the training. Several methods can be used to conduct the isolation step, and they are described in more detail in Chapter 4. Those consequences of doing something different are then converted to monetary value. There are 10 methods to choose from to conduct this step, and they are described in more detail in Chapter 5.

The next data you need includes the cost data. As Guiding Principle 10 tells us, the cost of the solution should be fully loaded for ROI analysis. So moving from Level 4 to Level 5, you will tabulate your fully loaded cost. Cost tabulation is described in more detail in Chapter 6. Next, you will identify the intangible benefits. Intangible benefits are those you choose not to convert to monetary value. Intangible benefits can be any additional benefits that you anticipate from the program you identified during your evaluation planning, or they can be pleasant surprises that were not anticipated. Chapter 5 discusses in detail how to identify intangible benefits. In the final step, data calculation, you calculate the return on investment by comparing your net monetary benefits to your fully loaded program costs.

How Do I Get the Data?

The next question to ask in planning your data collection is "How do we get the data?" Deciding how to collect the data depends on the type of data you plan to collect, the timing of the data collection, the cost you wish to expend for the data collection process, and the other Cfactors in Job Aid 3–1. Data collection decisions also must consider instrumentation design, development, and field testing, as well as the analysis that goes into it. Remember Guiding Principle 2, "When higher levels of evaluation are conducted, lower levels don't have to be comprehensive." This can ease your mind when you are considering the types of data collection instruments you use to collect data at the various levels.

Level 1: Reaction

The most prominent method of collecting data at Level 1 is the end-of-course feedback questionnaire. The questionnaire, as mentioned before, addresses key issues around the training process, the training materials, and the facilitator, but more importantly it includes utility measures such as relevance, importance, new information, and intent to use and to recommend to others. Figure 3–1 illustrates a typical Level 1 evaluation. Additional Level 1 instruments are in the tools section of the CD. See Figure 3–7 on the CD.

Level 2: Learning

Testing is the predominant way to measure learning. However, more subjective methods are often an accepted means to collect learning data. Again, when doing an ROI impact study, you want to conserve your resources for the higher levels of evaluation. However, you also want to ensure that you collect good data that can give you some indication that learning transpires during the learning engagement.

Methods for collecting Level 2 data include tests, such as norm-referenced tests, criterion-referenced tests, or performance testing.

Norm-Referenced Test

Norm-referenced tests compare participants with each other or with other groups rather than comparing test results with specific instructional objectives. They are characterized by using data to compare participants to the norm or the average. Although norm-referenced tests have only limited use in some training evaluations, they may be useful in programs involving large numbers of participants when average scores and relative rankings are important. In some situations, participants who score highest on the exams are given special recognition or awards or made eligible for other special activities.

Criterion-Referenced Test

The criterion-referenced test (CRT) is an objective test with a predetermined cutoff score. The CRT is a measure against carefully written objectives for the learning program. In a CRT, the interest lies in whether a participant meets the desired minimum standards, not how that participant ranks against others in the training program. The primary concern is to measure, report, and analyze participant performance as it relates to the instructional objectives.

Table 3–4 examines a reporting format based on criterion-referenced testing. This format helps explain how a CRT is applied to an evaluation effort. Four participants have completed a program with three measurable objectives. Actual test scores are reported, and the minimum standard is shown. For example, on the first objective, Participant 4 received a pass rating for a test that has no numerical value and is simply rated pass or fail. The same participant passed objective 2 with a score of 14 (10 was listed as the minimum

FIGURE 3–1

SAMPLE OF A LEVEL 1 (REACTION) EVALUATION QUESTIONNAIRE

Course Title:		Job No.	Date:
Company:		Location:	
Facilitator:		Setting: ☐ Classroom ☐ Workshop ☐ OJT ☐ Other	

Directions:

1. Rate each item listed below on a scale **of 1 to 7**

Strongly Disagree	Disagree	Mildly Disagree	Neutral	Mildly Agree	Agree	Strongly Agree
1	2	3	4	5	6	7

2. As appropriate, write comments for any evaluation item.

RATING   **COMMENTS**

A. COURSE CONTENT
1) Objectives matched the information presented.
2) Objectives were met.
3) Course was the right length or duration.
4) Was important for my job
5) I learned new information.

B. TRAINING MATERIALS/SETTING
1) Visual aids (handouts) were clear and easy to read.
2) Study materials were appropriate for my needs.
3) Classroom location promoted learning.

C. INSTRUCTOR
1) Was well prepared and organized for the class.
2) Clearly stated the course objectives.
3) Had a good knowledge/understanding of the subject.
4) Challenged me intellectually.
5) Presented material in a logical manner.
6) Used examples and comparisons.
7) Stressed safety issues associated with the subject.
8) Displayed courtesy and professionalism.
9) Kept me interested.
10) Sufficiently led discussion on how this training can be applied in the work setting.

D. PARTICIPANT
1) Training was related to my job.
2) I will recommend this program to others
3) This training will help me do my job better.
4) I will apply what I learned to my work setting.

Indicate how you will apply what you learned.

passing score). Participant 4 scored 88 on objective 3, but failed because the standard was 90. Overall, Participant 4 satisfactorily completed the program of study. The grid on the far right shows that the minimum passing standard for the program is at least two of the three objectives. Participant 4 achieved two objectives, the required minimum.

Criterion-referenced testing is a popular measurement instrument in WLP. Its use is becoming widespread and it is frequently used in e-learning. It has

TABLE 3–4

REPORTING FORMAT FOR (CRT) TEST DATA

	Objective 1 P/F	Raw Score	Objective 2 Std	P/F	Raw Score	Objective 3 Std	P/F	Total Obj's Passed	Minimum Program Standard	Overall Program Score
Participant 1	P	4	10	F	87	90	F	1	2 of 3	Fail
Participant 2	F	12	10	P	110	90	P	2	2 of 3	Pass
Participant 3	P	10	10	P	100	90	P	3	2 of 3	Pass
Participant 4	P	14	10	P	88	90	F	2	2 of 3	Pass
Totals 4	3 Pass 1 Fail			3 Pass 1 Fail			2 Pass 2 Fail	8 Pass 4 Fail		3 Pass 1 Fail

the advantage of being objective, precise, and relatively easy to administer. It does require programs with clearly defined objectives that can be measured by tests.

Performance Testing

Performance testing allows the participant to exhibit a skill (and occasionally knowledge or attitudes) learned in a WLP program. The skill can be manual, verbal, analytical, or a combination of the three. Performance testing is used frequently in job-related training in which the participants are allowed to demonstrate what they have learned. In supervisory and management training, performance testing comes in the form of skill practices or role-plays. Participants are asked to demonstrate discussion or problem-solving skills they have acquired.

For a performance test to be effective, the following steps are recommended for its design and administration:

- The test should be a representative sample of the key elements of the training program, and should allow the participant to demonstrate as many skills as possible that are taught in the program.
- Every phase of the test should be thoroughly planned, including the time, the preparation of the participant, the inventory of necessary materials and tools, and the evaluation of results.
- Thorough and consistent instructions are necessary. As with other tests, the quality of the instructions can influence the outcome of a performance test. All participants should be provided the same instructions.
- Acceptable standards must be developed for a performance test so that employees know in advance what they have to accomplish to satisfactorily complete the test.
- Information that may lead participants astray should not be included.

Using these general guidelines, performance tests can be developed into effective tools for program evaluation. Although more costly than written tests, performance tests are essential in situations where a high degree of conformity is required between work and test conditions. Pre- and postcourse comparisons using tests are quite common. The pretest/posttest is an easy way to collect learning data. Data are collected prior to the program to determine the baseline of participants knowledge, skill, or attitude. Immediately following the program an improvement in test scores shows the change in skill, knowledge, or attitude attributed to the program.

Along with testing, another way to measure learning is simulation. This method involves constructing and applying a procedure or test that simulates or models the activity addressed by the training program being conducted. The simulation is designed to represent as closely as possible the actual job situation. The advantages of simulations are:

- They are reproducible. Simulations permit tasks or jobs to be reproduced in a manner almost identical to the real setting.

- They are cost effective. Although sometimes expensive to construct, simulations can be cost effective in the long run. For example, in Panama, at the Panama Canal, boat pilots who are responsible for driving the boats through the canal are trained in three large simulators. One of the simulators replicates an actual barge that a pilot may feasibly drive through the canal. While standing in the simulator piloting the barge, various changes in the environmental setting are reproduced. Although expensive to develop at the outset, including the actual simulator as well as the technology necessary to implement the variety of environmental settings, the cost of on-the-job training in this same situation is prohibitive. Therefore, the simulator serves the purpose of testing learning before the pilot actually goes out onto the canal and drives an actual barge.
- Safety considerations. Safety is another advantage of using simulations. In the Panama Canal simulator example, safety is certainly an important issue. It would be too dangerous for the pilot to learn to steer the boat through the canal without doing it first in a simulator.

Various techniques for simulation exist. Some of the most common include electrical or mechanical simulation. This technique uses a combination of electronics and mechanical devices to simulate real-life situations and is used in conjunction with programs to develop operational and diagnostic skills. Our Panama Canal boat pilot simulator is an example of an electrical or mechanical simulation. Computer technology is also used for simulation techniques.

Another example is task simulation. This approach involves the performance of simulated tasks as part of an evaluation. For example, in an aircraft company, technicians are trained on the safe removal, handling, and installation of a radioactive source used in a nucleonic oil-quantity indicator gauge. These technicians attend a thorough training program on all the procedures necessary for this important assignment. To certify technicians to perform the task, a trained observer refers to a check-off card and observes technicians as they simulate the performance of all the necessary steps. Everything about the simulation is real except the radioactive source, which is replaced with a blank cartridge.

Another type of simulation is business games. Business games have grown in popularity in recent years. They represent simulations of a business enterprise in which participants change the variables of the business and observe the effect of those changes. The game not only reflects real-world situations but also represents a synopsis of the training program of which it is a part. Participants are given certain objectives, engage in the game, and have the output from their business decisions monitored. Their performance can usually be documented and measured. Participants who achieve objectives are those who usually have the highest performance in the program. In-baskets are another type of simulation technique. They are particularly useful in supervisory management training programs. Portions of the supervisor's job are simulated through a series of items that normally appear in the in-baskets. These items are typically memos, notes, letters, and reports that create realistic conditions facing the supervisor. Another example of simulation is the case study approach. Possibly less effective but still quite popular, case studies give a detailed description of a problem and usually contain a list of several questions to address issues presented by the case. The participant is asked to analyze the case and determine the best course of action. Types of case studies include:

- Exercise case studies, which provide the opportunity for participants to practice the application of a specific procedure.
- Situation case studies, which provide participants the opportunity to analyze information and make decisions about their particular situation.
- Complex case studies, which are an extension of situation case studies in which the participants are required to handle a large amount of data and information.
- Decision case studies, which require participants to go a step further than the previous categories and present plans for solving particular problems.
- Critical incident case studies, which provide a participant with a certain amount of information but withhold other information needed to move to the next phase or make a decision until the participant requests it.

Role-playing is sometimes referred to as skill practice, in which participants practice a newly learned skill as others observe them. Participants are given their assigned role with specific instructions that sometimes include an ultimate course of action. The participant then practices the skill with others to accomplish the desired objectives. Figure 3–8 on the CD illustrates an example of a role play performance test.

The assessment center method is a formal procedure in which feedback is provided by a group of specially trained observers—not the training staff members, as in the previous simulations. For years the assessment center approach has been an effective tool for employee selection and also shows great promise as a tool for evaluating the effectiveness of training programs.

Exercises, Problems, and Activities

Many training programs contain specific activities, exercises, or problems that must be explored, developed, or solved during the program. Some of these are constructed as team involvement exercises, while others require individual problem-solving skills. When these are integrated into the program, learning can be measured in several specific ways.

- The results of the exercise can be submitted for review and evaluated by the facilitator.
- The results can be discussed in a group with a comparison of various approaches and solutions.
- The group can reach an assessment of how much each individual has learned.
- The solutions to the problem or exercises can be shared with the group, and the participants can provide a self-assessment indicating the degree to which they have acquired skills or knowledge from the exercise.
- The facilitator can review the individual progress or success of each participant to determine the relative success.

Along with testing and simulations, there are other, less structured activities. Sometimes it is important to have an informal check of learning that provides some assurance that participants have acquired skills, knowledge, or perhaps even changes in attitude. For example, with your ROI impact study, these less structured activities may provide enough data to answer the questions, "Did the participants get it?" and "Are they confident about using the skills and knowledge taught in the program?"

This approach is appropriate when other levels of evaluation are pursued. For example, if a Level 3 on-the-job application evaluation is planned, it might not be crucial to have a comprehensive Level 2. An informal assessment of learning may be sufficient. After all, resources are scarce, and a comprehensive evaluation at all levels becomes quite expensive. The following are some alternative approaches to measuring learning that might suffice when inexpensive, low-key, informal assessments are needed.

Self-Assessment

In many applications, self-assessment may be appropriate. Participants are provided an opportunity to assess the extent of skills and knowledge acquisition. This is particularly applicable when Level 3, 4, and 5 evaluations are planned and it is important to know if learning has improved. A few techniques can ensure that the process is effective.

- The self-assessment should be made on an anonymous basis so that individuals feel free to express a realistic and accurate assessment of what they have learned.
- The purpose of the self-assessment should be explained, along with the plans for using the data. Specifically, if there are implications for course design or individual retesting, this should be discussed.
- If there has been no improvement or the self-assessment is unsatisfactory, there should be some explanation as to what that means and what the implications will be. This will help to ensure that accurate and credible information is provided.

Facilitator Assessment

A final technique is for facilitators to assess the learning that has taken place. Although this approach is subjective, it may be appropriate when a Level 3, 4, or 5 evaluation is planned. One of the most effective ways to accomplish this is to provide a checklist of the specific skills that need to be acquired in the course. Facilitators can then check off their assessment of the skills individually. Also, if a particular body of knowledge needs to be acquired, the categories could be listed with a checklist for assurance that individuals have a good understanding of those items.

This section provided an overview of the different methodologies for evaluating learning. Now your question is "How do I know which one to choose?" Again, one way of determining which method to choose is by asking yourself the extent to which you need the learning data. You certainly need learning data in conducting your ROI impact study so you can answer the simple questions "Did they get it?" and "Did they have the confidence to apply it?" These simple questions help you understand the extent to which participants are ready to apply learning on the job and can give you some indication of the extent to which application will occur. However, some programs require comprehensive testing regardless of the level to which they are being evaluated. For instance, a pharmaceutical company developing new products needs to know that its sales reps can have an intelligent discussion with physicians about product knowledge. Although taking the evaluation to ROI, a comprehensive Level 2 evaluation is still necessary. Criterion-referenced testing is often used in pharmaceutical firms to test sales representatives' knowledge of the pharmaceutical products they sell. In other situations, however, self-assessment may be satisfactory.

Level 3: Application and Level 4: Impact

Collecting data after the training program has been conducted is the part of the ROI process that can be the most disruptive to the organization. Fortunately, a variety of methods are available to capture data at the appropriate time after training. You should select the method(s) best suited to your purpose and needs while keeping in mind the 7Cfactors™ in Job Aid 3–1.

Ten methods are available to collect important follow-up data. Table 3–5 lists the methodologies along with the levels at which they are typically used. The remainder of this section will address each of these methods in more detail. There is often a tendency to want more data than you need. So be sure you know how you will use the data before you decide to collect it. If you have decided to use several methods and the cost and time to collect it exceeds the value or utility of the data, then perhaps you should abandon some of the methods.

TABLE 3–5

METHODS OF COLLECT LEVEL 3 AND LEVEL 4
FOLLOW-UP DATA

	Level 3	Level 4
Follow-up surveys	✓	
Follow-up questionnaires	✓	✓
Observation on the job	✓	
Follow-up interviews	✓	
Follow-up focus groups	✓	
Program assignments	✓	✓
Action planning	✓	✓
Performance contracting	✓	✓
Program follow-up session	✓	✓
Organization performance records	✓	✓

Questionnaires and Surveys

Probably the most common follow-up data collection method is the questionnaire. Ranging from short reaction forms to detailed follow-up tools, questionnaires can be used to obtain subjective information about participants, as well as to objectively document measurable business results for an ROI analysis. With this versatility and popularity and relatively low cost, the questionnaire is a preferred method for capturing Levels 1, 2, 3, and 4 data in many organizations. Of course, when Level 3 or Level 4 data is available from the organization's records, then this is the preferred method of collecting the data. This is especially true for Level 4 data.

Surveys represent a specific type of questionnaire, with several applications for measuring training success. Surveys are used when only attitudes, beliefs, and opinions are captured; in contrast, a questionnaire has much more flexibility and captures data ranging from attitudes to specific improvement measures and statistics. The principles of survey construction and design are similar to questionnaire design. The development of both types of instruments is covered in this section.

Types of Questions

In addition to the type of data sought, the types of questions distinguish surveys from questionnaires. Surveys can have yes or no responses when an absolute agreement or disagreement is required, or a range of responses on a Likert scale from "strongly disagree" to "strongly agree" may be used. A five-point scale is common.

A questionnaire may contain any or all of these five types of questions:

1. *Open-ended question:* has an unlimited answer. The question is followed by an ample blank space for the response.
2. *Checklist:* a participant is asked to check items that apply in the situation from a list.
3. *Two-way question:* has alternate responses, a yes/no, or other possibilities.
4. *Multiple-choice question:* has several choices, and the participant is asked to select the one most applicable.
5. *Ranking scale:* requires the participant to rank a list of items. Likert scales or numeric ranking can be used.

Questionnaire Design Steps

Questionnaire design is a simple and logical process. There is nothing more confusing, frustrating, and potentially embarrassing than a poorly designed or an improperly worded questionnaire. The following steps can ensure that a valid, reliable, and effective instrument is developed.

Determine the Specific Information Needed

As a first step in questionnaire design, the topics, skills, or attitudes presented in the program are reviewed for potential items for the questionnaire.

It is sometimes helpful to develop this information in outline form so that related questions or items can be grouped. Other issues related to the application of the program are explored for inclusion in the questionnaire.

Involve Management in the Process

To the extent possible, management should be involved in this process, either as a client, sponsor, supporter, or interested party. If possible, managers most familiar with the program or process should provide information on specific issues and concerns that often frame the actual questions planned for the questionnaire. In some cases, managers want to provide input on specific issues or items. Not only is manager input helpful and useful in questionnaire design, but it also builds ownership in the measurement and evaluation process.

Select the Type(s) of Questions

Using the previous five types of questions, the first step in questionnaire design is to select the type(s) that will best result in the specific data needed. The planned data analysis and variety of data to be collected should be considered when deciding which questions to use.

Develop the Questions

The next step is to develop the questions based on the type of questions planned and the information needed. Questions should be simple and straightforward to avoid confusion or leading the participant to a desired response. A single question should only address one issue. If multiple issues need to be addressed, separate the question into multiple parts, or simply develop a separate question for each issue. Terms or expressions unfamiliar to the participant should be avoided.

Check the Reading Level

To ensure that the questionnaire can be easily understood by the target audience, it is helpful to assess the reading level. Most word-processing programs have features that will evaluate the reading difficulty according to grade level. This provides an important check to ensure that the perceived reading level of the target audience matches the questionnaire design. Many organizations use eighth-grade reading level as a standard, but circumstances can dictate an even lower grade level.

Test the Questions

Proposed questions should be tested for understanding. Ideally, the questions should be tested on a sample group of participants. If this is not feasible, the sample group of employees should be at approximately the same job level and education as participants. Feedback, critiques, and suggestions are sought from the sample group to improve questionnaire design.

Address the Anonymity Issue

Participants should feel free to respond openly to questions without fear of reprisal. The confidentiality of their responses is of utmost importance because there is usually a link between survey anonymity and accuracy. Therefore, questionnaires should be anonymous unless there are specific reasons why individuals have to be identified. In situations where participants must complete the questionnaire in a captive audience, or submit a completed questionnaire directly to an individual, a neutral third party should collect and process the data, ensuring that the identity is not revealed. In cases where identity must be known (e.g., to compare output data with the previous data or to verify the data), every effort should be made to disguise the respondent's identity from those who may be biased in their actions.

Design for Ease of Tabulation and Analysis

Each potential question should be considered in terms of data tabulation, data summary, and analysis. If possible, the data analysis process should be outlined and reviewed in mock-up form and communicated to those who will be involved in analyzing the data. This should be transparent to the questionnaire respondents because they are not involved in the data analysis activity. This step avoids the problems of inadequate, cumbersome, and lengthy data analysis caused by improper wording or design.

Develop the Completed Questionnaire and Prepare a Data Summary

The questions should be integrated to develop an attractive questionnaire with proper instructions so that it can be administered effectively. In addition, a summary sheet should be developed so that the data can be tabulated quickly for analysis.

Questionnaire Content: Post Program

The following items represent a comprehensive list of questionnaire content possibilities for capturing follow-up data. The tools section on the CD contains a questionnaire in Figure 3–4, "Cyber International," used in a follow-up evaluation of a program on leadership development. This is not an actual questionnaire (it is too lengthy, but it does contain most of the questions actually used). It is used here to illustrate a range of questions that may be asked on a follow-up evaluation. It is designed to capture data for an ROI analysis when the primary method of data collection is a questionnaire. This example will be used to illustrate many of the issues involving potential content items for questionnaire design with emphasis on application (Level 3) and Impact (Level 4).

Progress with Objectives

Sometimes it is helpful to assess progress with the objectives in the follow-up evaluation, as is illustrated in question 1 of Cyber International. While this issue is usually assessed during the program (because it is Level 1 data), it can be helpful to revisit the objectives after the participants have had an opportunity to apply what they have learned. However, if you have collected this data at Level 1, then this question can be eliminated from the follow-up questionnaire, thus shortening the length.

Action Plan Implementation

If an action plan is required in the program, the questionnaire should reference the plan and determine the extent to which it has been implemented. If the action plan requirement is very low-key, perhaps only one question would be devoted to the follow-up on the action plan, as illustrated in question 2 of Cyber International. If the action plan is very comprehensive and contains an abundance of Level 3 and 4 data, then the questionnaire may take a secondary role and most of the data collection process will focus directly on the status of the completed action plan.

Relevance of Program Elements to the Job

It is helpful to know how participants respond to the program design elements. Question 3 addresses this in one way by listing the major design components and asking participants to rate the relevance of each component to their job. A similar approach can be used to determine the extent to which each design component contributes to participants' ability to learn the skills.

Use of Program Materials and Handouts

If participants are provided with materials to use on the job, it may be helpful to determine how much they use these materials. This is particularly helpful when operating manuals, reference books, and job aids have been distributed and explained in the program and are expected to be utilized on the job. Question 4 in Cyber International focuses on this issue.

Application of Knowledge or Skills

As shown in question 5 of Cyber International, it is helpful to determine the level of improvement in skills directly linked to the program. A more detailed variation of this question is to list each skill and indicate its frequency and effectiveness of use. For many skills, it is important to experience frequent use quickly after acquisition so that the skills become internalized. In this example, question 6 addresses the skill frequency issue.

Changes with Work

Sometimes it is helpful to determine what specific activities or processes in participants' work have changed as a result of the program. As question 7 in Cyber International illustrates, the participant explores how the skill applications (listed previously) have actually changed work habits, processes, and output.

Improvements and Accomplishments

Question 8 of Cyber International begins a series of four impact questions that are appropriate for most follow-up questionnaires. The first question in the series, question 8, seeks specific business outcomes resulting from the accomplishments and improvements provided by question 7. This question focuses on specific measurable successes that the participants can easily identify. Because this question is open ended, it can be helpful to provide examples that indicate the nature and range of responses requested. However, examples can also be constraining in nature and may actually limit the responses.

Monetary Impact

Perhaps the most difficult question (number 9 of Cyber International) asks participants to provide monetary values for the improvements identified in question 8. Only the first-year improvement is sought. Participants are asked to specify net improvements so that the actual monetary values will represent gains from the program. An important part of the question is the basis for the calculation, where participants specify the steps they take to develop the annual net value and the assumptions they make in the analysis. It is very important for the basis to be completed with enough detail to understand the process.

Improvements Linked with Program

The next question in the impact series (question 10 of Cyber International) isolates the effects of the training. Participants indicate the percent of the improvement directly related to the program. As an alternative, participants may be provided with the various factors that have influenced the results and are asked to allocate the percentages to each factor. This is covered in more detail in Chapter 4.

Confidence Level

To adjust for the uncertainty of the data provided in questions 8, 9, and 10, participants were asked to offer a level of confidence for the estimation, expressed as a percentage with a range of 0% to 100%, as shown in question 11 of Cyber International. This input allows participants to reflect their level of uncertainty with this process.

Investment Perception

The value of the program, from the viewpoint of the participant, can be useful information. As illustrated in question 12 of Cyber International, participants are asked if they perceive this program to represent an appropriate investment. Another option for this question is to present the actual cost of the program so that participants can respond more accurately from the investment perspective. It may be useful to express the cost as a per-participant cost. Also, the question can be divided into two parts, one reflecting the investment of funds by the company and the other an investment in the participants' time in the program.

Linkage with Output Measures

Sometimes it is helpful to determine the degree to which the program has influenced certain output measures, as shown in question 13 of Cyber International. In some situations, a detailed analysis may reveal specifically which measures this program has influenced by retrieving data from the organization's records. However, when this issue is uncertain, it may be helpful to list the potential business performance measures influenced by the program and seek input from the participants. The question should be worded so that the frame of reference is for the time period after the program was conducted.

Other Benefits

In most programs, additional benefits will begin to emerge, particularly in the intangible area. Participants should be asked to detail any benefits not presented elsewhere. In this example, question 14 shows the open-ended question for additional benefits.

Barriers

A variety of barriers can influence the successful application of the skills and knowledge learned in the training program. Question 15 of Cyber International identifies these barriers. As an alternative, the perceived barriers are listed and participants check all that apply. Still another variation is to list the barriers with a range of responses, indicating the extent to which the barrier inhibited results.

Enablers

Just as important as barriers, enablers are those issues, events, or situations that enable the process to be applied successfully on the job. Question 16 provides an open-ended question for enablers. The same options are available with this question as in the question on barriers.

Management Support

For most programs, management support is critical to the successful application of newly acquired skills. At least one question should be included on the degree of management support, such as 17. Sometimes this question is structured so that various descriptions of management support are detailed, and participants check the one that applies to their situation. This information is very beneficial to help remove or minimize barriers.

Other Solutions

A training program is only one of many potential solutions to a performance problem. If the needs assessment is faulty or if there are alternative approaches to developing the desired skills or knowledge, other potential solutions could be more effective and achieve the same success. In question 18 the participant is asked to identify other solutions that could have been effective in obtaining the same or similar results. This information can be particularly helpful as the training and development function continues to shift to a performance improvement function.

Target Audience Recommendations

Sometimes it is helpful to solicit input about the most appropriate target audience for the program. In question 19, the participants are asked to indicate which groups of employees would benefit the most from attending this program.

Suggestions for Improvement

As a final wrap-up question, participants are asked to provide specific suggestions for improving any part of the program or process. As illustrated in question 20, the open-ended structure is intended to solicit qualitative responses to be used to make improvements. Question 21 provides one last opportunity for other comments.

Improving the Response Rate for Questionnaires and Surveys

The content items of questionnaires represent a wide range of potential issues to explore in a follow-up. Obviously, asking all of the questions could reduce the response rate considerably. The challenge, therefore, is to tackle questionnaire design and administration for maximum response rate. This is a crucial issue when the questionnaire is the primary data collection method and most of the evaluation hinges on questionnaire results.

The following actions can be taken to increase response rate.

Provide Advance Communication

If appropriate and feasible, participants should receive advance communications about the requirement to complete a questionnaire. This minimizes some of the resistance to the process, provides an opportunity to explain in more detail the circumstances surrounding the evaluation, and positions the follow-up evaluation as an integral part of the program, not an add-on activity.

Communicate the Purpose

Participants should understand the reason for the questionnaire, including who or what has initiated this specific evaluation. Participants should know if the evaluation is part of a systematic process or a special request for this program.

Explain Who Will See the Data

It is important for participants to know who will see the data and the results of the questionnaire. If the questionnaire is anonymous, it should be clearly communicated to participants what steps will be taken to ensure anonymity. Participants should know if senior executives will see the combined results of the study.

Describe the Data Integration Process

Participants should understand how the questionnaire results will be combined with other data, if applicable. The questionnaire may be only one of the data collection methods used. Participants should know how the data is weighted and integrated in the final report.

Keep the Questionnaire As Simple As Possible

Although a simple questionnaire does not always provide the full scope of data necessary for an ROI analysis, the simplified approach should always be a goal. When questions are developed, and the total scope of the questionnaire is finalized, every effort should be made to keep it as simple and brief as possible.

Simplify the Response Process

To the extent possible, it should be easy to respond to the questionnaire. If the questionnaire is an online instrument, the ability to access it and navigate through the questionnaire should be simplified. If appropriate, a self-addressed stamped envelope should be included with hard copy questionnaires. Perhaps the e-mail system could be used for response, if it is easier. In still other situations, a response box is provided near the workstation.

Use Local Manager Support

Management involvement at the local level is critical to response rate success. Managers can encourage accessing the questionnaire online, distribute the hard copy themselves, make reference to the questionnaire in staff meetings, follow up to see if questionnaires have been completed, and generally show support for completing the questionnaire. This direct supervisor support will cause some participants to respond with usable data. Use caution that the nature of the responses are not influenced by management as they attempt to encourage return of the questionnaires.

Let the Participants Know They Are Part of the Sample

If appropriate, participants should know that they are part of a carefully selected sample and that their input will be used to make decisions about a much larger target audience. This action often appeals to a sense of responsibility for participants to provide usable, accurate data for the questionnaire.

Consider Incentives

A variety of incentives can be offered, and they usually fall into three categories. First, an incentive is provided in exchange for the completed questionnaire. For example, if participants return the questionnaire personally or through the mail, they will receive a small gift, such as a mouse pad or coffee mug. If identity is an issue, a neutral third party can provide the incentive. In the second category, an incentive is provided to make participants feel guilty about not responding. Examples are a dollar bill (or equivalent currency) clipped to the questionnaire or a pen enclosed in the envelope. Participants are asked to "take the money, buy a beverage, and fill out the questionnaire," or "please use this pen to complete the questionnaire." A third group of incentives is designed to obtain a quick response. This approach is based on the assumption that a quick response will ensure a greater response rate. If an individual puts off completing the questionnaire, the odds of completing it diminish considerably. The initial group of participants may receive a more expensive gift or they may be part of a drawing for an incentive. For example, in one study involving 75 participants, the first 25 returned questionnaires were placed in a drawing for a $500 credit card gift certificate. The next 25 were added to the first 25 for another drawing. After the first 50, there is no incentive. The longer a participant waits, the lower the odds of winning.

Have an Executive Sign the Introductory Letter

Participants are always interested in who sent the letter with the questionnaire. For maximum effectiveness, a senior executive who is responsible for a major area in which the participants work should sign the letter. Employees may be more willing to respond to a senior executive than to a member of the training and development staff.

Use Follow-up Reminders

A follow-up reminder should be sent one week and two weeks after the questionnaire is received. Depending on the questionnaire and the situation, these times could be adjusted. In some situations, a third follow-up is recommended. Sometimes the follow-up should be sent in different media. For example, a questionnaire may be sent through regular mail, whereas the first follow-up reminder is from the immediate supervisor and a second is sent through e-mail.

Send a Copy of the Results to the Participants

Even if in abbreviated form, participants should see the results of the study. More importantly, participants should understand that they will receive a copy of the study when they are asked to provide the data. This promise often increases the response rate, as some individuals want to see the results of the entire group along with their particular input.

Review the Questionnaire in the Session

It is critical for participants to understand the questionnaire as much as possible. It is extremely helpful for them to see a copy in advance. Ideally, the questionnaire should be distributed and reviewed during the training session prior to follow-up data collection. Each question should be briefly discussed and any issues or concerns about the questions need to be clarified. This not only helps the response rate but also improves the quality and quantity of data.

Consider a Captive Audience

The best way to have an extremely high response rate is to consider a captive audience. In a follow-up session, a preplan meeting, or just a session designed to collect data, the participants meet and provide input, usually in the first few minutes of the meeting. This is ideal in a follow-up training program that is a continuation in a series of the one being evaluated. Sometimes a routine meeting (such as a sales, technology, or management meeting) provides a good setting for collecting the data.

Communicate the Timing of the Data

Participants need be given specific deadlines for providing the data. They also need to know when they will receive something in return. The best approach is to give the exact date when the last questionnaires will be allowed, the date when the analysis is complete, the date that they will receive the results of the study, and the date the client will receive the results. The specific timing builds more respect for the process employed.

Select the Appropriate Medium

The medium for the survey (whether it's paper-based, Web-based, or e-mail) should match the culture of the target group, not necessarily selected for the convenience of the evaluator. Sometimes an optional response medium will be allowed. The important thing is to make it suitable for the audience.

Consider the Input to Be Anonymous

Anonymous data is often more objective, and sometimes more free flowing. If participants believe that their input is anonymous, they will be more constructive and candid in their feedback and their response rates will generally be higher.

Treat Data with Confidence

Confidentiality is an important part of the process. A statement should indicate that the participant's name will not be revealed to anyone other than the data collectors and those involved in analyzing the data. In some cases, it may be appropriate to indicate specifically who will actually see the raw data. Also, any particular steps taken to ensure the confidentiality of the data would be described here.

Pilot Testing

Consider a pilot test. One of the best ways to ensure that the questionnaire is designed properly, the questions flow adequately, and that they're clear and specific is to test the questionnaire with a typical target group. Pilot testing can be accomplished quickly with a very small sample size and can be very revealing. It is absolutely essential that the questions, issues, and flow of instrument be reviewed by someone with the same job level, job setting, and education as those in the target audience.

Explain How Long It Will Take to Complete the Questionnaire

Although this is a simple issue, participants need to have a realistic understanding of how long it will take them to provide the data. There is nothing more frustrating than to grossly underestimate how much time it will take to complete the questionnaire. The pilot test should provide the information needed to adequately allocate time for the response.

Personalize the Process, If Possible

Participants are more likely to respond to personal messages and requests. If possible, the letter with the questionnaire should be personalized. Also, if it's possible, a personal phone call works well as a follow-up reminder. The personal touch brings appropriate sincerity and responsibility to the process.

Provide an Update

In some cases it may be appropriate to provide an update on current responses and a progress report on the entire project. Although this may be appropriate for large projects, it is still helpful for the individuals to understand how others are doing. Sometimes this creates subtle pressure and a reminder to provide data.

Collectively, these items help boost response rates of follow-up questionnaires. Using all of these strategies can result in a 50% to 60% response rate, even with lengthy questionnaires that might take 30 minutes to complete.

Interviews

Another helpful collection method is the interview, although it is not used as frequently as questionnaires. The WLP staff, the participant's supervisor, or an outside third party can conduct interviews. Interviews can secure data not available in performance records, or data difficult to obtain through written responses or observations. Also, interviews can uncover success stories that can be useful in communicating evaluation results. Participants may be reluctant to describe their results in a questionnaire but will volunteer the information to a skillful interviewer who uses probing techniques. While the interview process uncovers reaction (Level 1), learning (Level 2), and impact (Level 4), it is primarily used to collect application (Level 3) data. A major disadvantage of the interview is that it is time consuming and requires interviewer preparation to ensure that the process is consistent.

Types of Interviews

Interviews usually fall into two basic types: (1) structured and (2) unstructured. A structured interview is much like a questionnaire. Specific questions are asked with little room to deviate from the desired responses. The primary advantages of the structured interview over the questionnaire are that the interview process can ensure that the data collection is completed and the interviewer understands the responses supplied by the participant.

The unstructured interview allows for probing for additional information. This type of interview uses a few general questions, which can lead to more detailed information as important data are uncovered. The interviewer must be skilled in the probing process.

Interview Guidelines

The design issues and steps for interviews are similar to those of the questionnaire. A few key issues need emphasis.

Develop Questions to Be Asked

After the type of interview is determined, specific questions need to be developed. Questions should be brief, precise, and designed for easy response.

Try Out the Interview

The interview should be tested on a small number of participants. If possible, the interviews should be conducted as part of the trial run of the training program. The responses should be analyzed and the interview revised, if necessary.

Prepare the Interviewers

The interviewer should have the appropriate level of core skills, including active listening, asking probing questions, and collecting and summarizing information.

Provide Clear Instructions to the Participant

The participant should understand the purpose of the interview and know how the information will be used. Expectations, conditions, and rules of the interview should be thoroughly discussed. For example, the participant should know if statements would be kept confidential.

Administer the Interviews According to a Scheduled Plan

As with the other evaluation instruments, interviews need to be conducted according to a predetermined plan. The timing of the interview, the individual who conducts the interview, and the location of the interview are all issues that become relevant when developing a plan. For a large number of participants, a sampling plan may be necessary to save time and reduce the evaluation cost.

Focus Groups

An extension of the interview, focus groups are particularly helpful when in-depth feedback is needed for a Level 3 evaluation. The focus group involves a small group discussion conducted by an experienced facilitator. It is designed to solicit qualitative judgments on a planned topic or issue. Group members are all required to provide their input, as individual input builds on group input.

When compared with questionnaires, surveys, tests, or interviews, the focus group strategy has several advantages. The basic premise of using focus groups is that when quality judgments are subjective, several individual judgments are better than one. The group process, in which participants stimulate ideas in others, is an effective method for generating qualitative data. It is inexpensive and can be quickly planned and conducted. Its flexibility makes it possible to explore a training program's unexpected outcomes or applications.

Applications for Evaluation

The focus group is particularly helpful when qualitative information is needed about the success of a training program. For example, the focus group can be used in the following situations:

- To evaluate the reactions to specific exercises, cases, simulations, or other components of a training program.
- To assess the overall effectiveness of program application.

- To assess the impact of the program in a follow-up evaluation after the program is completed.

Essentially, focus groups are helpful when evaluation information is needed but cannot be collected adequately with questionnaires, interviews, or quantitative methods.

Guidelines

Although there are no set rules on how to use focus groups for evaluation, the following guidelines are helpful:

Ensure That Management Buys into the Focus Group Process

Because this is a relatively new process for evaluation, it might be unknown to management. Managers need to understand focus groups and their advantages. This should raise their level of confidence in the information obtained from group sessions.

Plan Topics, Questions, and Strategy Carefully

As with any evaluation instrument, planning is critical. The specific topics, questions, and issues to be discussed must be carefully planned and sequenced. This enhances the comparison of results from one group to another and ensures that the group process is effective and stays on track.

Keep the Group Size Small

Although there is no magic group size, a range of 8 to 12 seems to be appropriate for most focus group applications. A group has to be large enough to ensure different points of view but small enough to provide every participant a chance to freely exchange comments.

Use a Representative Sample of the Target Population

If possible, groups should be selected to represent the target population. The group should be homogeneous in experience, rank, and job level in the organization.

Facilitators Must Have Appropriate Expertise

The success of a focus group rests with the facilitator, who must be skilled in the focus group process. Facilitators must know how to control aggressive members of the group and diffuse the input from those who want to dominate the group. Also, facilitators must be able to create an environment in which participants feel comfortable offering comments freely and openly. Because of this, some organizations use external facilitators.

In summary, the focus group is an inexpensive and quick way to determine the strengths and weaknesses of training programs, particularly with management and supervisory training. However, for a complete evaluation, focus group information should be combined with data from other instruments.

Observations

Another potentially useful data collection method is observing participants and recording any changes in their behavior. The observer may be a member of the WLP staff, the participant's supervisor, a member of a peer group, or an external party. The most common observer, and probably the most practical, is a member of the WLP staff.

Guidelines for Effective Observation

Observation is often misused or misapplied to evaluation situations, leaving some to abandon the process. The effectiveness of observation can be improved with the following guidelines.

The Observations Should Be Systematic

The observation process must be planned so that it is executed effectively without any surprises. The persons observed should know in advance about the observation and why they are being observed unless the observation is planned to be transparent.

The Observers Should Know How to Interpret and Report What They See

Observations involve judgment decisions. The observer must analyze which behaviors are being displayed and what actions the participants are taking. Observers should know how to summarize behavior and report results in a meaningful manner.

The Observer's Influence Should Be Minimized

Except for mystery observers and electronic observations, it is impossible to completely isolate the overall effect of an observer. Participants may display the behavior they think is appropriate, and they will usually be at their best. The presence of the observer must be minimized. To the extent possible, the observer should blend into the work environment or extend the observation period.

Select Observers Carefully

Observers are usually independent of the participants, typically a member of the WLP staff. The independent observer is usually more skilled at recording behavior and making interpretations of behavior. They are usually unbiased in these interpretations. Using them enables the WLP department to bypass training the observers and relieves the line organization of that responsibility. On the other hand, the WLP staff observer has the appearance of an outsider checking the work of others. There may be a tendency for participants to overreact and possibly resent this kind of observer. Sometimes it might be more plausible to recruit observers from outside the organization. This approach has the advantage of neutralizing any prejudice that enters the decisions.

Observers Must Be Fully Prepared

Observers must fully understand what information is needed and what skills are covered in the program. They must be trained for the assignment and provided a chance to practice observation skills.

Observation Methods

Five methods of observation are used, depending on the circumstances surrounding the type of information needed. Each method is described briefly.

Behavior Checklist and Codes

A behavior checklist can be useful for recording the presence, absence, frequency, or duration of a participant's behavior as it occurs. A checklist will not usually provide information on the quality, intensity, or possibly the circumstances surrounding the behavior observed. The checklist is useful because an observer can identify exactly which behaviors should or should not occur. Measuring the duration of a behavior may be more difficult and requires a stopwatch and a place on the form to record the time interval. This factor is usually not as important when compared with whether or not a particular behavior was observed and how often. The number of behaviors listed in the checklist should be small and listed in a logical sequence, if they normally occur in a sequence. A variation of this approach involves a coding of behaviors on a form. This method is less time consuming because the code that identifies a specific behavior is entered.

Delayed Report Method

With a delayed report method, the observer does not use any forms or written materials during the observation. The information is either recorded after the observation is completed or at particular time intervals during an observation. The observer attempts to reconstruct what has been observed during the observation period. The advantage of this approach is that the observer is not as noticeable, and no forms are being completed or notes being taken during the observation. The observer can blend into the situation and be less distracting. An obvious disadvantage is that the information written may not be as accurate and reliable as the information collected at the time it occurred. A variation of this approach is the 360-degree feedback process in which surveys are completed on other individuals based on observations within a specific time frame.

Video Recording

A video camera records behavior in every detail, an obvious advantage. However, this intrusion may be awkward and cumbersome, and the participants may be unnecessarily nervous or self-conscious when they are being videotaped. If the camera is concealed, the privacy of the participant may be invaded. Because of this, videorecording of on-the-job behavior is not frequently used.

Audio Monitoring

Monitoring conversations of participants who are using the skills taught in the training program is an effective observation technique. For example, in a large communication company's telemarketing department, sales representatives are trained to sell equipment by telephone. To determine if employees are using the skills properly, telephone conversations are monitored on a selected and sometimes random basis. Although this approach may stir some controversy, it is an effective way to determine if skills are being applied consistently and effectively. For it to work smoothly, it must be fully explained and the procedures clearly communicated.

Computer Monitoring

For employees who work regularly with a keyboard, computer monitoring is becoming an effective way to "observe" participants as they perform job tasks. Computer software monitors times, sequence of steps, and other activities to determine if the participant is performing the work according to what was learned in the training program. As technology continues to be a significant part of jobs, the use of computers holds promise of monitoring actual applications on the job. This is particularly helpful for Level 3 data.

Business Performance Monitoring

Data are available in every organization to measure business performance. Monitoring performance data enables management to measure performance in terms of output, quality, costs, and time. Performance is also measured in business metrics such as customer satisfaction, numerous customer service measures, employee grievances, absenteeism, turnover, and so on. All organizations have business performance measures readily available that are unique to that organization. In determining the use of data in the evaluation, the first consideration should be existing databases and reports. In most organizations, performance data suitable for measuring the improvement resulting from a training program are available. If not, additional record-keeping systems have to be developed for measurement and analysis. At this point, as with many other points in the process, the question of economics enters. Is it economical to develop the record-keeping system necessary to evaluate a training program? If the costs are greater than the expected return for the entire program, then it is meaningless to develop them.

Using Current Measures

The recommended approach is to use existing performance measures, if available. Specific guidelines are recommended to ensure that current measurement systems are easily developed.

Identify Appropriate Measures

Performance measures should be researched to identify those that are related to the proposed objectives of the program. Frequently, an organization has several performance measures related to the same item. For example, the efficiency of an operations unit can be measured in a variety of ways:

- Number of units produced per hour
- Number of on-schedule production units
- Percent use of equipment
- Percent of equipment downtime
- Labor cost per unit of production
- Overtime required per piece of production
- Total unit cost

Each of these, in its own way, measures the efficiency or effectiveness of the operations unit. All related measures should be reviewed to determine those most relevant to the training program.

Convert Current Measures to Usable Ones

Occasionally, existing performance measures are integrated with other data, and it may be difficult to keep them isolated from unrelated data. In this situation, all existing related measures should be extracted and retabulated to be more appropriate for comparison in the evaluation. At times, conversion factors may be necessary. For example, the average number of new sales orders per month may be presented regularly in the performance measures for the sales department. In addition, the sales costs per sales representative are also presented. However, in the evaluation of a training program, the average cost per new sale is needed. The two existing performance records are required to develop the data necessary for comparison.

Developing New Measures

In some cases, data are not available for the information needed to measure the effectiveness of a training program. The WLP staff must work with the participating organization to develop record-keeping systems, if this is economically feasible. In one organization, a new-employee orientation system was implemented on a companywide basis. Several measures were planned, including early turnover representing the percentage of employees who left the company in the first six months of their employment. An improved employee orientation program should influence this measure. At the time of the program's inception, this measure was not available. When the program was implemented, the organization began collecting early turnover figures for comparison. Typical questions when creating new measures are:

- Which department will develop the measurement system?
- Who will record and monitor the data?
- Where will it be recorded?
- Will forms be used?

These questions will usually involve other departments or a management decision that extends beyond the scope of the WLP department. Possibly the administration division, the HR department, or information technology section will be instrumental in helping determine if new measures are needed and, if so, how they will be collected. Often, management of the organization or department realizes that the data in question would also be useful for other purposes and the decision is made to support collecting data on the new measures.

ACTION PLANNING AND FOLLOW-UP ASSIGNMENTS

In some cases, follow-up assignments can develop Level 3 and Level 4 data. In a typical follow-up assignment, the participant is instructed to meet a goal or complete a particular task or project by the determined follow-up date. A summary of the results of these completed assignments provides further evidence of the program's impact. The action plan is the most common type of follow-up assignment and is fully described in this section. With this approach, participants are required to develop action plans as part of the program. Action plans contain detailed steps to accomplish specific objectives related to the program. The plan is typically prepared on a printed form such as the one shown in Figure 3–2. There are two completed samples on the Chapter 3 folder of the CD. (See Figure 3–6.) The action plan shows what is to be done, by whom, and the date by which the objectives should be accomplished. The action plan approach is a straightforward, easy-to-use method for determining how participants will change their behavior on the job and achieve success with training. The approach produces data that answers such questions as:

- What steps or action items have been accomplished and when?
- What on-the-job improvements or accomplishments have been realized since the program was conducted?
- How much of the improvement is linked to the program?

FIGURE 3–2
SAMPLE ACTION PLAN

Action Plan—*Part I*

Date: _____ Evaluation Period: _____ to _____

Participant Name: _____
Participant Function: _____
Instructor Name: _____

Objective: _____

Business Improvement Measure: _____
Current Performance: _____
Target Performance: _____

SPECIFIC ACTION STEPS: *I will do this* ⇗	END RESULT: *So that this occurs* ⇗	TARGET DATE
1.	1.	
2.	2.	
3.	3.	
4.	4.	
5.	5.	

Probable Barriers	Response to Probable Barriers	TARGET DATE
A	A	
B	B	
C	C	

COLLECTING THE DATA YOU NEED   101

FIGURE 3-2—*Continued*

SAMPLE ACTION PLAN

Action Plan—*Part II*

Participant Name: _____

Objective: _____

Business Improvement	Current Performance:	Target Performance: *(what*
Measure:	*(performance before you*	*you aim to obtain by the end of*
What are you measuring? _____	*created your action plan)*	*the evaluation period)*

RESULTS AND ANALYSIS

A. What is the unit of measure? _____ Does this measure reflect your performance alone?   Yes ☐   No ☐

   If not, how many employees are represented in the measure? _____

B. Define or estimate the monetary value (cost/value) of one unit of the measure? $ _____ (please attempt to determine a value)

C. How did you arrive at this value and what is the source? _____

D. Did you improve the measure?   Yes ☐   No ☐   How do you know? _____

   If yes, how much did this measure change during the last month of the evaluation period compared to the average before the coaching experience?

   _____

   _____

   What did you (or your team) do to cause this improvement? _____

   _____

E. What percentage of this change was actually caused by the application of the skills from the training? _____

   Between 100% and 0%. (100% = all of it happened because of the training and 0% = it would have happened anyway) _____ %

F. How confident are you in this information provided in B, C, D, and E above? (100%=Certainty and 0%=No Confidence) _____

G. If your measure is time savings, estimate the percentage of the time saved that was actually reallocated toward productive tasks.

   Between 100% and 0%. (100% = all of the time was reallocated/reinvested and 0% = none of the time was reallocated/reinvested) _____ %

- What may have prevented participants from accomplishing specific action items?
- What is the monetary value of the improvement?

With this information, training professionals can decide if a program should be modified and in what ways, while managers can assess the findings to evaluate the worth of the program.

Developing the Action Plan

The development of the action plan requires two tasks: (1) determining the areas for action and (2) writing the action items. Both tasks should be completed during the program. The areas or measures for action should originate from the need for the program and the content of the program, and at the same time they should be related to on-the-job activities. Participants can independently develop a list of potential areas for action, or a list may be generated in group discussions. The list may include a measure needing improvement or represent an opportunity for increased performance. Typical categories are:

- Productivity
- Sales, revenue
- Quality/process improvement
- Efficiency
- Time savings
- Cost savings
- Complaints
- Job satisfaction
- Work habits
- Customer satisfaction
- Customer service

The specific action items support the business measure and are usually more difficult to write than the identification of the action areas. The most important characteristic of an action item is that it is written so that everyone involved will know when it occurs. One way to help achieve this goal is to use specific action verbs. Some examples of action items are:

- *Learn* how to operate the new RC-105 drill press machine in the adjacent department, by *(date)*.
- *Identify* and *secure* a new customer account, by *(date)*.
- *Handle* every piece of paper only once to improve my personal time management, by *(date)*.
- *Learn* to talk with my employees directly about a problem that arises rather than avoiding a potential conflict, by *(date)*.

If appropriate, each action item should have a date for completion and indicate other individuals or resources required for completion. Also, planned

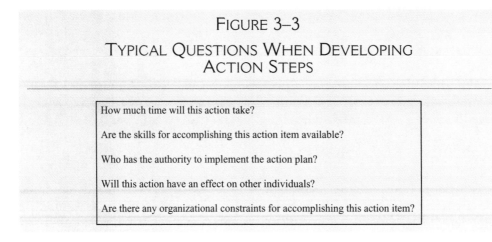

FIGURE 3–3
TYPICAL QUESTIONS WHEN DEVELOPING ACTION STEPS

How much time will this action take?

Are the skills for accomplishing this action item available?

Who has the authority to implement the action plan?

Will this action have an effect on other individuals?

Are there any organizational constraints for accomplishing this action item?

behavior changes should be observable. It should be obvious to the participant and others when it happens. Action plans, as used in this context, do not require the prior approval or input from the participant's supervisor, although it may be helpful.

Figure 3–3 provides some questions to ask when developing action steps.

Using Action Plans Successfully

The action plan process should be an integral part of the program and not an add-on or optional activity. To gain maximum effectiveness from action plans and to collect data for ROI calculations, the following steps should be implemented.

Communicate the Action Plan Requirement Early

One of the most negative reactions to action plans is the surprise factor often inherent in the way the process is introduced. When program participants realize that they must develop an unexpected detailed action plan, there is often immediate, built-in resistance. Communicating to participants in advance that the process is an integral part of the program often minimizes resistance. When participants fully realize the benefits before they attend the first session, they take the process more seriously and usually perform the extra steps to make it more successful. In this scenario, the action plan is positioned as an application tool—not an evaluation tool.

Describe the Action Planning Process at the Beginning of the Program

At the first session, action plan requirements are discussed, including an explanation of the purpose of the process, why it is necessary, and the basic requirements during and after the program. Some facilitators furnish a separate notepad for participants to collect ideas and useful techniques for their action plan. This is a productive way to focus more attention and effort on the process.

Teach the Action Planning Process

An important prerequisite for action plan success is an understanding of how it works and how specific action plans are developed. A portion of the program's agenda is allocated to teaching participants how to develop plans. In this session, the requirements are outlined, special forms and procedures are discussed, and a completed example is distributed and reviewed. Sometimes an entire program module is allocated to this process so that participants will fully understand it and use it. Any available support tools, such as key measures, charts, graphs, suggested topics, and sample calculations, should be used in this session to help facilitate the plan's development.

Allow Time to Develop the Plan

When action plans are used to collect data for an ROI calculation, it is important to allow participants time to develop plans during the program. Sometimes it is helpful to have participants work in teams so they can share ideas as they develop specific plans. In these sessions, facilitators often monitor the progress of individuals or teams to keep the process on track and to answer questions. In some management and executive development programs, action plans are developed in an evening session as a scheduled part of the program.

Have the Facilitator Approve the Action Plans

It is essential for the action plan to be related to program objectives and, at the same time, represent an important accomplishment for the organization when it is completed. It is easy for participants to stray from the intent and purposes of action planning and not give it the attention it deserves. Consequently, it is helpful to have the facilitator or program director actually sign off on the action plan, ensuring that the plan reflects all the requirements and is appropriate for the program. In some cases, a space is provided for the facilitator's signature on the action plan document.

Require Participants to Assign a Monetary Value to Each Improvement

Participants are asked to determine, calculate, or estimate the monetary value for each improvement outlined in the plan. When the actual improvement has occurred, participants will use these values to capture the plan's annual monetary benefits. For this step to be effective, it may be helpful to provide examples of typical ways in which values can be assigned to the actual data (Phillips, 2001).

Ask Participants to Isolate the Effects of the Program

Although the action plan is initiated because of the training program, the actual improvements reported on the action plan may be influenced by other factors. Thus, the action planning process should not take full credit for the improvement. For example, an action plan to reduce employee turnover in an agency could take only partial credit for an improvement because of other variables that influenced the turnover rate (Phillips, 2002). Although there are at least nine ways to isolate the effects of training, participant estimation is usually more appropriate in the action planning process. Consequently, the participants are asked to estimate the percent of the improvement actually related to this particular program. This question can be asked on the action plan form or on a follow-up questionnaire.

Ask Participants to Provide a Confidence Level for Estimates

Because the process of converting data to monetary values may not be exact and the amount of the improvement directly related to the program may not be precise, participants are asked to indicate their level of confidence in those two values. On a scale of 0% to 100%, where 0% means no confidence and 100% means complete confidence, this value provides participants a mechanism to express their uneasiness with their ability to be exact with the process.

Require Action Plans to Be Presented to the Group, If Possible

There is no better way to secure commitment and ownership of the action planning process than to have a participant describe his or her action plan in front of fellow participants. Presenting the action plan helps ensure that the process is thoroughly developed and increases the chances that it will be implemented on the job. Sometimes the process spurs competition among the group. If the number of participants is too large for individual presentations, perhaps one participant can be selected from the team (if the plans are developed in teams). Under these circumstances, the team will usually select the best action plan for presentation to the group, raising the bar for others.

Explain the Follow-up Mechanism

Participants must leave the session with a clear understanding of the timing of the action plan implementation and the planned follow-up. The method by which the data will be collected, analyzed, and reported should be openly discussed. Five options are common:

1. The group is reconvened to discuss the progress on the plans.
2. Participants meet with their immediate manager and discuss the success of the plan. A copy is forwarded to the training department.
3. A meeting is held with the program evaluator, the participant, and the participant's manager to discuss the plan and the information contained in it.

4. Participants send the plan to the evaluator and it is discussed in a conference call.

5. Participants send the plan directly to the evaluator with no meetings or discussions. This is the most common option. If this option is used, you should keep communication channels open in case you need to clarify an item on a participant's plan.

Although data can be collected in other ways, it is important to select a mechanism that fits the organization's culture, requirements, and constraints.

Collect Action Plans at the Predetermined Follow-up Time

Because it is critical to have a good response rate, several steps may be necessary to ensure that the action plans are completed and the data are returned to the appropriate individual or group for analysis. Some organizations use follow-up reminders by mail or e-mail. Others call participants to check progress. Still others offer assistance in developing the final plan. These steps may require additional resources, which have to be weighed against the importance of having more data. When the action plan process is implemented as outlined in this chapter, the response rates will normally be very high in the 60% to 90% range. Usually participants will see the importance of the process and will develop their plans in detail.

Summarize the Data and Calculate the ROI

If developed properly, each action plan should have annualized monetary values associated with improvements. Also, each individual has indicated the percent of the improvement directly related to the program. Finally, each participant has provided a confidence percentage to reflect uncertainty with the process and the subjective nature of some of the data.

Because this process involves some estimates, it may not appear to be credible. Several adjustments during the analysis make the process credible and believable. The following adjustments are made:

Step 1: For those participants who do not provide data, it is assumed that they had no improvement to report. This is a very conservative assumption. (Guiding Principle 6)

Step 2: Each value is checked for realism, usability, and feasibility. Extreme values are discarded and omitted from the analysis. (Guiding Principle 8)

Step 3: Because the improvement is annualized, it is assumed the program had no improvement after the first year. Some programs likely add value at years two and three. (Guiding Principle 9)

Step 4: The new values are then adjusted by the percent of the improvement related directly to the program using straight multiplication. This isolates the effects of training. (Guiding Principle 5)

Step 5: The improvement from step 3 is then adjusted by the confidence level, multiplying it by the confidence percent. The confidence level is actually an error suggested by the participants. (Guiding Principle 7). For example, a participant indicating 80% confidence with the process is reflecting a 20% error possibility. In a $10,000 estimate with an 80% confidence factor, the participant is suggesting that the value could be in the range of $8,000 to $12,000. To be conservative, the lower number is used. Thus, the confidence factor is multiplied by the amount of improvement.

The monetary values determined in these five steps are totaled to arrive at a total program benefit. This same process is used in making adjustments when questionnaires or interviews are used to collect Level 4 data. Because these values are annualized, the total of these benefits becomes the annual benefits for the program. This value is placed in the numerator of the ROI formula to calculate the ROI.

Level 5 ROI

To calculate ROI, we need to take two important steps. First, we should be capturing the fully loaded cost of the program as an ongoing part of the evaluation project. This should be entered on the Project Plan (see Chapter 2 on the CD). Someone should be assigned the responsibility to track and calculate costs. The cost categories and information needed are covered in Chapter 6, "Counting the Costs." Once the costs are collected, they are tabulated and totaled. The total is entered into the denominator of the formula. An important objective in capturing costs is to be certain not to understate costs. So, when we estimate such items as salaries, travel, or the cost of the facility and refreshments, we should be certain we use high-end estimates. Failing to do this will inflate the ROI.

Second, when we collect our Level 4 data, we have what we need to calculate ROI. We simply need to take the additional step of converting the data to a monetary value. This is covered in Chapter 5, "Converting Benefits to Money." As detailed in Chapter 5, we must decide which Level 4 data we will convert to a monetary value and which Level 4 data will be reported as intangible results. It is crucial to report both sets of data. The intangible results serve to support the idea that the ROI (if we are reporting an ROI) is actually understated. If an ROI is not being reported, then the Level 4 intangible results stand alone as the business impact of the program. As can be imagined, reporting intangibles is a challenge. We will be in the position of convincing our audience that the intangibles are significant enough to justify the investment in the training.

Who Do I Ask?: Sources of Data

When considering the possible data sources that will provide input on the success of a training program, six categories are easily defined.

Organizational Performance Records

The most useful and credible data source for ROI analysis is the records and reports of the organization. Whether individualized or group based, the records reflect performance in a work unit, department, division, region, or overall organization. This source can include all types of measures, which are usually available in abundance throughout the organization. Collecting data from this source is preferred for Level 4 evaluation (and ROI) because it usually reflects business impact data and it is relatively easy and inexpensive to obtain. However, sloppy record keeping by some organizations may make locating particular data or reports difficult.

Participants

A widely used data source for an ROI analysis is the program participants. Participants are frequently asked about reaction and satisfaction, extent of learning, and how they have applied skills and knowledge on the job. Sometimes they are asked to explain the impact of those actions. Participants are a rich source of data for Levels 1, 2, 3, and 4 evaluations. They are credible because they are the individuals who have been involved in the program and achieved the performance. Also, they are often the most knowledgeable of the work processes and other influencing factors. The challenge is to find an effective and efficient way to capture data in a consistent manner.

Supervisors of Participants

Individuals who directly supervise or direct program participants are another important source of data. This group often has a vested interest in the evaluation process because they approved the participants' attendance. Often, they observe the participants as they attempt to use the knowledge and skills acquired in the program. Consequently, they can report on successes as well as difficulties and problems associated with application and their input can be useful for both Level 3 and Level 4 improvements. It is important, however, for supervisors to maintain objectivity when assessing the performance of program participants.

Direct Reports of Participants

When supervisors and managers are being trained, their direct reports can provide information about perceived changes in observable behavior after the program was conducted. Input from direct reports is appropriate for Level 3 data (behavior), but not Level 4. While collecting data from this source can be very helpful and instructive, it is often avoided because of the potential biases that can enter into the feedback process.

Teams or Peer Groups

Those who serve as team members with the participant or occupy peer-level positions in the organization are another source of data for a few types of programs. Peer group members provide input on perceived behavioral changes of participants (Level 3 data). This source of data is more appropriate when all team members participate in the program and, consequently, they report on the collective efforts of the group or behavioral changes of specific individuals. Because this process is subjective and opportunities are limited to evaluate fully the application of skills, this source of data is somewhat limited.

Internal or External Groups

Internal or external groups, such as the training and development staff, program facilitators, expert observers, or external consultants, can sometimes provide input on how successfully individuals have learned and applied the skills and knowledge covered in the program. Sometimes expert observers or assessors may be used to measure learning (Level 2 data) and on-the-job observation (Level 3 data) after the training program has been completed. Collecting data from this source could have limited uses. Because internal groups may have a vested interest in the outcome of evaluation, their input may lose credibility.

When Do I Ask?

Level 1: Reaction

Level 1 data is usually collected during the learning engagement. If the learning program is delivered by desktop, the feedback instrument is built into completion of a module or program. Concerned that fewer participants respond to Web-based reaction instruments, some organizations require completion of the form before giving credit for completion. Of course, this tactic also runs the risk of the data being less than adequate. If the training is instructor-led, the Level 1 instrument is usually administered toward the end of the program.

Level 2: Learning

When tests or assessments are used to determine a baseline, they can be administered before or at the beginning of the training. When used to provide skill practice or to determine progress, administration occurs during the training engagement while a topic is being addressed. Tests are administered toward the end of a program if the purpose is to determine overall knowledge and skill.

Follow-Up Level 3: Application and Level 4: Business Impact Data

Collection of data at Level 3 must align with the participant's opportunity to exhibit the behavior or apply the knowledge and skills as intended. Therefore, the timing will vary. For example, a training program for call-center representatives on how to interact with customers to solicit information and provide answers about customer accounts involves the routine application of the knowledge and skills on a daily basis. This being the case, data can be collected relatively soon. Data collection could occur after a few weeks and certainly no longer than one or two months.

When knowledge and skills are broader in scope and have an application that does not occur on a daily basis, more time is needed to collect useful data. For example, a supervisor is trained in using the performance management process (setting expectations, coaching, providing feedback and recognition). Application of these skills occurs over a longer time frame, and several months could pass before useful data can be collected.

Another factor affecting the timing decision is the operational environment. For example, if a participant is observed during times that are not normal (i.e., in a crisis), the data collected may be distorted. Time of year could also be a factor because of workload or cyclical events in the work setting. The timing for collecting Level 3 data is always situational and should be discussed with the client and possibly other stakeholders before making a decision. The factors that affect normality should be identified and considered when making the decision on timing. On occasion, Level 3 data may be collected more than once. For example, you may want to collect data early just to see if the knowledge, skills, or processes are being used as intended or to identify any barriers to use. Then data is collected later to determine if use is sustained.

Another timing factor that often must be considered is convenience. Timing must be accommodated when people must provide data and there is a place, situation, or time frame that is more convenient for them. Another example of convenience is when the organization routinely collects Level 4 data. For example, an organization routinely collects customer satisfaction data in June and December. Our customer-service training program is completed in October with the objective of improving customer satisfaction. The customer satisfaction data is available in December, but this may be too soon to observe any change in the measure influenced by our program. The next available time frame is June of the following year. This is farther out than we would like. If collecting additional customer satisfaction data during a different time frame is too costly or too intrusive, then we must settle for June.

POTENTIAL CHALLENGES

Data collection poses many challenges. Among them is gathering enough data, particularly with questionnaires. This is often referred to as response rate. Table 3–6 provides helpful information on improving response rates for questionnaires.

Validity and reliability are other factors that can be challenging when designing data collection instruments. Probably the most important characteristic of an evaluation instrument is validity. A valid instrument measures what the instrument is designed to measure. Reliability refers to the consistency and stability of an instrument. A reliable instrument is consistent enough so that later measurements of an item provide approximately the same results. More information is available on validity and reliability in Jack J. Phillips' *Handbook of Training Evaluation and Measurement Methods,* (3rd edition), Burlington, MA: Butterworth-Heinemann, 1997.

TABLE 3–6

IMPROVING THE RESPONSE RATE FOR QUESTIONNAIRES

Administration:

✓	Use one or two follow-up reminders.
✓	Have the introduction letter signed by a top executive.
✓	Use local manager to distribute questionnaires, show support, and encourage response.
✓	Use a local coordinator to help distribute and collect questionnaires.
✓	Enclose a giveaway item with the questionnaire (pen, money).
✓	Provide an incentive (or chance of incentive) for quick response.
✓	Distribute questionnaire to a captive audience.
✓	Consider an alternative distribution channel such as electronic.
✓	Have a third party gather and analyze data.
✓	Keep questionnaire responses anonymous . . . or at least confidential.
✓	Make it easy to respond; include a preaddressed stamped envelope for hard-copy questionnaires.
✓	Provide options to respond (paper, e-mail, website).
✓	Allow completion of the survey during work hours.
✓	Consider paying for the time it takes to complete the questionnaire.

Communication:

✓	Provide advance communication about the questionnaire.
✓	Clearly communicate the reason for the questionnaire.
✓	Review the questionnaire at the end of formal session when practical.
✓	Provide an estimate of the time it should take to complete the questionnaire.
✓	Communicate the time limit for submitting responses.
✓	Communicate that you will send a summary of the results to participants.
✓	Let participants know what actions will be taken with the data.
✓	Indicate who will see the results of the questionnaire.
✓	If appropriate, let the target audience know that they are part of a carefully selected sample.

Other:

✓	Keep the questionnaire simple and as brief as possible.
✓	Carefully select the survey sample.
✓	Add emotional appeal.
✓	Design questionnaire to attract attention, with a professional format.
✓	Frame questions so participants can respond appropriately and make the questions relevant.

ACTION STEPS

- Review Part B of Premier Motors Case Study on the Chapter 3 folder of the CD. This may provide more insight as you complete your data collection plan.
- Complete Exercise 3–2, "Capturing ROI Data with Action Planning." This will give you a sneak preview of all the pieces coming together to collect, analyze data, and make adjustments to data to calculate ROI. After com-

EXERCISE 3–2. CAPTURING ROI DATA WITH
ACTION PLANNING

You are a member of a small team working on the ROI evaluation of the Leadership 101 training program. Thirty participants completed the three-day training program four months ago and you are now evaluating their follow-up results using action plans they were asked to implement. Action Plans were used as the tool to collect Level 4 and Level 5 data. Your team has almost finished the evaluation project.

You have already completed the analysis of 18 plans along with 10 others that submitted insufficient data. The data for the 18 participants has been entered below on the worksheet. Two completed plans arrived in the mail today. Your task is to analyze these two plans and complete the ROI calculation for Leadership 101. These two plans are on the Chapter 3 folder of the CD, "Figure 3–6, Sample Completed Action Plans."

- 30 participants participated in Leadership 101
- Data from 18 participants has already been analyzed, isolated, and annualized by your team (see benefits below)
- 10 participants did not provide data or provided insufficient data
- Two additional action plans must still be analyzed
  - Medicine Gelatin Manager: Plan just came in the mail
  - Bill Burgess: Plan just came in the mail

BENEFITS FROM LEADERSHIP 101 TRAINING

Medicine Gelatin Manager	$
Bill Burgess	$
18 other participants (isolated and annualized)	$52,765
10 other participants (no data submitted or insufficient data)	$
Total Benefits from Leadership Program	$
Total Fully Loaded Costs of Leadership Program: $60,000	

ROI = _____ %

pleting the exercise, check your answers with Exercise 3–2A Answers on the Chapter 3 folder of the CD.
- At the end of Chapter 2, you completed the objectives and measures at each level on the data collection plan. Return to your data collection plan and complete the remainder of the plan. There are examples of completed Data Collection Plans on the Chapter 2 folder of the CD, as well as in Figure 3–5 on the Chapter 3 folder of the CD.

CHAPTER SUMMARY

This chapter focused on collecting data at the four levels. Collecting data is perhaps the most crucial step of the ROI process because if you cannot collect data, then there will be no results to report. Planning and input/involvement of stakeholders is extremely important to a successful data collection effort. This chapter helped you:

- Develop the questions you plan to answer through your evaluation.
- Identify the appropriate data collection instruments for evaluating your program.
- Identify the sources of your data.
- Determine the timing of data collection.

The next chapter begins the analysis phase of the ROI process. Chapter 4 addresses isolating the effects and provides methods to determine the extent to which the training influences the selected business measures.

REFERENCES AND RESOURCES

Phillips, Jack J. *Handbook of Training Evaluation and Measurement Methods,* 3rd ed. Burlington, MA: Butterworth-Heinemann, 1997.

Phillips, Jack J. *Return on Investment in Training and Performance Improvement Programs,* 2nd ed. Burlington, MA: Butterworth-Heinemann, 2003.

Phillips, Jack J., and Adele O. Connell. *Managing Employee Retention: A Strategic Accountability Approach.* Burlington, MA: Butterworth-Heinemann, 2003.

Phillips, Jack J., and Ron Drew Stone. *How to Measure Training Results.* New York: McGraw-Hill, 2002.

Phillips, Patricia P. *The Bottomline on ROI,* Jack J. Phillips, series ed. Atlanta, GA: CEP Press, 2002.

Exercises and Case Study	Tools, Templates, and Job Aids
Exercise 3–1. Data Gathering	Figure 3–1. Sample Level 1 Questionnaire
Exercise 3–1A. Answers Data Gathering	Figure 3–2. Action Plan Form
Exercise 3–2. Capturing ROI Data with Action Planning	Figure 3–3. Typical Questions When Developing Action Steps
Exercise 3–2A. Answers Capturing ROI Data with Action Planning	Figure 3–4. Cyber International Follow-up Questionnaire
Case Study—Part B, Premier Motors International (PMI)	Figure 3–5. Sample Data Collection Plan— Performance Management
	Figure 3–6. Sample Completed Action Plans
	Figure 3–7. Sample B Level 1 Questionnaire
	Figure 3–8. Sample Level 2 Performance Observation
	Figure 3–9. Sample Level 3 Before and After Questionnaire
	Figure 3–10. Template L2 Performance Observation
	Figure 3–11. Sample Size Table
	Table 3–1. Level 1 Utility Measures
	Table 3–2. Hard Data
	Table 3–3. Soft Data
	Table 3–4 Level 2 CRT Reporting Format
	Table 3–5 Methods of Data Collection
	Table 3–6 Improving Response Rates
	Job Aid 3–1 7Cfactors™ of Data Collection

GIVING CREDIT WHERE CREDIT IS DUE

Addressing the extent to which an intervention influences business measures is an important issue for learning programs. The only way to know the connection between learning and business impact is to isolate the effects of learning on the specific business measures. This will ensure that the data analysis allocates only that part of the performance improvement that's connected to the learning. Without this important step, the study is perhaps invalid and worthless because other factors are usually present. At the same time a training program is being conducted, other factors—job redesign, incentives, rewards, compensation, technology, operational systems, and many other internal processes—may be influencing improvement in business measures. Factors external to the learning and HR area and to the organization can also influence job performance. Taking full credit for performance results by not accounting for other factors is unacceptable. Only the results influenced by the learning engagement should be reported to stakeholders. This chapter explores the methods of isolation with an emphasis on examples and actions.

In this chapter, you will learn to:

- Understand and itemize the importance of isolating the effects of learning.
- Discuss the examples of the use of the methods to isolate the effects of learning.
- Identify the challenges faced in addressing this important issue.
- Formulate questions that must be addressed to determine which specific method should or could be used.
- List the particular action steps needed to make the process successful.

Isolating the effects of learning can be a confusing process and is certainly one of the most difficult issues to address, but it is absolutely essential to sort out the causes of the business performance improvement. An exercise will illustrate the need for this isolation.

First Bank

First Bank, a large commercial bank, had experienced a significant increase in consumer loan volume for the quarter. In an executive meeting, the chief executive officer asked the executive group why the volume increased.

- The executive responsible for consumer lending started the discussion by pointing out that his loan officers are more aggressive. "They have adopted an improved sales approach. They all have sales development plans in place. We are being more aggressive."
- The marketing executive added that she thought the increase was related to a new promotional program and an increase in advertising during the period. "We've had some very effective ads," she remarked.
- The chief financial officer thought it was the result of falling interest rates. He pointed out that interest rates fell by an average of 1% for the quarter and added, "Each time interest rates fall, consumers will borrow more money."
- The executive responsible for mergers and acquisitions felt that the change was the result of a reduction in competition. "Two bank branches were closed during this quarter, which had an impact on our market areas. This has driven those customers over to our branches." She added, "When you have more customers you will have more loan volume."
- The human resources vice president spoke up and said that the consumer loan referral incentive plan had been slightly altered with an increase in the referral bonus to all employees who refer legitimate customers for consumer loans. This new bonus plan, in her opinion, had caused the increased consumer loan value. She concluded, "When you reward employees to bring in customers, they will bring them in . . . in greater numbers."
- The human resource development vice president said the Consumer Lending Seminar delivered to loan officers caused the improvement. He indicated that it has been revised and is now extremely effective, with appropriate strategies to increase customer prospects. He concluded, "When you have effective training and build skills in sales, you will increase loan volume."

These responses left the CEO wondering just what had caused the improvement. Was it one or all of the factors? If so, how much of the improvement was influenced by each?

In this situation, the process owners are all claiming credit for the improvement; yet, realistically, each could rightfully claim only a share, if any, of the actual improvement. The challenge is to determine which isolating method would be most appropriate. Unfortunately, because the situation has already occurred, it is difficult to address this issue with some of the methods. It could be helpful to go back and review some of the data to see if, in a sensitivity analysis, you could determine the various influences and what impact might have been generated at that time. It is too late for a control group arrangement because all parts of the bank were subject to these various influences. It is also important to note that the people who understand this issue best—the actual loan officers who received the training—are being omitted from consideration. Among the many available techniques, asking the participants (the actual performers) to isolate the effects of a particular program or influence may be the most credible and perhaps only way that this can be accomplished in this situation. Ironically, in this setting, it was ignored altogether. Incidentally, the CEO concluded the meeting with a request for additional details from each of the participants. Unfortunately, only one person provided data: the chief financial officer. In his response, he said that data from the American Banker's Association indicated that when consumer loan interest rates fall, consumer loans, by volume, go up. He applied this to the bank's situation to account for a large portion of the increase in volume. The other owners of processes did not respond, so only a few very important conclusions could be drawn:

1. The issue must be addressed to gain credibility for any of the functions or processes designed to improve consumer loan volume.
2. Sometimes the most important persons in this analysis are the end users, performers, or people who are actually involved in the process.
3. Failure to do this leaves a concern or even a cloud over their particular option—doing nothing is not an option.
4. This issue must be addressed early in the process so that many options to isolate the effects can be considered.

As the past discussion on the ROI Methodology has explained, a variety of techniques are available to isolate the effects of learning. Figure 4–1 shows a list of these techniques.

Although these are the most theoretically possible ways, they can actually be condensed into a smaller number of manageable categories: control groups, trends and forecast, and estimates. These are addressed in this section.

Control Groups

The control group arrangement is a classic experimental design where one group of participants is involved in a training program and a similar group is not. These groups are often called the pilot or experimental group (they receive the training) and the comparison group. Figure 4–2 shows the preferred control group design, which is a posttest-only control group arrangement.

The first step in this process is to identify the measure that will be influenced by the learning solution. This is a measure that matters—the Level 4 measure that is being monitored and compared between the two groups. Next, selection criteria are identified that define the various factors that will influence this

FIGURE 4–1

TECHNIQUES FOR ISOLATING THE EFFECTS OF LEARNING

- Use of a control group arrangement

- Trend line analysis of performance data

- Use of forecasting methods of performance data

- Participant's estimate of impact (percent)

- Supervisor's estimate of impact (percent)

- Management's estimate of impact (percent)

- Use of experts/previous studies

- Calculate/Estimate the impact of other factors

- Use of customer input

FIGURE 4–2

PREFERRED CONTROL GROUP DESIGN

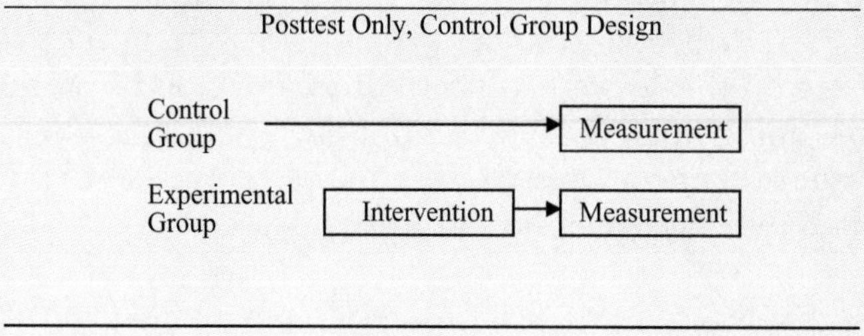

Posttest Only, Control Group Design

measure. These become the criteria for selecting the two groups. Then you apply the criteria to select the groups that will be in your study. This process is best explained by examining several examples. Each of the following examples is structured to quickly show a particular application.

Control Group Example 1—Retail Merchandise Company

Setting

Retail Merchandise Company (RMC) is a national chain of 420 stores, located in most major U.S. markets. RMC sells small household items, gifts of all types, electronics, and jewelry, as well as personal accessories. It does not sell clothes or major appliances. RMC executives have been concerned about the slow sales growth and were experimenting with several programs designed to boost sales. One of the concerns focused on interaction with customers. Sales associates were not actively involved in the sales process. They usually waited for a customer to make a purchasing decision and then processed the sale. Several store managers had analyzed the situation to determine if more communication with the customer would boost sales. The analysis revealed that the use of very simple techniques to probe and guide the customer to a purchase should boost sales in each store.

The senior executives asked the training and development function to experiment with a very simple customer interactive skills program for a small group of sales associates. A program produced by an external supplier was preferred to avoid the cost of development, particularly if the program proved to be ineffective. The specific charge from the management team was to implement the program in three stores, monitor the results, and make recommendations. If the program increased sales and presented a significant payoff for RMC, it would be implemented in other stores.

Audience

The participants in the audience (sales associates) were typical of retail store employees: Few if any were college graduates, and most had only a few months of retail store experience. They were not considered to be professional level but more clerical and administrative employees. Historically, they had not been involved in discussing sales with customers except in processing transactions. This training is designed to shift that paradigm so that they will be more actively involved in the sales experience.

Learning Solution

Based on the needs analysis, the sales staff does not have the necessary skills; therefore, a program called Interactive Selling Skills was selected with significant use of skill practices. The program consisted of two days of training, in which participants had an opportunity to practice each of the skills with a fellow classmate. This was followed by three weeks of on-the-job application. The third and final day of training included a discussion of problems, issues, barriers, and concerns about using the skills. Additional practice and fine-tuning of skills was a part of this final session. The program, an existing product from an external training supplier, would be applied in the electronics area of three stores. The program was taught by the staff of the training supplier for a predetermined facilitation fee.

Measures that Matter

The particular measure in question for this analysis is the average weekly sales per associate. This measure is readily available in the store's sales receipts and the organization's payroll records by store and by individual. A history of sales data is available.

Selection Criteria

Although many different factors could influence sales, four criteria were selected after some discussion with several store executives. These are:

1. Previous store performance. Tracking the actual weekly sales per associate for potential comparison stores enabled the group to select only those stores that matched up.
2. Sales volume. Although sales volume can vary significantly from one store to another, it was used as matching criteria. In other words, stores were selected with the same sales volume for each group.
3. Traffic flow. It was routine to monitor customers as they came in and out of the store for security purposes. This measure became the traffic flow. Consequently, stores with the same traffic flow were used in the matching groups.
4. Market. Stores were selected with the same basic market setting, which is defined as average household disposable income. This is available in the marketing database and was one of the key measures that drove the selection of each store's location at the start.

These four factors were used to select the two matching groups (three stores received the training; three stores did not). These factors were selected because, together, they influenced sales significantly more than any other factors.

Size of Groups

There were 16 people in each store for an equal size of 48 in the experimental group and 48 in the control group. This would be enough to see if differences occurred, yet would not be too expensive.

Duration of Experiment

The experiment ran for three months. The evaluation team thought that was enough time to see the impact of these simple skills on sales. Participants would have ample opportunity during the three months to utilize the skills in a variety of situations with a significant number of customers.

Control Group Example 2—Federal Information Agency

Setting

The Federal Information Agency (FIA) collects and distributes many types of important and sensitive information to a variety of stakeholders. FIA was experiencing an unacceptable rate of employee turnover for a group of technology communication specialists—averaging 38% in the preceding year alone. This was placing a strain on the agency to recruit trained replacements. An analysis of exit interviews revealed that employees were leaving for jobs providing higher salaries. Because FIA was somewhat constrained in its ability to provide competitive salaries, it was having difficulty competing with the private sector. Although salary increases and adjustments in pay would be necessary to avoid turnover, FIA was exploring other options. The annual feedback survey indicated much interest in employees attending an on-site master's degree program on agency time.

Audience

The individuals targeted were 1,500 communications specialists who had degrees in various fields: communications, computer science, and electrical engineering. Only a few had master's degrees in their specialty. Among these 1,500, roughly a third were considered high-potential employees that were destined for more important leadership assignments in the organization. The others were needed to continue to work in their assigned positions.

Solution

The solution was an in-house master's degree program offered by a regional state university. The program would be presented at no cost to the participating employees and conducted during normal work hours. Both morning and afternoon classes were available, each representing three hours' class time per week. Participants were allowed to take one or two courses per semester, with one course in the summer session, but were discouraged from taking more than two courses per term. With this schedule, the program would be completed in three years.

Measures that Matter

The measure that was monitored was the voluntary employee turnover rate. Of particular interest were those employees in the first five years of employment. The records clearly showed that once an individual stayed five years, he or she would usually stay much longer and the turnover rate went down considerably.

Selection Criteria

The experimental group consisted of participants in the program, and a matching group was selected. Although many factors could effect an employee's decision to leave, three were used as criteria:

1. The employees were matched along the same degree of specific measure so that their background was comparable.
2. The job status—that is, job title and pay grade—was matched.
3. The length of service with the company was matched.

These three factors were used to select the two groups.

Size of the Group

One hundred individuals were selected for the program and 100 matching control group participants were selected. The individuals were not in the program but matched along the three criteria identified previously.

Duration of Experiment

The experiment ran for four years—three years taking the first group through the program and one year post-program to continue to measure turnover.

Control Group Example 3—Midwest Electric, Inc.

Setting

Midwest Electric, Inc. (MEI) is a growing electric utility serving several midwestern states. Since deregulation of the industry, MEI has been on a course of diversification and growth. Through a series of acquisitions, MEI moved outside its traditional operating areas into several related businesses. MEI had been experiencing significant workplace changes as it transformed from a bureaucratic, sluggish organization into a lean, competitive force in the marketplace. These changes have placed tremendous pressure on employees to develop multiple skills and perform additional work. Employees, working in teams, must constantly strive to reduce costs, maintain excellent quality, boost productivity, and generate new and efficient ways to supply customers and improve service.

As with many industries in a deregulated environment, MEI has detected symptoms of employee stress. The safety and health function in the company suggested that employee stress has lowered productivity and reduced employee effectiveness. Stress is also considered to be a significant employee health risk. Research has shown that high levels of stress are commonplace in many work groups and that organizations are taking steps to help employees and work groups reduce stress in a variety of ways. The vice president of human resources has asked the training and education department, with the help of the safety and health department, to develop a program for work groups to help them alleviate stressful situations and deal more productively and effectively with job-induced stress.

Needs Assessment

Because of its size and sophisticated human resource systems, MEI has an extensive database on employee-related measures. MEI prides itself on being one of the leaders in the industry in human resources practices. Needs assessments are routinely conducted, and the HR vice president is willing to allow sufficient time for an adequate needs assessment before proceeding with the program.

The overall purpose of the needs assessment was to identify the causes of a perceived problem. The needs assessment would:

- Confirm that a problem does exist with stress and provide an assessment of the actual impact of this problem.
- Uncover potential causes of the problem within the work unit, company, and environment. Provide insight into potential remedies to correct the problem.

The sources of data for the needs assessment included company records, external research, team members, team leaders, and managers. The assessment began with a review of external research that identified the factors usually related to high stress and the consequences of high stress in work groups. The consequences uncovered specific business measures that could be identified at MEI.

This external research led to a review of several key data items in company records, including attitude surveys, medical claims, Employee Assistance Plan (EAP) utilization, safety and health records, and exit interviews. The attitude survey data represented the results from the previous year and were reviewed for low scores on the specific questions that could yield stress-related symptoms. Medical claims were analyzed by codes to identify the extent of those related to stress-induced illnesses. Employee Assistance Plan data were reviewed to determine the extent to which employees were using provisions and services of the plan perceived to be stress related. Safety records were reviewed to determine whether specific accidents were stress related or causes of accidents could be traced to high levels of stress. In each of the above areas, the data were compared to the previous year to determine whether stress-related measures were changing. Also, where available, data were compared to expected norms from the external research. Finally, exit interviews for the previous six months were analyzed to determine the extent to which the stress-related situations were factors in an employee's decision to voluntarily leave MEI.

A small sample of employees (10 team members) was interviewed to discuss their work-life situations and uncover symptoms of stress at work. Also, a small group of managers (5) was interviewed with the same purpose. To provide more detail on this input, a 10% sample of employees received a questionnaire to explore the same issues. MEI has 22,550 employees with 18,220 nonsupervisory team members.

Audience

The audience for this group was members of intact work teams who voluntarily enrolled in this program to reduce stress management. These teams had to be experiencing high levels of stress and willing to participate in a program of planned stress reduction.

Solution

The program, entitled "Stress Management for Intact Work Teams," involved several activities in 10 sessions. Initially, the entire group completed the comprehensive self-assessment tool called StressMap® so they could see where they stood on a scale of 21 stress factors. Then a three- to four-hour StressMap® debriefing session was conducted, designed to help individuals interpret their scores. This was followed by a four-hour module suited to the needs of the group. All of this was done in one day. The program was basically an organization development solution involving only half days of consulting time and follow-up one to two weeks later onsite or by phone. Approximately three to four hours of telephone follow-up was included in the process.

Measures that Matter

This program had multiple measures: unplanned and unexpected absenteeism, voluntary turnover, monthly health care costs for employees, and safety and health costs for employees.

Selection Criteria

Several criteria were available for selecting the control group.

1. The first is to select groups that had the same types of measures in their operating group.
2. A particular exercise was implemented to identify these groups. At least 75% of the measures had to be common between the two groups. This action provided an opportunity to compare performance in the six months preceding the program.
3. Each intact team and experimental group had to have the same function code. At MEI, all groups were assigned a code depending on the type of work they performed, such as finance and accounting, engineering, or plant operations.
4. Group size was also a factor. The number of employees in the group had to be within a 20% spread.
5. Average tenure was also used as final selection criteria and had to be within a two-year range. At MEI, as well as many other utilities, there was a high average tenure rate.

Size of the Group

The six pairs of groups represented a total level of employment of 138 team members for the experimental groups and 132 team members and six managers for the control groups.

Duration

The duration was a six-month review of the data for all four measures, which were then extrapolated for a complete year to determine an annual impact.

Control Group Example 4—International Software Company

Setting

International Software Company (ISC) produces payroll software for companies with a small number of employees. Packaged as standard payroll processing software, several enhancements can be purchased to perform other routines involving employee statistics and data. In some cases, data gets into staffing and manpower-planning issues. The company enjoys a customer database of over 1,500 users. For the most part, the customers use only the payroll functions.

Each year ISC hosts a conference where the users discuss issues they've encountered with implementation, new uses of the software, and how it can be adjusted, modified, or enhanced to add value to the organization. This is also an opportunity for ISC to get referrals and sell enhanced versions of the software.

Audience

The audience for this project is the individuals who attend the users' conference. To attend the conference they must be a current purchaser of the software and use it primarily for the payroll option.

Solution

The solution is the two-day conference designed to improve customer satisfaction with the current use of the software, upgrade particular software users to other options, and obtain referrals for other potential clients. There is no charge for the participants to attend; however, the participants must handle their own travel arrangements and hotel accommodations.

Measures that Matter

Several measures are monitored in a control group arrangement to ensure the success of this program.

1. Enhanced sales of upgrading options to current customers (increased sales of existing clients).
2. Referrals for new clients.
3. Increase in customer satisfaction as measured on the annual satisfaction survey.

Selection Criteria

Four specific criteria were used to select individuals for the comparison group. The user group attendees became the experimental group, and a comparison group of users that did not attend the conference became the control group. The two groups were matched using the following criteria:

1. The type of organization. This was basically matching the type of business by standard industrial classification.
2. The extent of use. The extent to which the customers are using upgraded software options beyond the standard, basic payroll processing.
3. The actual sales volume to date, which reflected the number of employees.
4. The actual longevity of the customer measured in years of using the current software.

Size of Groups

One hundred twenty-four users attended the conference, and a matching group of 121 were selected with the criteria outlined above.

Duration of Experiment

The experiment lasted for one year to track the three measures identified to compare the performance in the years after the program (i.e., the average referrals from other channels compared with referrals coming through the conference as well as the actual upgrade from other users groups compared to those who attended the conference). Finally, the customer satisfaction data were compared for the two groups.

Questions to Determine If a Control Group Is Possible

1. Is the population large enough to divide into groups?
2. Is the population homogeneous—representing similar jobs and similar environments?
3. What is the particular measure that matters to the organization?
4. What criteria may be affecting the measure that matters? These criteria are used to actually select the comparison groups for the control group arrangement (see example in Part C of PMI Case Study on the CD).
5. Using the 80/20 rule, which of the factors account for 80% or more of the difference between the groups?
6. Can the training and learning program be withheld from a particular group? Sometimes this is a naturally occurring situation because it may take a long time to roll out a particular program. Employees who receive the training program last may be as many as three to six months behind

those who receive the training first, creating an opportune time to compare the last group with the first group.

7. Is a pilot offering planned and could the pilot group be matched up with other groups for comparison purposes?

Rules for Working with Control Groups

1. Keep the groups separated by different locations, different buildings, different cities, if possible, maybe even different shifts, but certainly different floors.
2. Minimize communication between the groups.
3. Do not let the control or experimental group know they are part of an experiment and being compared with others.
4. Monitor data on a short-term basis to check for improvements for both groups.
5. Watch out for the Hawthorne effect from the experimental group. Minimize the attention paid to the group other than that required by the program design.
6. Minimize the effect of the self-fulfilling prophecy by not creating expectations beyond the norm that may drive results (example: do not tell people they are a special group and top performance is expected).

Trend Line Analysis

The primary reference books show this process in more detail. Trend line approaches are used to compare a group's preprogram performance with performance after the training. Trend line analysis has limitations and can only be used when certain conditions are met. Here are some examples of how to use trend analysis to isolate the effects.

Trend Analysis Example 1—Micro Electronics

Setting

In an improvement effort for Micro Electronics, an electronics components manufacturer, a series of training programs has been conducted. One measure of quality is the reject rate—the percent of items returned for rework. Because of the overall emphasis on quality for the last year, there has been a downward trend in the reject rate. However, the movement is gradual, and there is still significant room for improvement.

Audience

In one work unit, a continuous improvement program (CPI) was conducted to improve the reject rate. All employees were involved in the program. In this example, the employees were in a particular process unit (26 employees were involved).

Solution

The solution was a continuous process improvement program, conducted two hours per day over a one-week period. In this program, employees examine each of the process variables in the work unit and discuss and brainstorm ways to make improvements. The result is usually improvement in one or more of the processes, which include the measure in question.

Measures That Matter

The measure is the reject rate in the work unit, which has been as high as 2% at times. The goal is to get this as close to zero as possible.

Plot

Figure 4–3 shows a plot of the data.

Conditions Test

The employees, quality-control staff, and the team leader knew of no additional influence that entered into the process during the evaluation period. They also concluded that the downward trend would most likely continue—at least for the six months in the evaluation period. With these two conditions met, the difference of 1.45% and 0.7% is the amount attributed to this process improvement program.

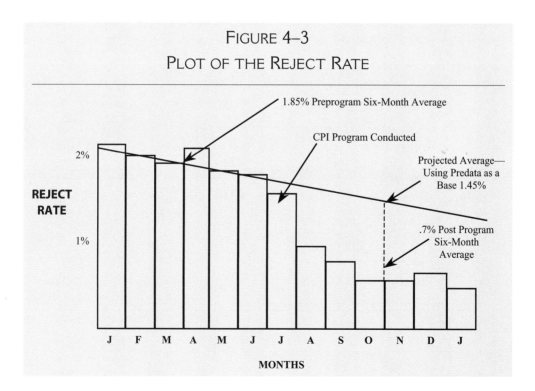

FIGURE 4–3
PLOT OF THE REJECT RATE

1.85% Preprogram Six-Month Average

CPI Program Conducted

Projected Average—
Using Predata as a
Base 1.45%

REJECT RATE

2%

1%

.7% Post Program
Six-Month
Average

J F M A M J J A S O N D J

MONTHS

Trend Analysis Example 2—Healthcare, Inc.

Setting

Healthcare, Inc. (HI) is a regional provider of a variety of health care services through a chain of hospitals, HMOs, and clinics. HI has grown steadily in the last few years and has earned a reputation as a progressive and financially sound company. HI is publicly owned with an aggressive management team poised for additional growth.

In the United States, sexual harassment continues to grow as an important and significant employee relations issue. Sexual harassment claims throughout the nation and in the health care industry continue to increase, sparked in part by increased public awareness of the issue and the willingness of the victims to report harassment complaints. HI has experienced an increasing number of sexual harassment complaints, with a significant number of them converting to charges and lawsuits. Executives considered the complaint record excessive and a persistent and irritating problem. In addition, HI was experiencing an unusually high level of turnover, which may have been linked to sexual harassment.

Audience

The audience would be all HI employees. The nonsupervisory employment level is at 6,844. First- and second-level managers number 655, while the senior management team numbers 41.

Solution

A detailed analysis indicated the major causes of the problem were a lack of understanding of the company's sexual harassment policy and what constitutes inappropriate and illegal behavior. Consequently, a one-day sexual harassment workshop was designed for all first- and second-level managers. After the managers attended the program, they were required to conduct a meeting with employees and disseminate information about the policy and discuss what constitutes inappropriate behavior. In essence, the program reaches every employee using this process, and all 17 one-day workshops were conducted in a 45-day period, with a total of 655 managers.

Measures That Matter

Two particular measures were critical for this analysis. First is the number of internal sexual harassment complaints filed with the human resources manager. This is a formal written complaint that had to be investigated. Some resolution had to be reached, whether sexual harassment was confirmed or not. The second measure is avoidable employee turnover, which is turnover for employees leaving voluntarily and turnover that could have been prevented in some way.

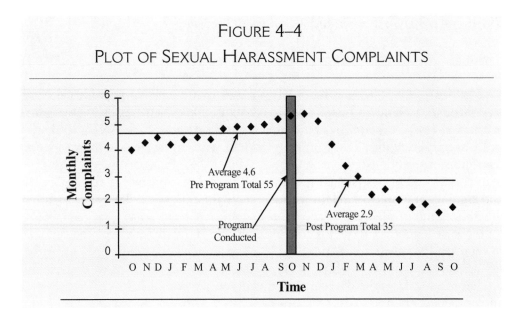

FIGURE 4–4

PLOT OF SEXUAL HARASSMENT COMPLAINTS

Plot

Figure 4–4 shows a plot of sexual harassment complaints.

Conditions Test

The human resources staff, including the HR manager, reviewed the climate during the one-year period after the program had been conducted. The group concluded the following:

1. The upward trend of sexual harassment complaints would probably have continued if the company had not implemented this program.
2. They could not identify any other new influence that could have prevented sexual harassment complaints; thus, the difference in the trend and the actual was the number of complaints that could be attributed to the sexual harassment prevention program.

Trend Analysis Example 3—National Book Company

Setting

National Book Company, a publisher of specialty books, is experiencing some productivity problems in their shipping department. On any given day, many of the scheduled shipments are not sent out, creating delays in getting promised shipments to some customers. The organization development function explored the issue, analyzed the problem, and addressed the issue in a team program.

Audience

The audience was all the employees in the shipping department, including the three supervisors.

Solution

The solution is an off-the-job meeting with an organization development consultant in which they explored the problem, causes, suggestions, and commitments to make changes and improvement. The results were reported back to the audience on a routine basis. Individual and collective follow-up sessions spanned another two-week period.

Measures That Matter

The measure is the actual shipment productivity, measured as a percent of scheduled shipment.

Plot

Figure 4–5 shows the shipment productivity.

Conditions Test

Collectively, all the team members could not identify any other influences that could have affected the shipment productivity measures, but they concluded the following:

FIGURE 4–5
PLOT OF SHIPMENT PRODUCTIVITY

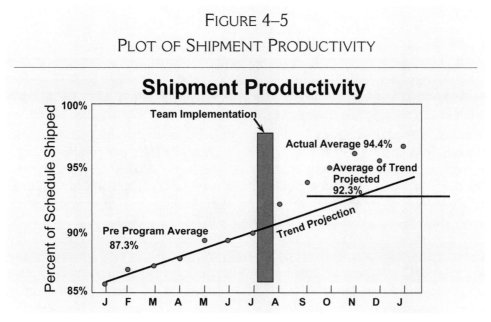

1. The upward trend improvement that was started would probably have continued because of the concern over productivity and the discussion of productivity in similar meetings.
2. No other new influence has occurred during the evaluation period, so the total improvement could be attributed to the team-building program. Thus, the actual average of 94.4% and projected average of 92.3% comprise the improvement directly connected to this program.

Trend Analysis (Forecasting) Example 4—Retail Sales

A more analytical approach to trend line analysis is to use forecasting methods to predict a change in performance variables. This approach represents a mathematical interpretation of the trend line analysis discussed above when other variables enter the situation at the time of training. A linear model, in the form of $y = ax + b$, is appropriate when only one other variable influences the output performance and that relationship is characterized by a straight line. Instead of drawing the straight line, a linear equation is developed from which to calculate a value of the anticipated performance improvement.

An example will help explain the application of this process. A large retail store chain implemented a sales training program for sales associates. The three-day program was designed to enhance sales skills and prospecting techniques. The application of the skills should increase the sales volume for each sales associate. An important measure of the program's success is the sales per employee six months after the program compared to the same measure prior to the program. The average daily sales per employee prior to training, using a one-month average, was $1,100. Six months after the program, the average daily sales per employee was $1,500. Two related questions must be answered: Is the difference in these two values attributable to the training program? Did other factors influence the actual sales level?

After reviewing potential influencing factors with several store executives, only one factor, the level of advertising, appeared to have changed significantly during the period under consideration. When reviewing the previous sales per employee data and the level of advertising, a direct relationship appeared to exist. As expected, when advertising expenditures were increased, the sales per employee increased proportionately.

Using historical values to develop a simple linear model yielded the following relationship: $y = 140 + 40x$, where y is the daily sales per employee and x is the level of advertising expenditures per week (divided by 1,000). Developing this equation is a process of deriving a mathematical relationship between two variables using the method of least squares. This is a routine option on some calculators and is included in many software packages.

The level of weekly advertising expenditures in the month preceding training was $24,000, and the level of expenditures in the sixth month after training was $30,000. Assuming that other factors that might influence sales were insignificant, as concluded by the store executives, the impact of the training program is determined by plugging in the new advertising expenditure amount,

FIGURE 4–6

DAILY SALES VERSUS ADVERTISING

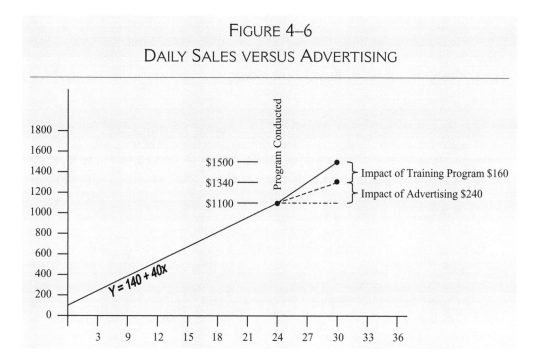

30, for x and calculating the daily sales, which yields $1,340, as shown in Figure 4–6.

Thus, the new sales level caused by the increase in advertising is forecast to be $1,340, as shown in Figure 4–6. Since the new actual value is $1,500, then $160 ($1,500—$1,340) must be attributed to the training program. Figure 4–6 shows graphically the effect of both the training and advertising.

A major disadvantage with this approach occurs when many variables enter the process. The complexity multiplies, and using sophisticated statistical packages for multiple variable analysis is necessary. Even then, a good fit of the data to the model may not be possible. Unfortunately, some organizations have not developed mathematical relationships for output variables as a function of one or more inputs. Without them, the forecasting method is difficult to use.

The primary advantage of this process is that it can predict business performance measures without training, if appropriate data and models are available.

Questions to Ask when Considering the Use of Trend Line Analysis

To use trend line analysis to isolate effects, a yes answer is necessary for these four questions:

1. Is historical data available for the measure at hand?
2. Are at least six data points available?
3. Do the historical data appear to be stable when they are plotted over time?

4. Is it anticipated that there will be no other influences, factors, or processes implemented at the same time of the training?

Rules for Working with Trend Line Analysis

1. Use the trend data to actually draw the trend line.
2. Trend lines are easily developed in Microsoft Excel. Input the data in columns and then develop the graph using the chart wizard.
3. Check with the process owners to see if the trend had begun before the onset of the program. Ask if the trend probably would have continued during the postanalysis period if the program had not been implemented. If the answer is no to this question, trend line analysis cannot be used for the measure under consideration.
4. Following the training, check to see if any other factors have entered into the process during the evaluation time period. If other factors have likely influenced the measure being tracked, trend line analysis cannot be used for the measure under consideration.
5. If we can pass checks 3 and 4, a trend line analysis becomes a very credible way of isolating the effects.

Estimations

Because at times neither the control group nor the trends and forecasting methods work, other methods must be used. The remaining methods involve estimations from the appropriate group. Two very important principles have to be followed when using estimates. First, data must be captured from the most credible group—those who are capable of providing this estimate. Second, the estimates must be adjusted for the error of that estimate. This method, although criticized by some, is considerably better than doing nothing, which would be even less credible. The estimates will come from a variety of groups, and each is explained with an example. However, the estimate itself can be obtained in two different ways. First is the focus group approach, where the individuals providing the data meet as a small focus group. The following steps are recommended:

1. Explain the task. The task of the focus group meeting is outlined. Participants should understand that performance has improved. While many factors could have contributed to the performance, the task of this group is to determine how much of the improvement is related to the training.
2. Discuss the rules. Each participant should be encouraged to provide input, limiting his or her comments to two minutes (or less) for any specific issue. Comments are confidential and will not be linked to a specific individual.
3. Explain the importance of the process. The participants' role in the process is critical. Because it is their performance that has improved, the participants are usually in the best position to indicate what has caused this improvement; they are the experts in this determination. Without

quality input, the contribution of this training (or any other processes) may never be known.

4. Select the first measure and show the improvement. Using actual data, show the level of performance prior to and following training; in essence, the change in business results—the Δ—is reported.

5. Identify the different factors that have contributed to the performance. Using input from experts—others who are knowledgeable about the improvements (including participants)—identify the factors that have influenced the improvement (e.g., the volume of work has changed, a new system has been implemented, or technology has been enhanced). If these are known, they are listed as the factors that may have contributed to the performance improvement.

6. The group is asked to identify other factors that have contributed to the performance. In some situations, only the participants know other influencing factors and those factors should surface at this time.

7. Discuss the linkage. Taking each factor one at a time, the team members individually describe the linkage between that factor and the business results. For example, for the training influence, the participants would describe how the training has driven the actual improvement by providing examples, anecdotes, and other supporting evidence. Participants may require some prompting to provide comments. If they cannot provide dialogue on a particular issue, there's a good chance that that factor had no influence.

8. The process is repeated for each factor. Each factor is explored until all the participants have discussed the linkage between all the factors and the business performance improvement. After this linkage has been discussed, the participants should have a clear understanding of the cause-and-effect relationship between the various factors and the business improvement.

9. Allocate the improvement. Participants are asked to allocate the percent of improvement to each of the factors discussed. Participants are provided a pie chart, which represents a total amount of improvement for the measure in question, and are asked to carve up the pie, allocating the percentages to different improvements with a total of 100%. Some participants may feel uncertain with this process but should be encouraged to complete this step using their best estimate. Uncertainty will be addressed later in the meeting.

10. Provide a confidence estimate. The participants are then asked to review the allocation percentages and, for each one, estimate their level of confidence in it. Using a scale of 0%–100%, where 0% represents no confidence and 100% is certainty, participants express their level of certainty with their estimates in the previous step. A participant may be more comfortable with some factors than others, so the confidence estimate may vary. This confidence estimate serves as a vehicle to adjust results.

11. Participants are asked to multiply the two percentages. For example, if an individual has allocated 35% of the improvement to team building and is 80% confident, he or she would multiply 35% by 80%, which

is 28%. In essence, the participant is suggesting that at least 28% of the team's business improvement is linked to the team-building process. The confidence estimate serves as a conservative discount factor, adjusting for the error of the estimate. The pie charts with the calculations are collected without names and the calculations are verified. Another option is to collect pie charts and make the calculations for the participants.

12. Report results. If practical, the average of the adjusted values for the group is developed and communicated to the group. Also, the summary of all of the information should be communicated to the team as soon as possible.

Another approach is to use questionnaires. The questions are provided as an add-on to the follow-up questionnaire and a chain of impact questions, as illustrated below. First, we ask for results data in questions 1 through 7. Question 8 prompts the respondent to think about other factors that may influence the measure being addressed. Question 9 addresses the isolation issue directly. Question 10 adjusts for confidence level (because we are dealing with estimates). Question 11 seeks information which may identify other sources that could assist in providing results and other answers.

IMPACT QUESTIONS

1. How have you and your job changed as a result of attending this program?
2. What business impact do these changes bring to your work or work unit?
3. How is this impact measured (specific measure)?
4. How much did this measure change after you participated in the program (monthly, weekly, or daily amount)?
5. What is the unit value of the measure?
6. What is the basis for this unit value? Please indicate any assumptions made in the specific calculations you performed to arrive at the value.
7. What is the annual value of this change or improvement in the work unit (for the first year)?
8. We recognize that many other factors influence output results in addition to training. Please identify the other factors that could have contributed to this performance.
9. What percent of this improvement can be attributed directly to the application of skills and knowledge gained in the program? (0% = none; 100% = all of it)
10. What confidence do you have in the above estimate and data, expressed as a percent? (0% = no confidence; 100% = certainty)
11. What other individuals or groups could estimate this percentage or determine the amount?

This process can be described in more detail in an example. Several examples are provided below. Several samples showing how estimates can be addressed are also provided on the CD folder for Chapter 4. The CD folder for Chapter 3 includes the Cyber International questionnaire, which also shows a string of impact questions similar to these. Figure 4–11 provides a template for this string of questions.

Estimations Example 1—National Bank

Setting

National Bank is on a carefully planned growth pattern through acquisitions of smaller banks. One recent acquisition was quite large, representing almost £1 billion in total assets. After the acquisition, record-keeping systems and performance-monitoring processes were implemented at all locations. Each branch in the network has a scorecard where performance is tracked using several measures such as new accounts, total deposits, and growth by specific products.

National Bank has an excellent reputation as having a strong sales culture. Through a competency-based learning program, all branch personnel are taught how to aggressively pursue new customers and cross-sell existing customers in a variety of product lines. The bank uses sales training coupled with incentives and management reinforcement to ensure that ambitious sales goals are met. Six months after the performance monitoring systems were in place in the new acquisition, management was ready to implement the sales culture, including the training program for all branch personnel.

Recognizing that several factors have influenced scorecard results, management decided to let the program participants estimate the impact of the learning program. Branch management initially identified the following factors as having a significant influence on sales output: (1) the sales program, (2) incentive systems, (3) management reinforcement/management emphasis, (4) market fluctuations. Management tracked the improvements by product category after the program was implemented. Here, management used scorecard results by product.

Audience

The audience was all the employees in the branches. In this situation, there are 30 branches and the branch manager, including the tele-supervisors. This amounts to about 900-plus employees.

Solution

The solution is a sales training program that consists of both product knowledge training (products were adjusted slightly from the previous product offerings) and sales techniques (explaining the features and benefits of the product, overcoming resistance to the sale, and pointing out comparisons with competitors' products). The training lasted a total of one and a half days in half-day increments.

Measures

All major measures were monitored in the branch, including the number of new credit cards and checking accounts, an increase in deposits or product line, and increasing consumer loans. Although other measures are related to the products, these were the ones that the staff could most directly influence, indicating the payoff measures.

Estimates Provided

The entire team (by branch) provided estimates in a focus group setting. The branch manager was trained in the focus group process and actually conducted the meeting, capturing the data from each of the 30 branches. Thus, it became a collective input of the entire group using a summary of each person's individual improvement for each measure.

Credibility Check

To ensure that the most credible persons provided this estimate, the evaluation team decided that the branch staff would provide the measures. It is their performance that is being evaluated, and they should know more than anyone else what has caused their performance.

Methodology

The branch managers in the target metro area were contacted by questionnaire and asked to involve the team in estimating the percent of improvement that could be attributable to each of the factors above. All branch employees provided input in a meeting that the manager facilitated. In the carefully organized meeting, the branch manager:

- Described the task.
- Explained why the information was needed and how it will be used.
- Had employees discuss the linkage between each factor and the specific output measure.
- Provided employees with any additional information needed to estimate the contribution of each factor.
- Asked employees to identify any other factors that may have contributed to the increase.
- Obtained the actual estimate of the contribution of each factor. The total had to be 100%. Several consensus-reaching tools were offered.
- Obtained the confidence level from each employee for the estimate for each factor (100% = certainty; 0% = no confidence). The values are averaged for each factor.

Estimations Example 2—Global Financial Services

Setting

Global Financial Services, Inc., is a large international firm that offers a variety of financial services to clients. After analyzing its current sales practices and results, the firm identified the need to manage sales relationships more effectively. A task force comprised of representatives from field sales, marketing, financial consulting, information technology, and education and training examined several solutions for improving relationships, including customer contact software packages. The firm chose to implement a software package called ACT!™. This software, developed by Symantec, is designed to turn contacts into relationships and relationships into increased sales. The program features a flexible customer database, easy contact entry, a calendar, and a to-do list. ACT!™ enables quick and effective customer communication and is designed for use with customized reports. It also has built-in contact and calendar sharing and is Internet-ready.

Audience

The audience consisted of 4,000 relationship managers. Global Financial Services evaluated the success of the software on a pilot basis using three groups, each composed of 30 relationship managers. These managers were basically sales reps who had direct contact with the customers.

Solution

A one-day workshop was designed to teach these relationship managers how to use the software. The ACT!™ software was distributed and used at the workshop. If the program proved successful, yielding the appropriate return on investment, GFS planned on implementing the program for all of its relationship managers.

Measures

Particular measures were tracked in four categories:

1. Increased sales for existing customers.
2. Reduction of customer complaints regarding missed deadlines, late responses, and failure to complete transactions.
3. Increase customer satisfaction composite survey on the next customer survey data.
4. Reduction in time to respond to customer inquiries and requests.

Estimation Provided

The relationship managers provided the estimate in a focus group meeting. Five groups—12 in each group—for a total of 60.

Credibility Check

It was concluded that the relationship managers were the most credible source of data for this estimation. It is their performance being judged and, therefore, they should know this better than anyone.

Methodology

The method for the estimation is the focus group approach outlined earlier.

Estimations Example 3—Cracker Box

Setting

Cracker Box, Inc., is a large, fast-growing restaurant chain located along major interstates and thoroughfares. In the past 10 years, Cracker Box has grown steadily and now has over 400 stores, with plans for continued growth. Each store has a restaurant and a gift shop. A store manager is responsible for both profit units. Store manager turnover is approximately 25%—lower than the industry average of 35%—but still excessive. Because of the store's growth and manager turnover, there is a need to develop almost 150 new store managers per year.

Store managers operate autonomously and are held accountable for store performance. Using the store team, managers control expenses, monitor operating results, and take action as needed to improve store performance. Each store has dozens of performance measures reported in a monthly operating report. Some measures are reported weekly.

Store managers are recruited both internally and externally and must have restaurant experience. Many have college degrees. The training program for new managers usually lasts nine months. When selected, the store manager trainee reports directly to a store manager who serves as a mentor to the trainee. Trainees are usually assigned to a specific store location for the duration of manager training. During the training period, the entire store team reports to the manager trainee as the store manager coaches the trainee. As part of the formal training and development, each manager trainee is required to attend at least three one-week programs offered by the company's corporate university. One of those programs is the Performance Management Program.

Audience

The audience consists of new store managers attending the Performance Management Training program. They're newly appointed to their restaurant manager's job and participating in this nine-month training program.

Solution

The Performance Management Program teaches new store managers how to improve store performance. Program participants learn how to establish measurable goals for employees, provide performance feedback, measure progress toward goals, and take action to ensure that goals are met. The program focuses on using the store team to solve problems and improve performance. Problem analysis and counseling skills are also covered. The one-week program is residential, and evening assignments are often part of the process. Skill practice sessions are integrated throughout the sessions during the week. The program is taught by both the corporate university staff and operation managers. Program sessions take place at the corporate university near the company's headquarters.

Measures

The measures in this example vary significantly, depending on where the manager is located and particular operational issues that are a concern to both the manager and his or her direct reporting manager. They can include sales and customer service, store operations and efficiency, safety and health, absenteeism and turnover, or any other measures that may be appropriate.

Estimate Provided

The actual store managers provide the estimate. Essentially, it is the team's performance that is being measured and the teams report directly to these managers.

Credibility Check

The evaluation team concluded that these store managers were the most credible source of input regarding the different factors that could have contributed to their store's improvement.

Methodology

The data were obtained on the action-planning document, on which the manager was asked to indicate the percent of improvement directly related to the program. Their adjustment was also provided.

Estimations Example 4—International Car Rental

Setting

The International Car Rental (ICR) Company operates in 27 countries and has 27,000 employees. The U.S. division has 13,000 employees and operates in most major U.S. cities. The learning and development (L&D) staff at ICR has developed a new program for all first-level managers.

Audience

The Leadership Challenge is designed for team leaders, supervisors, and managers who are responsible for those who actually do the work (i.e., first-level management). Program participants may be located in rental offices, service centers, call centers, regional offices, and headquarters. Most functional areas are represented, such as operations, customer service, service and support, sales, administration, finance and accounting, and IT. Essentially, this is a cross-functional program for this important job in the organization.

Solution

The Leadership Challenge involves four days of off-the-job learning with input from the immediate manager who serves as a coach for some of the learning processes. An online prework instrument and a short book must be completed before attending the program.

Measures

The program focuses on typical competencies such as problem solving, counseling, motivation, communication, goal setting, and feedback. In addition to developing skills, the WLP staff attempted to focus directly on job performance and business needs. Consequently, prior to attending the program, each manager was asked to identify at least two business measures in the work unit that represent an opportunity for improvement. The selected measures had to meet an additional test. Each measure had to have the potential to be influenced by team members with the manager using the competencies in the program.

Estimates Provided

Participants provided the estimates and then gave a confidence factor.

Method

Estimations were provided through questionnaires.

Estimations Example 5—Litton Industries

Setting

Litton Industries' Salt Lake City Plant assembles, integrates, tests, and delivers the inertial navigation systems required to give extremely accurate guidance to military aircraft and missiles. The work is highly detailed and quality sensitive. There is little room for error, and the work must be done right the first time.

Litton traditionally had a top-down management structure. As the product line expanded and the plant grew in size and employment, quality slipped and management saw the need to get workers more involved by participating more in the decision-making process to improve quality and productivity.

Top management expressed a total commitment to a plantwide imperative that would focus on continuous improvement and redistribute decision making to the lowest levels through teams.

Audience

All employees in the plant were grouped into teams of 8 to 15 and trained in the Perfect Teams course. This course included section managers and supervisors.

Solution

After some experimentation with weekly meetings (and minimal training) to provide teams more flexibility to become productive and to discuss quality issues, management was finally sold on the need to roll out the self-directed team training called the Perfect Teams course. The three-day course consisted of a vision of transformation, clarification of team roles, and training in needed team skills such as group communication, problem solving, and self-management.

Measures

The team concept and the training were aimed at improving quality, processes, and productivity.

Estimates Provided

Sometimes it is helpful to push the estimation process up an even higher level to the senior management team. The evaluation of the self-directed team process had been conducted, but senior management felt the results may have been overstated. Although every influencing factor that could be identified was accounted for, the results still appeared to be unbelievable, excessive, and difficult for the senior team to accept. Although they believed that no other factors could have caused this improvement and the analysis was conservative, they assumed something else must exist, so the senior management team was asked to indicate an adjustment factor. Essentially they were asked to tell how much of this improvement was related to this program. Collectively, this group took away 40% of the results, still yielding a very impressive 750% ROI. This technique is not recommended because there's very little basis for this type of estimate. It may be used as a last resort when the values are quite high and there's a feeling that some other factors must be influencing the measures but cannot be identified.

Method

The method used was a brief focus group meeting to determine senior management estimates.

Estimations Example 6—Public Bank of Malaysia

Setting

At times it may be helpful to go directly to the customer. Consider the case of Public Bank of Malaysia. It began offering a new deposit savings product and was interested in measuring the impact of the new product.

Audience

Customer service representatives were targeted for the training on the new product.

Solution

Customer service representatives received training on the new deposit savings product, with the goal of convincing customers to buy the product.

Measures

The only measure was the sales of the deposit savings product.

Estimates Provided

As customers entered the branches and decided to put their money into this savings product, they were asked to complete a card and leave it in a box as they exited the branch.

Method

The equivalent of a questionnaire was used by administering the card as customers bought the product. The card had places to indicate the reasons why the customers selected this product at this time. The customer could check any or all of these factors. One of the factors was the sales capability of the customer service representative in convincing them to buy the product. This is the part that would be directly related to the training, assuming that no other factors had influenced those skills. This can be credible because it comes directly from the customers' estimate. However, customers may not be as accurate as employees as they try to understand their own performance. The impact of estimates and how they can add additional credibility is underscored in many other examples.

Estimations Example 7—Multi National, Inc.

Setting

Multi National, Inc. (MNI) is a large global firm with manufacturing and support facilities in more than 25 countries. MNI has experienced tremendous growth and is poised for additional growth in the future. MNI's comprehensive training and education program include a series of programs for the executives. One executive education program, Leadership and Shareholder Value, focused on using leadership and management principles to add shareholder value to the company.

As the program was developed, the company's chief financial officer was asked to sponsor the program. Because the nature of the program was intriguing, he accepted the challenge and became involved in some of the design issues and the complete implementation of the program. He made a personal visit to as many programs as he could fit into his schedule. His work with the program turned into enthusiasm as he saw an opportunity for a training program to have a measurable business impact, something that he has not seen previously.

Built into this three-day program was a detailed action plan that participants had to develop and implement. The action plan focused on a project that would add shareholder value to the company.

Because of his enthusiasm about the program and his sincere belief that the program was adding significant value to the company, the chief financial officer asked the program designers to follow up on the action plans and determine the success of the program in monetary terms. Two groups were targeted and contacted to obtain information on their accomplishments from the action-planning process. Much to the designers' pleasure, significant improvements were identified as important projects were implemented as a result of the program. Input from the participants was reviewed and the project items were tallied. To be consistent, only annual values converted to margin were used in the analysis. It was assumed that all of the improvements reported were linked directly to the program. The total came to a surprising £3 million for the two groups.

The chief financial officer was unsure of the actual cost of the program but was quite convinced that its benefit exceeded the costs. Eager to show the success of the program, he sent a brief report to senior executives, highlighting the success of the program. Because the executive group had never seen monetary values attached to a training program, the response was extremely favorable.

Audience

Executives from various functions were the targeted group.

Solution

In an attempt to bring more accountability to the training and education process, MNI engaged the services of a leading consulting firm that specializes in training measurement and evaluation. The consulting firm was asked to calculate the actual return on investment in several programs, including the executive education program that focused on achieving shareholder value. The program, Leadership and Shareholder Value, had achieved some notoriety because of its apparent success in adding value to the company's bottom line. An earlier follow-up indicated that savings of $3 million was generated through action plans implemented by two separate groups of the program.

Measures

The program did not focus on specific measures but instead asked participants to set objectives with an action-planning process. As they set objectives, they determined specific measures that would be influenced, ranging from output to quality to customer service measures.

Estimates Provided

The consulting firm explored several options to calculate the ROI, including the use of control groups, trend line analysis, and estimates obtained directly from participants. Because of the scheduling of the sessions, a control group evaluation was not feasible. Also, because the program did not directly influence a specific set of performance measures, trend line analysis was not feasible. Consequently, estimates from participants were used to approximate the impact of the program.

Participants were asked to describe their specific accomplishments and measurable results. They were asked a series of impact questions that yielded annualized values for the improvement. In addition, the questionnaire captured input on the participants' confidence in the data provided. Finally, participants estimated the amount of the improvement that was directly related to the program, expressed as a percent. The value of each participant's improvement was adjusted by the confidence-level percentage and by the percentage attributable to the program. The total value for improvements reported by the participants, after these adjustments, was $950,000. The overall cost of the program, on a per-participant basis, was $3,700. Fifty participants attended the two programs.

Method

A detailed questionnaire and action plan were used to describe specific accomplishments and to estimate the extent to which the training influenced the various measures.

Wisdom of Crowds

It is helpful to look at another exercise that reflects the importance of estimates. One day in the fall of 1906, the British scientist Francis Galton left his home in the town of Plymouth and headed for a country fair (this narrative is adapted from Surowicki, 2004). Galton was 85 years old and beginning to feel his age, but he was still brimming with the curiosity that had won him renown—and notoriety—for his work on statistics and the science of heredity. And on that particular day, Galton was curious about livestock.

Galton's destination was the annual West of England Fat Stock and Poultry Exhibition, a regional fair where the local farmers and townspeople gathered to appraise the quality of each other's cattle, sheep, chickens, horses, and pigs. Wandering through rows of stalls examining workhorses and prize hogs may seem to have been a strange way for a scientist to spend an afternoon, but there was a certain logic to it. Galton was a man obsessed with two things: the measurement of physical and mental qualities, and breeding. And what, after all, is a livestock show but a big showcase for the effects of good and bad breeding?

Breeding mattered to Galton because he believed that only a very few people had the characteristics necessary to keep societies healthy. He had devoted much of his career to measuring those characteristics, in fact, in order to prove that the vast majority of people did not have them. His experiments left him with little faith in the intelligence of the average person, "the stupidity and wrong-headedness of many men and women being so great as to be scarcely credible." Only if power and control stayed in the hands of the select, well-bred few, Galton believed, could a society remain healthy and strong.

As he walked through the exhibition that day, Galton came across a weight-judging competition. A fat ox had been selected and placed on display, and members of a gathering crowd were lining up to place wagers on what the weight of the ox would be *after* it had been slaughtered and dressed. For sixpence, you could buy a stamped and numbered ticket, where you filled in your name, occupation, address, and estimate. The best guesses would receive prizes.

Eight hundred people tried their luck. They were a diverse lot. Many of them were butchers and farmers, who were presumably experts at judging the weight of livestock, but there were also quite a few people who had no insider knowl-edge of cattle. "Many non-experts competed," Galton wrote later in the sci-entific journal *Nature*. "The average competitor was probably as well fitted for making a just estimate of the dressed weight of the ox, as an average voter is of judging the merits of most political issues on which he votes," he wrote.

Galton was interested in figuring out what the "average voter" was capable of because he wanted to prove that the average voter was capable of very little. So he turned the competition into an impromptu experiment. When the contest was over and the prizes had been awarded, Galton borrowed the tickets from the organizers and ran a series of statistical tests on them. Galton arranged the guesses (which totaled 787 in all, after he had to discard 13 because they were illegible) in order from highest to lowest and graphed them to see if they would form a bell curve. Then, among other things, he added all the contestants' esti-mates, and calculated the mean of the group's guesses. That number repre-sented, you could say, the collective wisdom of the Plymouth crowd. If the crowd were a single person, that was how much it would have guessed the ox weighed.

Galton undoubtedly thought that the average guess of the group would be way off the mark. After all, mix a few very smart people with some mediocre people and a lot of dumb people, and it seems likely you'd end up with a dumb answer. But Galton was wrong. The crowd had guessed that the ox, after it had been slaughtered and dressed, would weigh 1,197 pounds. After it had been slaughtered and dressed, the ox weighed 1,198 pounds. In other words, the crowd's judgment was essentially perfect. The "experts" were not close. Perhaps breeding did not mean so much after all. Galton wrote later: "The result seems more creditable to the trustworthiness of a democratic judgment than it might have been expected." That was, to say the least, an understatement.

What Francis Galton stumbled on that day in Plymouth was a simple but powerful truth: under the right circumstances, groups are remarkably intelligent, and are often smarter than the smartest people in them. Groups do not need to be dominated by exceptionally intelligent people in order to be smart. Even if most of the people within a group are not especially well informed or rational, it can still reach a collectively wise decision.

Questions to Ask When Considering the Use of Estimations

1. Can other approaches work? (Remember, estimates are a fallback position.)
2. Is the group providing estimates credible in terms of providing input?
3. Is this group accessible; that is, can we get to this group either by a focus group or questionnaire?
4. Which is the most practical and appropriate method to collect the data; a focus group or a questionnaire? Proceed with the acceptable method.

Rules for Working with Estimations

1. Data must be captured from the most credible group—those who are capable of providing this estimate. This follows Guiding Principle 3, "When collecting and analyzing data, use only the most credible sources." The group that is most credible to isolate the effects may not be the same group that is most credible to provide other types of data. Remember, the isolation question is a *why* question.
2. When two or more groups or sources provide estimates to isolate the effects and the data differ, unless a compelling reason exists to do otherwise, Guiding Principle 4 should be considered: "When analyzing data, choose the most conservative alternative for calculations".
3. Adjust the estimate for the possibility of error. This follows Guiding Principle 7: "Estimates of improvements should be adjusted for the potential error of the estimate."

These rules may be applied in several ways. Let's look at some possibilities. The FDA recently approved a new drug (Salustatin) for a large pharmaceutical firm. A training program was conducted for 150 sales representatives prior to marketing the drug. The program was evaluated for impact by using a follow-up questionnaire. Table 4–1 reports the isolation factor as consolidated results based on estimates provided by sales managers and sales representatives

TABLE 4–1

ESTIMATES OF THE FACTORS THAT INFLUENCED PERFORMANCE IMPROVEMENT

Several factors often contribute to performance improvement. In addition to the Salustatin training, some of the other potential factors are identified below. We asked participants and managers to look at the factors and indicate what percentage they attributed to each toward overall performance improvement during the past four months. They were asked not to assign a percentage to a factor if they thought it had no influence. *The total of all selected items had to equal 100%.*

The Question	The Results	
Please select the items that you feel are appropriate by writing in your estimated percentages as they apply. The total of all selected items must equal 100%.	The percentage attributed to each item	
	Sales Reps	Sales Managers
A) Physician seminars promoting Salustatin as treatment of choice	21%	20%
B) Other local promotions of Salustatin	10%	11%
C) Salustatin training for sales representatives	24%	16%
D) Market conditions	14%	25%
E) Salustatin physicians seeing more patients with associated indications	6%	4%
F) Improved sales brochures supporting the core promotional message	11%	12%
G) Lack of competing products from our competitors	4%	3%
H) Other training initiatives: <u>Shyomine training frequently mentioned</u>	7%	8%
I) Other: _____ *please specify*	3%	1%
Total of all selected items must = 100%	**100%**	**100%**

on the questionnaire. Item C in the table denotes the training. A questionnaire was administered to both groups, and these are their respective results for the isolation question.

Rules 1 and 2 both come into play here. Both sources seem credible. The answers from both sources are quite similar except for items C and D in the table. The sales reps are often best able to determine *why* their performance improved. So, one approach is to go with the 23% isolation factor provided by sales reps. This seems like a logical approach since it follows Guiding Principle 3. Another possibility is to average the two responses from item C, which would give us an isolation factor of 20%. A third possibility is to take a weighted average of the two. Thus, if there are more sales reps responding than managers, then the percentage we use would be weighted more toward 24% (or vice versa if more managers). These latter two approaches are not covered by the guiding principles but may be a compromise to satisfy several stakeholders.

A fourth possibility may exist. Suppose we ask why responses C and D are at such variance between the reps and managers. This is certainly an important question. Suppose the answer is that the managers are aware of market conditions the sales reps are not in a position to know about. We could then conclude that the managers may be in the best position to know about *all* of the influences, especially market conditions. Given this compelling reason, we could possibly decide to use the 16% isolation attribution provided by the managers.

So if total sales were $10,000,000, our adjustment using the sales reps' responses would yield $2,400,000 in sales attributed to the training. If we use the managers' responses to make the adjustment, it would yield $1,600,000 attributed to the training. Quite a difference exists between these two numbers, and this would certainly influence the ROI calculation. Figure 4–9 on the CD includes an isolation template using estimates as the method. Figure 4–10 illustrates how estimates are adjusted for isolation and confidence level.

Identify the Forces for Other Factors

During a given time frame when we are conducting an evaluation, we need to identify the factors that may influence the performance measures we are addressing. During our evaluation planning process it is important to identify who can provide input on all the factors that may be influencing a specific measure. This is helpful, particularly in trend line analysis, forecasting, and estimation, to ensure a correct and complete list of the factors as we are planning our evaluation strategy. The participants themselves are often the most credible source for this data. During our planning phase, we should also determine the need for input from others:

1. Analysts who have identified the problem and the solution to begin with may have some excellent input on the other factors that could be influencing the business measure.
2. The developers and designers often understand the situation and the dynamics of the workplace and may be able to contribute.
3. The facilitators who teach the program. An experienced facilitator should be very familiar with the work environment—often coming out of that environment—and may have a good feel for the potential factors that may be involved.
4. The supervisors and managers of participants will sometimes have a larger scope to work with and are often positioned to view more of the various factors that can influence results.
5. Process owners who understand their processes can usually tell us what may need to be considered. Examples include IT or operations groups for automated operating systems and processes; quality departments for quality issues; HR groups for rewards and recognition systems, job design, and compensation; and marketing and sales departments for promotional campaigns, advertising, product pricing, and consumer behavior.
6. Managers at high levels or other areas who have insight into all the dynamics of the worksite may be able to add value.

POTENTIAL CHALLENGES

Isolating the effects of learning is a very challenging process. It is probably the most difficult area of all the analysis components and often keeps people from pursuing it. More specifically, the following five challenges must be overcome:

1. It is difficult for some people to address because it involves thinking outside the box to make sure they've identified only the part where improvement is connected to the program. Some of the techniques get into analytical and research-based methods and involve some statistical techniques that some may find quite difficult.
2. Some researchers, even well-trained ones, give up if they cannot use a control group or trend line analysis. This is unfortunate; just because those methods cannot be used does not mean the issue goes away. If we do not address this issue, we will continue to disappoint management (and ourselves) by failing to demonstrate how our solutions contribute to the business.
3. The use of some methods—such as estimates—may be uncomfortable for some because it is not as precise as desired. This will have to be fully explored and confidence will have to be built when using estimates, but only if they are used properly, according to the methods outlined in this chapter.
4. When organizations begin to use estimates, there may be too much reliance on estimates, so, as a caution, always use the most credible value.

In summary, these challenges make this a very difficult topic, but doable within most evaluation situations.

ACTION STEPS

- Complete Exercise 4–1, "Isolation and ROI Calculation," which follows. The answers are on the Chapter 4 folder of the CD.
- Review Part C of Premier Motors Case Study on the Chapter 4 folder of the CD. This may provide more insight as you begin to populate your ROI Analysis Plan by choosing a method to isolate the effects of your selected program.
- At the end of Chapter 3, you completed the data collection plan. You should now begin the development of your ROI Analysis Plan. Begin by copying your Level 4 measures from your Data Collection Plan and place them in the first column of your ROI Analysis Plan. The first column is labeled "Data Items." The blank ROI Analysis Plan form (Figure 4–7) is on the Chapter 4 folder of the CD. Figure 4–8 provides an example of a completed ROI Analysis Plan.
- As you begin to consider the method(s) you will use to isolate the effects for your program, review Job Aid 4–1, "Steps to Determine Isolation Method,"

EXERCISE 4–1. ISOLATION AND ROI CALCULATION

You are a member of the training and education department evaluation team. The last session of an extensive Leadership Development program was delivered in the organization four months ago. The 30 participants were asked to provide follow-up improvement data four months after the program through a follow-up questionnaire. You have just finished collecting and analyzing their data.

A series of questions on the questionnaire asked participants to provide their results, how they were achieved, and the monetary value of the results. Monetary results were achieved by 18 participants, ranging from direct cost savings to quality improvements with several work processes. The monetary benefits ranged from a low of $2,000 annually to a high of $310,000 annually. The total monthly monetary benefits from the 18 participants are $185,000 before isolating the effects. Following the above series of questions about results on the questionnaire, question 9 below was presented, asking participants to isolate the effects *(For purposes of this exercise, the answers to the isolation factor have been consolidated in the right column).*

Your Task: Using the consolidated results shown below that include the average isolation factor of 30% reported by the participants, calculate the total annualized benefits attributable to the Leadership Program and calculate the ROI. The fully loaded cost of the Leadership Program is $500,000.

Question 9: Many factors often contribute to performance improvement. In addition to the Leadership Development program, some of the other potential factors are identified below. Look at the factors and estimate what percentage you attribute to each toward the improvements you reported above. If you feel that some of the factors had no influence, then do not assign them a percentage. *The total of all selected items must equal 100%.*

Please select the items that you feel are appropriate by writing in your estimated percentages as they apply	Write in the percentage attributed to appropriate items:
A) Mentor guidance and support	25%
B) Leadership Development Program	30%
C) Coaching by immediate supervisor	20%
D) Incentives for cost-savings recommendations	5%
E) Implementation of self-learning plan	15%
F) Other: _____	5%
please specify	
Total of all selected items must = 100%	**Total 100%**

Your Answer: Total annualized monetary benefits attributable to Leadership program =

$_____

ROI = _____%

on the Chapter 4 folder of the CD. Use the Job Aid to make your decision. If you have more than one Level 4 measure, then you should repeat the process for each measure. Your method may be different for different measures. Worksheet 4–1 is also included on the CD to assist you in making a decision on your method of isolation.

CHAPTER SUMMARY

This chapter addresses the most critical and challenging issue facing evaluators of learning solutions. Isolating the effects of learning is an issue that must be addressed for the data to have credibility. If it is omitted, the study will probably be invalid. If it is addressed, a variety of techniques are available. These techniques were briefly explored in this chapter through examples and tools. The processes are basically in three categories: control groups, trends in forecast, or estimations. Estimations are considered the fallback position and used only if the other two options are not available. Estimates from the actual participants represent the default position and can always be used if nothing else works.

REFERENCES AND RESOURCES

Phillips, Jack J. *Handbook of Training Evaluation and Measurement Methods,* 3rd ed. Woburn, MA: Butterworth-Heinemann, 1997.

Phillips, Jack J. *Return on Investment in Training and Performance Improvement Programs,* 2nd ed. Woburn, MA: Butterworth-Heinemann, 2003.

Phillips, Jack J., and Ron Drew Stone. *How to Measure Training Results.* New York: McGraw-Hill, 2002.

Phillips, Patricia P. *The Bottomline on ROI.* Jack J. Phillips, series ed. Atlanta, GA: CEP Press, 2002.

Surowicki, James. *The Wisdom of Crowds: Why the Many Are Smarter Than the Few and How Collective Wisdom Shapes Business, Economics, Societies and Nations.* New York: Doubleday, 2004.

Exercises and Case Study	Tools, Templates, and Job Aids
Exercise 4–1. Isolation and ROI Calculation	Figure 4–1. Techniques to Isolate the Effects
Exercise 4–1A. Answers: Isolation and ROI Calculation	Figure 4–2. Control Group Design
Case Study—Part C, Premier Motors International (PMI)	Figure 4–3. Plot of Reject Rate
	Figure 4–4. Plot of Sexual Harassment Complaints
	Figure 4–5. Plot of Shipment Productivity
	Figure 4–6. Daily Sales vs Advertising
	Figure 4–7. ROI Analysis Plan form
	Figure 4–8. Sample ROI Analysis Plan— Performance Management
	Figure 4–9. Template–Isolation Using Estimates
	Figure 4–10. Sample—Isolation: Adjusting Participants' Estimates from a Leadership Program
	Figure 4–11. Sample—Isolation: Impact questions and Adjustments
	Table 4–1. Estimates of Factors that Influenced Performance Improvement
	Job Aid 4–1. Steps to Determine Isolation Methods
	Worksheet 4–1. Selecting the Isolation Method

5

CONVERTING BENEFITS TO MONEY

Before we can calculate the actual ROI, the first step is converting data to monetary value. Five simple steps lead the way. An important part of the process is deciding which data to convert to monetary value and which to report as intangible measures. Review of this chapter will help you understand how to do this.

In this chapter you will learn to:

- ❑ Distinguish between tangible and intangible measures.
- ❑ Convert data to monetary value, using the five steps.
- ❑ Decide when to convert and when not to convert data to monetary value.

THE FUNDAMENTALS

To move from Level 4 to Level 5 evaluation, we take five simple steps:

1. Identify program benefits after all adjustments are made, including isolation.
2. Convert those benefits to monetary value.
3. Tabulate program costs.
4. Identify intangible benefits.
5. Compare the monetary benefits to the costs by applying the ROI formula.

The first step, identify program benefits, represents our Level 4 measures in the five-level framework. These measures, called impact measures (results or benefits), are defined as the consequence of doing something differently as a result of the program. To review your knowledge of these types of measure, complete Exercise 5–1, Identify Level 4 Measures.

As you can see by responding to the exercise, Level 4 measures are often characterized as hard data or soft data. You will remember this from Chapter 3. For instance, if you look at Objective 1 in Exercise 5–1, decrease error rates on reports by 20%, you might assume error rates are considered hard data. Many people suggest that error rates are hard data because errors can be easily observed and counted. On the other hand, Objective 8, increase the external customer satisfaction index by 25% in three months, is easily counted. Although this is easily recognizable as a consequence of doing something different (therefore a Level 4 measure), the measure itself, external customer satisfaction, is often considered soft data. This is because the measure does not have a quantitative nature. That is, the organization typically does not associate a monetary value with the measure. Improving the measure is extremely important, but we cannot be certain how important if we do not know the monetary value. If we are not certain of the importance, it becomes more difficult and risky to allocate funds to improve it. Lack of a monetary value makes reporting the measure more subjective and puts it into the soft category. Before proceeding, consider refreshing your knowledge by reviewing hard and soft data examples in Table 3–2 and Table 3–3 on the Chapter 3 folder of the CD.

As shown in Table 3–2, hard data measures are categorized into output, quality, cost, and time, whereas in Table 3–3, soft data measures are catego-

---

EXERCISE 5–1. IDENTIFY LEVEL 4 MEASURES

Select the Level 4 Measures

Instructions: Review the program objectives below. Select the Level 4 measures by circling "Yes" if the objective represents a Level 4 measure; "No" if it does not.

Level 4 Measures are Defined As: *The consequence of doing something different as a result of the program*

Objective	Level 4?	
1. Decrease error rates on reports by 20%	Yes	No
2. Increase the use of disciplinary discussion skills in 90% of discussions	Yes	No
3. Achieve a posttest score increase of 30% over pretest	Yes	No
4. Initiate at least three cost reduction projects	Yes	No
5. Decrease the amount of time required to complete a project	Yes	No
6. Achieve a 2:1 benefit to cost ratio one year after program implementation	Yes	No
7. Receive an instructor rating from participants of at least 4.5	Yes	No
8. Increase the external customer satisfaction index by 25% in 3 months	Yes	No
9. Achieve a work simulation test score average of 75	Yes	No
10. Reduce litigation costs by 24%	Yes	No
11. Increase the employee loyalty index by 30% in 9 months	Yes	No
12. Reduce the absenteeism rate by 20% in 6 months	Yes	No

rized into work habits, customer service, work climate/satisfaction, employee development/advancement, initiative/innovation, and job attitude. As Chapter 3 notes, every soft data item will influence at least one measure in one of the hard data categories. However, we often fail to connect soft data to the hard data measures. For example, innovation is often considered a soft measure because you can't count it. However, what is the intent of innovation? In his book *Wow! That's a Great Idea!*, Ed Bernacki clearly shows that innovation is a tool organizations can use to enhance financial performance. Whether that financial performance is increase in revenue or increase in efficiency, it takes place through innovation. But it's the implementation or the action of that innovation that results in these consequences.

When soft data Level 4 measures are identified up front as a target to be influenced by the training, a discussion should ensue regarding which hard data category is influenced. How is the Level 4 soft data measure linked to at least one Level 4 hard data measure? This is the beginning of designing and delivering the training in the proper context. Allowing ourselves and others to discuss soft data in elusive terms will continue to limit our ability to properly analyze and report tangible results.

So, as in the example of innovation, we need to be able to make the leap from soft data measures to hard data measures. An example would be employee satisfaction—why do we want employees to be satisfied? Typically it is to build teamwork or to enable employees to become more productive or to improve work quality. So if we are trying to build teamwork, we have to look carefully and ask, "Why do we want teamwork?" To improve productivity or quality—both hard data measures. For purposes of converting data to a monetary value, the improvement of hard and soft data measures is going to contribute to either profit or cost savings. Our challenge is to determine how this should occur and then answer the question, Did it occur?

For example, improved quality can result in improved products or services, which in turn can result in increased sales. Increased sales can either increase profits or improve the profit margin. Improved quality can also contribute to cost savings by reducing the amount of time or cost to acquire facilities and materials or to design, process, produce, store, market, account for, and deliver the product or service. This same logic follows for any measure in either of the hard data or soft data categories. Often, standard values for output and quality measures are available in the organization. The internal finance/accounting function is usually the source of these standard values. If a standard value does not exist, conferring with stakeholders or experts can sometimes determine a credible monetary value.

Rather than talk about hard data measures versus soft data measures, another frame of reference is to refer to data as tangible or intangible. Tangible data are those data we choose to convert to a monetary value. Intangible data are those data we choose not to convert to monetary value.

Credibility of Data

As mentioned above, we can convert any measure into tangible data. If, for example, you want to convert organization commitment into monetary value, you and a partner can go out into the hall and come up with a value that you think should be placed on organization commitment. The question to consider, however, is how credible is your value? Will others believe in your value?

Exercise 5–2 provides more emphasis on credibility of data. Complete the exercise and review the answers on the Chapter 5 folder of the CD.

As you can see by the examples in Exercise 5–2, understanding the complete story is imperative in recognizing the credibility of our data. In some cases, data sources have immediate credibility. Others, however, lack credibility. But even for those sources we think are credible, when we dig down deep enough, bias can bleed through. We may also see that estimates are used somewhere along the way. So what appeared to be objective data is often based on a subjective process.

As we noted at the outset of the fieldbook, Guiding Principle 3 tells us to go with the most credible source of data. How do we do that? Credibility of data is influenced by nine factors, as shown in Table 5–1.

Reputation of Source of Data

The first factor, the reputation of the source of the data, tells us that while we may consider our data source as credible, we need to consider its reputation in the organization. Are the sources well positioned to know about the data they have provided? How reputable is this source to those people to whom we are going communicate the results?

Reputation of Source of Study

The second factor, the reputation of the source of the study, tells us to consciously consider the person(s) or group who are completing the evaluation. It is not their data. They gathered the data from other sources. But because they analyzed the data and reported it, their credibility is also important. How credible are they? What work have they done in the past? How valuable was the work in the past? And how credible were the results of previous studies?

TABLE 5–1

NINE INFLUENCES ON CREDIBILITY OF OUTCOME DATA

1. Reputation of the source of the data
2. Reputation of the source of the study
3. Motives of the researchers
4. Personal bias of the audience
5. Methodology of the study
6. Assumptions made in the analysis
7. Realism of the outcome data
8. Type of data
9. Scope of the analysis

EXERCISE 5–2. CREDIBILITY OF DATA

A. Smoking costs the USA $130 billion a year in shortened working lives and additional health care spending.
   Source: U.S. Treasury Department. Reported in The Wall Street Journal. ❏

B. Vulcan Materials Company produced 195 million tons of crushed stone last year.
   Source: Annual Report. ❏

C. Yellow Freight Systems receives 1115% ROI for training program.
   Source: Measuring Return on Investment, In Action Series, Jack J. Phillips (Editor), American Society for Training and Development ❏

D. Annual cost of absenteeism and diminished productivity resulting from employee depression is $23.8 billion.
   Source: MIT study reported in Nation's Business ❏

E. Alcohol-related problems cost the USA employers $27 billion a year in productivity losses alone.
   Source: National Institute for Alcoholism and Alcohol Abuse ❏

Discussion Questions

1. Which of these items have the most credibility? Select the two you believe are most credible. Rank the most credible as 1 and the next one as 2.

   _____
   _____
   _____

2. Why are these items credible or not credible?

   _____
   _____
   _____

3. List all the factors that influence the credibility of data.

   _____
   _____
   _____

4. Why are we uncomfortable in using estimates in our programs?

   _____
   _____
   _____

Motives of Researcher

The third item, the motives of the researcher, is a clear link to us, the discipline of measurement and evaluation. Why are we evaluating the program? Are we evaluating it ourselves? What is our motive for evaluation—are we trying to kill the program or prove its value to the organization?

Personal Bias of Audience

The next item, the personal bias of the audience, increases our pressure to ensure that we report only the most credible results. For instance, assume you are presenting your data to a group of executives and an operations manager is sitting in the audience. You tell the operations manager that your training program increased productivity 25% and that when you converted that 25% to monetary value, you saw a $3 million improvement. Now unless you have provided that operations manager some clear evidence that this value is true, you are going to immediately lose credibility with that audience.

Evaluation Methodology

The next item, evaluation methodology, suggests that we clearly consider the method we use to evaluate the program. Is our methodology systematic? Do we have standards with our methodology, and did we apply them to this study? How did we arrive at the monetary value of the program? How did we arrive at the changes in the Level 4 impact measure? How did the Level 3 data influence the Level 4 business measure? Methodology of the study is crucial. Although qualitative data provides a lot of evidence, we often need to go to performance records, thereby increasing the objectivity of our study. The credibility of our methodology is clearly dependent upon the organization. An organization that values subjectivity and qualitative data will accept more subjective processes. However, an organization that values quantitative measures will view subjective methods as less credible than methods such as performance monitoring and organizational records.

Assumptions

The next item, assumptions made in the analysis, tells us that we must clearly define the assumptions we make. Depending on what the assumptions are, they can influence how people feel about the completeness of the study and therefore its credibility.

Realism of Outcome Data

Another item that influences credibility is the realism of the outcome data. A recent *Chief Learning Officer* magazine stated that IBM achieved a 2,240% return on investment and a two-week payback period on an e-learning initiative. When I pointed out this example to a group and asked for their opinion, 42% suggested they would like to know how they achieved an ROI this high, and 38% suggested there was no way they could achieve it. On any program, a 2,200% ROI is quite high. However, some comments from the audience indicated that 2,200% ROI appeared to be credible given that it was IBM; hence, the source of the data was an important factor. However, for the other 38% who suggested "no way," the 2,200% was extraordinarily high and unbelievable. If the audience understands the relationship between the beginning performance gap, a successful solution, and the ultimate benefits achieved, a high ROI may be more believable. Although there may be many high ROIs, it is important to remember that ROI is one measure of success of our programs. The additional measures that make up the chain of impact are critical in telling the complete story of program success.

Method of Converting Data

The next item addresses the method used to convert our data to monetary benefit. Again, this goes back to the issue of hard data versus soft data. As we mentioned, all soft data can be linked to a hard data measure as either cost savings (time or quality) or improved profit. Sometimes soft data are indirect measures, and although the linkage may be clear to you, it may not be clear to your stakeholders. Conversion of soft measures is more suspect and less believable; therefore, we are selective in choosing when to report it as intangible.

Scope of Analysis

The final item that influences the credibility of data is the scope of the analysis. How large was the scope of the evaluation project? How comprehensive was it? The larger the scope, the more difficult to control the standard way the data is collected and reported. In large studies, more assumptions are usually made. It is difficult to know what assumptions were made and how they affected the collection, analysis, and reporting of the data. This makes the data highly suspect and therefore less credible.

Methods of Data Conversion

There are 10 methods we can use to convert data to a monetary value. Table 5–2 lists these 10 methods. The first three methods, converting output to contribution, converting the cost of quality, and converting employees' time, are typically standard values within the organization.

Output

When converting output to contribution, for instance, we are typically talking about revenue generation or sales converted to profit contribution. This is often a standard value. Profit is usually expressed as a percentage of revenue and is available from the finance/accounting department. Another output measure may be productivity. We first need to define what productivity is and then determine if there is a standard value for that productivity measure.

TABLE 5–2

METHODS OF CONVERTING DATA TO MONETARY VALUES

- Converting output to contribution—using standard value (profit/savings)
- Converting the cost of quality—using standard value of quality
- Converting employee's time—using standard values of compensation
- Using historical costs/savings
- Using internal and external experts
- Using data from external databases/studies
- Linking with other measures
- Using participants' estimates
- Using supervisors' and managers' estimates
- Using training/performance improvement staff estimate

Quality

The cost of quality is often another standard value. Many organizations have placed a value on quality. We first need to decide, however, what we mean by quality and then determine if the organization has placed an acceptable value on this quality measure. For example, operational measures of quality—such as product defects, shipping errors, order fulfillment errors, and patient or guest wait time—may have a standard value. Organizations often place standard values on measures associated with their core business.

However, other types of quality measures that are not on the operational side of the business may not be assigned a standard value. Quality measures—such as errors on invoices, errors on reports, incomplete proposals, inadequate engagement of teams, and inadequate recognition of employees—may fit in this category. Other methods will need to be used to convert improvements/savings in these areas.

Time Savings

And finally we can convert using employees' time. Many of our cost-savings improvements can be converted using employee time along with the benefits factor. This is also considered a standard value. We pay employees salaries or wages plus a percentage of salaries for benefits. The cost of employee benefits include items like medical plan coverage, life insurance, sick leave provisions, vacation pay, workers' compensation costs, pensions, and matching Social Security payments. The cost of these items is expressed as a benefits factor calculated as a percentage of salaries/wages. It ranges from 20% to about 40% in the United States. In Europe it may be in the high 30% or 40% range. Human resource and finance departments are usually quite familiar with the exact percentage in their organization.

When working with these three standard values, data conversion can be quite efficient and reasonably accurate. However, sometimes we don't have a standard value. In some cases, a measure has not been converted within the organization and there is no acceptable value for it. When that is the case, we must move to more operational methods of data conversion. The last seven items in Table 5–2 represent these operational methods.

Historical Costs

Historical costs represent costs incurred in the past for similar improvement in a particular measure. An example would be litigation—what has litigation for a similar act cost the organization? We can often go to our legal services department to find the answer—by looking at historical litigation costs.

Internal or External Experts

Sometimes, an expert within the organization can quickly and efficiently place a value on a particular measure. Figure 5–1 shows an example of combining historical costs and expert input to convert the cost of a sexual harassment complaint. In this scenario, a local hospital had a high rate of sexual harassment complaints. These complaints ultimately resulted in significant turnover of nurses. In addition to the behavior being inappropriate, the hospital (1) did not need the publicity and (2) it was losing nurses. Accordingly, a program was initiated to reduce the number of complaints. After implementing the program and isolating the effects of the program, a reduction of 35 complaints was achieved. To convert these complaints to monetary value (meaning to analyze the cost of those complaints), two methods were used— historical costs and expert input.

Historical costs were obtained from the legal department. The organization looked at the actual costs from records. These costs included legal fees, settlements, losses, materials, and direct expenses. The costs of the complaint were also defined as the cost to the EEO staff in the HR department. Experts in the

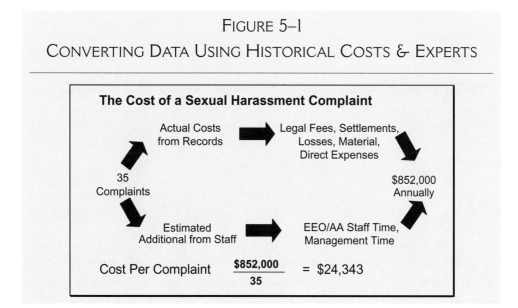

FIGURE 5–1

CONVERTING DATA USING HISTORICAL COSTS & EXPERTS

EEO organization estimated these costs, including staff time and management time. As a result, the annualized value of costs avoided by eliminating 35 complaints was $852,000. As shown at the bottom of Figure 5–1, each complaint cost the organization $24,343. So by reducing complaints, the program saved the organization $852,000 annually.

External Databases and Studies

Another method for converting data to monetary value is using data from external databases. The Internet provides a wealth of resources to help us convert data to monetary value. One database in particular, ERIC, which can be retrieved through the EBSCO host on a university or public library computer database, provides such opportunities. For example, an organization was losing its middle managers, whose salary was $70,000. The cost of turnover or losing the middle manager, based on data retrieved from an external database, was 150% of the manager's salary. Thus, the total cost of turnover was $105,000 per manager. By reducing one turnover of a manager at this level, an organization could save $105,000. Just think what the organization could achieve if it reduced two unnecessary turnovers.

Linking with Other Measures

Another method, linking with other measures, is often used to convert data to monetary value. However, it can sometimes be a very complicated and expensive process. One rule of thumb is that we don't expend more resources on data conversion than we expend on the evaluation itself. However, several years ago, Sears implemented a process for linking employee satisfaction to customer satisfaction and tying that to revenues converted to profit. Figure 5–2 illustrates this linkage. The study took about 18 months to complete. A review of this illustration reveals that the study was quite large. It is highly likely that many assumptions were made in a study of this magnitude.

Another example of linking that is much less complicated involves a situation in which overtime costs are excessive because of excessive absenteeism. A solution is implemented and absenteeism is reduced by 50%. The increased availability of the team to complete the work reduces overtime by 60%. The reduction in overtime cost becomes the value used to calculate the savings. Because the overtime reduction is a direct cost savings, conversion is not necessary. We simply use the savings as our monetary benefit.

Using Estimates

Other methods of data conversion include participant estimates, supervisor/manager estimates, and staff estimates. Although these represent four different sources of data, the estimation process is the same. An example is absenteeism. When we look at the cost of absenteeism, we have to consider all the costs. Yes, we lose salary and benefits because that is the value of the productivity of the job, but we also have to look at makeup costs—the cost of the work being assigned to other staff, the cost of the work assigned to the

FIGURE 5–2

LINKAGE WITH OTHER MEASURES

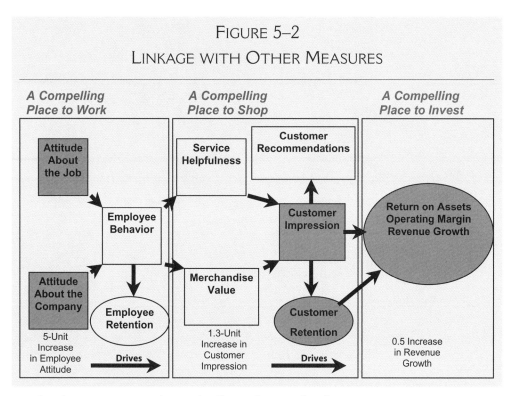

Used with permission. President and Fellows of Harvard College, 1998.

manager, the cost of the work not being done, customer dissatisfaction, and other key variables. So in converting absenteeism to monetary value, one source of data that is often considered the most credible is the supervisor estimate. So, if we have an absenteeism problem, and we need to convert this measure to monetary value, one method of doing so may be to pull our supervisors into a room (6 to 10 supervisors at a time) and explain the need to place a value on absenteeism. The facilitator of the focus group asks each supervisor to explain everything that happens when an employee is unexpectedly absent. Each supervisor states his or her case. In some cases, it is important to go back around and get additional input from each supervisor after the other supervisors present their views. Once the cases are laid out, there is a clear understanding of all consequences of an unexpected absence.

The facilitator then asks each supervisor to place a value or cost on those consequences. For instance, Supervisor One is asked, "Okay, you have heard all the things that take place when an unexpected absence occurs. Now how much do you think this costs the organization?" Supervisor One provides the cost and they write it down. Then the other supervisors are asked to estimate a cost to the organization for this unexpected absence. In the third round, you go to each supervisor and say, "Okay, how confident are you in your estimate of the cost of the unexpected absence on a scale of 0% to 100% (0% = no confidence, 100% = absolutely sure)?" Supervisor One suggests she's 50% confident, so you ask Supervisor One to multiply her $1,000 cost estimate by the 50% to get $500—this is the value estimated by Supervisor One of the cost of an unexpected absence. You then ask the other supervisors the same question.

TABLE 5–3
SUPERVISOR ESTIMATES USED TO CONVERT ABSENTEEISM

Supervisor	Est. Per Day Cost	% Confidence	Adjusted Per Day Cost
1	$1,000	70%	$700
2	$1,500	65%	$975
3	$2,300	50%	$1,150
4	$2,000	60%	$1,200
5	$1,600	80%	$1,280
			$5,305
Average adjusted per day cost of 1 absence			$1,061

Each supervisor adjusts the estimate by level of confidence. This, in essence, is adjusting for the error in their estimate.

After all the adjustments are made, the value identified by the supervisors is added up and divided by the number of supervisors in the group to get the average cost for the estimate of an unexpected absence. This estimation process, while not the most favored process, is often the most conservative process of converting data. We are taking some of the subjectivity out of the estimate and creating a very conservative value for our program benefit. Table 5–3 presents the results of this estimation focus group in table form to clarify how the values are calculated.

Five Steps to Data Conversion

The previous section described the methods of data conversion. Now we want to take a look at the five steps necessary to convert a measure to monetary value. The five steps include:

1. Focus on a unit of measure.
2. Determine the value of each unit.
3. Calculate the change in performance of the measure.
4. Determine the annual amount of the change.
5. Calculate the total annual value of the improvement.

These steps are also included as Job Aid 5–1 on the CD in Chapter 5. Keep in mind, as Guiding Principle 9 tells us, for a short-term program we want to calculate annual benefits. It is common practice in ROI to analyze data over a short time frame and annualize the benefits. An example of these five steps appears below.

HMH Corporation had a grievance problem. The number of grievances was extraordinary. Because of that, a supervisor training program was implemented to help supervisors improve communication with their staff to better engage their team. The program was implemented and grievances were reduced. Because HMH wanted to calculate the ROI for the program, they needed to

Step 1	**Focus on a unit of measure**
Step 2	**Determine the value of the unit of measure**
Step 3	**Determine/calculate the change in performance of the measure**
Step 4	**Calculate the annual change**
Step 5	**Calculate the total annual value of the improvement**

convert the improvement in grievances to monetary value. To do so, they followed the five steps to data conversion.

- Step 1: Focus on a unit of measure. The unit of measure was one grievance.
- Step 2: Determine the value of the unit of measure. The value of one grievance, based on internal experts, is $6,500.
- Step 3: Determine/calculate the change in performance of the measure. It was determined through the evaluation that on average, 10 grievances per month were avoided during the posttraining six-month follow-up. Isolating the effects revealed that 7 out of the 10 reductions related to the training program. So the change in performance equals seven.
- Step 4: Calculate the annual change. Because the program reduced the number of grievances by an average of seven per month, the annual change in performance equaled 84 (12×7).
- Step 5: Here we calculate the total annual value of the improvement. In this case, the annual change in performance was 84 times the value of $6,500. This gives us an annual value improvement of $546,000 due to the training program. Job Aid 5–1A summarizes these steps using the grievance example.

Now it is time for you to try this Job Aid. Exercise 5–3 gives you the opportunity to use these five steps.

Take a look at the Exercise 5–3 answer on the Chapter 5 folder of the CD. There are some decisions to make here regarding the value of one unit of the measure for absenteeism. The answer discusses this decision.

EXERCISE 5–3. PACKAGE DELIVERY CO.

At Package Delivery Co., a Supervisor Development program was conducted with 15 branch managers. One of the objectives of the program was to reduce the absenteeism in each work group using interactive skill-building sessions. Before the program was conducted, the average absenteeism rate for the employees in the branch was 7%. It was determined in the follow-up evaluation that the new average rate was 4%. In a post-program follow-up, managers estimate that 40% of the reduction was directly related to the program.

A total of 120 employees work for the 15 branch managers. During the learning program, the managers (program participants) estimated the costs of a single absence to be $81. (This is the average value from all 15 managers.) External studies have shown that the cost of a single absence ranges from $60 to $70, depending on the industry and specific job. Assume that employees are expected to work 240 days per year.

Questions for Discussion

1. Calculate the annual savings from the improvement.

   _____

   _____

   _____

2. Is this a credible process?

   _____

   _____

   _____

POTENTIAL CHALLENGES

One of the biggest challenges in converting data to monetary value is determining whether or not to do it. When we are converting our Level 4 measures to monetary value, we are in effect increasing our ROI with each measure we convert. We are building monetary benefits to place in the numerator. Ideally, we like to convert all measures to monetary benefit, but because of credibility issues, the conservative nature of our process, and the cost of converting some measures, we often choose not to. In determining whether to convert a data item to monetary value, we take a four-part test. The four-part test answers these four critical questions:

1. Is there a standard value?
2. Is there a method to get there?
3. Can we get there with minimum resources?
4. Can we convince our executives in two minutes or less that the value is credible?

As shown in Job Aid 5–2, this four-part test helps us make the decision to add a converted value to the numerator or to report improvement in the measure as an intangible benefit.

The first question is, "Is there a standard value?" If there is a standard value, we immediately convert that measure to monetary benefit. The standard value has been accepted within the organization. If there is no standard value, we then ask, "Is there a method to get there?" As shown in the previous section, there are seven operational methods that will get us to a monetary value. We review these methods and consider their credibility. If we see there is not a method to get there, we report the improvement in this measure as an intangible benefit. However, if there is a method that will get us there, we then ask the third question "Can we get there with minimum resources?"

As noted earlier, a rule of thumb is that we don't want to spend more on data conversion than we expend on the entire evaluation. If we cannot convert the measure using one of the techniques selected within the limits of our resources, we then report the measure as an intangible benefit. If we can convert the measure, we ask the final question, "Can we convince our executives in two minutes or less that this value is credible?" If we cannot, we report the improvement in the measure as an intangible benefit. If we can convince our executives, we convert it to monetary value. Again, converting data to monetary value is critical in calculating our actual return on investment, but

JOB AID 5–2
TO CONVERT OR NOT TO CONVERT?

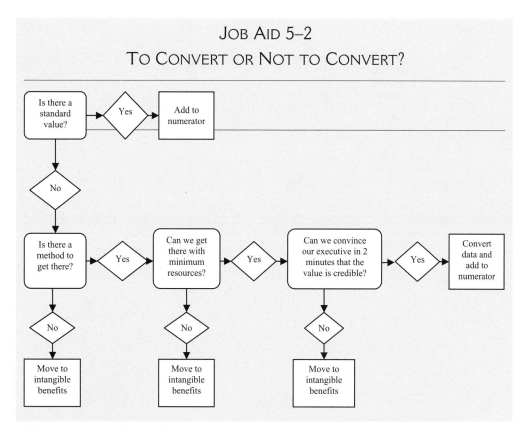

©2002 Patricia Pulliam Phillips

TABLE 5–4

TURNOVER COSTS SUMMARY

Job Type/Category	Turnover Cost Ranges as a Percent of Annual Wage/Salary
Entry Level—Hourly, Non Skilled (e.g., Fast Food Worker)	30%–50%
Service/Production Workers—Hourly (e.g., Courier)	40%–70%
Skilled Hourly (e.g., Machinist)	75%–100%
Clerical/Administrative (e.g., Scheduler)	50%–80%
Professional (e.g., Sales Representative, Nurse, Accountant)	75%–125%
Technical (e.g., Computer Technician)	100%–150%
Engineers (e.g., Chemical Engineer)	200%–300%
Specialists (e.g., Computer Software Designer)	200%–400%
Supervisors/Team Leaders (e.g., Section Supervisor)	100%–150%
Middle Managers (e.g., Department Manager)	125%–200%

Notes:
1. Percents are rounded to reflect the general range of costs from studies.
2. Costs are fully loaded to include all of the costs of replacing an employee and bringing him/her to the level of productivity and efficiency of the former employee. The turnover included in studies is usually unexpected and unwanted. The following costs categories are usually included:

   —Exit cost of previous employee   —Lost productivity
   —Recruiting cost   —Quality problems
   —Employee cost   —Customer dissatisfaction
   —Orientation cost   —Loss of expertise/knowledge
   —Training cost   —Supervisor's time for turnover
   —Wages and salaries while training   —Temporary replacement costs
3. Turnover costs are usually calculated when excessive turnover is an issue, and turnover costs are high. The actual cost of turnover for a specific job in an organization may vary considerably. The above ranges are intended to reflect what has been generally reported in the literature when turnover costs are analyzed.

Sources of Data
The sources of data for these studies follow 3 general categories:

1. Industry and trade magazines have reported the cost of turnover for a specific job within an industry.
2. Publications in general management (academic and practitioner), human resources management, human resources development training, and performance improvement often reflect ROI cost studies because of the importance of turnover to senior managers and human resources managers.
3. Independent studies have been conducted by organizations and not reported in the literature. Some of these studies have been provided privately to the ROI Institute. In addition, the Institute has conducted several turnover cost studies, and these results are included in these analysis.

Copyright © 2004, The ROI Institute. All rights reserved. May be used as a reference.

another rule of thumb with regard to the numerator applies: "When in doubt, leave it out." We want to maintain the credibility of our process, the credibility of our monetary values, and the conservative nature of the evaluation methodology.

Keep in mind that the two-minute guideline is only a guideline. Executive interest in the monetary value or their interest in the program may extend their patience. For example, suppose you are placing a value on employee satisfaction. This could be a measure that management has a high interest in. Additionally, if an acceptable value existed, management could use that value in many other situations. A discussion with executives up front during the evaluation planning phase may result in additional time and resources to convert this important measure.

The CD includes a worksheet to go along with the Job Aid to further help you decide whether to convert a measure to monetary value.

ACTION STEPS

- Review Part D of Premier Motors Case Study on the Chapter 5 folder of the CD. This may provide more insight as you complete your ROI Analysis Plan.
- At the end of Chapter 4, you completed the isolation column and several other columns on your ROI Analysis Plan. Return to your ROI Analysis Plan and complete the column on conversion and the column on intangible benefits. If you are in the planning stages of your evaluation, list the technique on your data analysis plan as the technique you have chosen to use to convert that measure to monetary value.

  If you have already collected your data, look at the improvements in your Level 4 measures. Is there a standard value that can be used to convert these measures to monetary value? If not, can you use one of the operational techniques? Look at each measure individually. If you can, begin the five steps to data conversion. Focus on one unit of that measure. Then, using your selected technique, place a value on that measure. How much did that measure improve as a result of your program? What is the annual change in that improvement? Now multiply your annual change in improvement times the value you have placed. You then have your monetary benefit for the improvement of that program. This value will go into your numerator.

  The intangible benefits are any Level 4 measures your program will influence that you have decided not to convert and any additional intangibles that you expect will be influenced by your program.

- Okay, how about one final exercise just to fine-tune your skills. Good, I knew you would be delighted. Exercise 5–4, which follows, is a scenario in which you have worked with a team to evaluate an intervention delivered to executives. The intervention addressed the actions and programs executives should sponsor directly and indirectly to reduce a turnover problem the organization was having with middle managers. The answers to this exercise and the other exercises are on the Chapter 5 folder of the CD.

EXERCISE 5–4. CONVERTING DATA USING EXTERNAL STUDY

Your team designed and implemented an intervention with executives to reduce a turnover problem of middle managers in your organization. The average salary for a middle manager in your organization is $75,000. The intervention has been completed and one year later it has influenced a reduction in turnover of 10 middle managers. This result has been tied directly to the intervention by an isolation strategy. Apply Job Aid 5–1 (recreated below) to calculate the total annual monetary value of the turnover reduction.

Step 1: Unit of Improvement _____

Step 2: The Cost (Value) of One Turnover Is* _____

Step 3: Performance Level Change _____

Step 4: Annual Change in Performance _____

Step 5: Total Annual Value of the Improvement _____

*Use Table 5–4, Turnover Cost Summary, (an external study on the Chapter 5 folder of the CD) to determine the cost (value) of one turnover. Be sure and follow the Guiding Principles.

CHAPTER SUMMARY

In this chapter, we took a look at converting data to monetary benefits. You learned the 10 methods of data conversion and the five steps to data conversion, and you were introduced to a four-part test to help you decide whether or not to convert the data to monetary value. Two rules of thumb were mentioned. First, don't expend more resources on data conversion than you expend on the entire evaluation. And finally, when in doubt, leave an improvement out.

This chapter also addressed three of our guiding principles: Guiding Principle 3, Use only the most credible source for your data; Guiding Principle 4, When analyzing data, choose the most conservative among alternatives; and Guiding Principle 9, For short-term programs, annualize the benefits. Our next chapter, Chapter 6, takes us one step closer to the ROI calculation. Here we will address tabulating our fully loaded costs.

REFERENCES AND RESOURCES

Bernacki, Ed. *Wow! That's a Great Idea!* Melbourne, Victoria, Australia: Perspectives, 2001.

Phillips, Jack J. *Handbook of Training Evaluation and Measurement Methods,* 3rd ed. Woburn, MA: Butterworth-Heinemann, 1997.

Phillips, Jack J. *Return on Investment in Training and Performance Improvement Programs,* 2nd ed. Woburn, MA: Butterworth-Heinemann, 2003.

Phillips, Jack J., and Adele O. Connell. *Managing Employee Retention: A Strategic Accountability Approach.* Woburn, MA: Butterworth-Heinemann, 2003.

Phillips, Jack J., and Ron Drew Stone. *How to Measure Training Results.* New York: McGraw-Hill, 2002.

CD ⊛

Exercises and Case Study	Tools, Templates, and Job Aids
Exercise 5–1. Identify Level 4 Measures	Figure 5–1. Experts and Historical Costs
Exercise 5–1A. Answers: Identify Level 4 Measures	Figure 5–2. Linking to Other Measures
Exercise 5–2. Credibility of Data	Table 5–1. Influences on Credibility of Outcome Data
Exercise 5–2A. Answers: Credibility of Data	Table 5–2. Methods of Converting Data
Exercise 5–3. Package Delivery	Table 5–3. Supervisor Estimates
Exercise 5–3A. Answers: Package Delivery	Table 5–4. Turnover Cost Summary
Exercise 5–4. Converting Data with External Study	Job Aid 5–1. Five Steps to Convert Data
Exercise 5–4A. Answers: Converting Data With External Study	Job Aid 5–1A. Answers: Five Steps to Convert Data
Case Study—Part D, Premier Motors International (PMI)	Job Aid 5–2. To Convert or Not Convert
	Worksheet 5–1. To Convert or Not Convert

COUNTING THE COSTS

In Chapter 5, you learned how to convert data to a monetary value. This is a key step in moving from impact to ROI. But you cannot get to ROI without incorporating the costs of the program. When we say *costs,* we mean fully loaded costs—all of them. But what are these costs? Once we account for the fully loaded costs, how do we present them and what cautions are in order? These and other questions about costs are answered in this chapter.

In this chapter you will:

❑ Learn the importance of accounting for fully loaded costs.
❑ Identify the cost categories necessary to calculate a credible ROI.
❑ Learn how to report costs.

THE FUNDAMENTALS

The cost of providing training and performance solutions is becoming an increasingly larger slice of the budget for many organizations. The larger this budget becomes, the more scrutiny training will receive. Additionally, most organizations are becoming more sensitive to the cost and operational consequences of employees being taken off the job for training. And finally, with more executives requiring return on investment data, comparing the benefits of training costs requires that costs be fully loaded and tracked for reporting purposes.

Fully loaded cost means that the cost profile goes beyond the direct costs and includes all indirect costs. Fully loaded cost information is used to manage resources, develop standards, measure efficiencies, calculate ROI, and examine alternative delivery processes. Tabulating program costs is an essential step in developing the ROI calculation because it represents the denominator in the

ROI formula. It is just as important to focus on costs as it is on benefits. In practice, however, costs are often more easily captured than benefits. This chapter explores the steps in accumulating and tabulating costs, outlining the specific costs that should be captured. Economic ways to develop costs are also addressed.

Importance of Accounting for Fully Loaded Costs

Many training professionals ask, "Why include items such as salaries and in-house training facilities when reporting costs?" They rationalize that salaries are paid and in-house facility costs are incurred whether we deliver the training or not. Many reasons demonstrate why we should report these costs. Perhaps the most compelling reason to account for salaries, training facilities, and other cost items is that if we do not, then we will likely overstate the return on investment. To see an example of this, let's look at the contrasting approaches in Table 6–1. We have conducted a two-day training class for a

TABLE 6–1

COMPARISON OF COST SCENARIOS

Negotiation Skills Training
Level 4 annualized benefits from 36 participants after isolation is $240,000

Approach A: Cost Tabulation *Training manager cost calculation*		Approach B: Cost Tabulation *Client cost calculation*
Needs assessment (one time cost)	$12,000	$12,000
Design and development (minimal redesign required to revise role plays)	$2,000	$2,000
Delivery		
▪ Facilitator and coaching fees	$38,000	$38,000
▪ Facilitator travel expenses	$2,900	$2,900
▪ Materials	$5,000	$5,000
▪ Refreshments	$900	$900
▪ Salaries/benefits—coordinator	$317	$317
▪ Travel expenses—coordinator	$700	$700
▪ Salaries/benefits–participants	$33,413	N/A
▪ Travel expenses—participants	$3,600	$3,600
▪ Traning facility and AV cost	$1,100	N/A
Evaluation (one-time cost)	$9,000	$9,000
Overhead (2% of total program cost)	$2,179	$1,448
TOTAL	$111,109	$75,905

client on negotiation skills. This was a one-time offering that included all 36 professional employees reporting to the manager (client). The program was delivered by a training supplier using the supplier's materials and process. The annualized monetary benefit for the 36 participants after using their improved skills to make a difference is £240,000. The table shows two approaches where the costs are calculated differently by the training manager (Approach A) and the client (Approach B).

Using both cost scenarios, the ROI calculation comparisons are shown below. Approach B, which does not include participant salaries and facilities cost, yields an ROI that is almost twice that of Approach A, which is fully loaded. This ROI is significantly overstated in Approach B.

ROI using Approach A cost tabulation:

$$\text{ROI} = \frac{\text{Net Benefits}}{\text{Costs}} = \frac{\$240,000 - \$111,109}{\$111,109} = 116\%$$

ROI using Approach B cost tabulation:

$$\text{ROI} = \frac{\text{Net Benefits}}{\text{Costs}} = \frac{\$240,000 - \$75,905}{\$75,905} = 216\%$$

Executives frequently review salaries and benefits in connection with other organization costs. For example, every time there is a request to hire additional personnel, the central issue is to justify the added resource. That is, how will this newly incurred cost bring a benefit to the organization? The personnel expenditure is viewed in terms of "loaded cost," or the cost of one FTE (full-time equivalent). Even the expenses that will likely be incurred by the new resource are detailed as a separate item, which increases the justification requirement for the resource. Executives are accustomed to dealing with "all costs," direct and indirect. Anything short of this would be viewed as inadequate accounting.

So, just as executives weigh all costs of adding additional head count, we must do the same. In principle, to account for fully loaded costs when evaluating a specific training program, we must include every cost incurred to acquire and deliver the program. Guiding Principle 10 states that "project/program costs should be fully loaded for ROI analysis."

When fully loading costs, all costs that can be identified and linked to a particular program are included. The philosophy is simple: When in doubt in the denominator, put it in (i.e., if it is questionable whether a cost should be included, it is recommended that it be included, even if the cost guidelines for the organization do not require it). This parallels a rule for the numerator, which states, "When in doubt, leave it out" (i.e., if it is questionable whether a benefit should be included in the numerator, it should be omitted from the analysis). When an ROI is calculated and reported to target audiences, the process should withstand even the closest scrutiny in terms of its accuracy and credibility. The only way to meet this test is to ensure that all costs are included. Of course, from a realistic viewpoint, if the controller or chief financial officer insists on not using certain costs, then it is best to leave them out.

Controlling Costs

To improve the efficiency of the training function, controlling costs is necessary. Competitive pressures place increased attention on efficiencies in for-profit organizations. In nonprofit organizations pressure comes from budget constraints, public and political pressure, and agency competition for scarce funds. Most training departments have monthly budgets with cost projections listed by various accounts and, in some cases, by program. Cost monitoring identifies problem areas so that corrective action can be taken. In the practical and classical management sense, the accumulation and accounting of cost data is a necessity.

Capturing costs is challenging because the figures must be reliable. Although the total training direct budget is usually a number that is easily developed, it is more difficult to determine the specific costs of a program, including its indirect costs. To develop a realistic ROI, costs must be accurate and credible. Otherwise, the painstaking difficulty and attention to the training's benefits will be wasted because of inadequate or inaccurate costs. Cost accounting systems are a necessary part of the business.

Cost Categories

The most important task is to define which specific costs to include in the program costs. This task involves decisions that will be made by the workforce learning and performance (WLP) staff and usually approved by department management. If appropriate, the finance and accounting staff may need to approve the list just to ensure it is compatible with internal accounting systems. Table 6–2 shows the recommended cost categories for a fully loaded, conservative approach to estimating costs. Each category is either a direct expense

TABLE 6–2
RECOMMENDED COST CATEGORIES

Category	Prorated	Expensed
A. Needs assessment and analysis	✓	
B. Design and development	✓	
C. Acquisition	✓	
D. Technology support	✓	
E. Delivery/implementation		✓
■ Salaries/benefits—Facilitators		✓
■ Salaries/benefits—Coordinators		✓
■ Program materials and fees		✓
■ Salaries/benefits—Participants (contact hours while being paid)		✓
■ Travel/lodging/meals		✓
■ Training facilities		✓
F. Evaluation	✓	*
G. Overhead/training and development	✓	

or possibly prorated. Prorated items are those that benefit all current year and future year offerings of the training. Each category is described below.

Needs Assessment and Analysis

One of the most often overlooked items is the cost of conducting a needs assessment. In some programs this cost is zero because the program is conducted without a needs assessment. However, as more organizations focus increased attention on needs assessment, this item will become a more significant cost. All costs associated with the needs assessment should be captured to the fullest extent possible. These costs include the time of staff members conducting the assessment, direct fees and expenses for external consultants who conduct the needs assessment, and internal services and supplies used in the analysis. The total costs are usually prorated over the life of the program. Depending on the type and nature of the program, the shelf life should be kept to a very reasonable number in the one- to two-year time frame. Of course the exception would be very expensive programs that are not expected to change significantly for several years.

Design and Development Costs

One of the more significant items is the cost of designing and developing the program. These costs include internal staff time in both design and development and the purchase of supplies, videos, CDs, and other materials directly related to the program. It would also include the use of consultants. As with needs assessment costs, design and development costs are usually prorated, perhaps using the same time frame. One to two years is recommended unless the program is not expected to change for many years and the costs are significant.

When pilot programs are implemented, a prorating dilemma may surface. For very expensive pilots, the complete design and development costs could be significant. If all those costs are included in the ROI analysis, it may be difficult, if not impossible, for a project to produce a positive ROI. In this situation, prorating is not an issue because the pilot is completely at risk. The following guidelines can help work through this dilemma.

1. If the pilot project is completely at risk, all the costs should be placed in the evaluation, (i.e., if the pilot does not have a positive ROI with all the costs included, it will not be implemented). This is often an unreasonable request, but if it must be approached this way, it is best to keep the design and development costs to a minimum. Perhaps the program could be implemented without all of the "bells and whistles." The videos, CDs, and other expensive development tools may be delayed until the basic premise of the skills and content are proven.

2. If program implementation is not at risk, the cost of the development should be prorated over the anticipated life cycle. This is the approach in most situations. It is plausible to have a significant investment in the design and development of a pilot when it is initiated with the under-

standing that if it is not adding value, it can be adjusted, changed, or modified to add value. In these cases, a prorated development cost would be appropriate.

Acquisition Costs

In lieu of development costs, many organizations purchase programs to use directly or in a modified format. The acquisition costs for these programs include the purchase price for the instructor materials, train-the-trainer sessions, licensing agreements, and other costs associated with the right to deliver the program. These acquisition costs should be prorated using the same rationale above; one to two years should be sufficient. If the program has to be modified or some additional development is required, these costs should be included as development costs. In practice, many programs have both acquisition costs and development costs.

Technology Support

Some programs require technology support. For example, computers may be used to deliver the content. The finance and accounting department can provide information on how to spread these costs over the life of the program based on how the equipment has been depreciated. Some training programs are associated with new work processes or technology implementation where a help desk is used for some period of time following the training. When it is appropriate to capture these costs, they may also be prorated.

Delivery/Implementation Costs

Usually the largest segment of training costs are those associated with delivery. Five major categories are included:

- *Salaries of facilitators and coordinators.* The salaries of facilitators or program coordinators should be included. If a coordinator is involved in more than one program, the time should be allocated to the specific program under review. If external facilitators are used, all charges should be included for the session. The important issue is to capture all the direct time of internal employees or external consultants who work directly with the program. The benefits factor, expressed as a percentage of salaries, should be included each time direct labor costs are involved.
- *Program materials and fees.* Specific program materials such as notebooks, textbooks, CDs, case studies, exercises, and participant workbooks should be included in the delivery costs, along with license fees, user fees, and royalty payments. Pens, paper, certificates, calculators, and personal copies of software are also included in this category.
- *Travel, lodging, and meals.* Direct travel for participants, facilitators, or coordinators are included. Lodging and meals are included for participants during travel, as well as meals during the stay for the program. Refreshments should also be included.

- *Facilities.* The direct cost of the facilities should be included. For external programs, this is the direct charge from the conference center, hotel, or motel. If the program is conducted in-house, the conference room represents a cost for the organization, and the cost should be estimated and included even if it is not the practice to include facilities' cost in other reports. The cost of internal facilities can easily be estimated by obtaining a room rental rate of the same size room at a local hotel. The hotel includes their profit in their quote so the value will be conservative for our purposes. Sometimes this figure is available internally on a square-foot basis from the finance and accounting staff, that is, the actual value of the square footage on a daily basis. In other situations, the cost of commercial real estate on a square-foot basis could be determined locally from commercial real estate directors or the newspaper. The important point is to quickly come to a credible estimate for the value of the cost of the room. This is not a difficult task. Facility cost is an important issue that is often overlooked. Some WLP staff members, with a confirmation from the finance and accounting staff, do not charge for the use of the facilities. The argument is that the room would be used regardless; however, the true, complete cost of training should include the item because the room would probably not be there unless there was routine training taking place. In the scheme of things, this is a minor charge. It might have more value from the gesture than from influencing the actual output of the ROI calculation.
- *Participants' salaries and benefits.* The salaries plus employee benefits of participants represent an expense that should be included. When the program has been conducted, these costs can be estimated using average or midpoint values for salaries in typical job classifications. When a program is targeted for an ROI calculation, participants can also provide their salaries directly and confidentially if necessary. The time that is captured is the time the employees are away from their normal job. For example, employees work a normal eight-hour day. A remote offsite training program is conducted for two days with six hours each day. Participants are absent from work for 16 hours while traveling to and from and attending the training. The participant's time captured and charged to the training is 16 hours, not 12 hours, because the other four hours are a consequence of the training.

The benefits factor is usually well known in the organization and is used in other costing formulas. It represents the cost of all employee benefits expressed as a percentage of base salaries. In some organizations this value is as high as 50%–60%. In others, it may be as low as 25%–30%. The U.S. average is approximately 38% (*Nation's Business*, 2002). European countries are usually slightly higher. Here is an example of calculating the benefits factor. A two-day training program is offered and 30 participants attend. The average salary of the participants is $320 per day. Total salaries are $19,200 ($640 × 30). The HR department provides a benefits factor of 36%. The benefits for our group of participants equate to $6,912 ($19,400 × 0.36). Total salaries and benefits becomes $26,112 ($19,200 + $6,912).

For major training and development programs, there may be a separate category for implementation. If the program involves a variety of meetings, follow-ups, manager reinforcement, and a variety of other activities beyond the specific training program, an additional category for implementation may be appropriate. In some extreme examples, on-site coordinators make sure the program is working and provide assistance and support for the program as it is implemented throughout the region, branch, or organization. These implementation expenses should be calculated; however, in most situations, the implementation is considered part of the delivery and is placed in that category. The specific cost categories and implementation are often mirrored in the delivery categories. Most organizations would lump delivery and implementation together.

Evaluation

Usually the total evaluation cost is included in the program costs to compute the fully loaded cost. ROI costs include the cost of developing the evaluation strategy, designing instruments, collecting data, data analysis, and report preparation and distribution. Cost categories include time, materials, purchased instruments, or surveys. A case can be made to prorate the evaluation costs over several programs instead of charging the total amount as an expense. For example, if 25 sessions of a program are conducted in a three-year period and one group is selected for an ROI calculation, then the ROI costs could logically be prorated over the 25 sessions, because the results of the ROI analysis should reflect the success of the other programs and will perhaps result in changes that will influence the other programs as well. *However, there may be situations in which a stakeholder would prefer that the evaluation cost be expensed. For example, if a pilot program is being conducted and a go/no go decision will be made to roll out the program to others based on the pilot results, it may be appropriate to expense the evaluation costs.

Overhead

A final charge is the cost of overhead, the additional costs in the training function not directly related to a particular program. The overhead category represents any training department cost not considered in the above calculations. Typical items include the cost of clerical support, the departmental office expenses, salaries of training managers, and other fixed costs. Some organizations obtain an estimate for allocation by dividing the total overhead by the number of program participant training days or hours for the year. This becomes a standard value to use in calculations.

The example in Table 6–3 illustrates the simplicity of this approach.

An organization anticipates delivering 100 training programs this year. All the expenditures in the budget not allocated directly to a particular program are calculated. This total unallocated part of the budget is then viewed as total overhead, unallocated to specific training and development programs. Suppose this number is $500,000. This number is then divided by the total number of participant days or hours for the budget year. The hours approach may be helpful if there's a lot of e-learning and participants are involved in programs

TABLE 6–3

CALCULATING OVERHEAD COSTS: EXAMPLE

Name of program	Program length ×	No. time offered this year =	Total days this year
#1 Leadership Advantage	5 days	10 times	50 days
#2 Negotiation Skills	1 day	30 times	30 days
etc.	etc.	etc.	etc.
etc.	etc.	etc.	etc.
etc.	etc.	etc.	etc.
etc.	etc.	etc.	etc.
etc.	etc.	etc.	etc.
etc.	etc.	etc.	etc.
#100 Listening Skills	1 day	25 times	25 days
Total Contact Days This Year for 100 Programs Delivered			**10,000 Days**

an hour at a time. The allocation of days may be appropriate in others. As shown in Table 6–3, if a particular 5-day program is offered 10 times a year, 50 days should be put in the total days category. When all 100 programs are entered, this total amount is 10,000 days in the example. Thus, in this example, the total unallocated overhead cost of $500,000 divided by 10,000 days equals $50. Each program will be charged $50 per delivery day to account for departmental overhead.

Cost Categorization Example

Perhaps it is best to show an example of the allocation of the costs using an actual case study. Table 6–4 shows the cost for a major executive leadership program (Phillips, 2001). This was an extensive program involving four one-week off-site training sessions with personal coaches and learning coaches assigned to the participants. Participants worked on projects that were of critical importance to the organization. They attempted to cost a particular project and report the results to management. The project teams could hire consultants as well. These are listed as project costs. The cost for the first session involving 2,200 participants is detailed in the table.

The issue of prorating costs was an important consideration. In this case, it was reasonably certain that a second session would be conducted. The analysis, design, and development expenses of $580,657 could therefore be prorated over two sessions. Consequently, in the actual ROI calculation, half of this number was used to arrive at the total value ($290,328). This left a total program cost of $2,019,598 to include in the analysis ($2,309,926–$290,328). On a participant basis, this is $91,800, or $22,950 for each week of formal sessions. Although this was expensive, it was still close to a rough benchmark of weekly costs of several senior executive leadership programs involving the same time commitments.

TABLE 6–4

EXECUTIVE LEADERSHIP DEVELOPMENT PROGRAM COSTS

Program Costs	
Analysis/Design/Development	
External consultants	$525,330
Training department	$28,785
Management committee	$26,542
Delivery	
Conference facilities (hotel)	$142,554
Consultants/external	$812,110
Training department salaries and benefits (for direct work with the program)	$15,283
Training department travel expenses	$37,500
Management committee (time)	$75,470
Project costs ($25,000 × 4)	$100,000
Participant salaries and benefits (class sessions) (Average daily salary × benefits factor × number of program days)	$84,564
Participant salaries and benefits (project work)	$117,353
Travel and lodging for participants	$100,938
Cost of materials (handouts, purchased materials)	$6,872
Research and Evaluation	
Research	$110,750
Evaluation	$125,875
Total Costs	$2,309,926

Cost Accumulation and Estimation

Costs can be accumulated in two basic ways. One is by a description of the expenditure, such as labor, materials, supplies, travel, and so forth. These are expense account classifications. The other is by categories in the training process or function, such as program development, delivery, and evaluation. An effective system monitors costs by account categories according to the description of those accounts but also includes a method for accumulating costs by the training process/functional category. Many systems stop short of this second step. Although the first grouping sufficiently gives the total program cost, it does not allow for a useful comparison with other programs or indicate areas where costs might be excessive by comparison.

Cost Classification Matrix

Costs are accumulated under both of the above classifications. The two classifications are obviously related, and the relationship depends on the organization. For instance, the specific costs that comprise the analysis part of a program may vary substantially with the organization.

An important part of the classification process is to define the kinds of costs in the account classification system that normally apply to the major process/functional categories. Table 6–5 is a matrix that represents the cate-

TABLE 6–5

COST CLASSIFICATION MATRIX

Expense Account Classification	Process/Functional Categories			
	Analysis	Development	Delivery	Evaluation
00 Salaries and Benefits—WLP Staff	X	X	X	X
01 Salaries and Benefits—Other Staff		X	X	
02 Salaries and Benefits—Participants			X	X
03 Meals, Travel, and Incidental Expenses—WLP Staff	X	X	X	X
04 Meals, Travel, and Accommodations—Participants			X	
05 Office Supplies and Expenses	X	X		X
06 Program Materials and Supplies		X	X	
07 Printing and Copying	X	X	X	X
08 Outside Services	X	X	X	X
09 Equipment Expense Allocation	X	X	X	X
10 Equipment—Rental		X	X	
11 Equipment—Maintenance			X	
12 Registration Fees	X			
13 Facilities Expense Allocation			X	
14 Facilities Rental			X	
15 General Overhead Allocation	X	X	X	X
16 Other Miscellaneous Expenses	X	X	X	X

gories for accumulating all training-related costs in the organization. Those costs, which normally are a part of a process/functional category, are checked in the matrix. Each member of the training staff should know how to charge expenses properly. For example, equipment is rented to use in the development and delivery of a program. Should all or part of the cost be charged to development? Or should it be charged to delivery? More than likely the cost will be allocated in proportion to the extent to which the item was used for each category.

Cost Accumulation

With expense account classifications clearly defined and the process/functional categories determined, it is easy to track costs on individual programs. This is accomplished by using special account numbers and project numbers. An example illustrates the use of these numbers.

A project number is a three-digit number representing a specific training program. For example:

New Professional Associates' Orientation	112
New Team Leader Training	215
Statistical Quality Control	418
Valuing Diversity	791

Numbers are assigned to the process/functional breakdowns. Using the example presented earlier, the following numbers are assigned:

Analysis	1
Development	2
Delivery	3
Evaluation	4

Using the two-digit numbers assigned to account classifications in Table 6–5, an accounting system is complete. For example, if workbooks are reproduced for the Valuing Diversity workshop, the appropriate charge number for that reproduction is 07-3-791. The first two digits denote the account classification, the next digit is the process/functional category, and the last three digits the project number. This system enables rapid accumulation and monitoring of workforce learning costs. Total costs can be presented by:

- Training program (Valuing Diversity workshop),
- Process/functional categories (delivery), and
- Expense account classification (printing and reproduction).

Cost Estimation

The previous sections covered procedures for classifying and monitoring costs related to training programs. It is important to monitor and compare ongoing costs with the budget or with projected costs. However, a significant reason for tracking costs is to predict the cost of future programs. Usually this goal is accomplished through a formal cost estimation method unique to the organization.

Some organizations use cost estimating worksheets to arrive at the total cost for a proposed program. Figure 6–1 shows an example of a cost estimating worksheet that calculates analysis, development, delivery, and evaluation costs. The worksheets contain a few formulas that make it easier to estimate the cost. In addition to these worksheets, current charge rates for services, supplies, and salaries are available. These data become outdated quickly and are usually prepared periodically as a supplement.

Figure 6–1
COST ESTIMATING WORKSHEET

Analysis Costs	**Total**
Salaries & Employee Benefits—WLP Staff (No. of people × Average salary × Employee benefits factor × No. of hours on project)	
Meals, travel, and incidental expenses	_____
Office supplies and expenses	_____
Printing and reproduction	_____
Outside services	_____
Equipment expenses	_____
Registration fees	_____
General overhead allocation	_____
Other miscellaneous expenses	_____
Total Analysis Cost	=============

Development Costs	**Total**
Salaries & employee benefits (No. of people × Average salary × Employee benefits factor × No. of hours on project)	_____
Meals, travel, and incidental expenses	_____
Office supplies and expenses	_____
Program materials and supplies	_____
CDs	_____
Videotapes	_____
Audiotapes	_____
Slides	_____
Manuals and materials	_____
Other	_____
Printing and reproduction	_____
Outside services	_____
Equipment expense	_____
General overhead allocation	_____
Other miscellaneous expense	_____
Total Development Costs	=============

Figure 6–1—*Continued*
COST ESTIMATING WORKSHEET

Delivery Costs	Total
Participant costs (A)*	
Salaries & employee benefits (No. of participants × Average salary × Employee benefits factor × Hrs. or days of training time)	_____
Meals, travel, & accommodations (No. of participants × Average daily expenses × Days of training)	_____
Program materials and supplies	_____
Participant replacement costs (if applicable) (B)*	_____
Lost production (explain basis) (C)**	_____
Facilitator costs	_____
Salaries & benefits	_____
Meals, travel, & incidental expenses	_____
Outside services	_____
Facility costs	_____
Facilities rental	_____
Facilities expense allocation	_____
Equipment expense	_____
General overhead allocation	_____
Other miscellaneous expense	_____
Total Delivery Costs	_____

Evaluation Costs	Total
Salaries & employee benefits—WLP staff (No. of people × Average salary × Employee benefits factor × No. of hours on project)	_____
Meals, travel, and incidental expenses	_____
Participant costs	_____
Office supplies and expense	_____
Printing and reproduction	_____
Outside services	_____
Equipment expense	_____
General overhead allocation	_____
Other miscellaneous expenses	_____
Total Evaluation Costs	_____
TOTAL PROGRAM COSTS	_____

*Note: Use (A) and (B) only if (B) has an excess cost associated with it. Example: Employee Bill Bennett is participating in training on paid time (Employee Bill earns $20 per hour). Temporary employee Stacy Locke is brought in to take over the job duties while Bill is participating in the training. Stacy is paid $22 an hour ($2 an hour more than Bill makes). *Calculation:* Count the salary of Bill ($20 per hour) and the additional $2 per hour for Stacy. Do not count the remainder of Stacy's salary ($20) because she is producing the work. The work is not sacrificed.

**Note: Use (A) and (C) when it can be determined that production (any type of output) is lost because an employee is participating in training. The value of the lost production should be added to the salary cost. To see an example of this, go to Part E of the PMI Case Study on the Chapter 6 folder of the CD.

The most appropriate basis for predicting costs is to analyze the previous costs by tracking the actual costs incurred in all phases of a program, from analysis to evaluation. This way, it is possible to see how much is spent on programs and how much is being spent in the various categories. Until adequate cost data are available, it is necessary to use the detailed analysis in the worksheets for cost estimation.

Prorated vs. Direct Costs

Usually all costs related to a program are captured and expensed to that program. However, three categories are usually prorated over several sessions of the same program. Needs assessment, design and development, and acquisition are all significant costs that should be prorated over the shelf life of the program. Using a conservative approach, the shelf life should be very short. Some organizations will consider one year, others may consider two or three years. If there is some dispute about the specific time period to be used in the prorating formula, the shorter period should be used. If possible, the finance and accounting staff should be consulted for their opinion.

A brief example will illustrate how to prorate costs. Review Exercise 6–1 to see how this works.

A large telecommunications company developed a computer-based training program at a cost of $120,000. It was anticipated that it would have a three-year life cycle before it would have to be updated. The revision costs at the end of the three years were estimated to be about half of the original development costs, or $60,000. The program would be delivered to 500 people in a three-year period with an ROI calculation planned for one specific group of 40 people. Since the program would retain half of its residual value at the end of three years, half of the cost should be written off for this three-year period. Thus, the $60,000, representing half of the development costs, would be spread over the 500 participants as a prorated development cost. Thus, an ROI for a group of 40 people would have a development cost of $4,800 included in the cost profile.

Prorating costs is simply a matter of totaling the costs from all categories to be prorated, then applying the total to the steps in the exercise to determine the amount allocated to the training under review.

Reporting the Costs

Costs should be presented in a way that leaves no doubt about being fully loaded. Consider the following scenario during a 15-minute presentation to several executives as we are presenting our impact study and ROI.

- *Training Vice President, Amber Locke:* The graphic on this slide illustrates our total cost for 40 participants was $120,000. You can also see the categories where we derived the cost. Now, let's see how . . .
- *Executive 1, Senior VP of Operations, Sam Hinkle:* Excuse me, Amber! I don't see a category for employee salaries while they were in training. Did you account for salaries?

EXERCISE 6–1. PRORATING COSTS

A. Type of program		E-learning
B. Development costs		120,000
C. Life cycle of program		3 years
D. Estimated value at the end of year 3		$60,000
E. Write-off during 3-year implementation (B minus D)		$60,000
F. Number of participants during 3 years		500
G. Number of participants included in ROI study		40
H. Value per participant (item E divided by item F)	60,000/500	$120.00
I. Value per participant for ROI study (H multiplied by G)	$120.00 × 40	$4,800
Development cost to be allocated to ROI study		**$4,800**

You try it.

A. Type of program	
B. Development costs	_____
C. Life cycle of program	_____
D. Estimated value at the end of year 3	_____
E. Write-off during 3-year implementation (B minus D)	_____
F. Number of participants during 3 years	_____
G. Number of participants included in ROI study	_____
H. Value per participant (item E divided by item F)	_____
I. Value per participant for ROI study (H multiplied by G)	_____
Development cost to be allocated to ROI study	_____

- *Training VP, Amber Locke:* Actually, we decided since the participants were being paid whether they were involved in training or not, we did not see the need . . .
- *Executive 2, Senior VP of Quality, Amanda Noel:* Interrupting, I agree with Sam. Participant salaries should be included. The work is being vacated while they are in training and they are still being paid.
- *Executive 3, CFO, Madison Heller:* That brings up another issue, what about opportunity costs?
- *Executive 1, Sam Hinkle:* These are all good points. I don't see facility costs as a category either. Did we conduct this training under a shade tree?

Well, you get the idea. Our 15 minutes of fame just turned into 15 minutes of shame. We will get very little, if any, opportunity to discuss the benefits of the training process because everyone is now focused on costs. And we may have lost some degree of credibility with the executive group. We want to spend minimal time in our presentation discussing cost details. We want to conserve our time to discuss the benefits of the training, how the ROI was achieved, and how the training process can be improved to achieve greater contribution. A word to the wise: Fully load the costs and leave no doubt that you have done so. Show the categories and the breakdown of costs in your report and on your presentation slides and emphasize "fully loaded." Leave the slide up just long enough so that all can see the categories. You may even briefly bring attention to how the costs are fully loaded using just a few short examples. Then move on to the training's benefits.

POTENTIAL CHALLENGES

If a system is not in place to capture and allocate costs, then this presents many challenges. It is difficult to adopt cost standards if you have no structure to begin with. The training organization is at serious risk if costs cannot be identified. Additionally, if one WLP staff member uses one type of standard or basis to identify costs and another staff member uses another standard or basis, we will be inconsistent. We will also be seen as lacking in business acumen.

ACTION STEPS

- Review Part E of Premier Motors Case Study on the Chapter 6 folder of the CD. This will provide more insight into capturing costs.
- Carefully review the cost categories you will include with your program. Insert the cost categories for your program in the ROI Analysis Plan. This completes the planning component of your impact study.
- Practice prorating costs using Exercise 6–1 on the CD.

CHAPTER SUMMARY

Costs are important for a variety of uses and applications. They help the WLP staff manage the resources carefully, consistently, and efficiently. They also allow for comparisons between different elements and cost categories. Cost categorization can take several different forms; the most common are presented in this chapter. More important, costs should be fully loaded for ROI calculation. From a practical standpoint, including some of the costs may be optional, based on the organization's guidelines and philosophy. However, because of the scrutiny involved in ROI calculations, it is recommended that all costs be included, even if doing so goes beyond the requirements of the company policy. When presenting an ROI from an impact study, we want to maximize the time with executives to discus the training's benefits. If we leave any doubts about the inclusion of fully loaded costs, precious time will be diverted to discussing the cost issue.

REFERENCES AND RESOURCES

Books

Phillips, Jack J. *Handbook of Training Evaluation and Measurement Methods,* 3rd ed. Woburn, MA: Butterworth-Heinemann, 1997.

Phillips, Jack J. *Return on Investment in Training and Performance Improvement Programs,* 2nd ed. Woburn, MA: Butterworth-Heinemann, 2003.

Software for Calculating Costs

- Microsoft Excel
- Learning Management Systems (some LMS have capability to track costs)
- Project Management Software (some PM software has capability to track costs)

CD 🛠

Exercises and Case Study	Tools, Templates, and Job Aids
Exercise 6–1. Prorating Costs	Figure 6–1. Cost Estimating Worksheet
Case Study—Part E, Premier Motors International (PMI)	Table 6–1. Comparison of Cost Scenarios
	Table 6–2. Recommended Cost Categories
	Table 6–3. Calculating Overhead Costs—Example
	Table 6–4. Executive Leadership Development Program Costs
	Table 6–5. Cost Classification Matrix

CALCULATING THE RETURN ON INVESTMENT

Now that monetary benefits are known along with the costs, the next critical step is to calculate the actual return on investment. Although this is an easy step—following two specific formulas—the ROI itself deserves much care and attention. Taken alone, the ROI calculation has very little value. When considered in conjunction with the other measures, it provides additional insight. This chapter explores the calculation, use, and abuse of ROI. It underscores how it should be interpreted and utilized to become an important part of the evaluation mix.

In this chapter, you will learn to:

❑ Calculate the benefit cost ratio and its interpretation.
❑ Calculate the actual ROI as a percent and its interpretation.
❑ Discuss and use ROI data appropriately.
❑ Address the various concerns about the ROI calculation.
❑ Properly confront a negative ROI study.

THE FUNDAMENTALS

The Formulas

The return on investment is calculated using the program benefits and costs. The benefit/cost ratio (BCR) is the program benefits divided by cost. In formula form it is:

$$BCR = \frac{\text{Program benefits}}{\text{Program costs}}$$

The return on investment uses the net benefits divided by program costs. The net benefits are the program benefits minus the costs. In formula form, the ROI becomes:

$$\text{ROI}(\%) = \frac{\text{Net program benefits}}{\text{Program costs}} \times 100$$

Annualized Values

All the formulas presented in this chapter use annualized values so that the first-year impact of the program investment is developed. Although the data may be collected over a shorter time frame (several weeks or months), it is annualized to develop the ROI value. Using annual values is becoming a generally accepted practice for developing the ROI in many organizations. This approach is a conservative way to develop the ROI, because many short-term training programs have added value in the second or third year. For long-term training programs, annualized values are inappropriate and longer time frames need to be used. For example, in an ROI analysis of a program to send employees of a Singapore-based company to the United States to obtain MBA degrees, a seven-year time frame was used. The program itself required two years and a five-year impact, with postprogram data used to develop the ROI. However, for most programs that last one day to one month (total hours), first-year values are appropriate.

When selecting the approach to measure ROI, it is important to communicate to the target audience the formula used and the assumptions made to arrive at the decision to use it. This action can avoid misunderstandings and confusion surrounding how the ROI value was developed. Although several approaches are available, two stand out as the preferred methods: the benefit/cost ratio and the basic ROI formula, described earlier.

Fully Loaded Costs

When benefits are compared to costs, it is important to include *all* the costs. The conservative approach to calculating the ROI has a direct connection to cost. Guiding Principle 10 focuses directly on this issue: Project/program costs should be fully loaded for ROI analysis.

When an ROI is calculated and reported to target audiences, the process should withstand even the closest scrutiny in terms of its accuracy and credibility. The only way to meet this test is to ensure that all costs are included. Of course, from a realistic viewpoint, if the controller or chief financial officer insists on not using certain costs, it is best to leave them out.

Example 1—Global Financial Services

This is a program for relationship managers, designed to teach them how to use customer-contact-management software. This is a one-day workshop, and 120 managers are trained on a pilot basis.

Payoff Measures: increased sales from existing customers; reduction in customer complaints
Key Intangibles: less time to respond to customer; customer satisfaction
Business Impact Measure

Value of reduced customer complaints	$575,660
Value of increased sales to existing customers	$539,280
Total	$1,114,940

Project Costs

Development costs	$10,500
Materials/software	$18,850
Equipment	$6,000
Instructor (including expenses)	$7,200
Facilities/food/refreshments 60 × $58	3,480
Participants time (lost opportunity) 58 × $385	$22,330
Coordination/evaluation	$15,600
Total	$83,960

ROI Calculation

$$\text{ROI}(\%) = \frac{\$1,114,940 - \$83,960}{\$83,960} \times 100 = 1,228\%$$

Example 2—Healthcare, Inc.

The program was a one-day sexual harassment prevention workshop designed for all first- and second-level supervisors and managers, conducted over a 45-day period with 17 sessions involving 655 managers.

Payoff Measures: reduced number of sexual harassment complaints, reduced turnover
Key Intangibles: job satisfaction, absenteeism, stress reduction, image of Healthcare, Inc., and recruiting
Business Impact Measure

Internal complaints	$360,276
Turnover reduction	$2,840,632
Total	$3,200,908

Program Costs

Needs assessment (estimated cost of time)	$9,000
Program development/acquisition	$15,000
Program coordination/facilitation time	$9,600
Travel and lodging for facilitation and coordinators	$1,520

Program materials (655 × $12)	$7,860
Food/refreshments (655 × $30)	$19,650
Facilities (17 × $150)	$2,550
Participant salaries and benefits ($130,797 × 1.39)	$181,807
Evaluation	$31,000
	$277,987

ROI Calculation

$$\text{ROI} = \frac{\text{Net benefits}}{\text{Costs}} = \frac{\$3,200,908 - \$277,987}{\$277,987} = 1,052\%$$

Example 3—Metro Transit Authority

This program initiated two processes: A no-fault disciplinary system was implemented, and the selection process for new drivers was modified. This program was implemented throughout the entire company of 2,900 drivers.

Payoff Measures: reduced driver absenteeism
Key Intangibles: Improve customer service and satisfaction with a reduction in schedule delays caused by absenteeism
Business Impact Measure

The contribution of the no-fault policy	$518,000
The contribution of the new screening process	$144,000
	$662,000

Program Costs

Cost of screening process	
Development cost	$20,000
Interviewer preparation	$5,000
Administrative time (1,200 × $7.25)	$8,700
Materials (1,200 × $2.00)	$2,400
Total	$36,100

Cost of no-fault policy	
Development cost	$11,000
Materials	$3,800
Meeting time	$16,500
Total	$31,300

ROI Calculation

$$\text{ROI} = \frac{\text{Net benefits}}{\text{Costs}} = \frac{\$662,000 - \$67,400}{\$67,400} = 882\%$$

Example 4—Midwest Electric

In this stress management program, managers and representative employees participated in focus groups to identify work satisfiers and de-stressors and then collaborated on alleviating systemic sources of stress.

> *Payoff Measures:* reduced medical care costs, reduced absenteeism, reduced turnover
> *Key Intangibles:* improved communication, time savings, fewer conflicts, teamwork, and improvement in problem solving.
> *Business Impact Measure*

Reduced medical costs	$198,720
Improvement for absenteeism	$67,684
Improvement for turnover	$157,553
Total	$423,957

Project Costs

Needs assessment	$16,500
Program development	$4,800
Program materials (144 × $95)	$13,680
Participant salaries/benefits (based on 1 day)	$24,108
Travel and lodging (144 × $38)	$5,472
Facilitation, coordination, T&E overhead	$10,800
Meeting room, food, and refreshments 144 × $22	$3,168
Evaluation costs	$22,320
Total	$100,848

ROI Calculation

$$\text{ROI}(\%) = \frac{\$423,957 - \$100,848}{\$100,848} \times 100 = 320\%$$

Example 5—Federal Information Agency

This program offered 1,500 communication specialists the opportunity to receive their master's degree. Participants were asked to prepare for classroom activities on their own time but were allowed to attend classes on the agency's time.

> *Payoff Measures:* reduced turnover
> *Key Intangibles:* improved job satisfaction, improved operational commitment, career enhancement, enhanced agency capability, technology upgrade
> *Business Impact Measure*

Improved capability and operations	$1,580,000
Improvement for turnover	$8,365,000
Total	$9,945,000

Project Costs

Initial analysis (prorated)	$5,000
Development (prorated)	$10,000
Tuition—regular	$915,000
Tuition—premium	$152,500
Salaries/benefits (participants)	$2,497,023
Salaries/benefits (program administrator)	$167,474
Program coordination	$45,000
Facilities	$120,960
Management time	$9,000
Evaluation	$10,000
Total	$3,931,957

ROI Calculation

$$\text{ROI}(\%) = \frac{\$9,945,000 - \$3,931,957}{\$3,931,957} \times 100 = 153\%$$

Interpretation of ROI

1. *Choose the right formula.* What quantitative measure best represents top management goals? Many managers are preoccupied with the measures of sales, profits (net income), and profit percentages (the ratio of profits to dollar sales). However, the ultimate test of profitability is not the absolute amount of profit or the relationship of profit to sales. The critical test is the relationship of profit to invested capital. The most popular way of expressing this relationship is by means of a rate of return on investment (Anthony and Reece, 1983).

Profits can be generated through increased sales or cost savings. In practice, there are more opportunities for cost savings than profit. For example, cost savings can be generated when there is improvement in output, quality, efficiency, cycle time, or an actual cost reduction. In more than 1,000 studies the authors have been involved in, the vast majority pay off on cost savings. Approximately 85% of the studies pay off on output, quality, efficiency, time, or cost reduction. The other 15% pay off on sales increases, in which the earnings come from the profit margin. This opportunity is important for nonprofits and public-sector organizations in which the profit opportunity is often unavailable. Most training and performance improvement initiatives are connected directly to the cost savings portion; thus, ROIs can still be realized in those settings.

Return on investment is defined as net income (earnings) divided by investment. The term *investment* is used in three different senses in financial analysis, thus giving three different ROI ratios: return on assets (ROA), return on owners' equity (ROE), and return on capital employed (ROCE).

Financiers and others have used the ROI approach for centuries. Still, this technique did not become widespread in industry for judging operating performance until the early 1960s. Conceptually, ROI has innate appeal because it blends all the major ingredients of profitability in one number; the ROI statistic by itself can be compared with opportunities elsewhere (both inside and outside). Practically, however, ROI is an imperfect measurement that should be used in conjunction with other performance measurements (Horngren, 1982).

In the context of training and performance improvement, net income is equivalent to net monetary benefits (program benefits minus program costs). Investment is equivalent to program costs.

It is important for organizations to use this formula (outlined above). Deviations from or misuse of the formula can create confusion not only among users but also among the finance and accounting staff. The chief financial officer (CFO) and the finance and accounting staff will become integral partners in making the ROI Methodology a success. Without their support, involvement, and commitment, it would be difficult to use ROI on a wide-scale basis. Consequently, it is important that the same financial terms be used as those used and expected by the CFO. Table 7–1 shows some misuse of financial terms that appear in the literature.

Terms such as return on intelligence (or information) abbreviated as ROI do nothing but confuse the CFO who's thinking that ROI is the actual return on investment described above. Sometimes return on expectations (ROE), return on anticipation (ROA), or return on client expectations (ROCE) are used, confusing the CFO who is thinking return on equity, return on assets, and return on capital employed, respectively. Use of these terms in calculating the payback of a training and performance improvement program will do nothing but confuse and perhaps lose the support of the finance and accounting staff. Other terms such as return on people, return on resources, return on training, and return on web are often used with almost no consistent financial calculations.

TABLE 7–1

MISUSE OF FINANCIAL TERMS

Term	Misuse	CFO Definition
ROI	Return on Information or Return on Intelligence	Return on Investment
ROE	Return on Expectation	Return on Equity
ROA	Return on Anticipation	Return on Assets
ROCE	Return on Client Expectation	Return on Capital Employed
ROP	Return on People	??
ROR	Return on Resources	??
ROT	Return on Training	??
ROW	Return on Web	??

The bottom line: Don't confuse the CFO. Consider this person to be an ally and use the same terminology, same processes, and the same concepts when applying financial returns for programs.

2. *What it means.* The ROI calculation shows the efficient use of capital invested in a process. In this case, it shows the actual earnings (benefits minus costs) from the invested human capital (cost of the program). This is the same basic formula used to calculate the investments in plants, equipment, and start-up companies.

3. *It is not perfect.* By itself, the ROI calculation is flawed and should never be used without other supporting data. Even the classic finance and accounting text will make this important point. Although ROI shows efficiency when investing in capital, it is weak as the only measure of success; it must be used in conjunction with other measures.

4. *There are six types of data.* It is important to remember that the ROI Methodology collects six types of data, with ROI being only one of them. The other types of data, specifically Level 3, Level 4, and intangibles, may be just as important if not more important than the ROI calculation. The stakeholders should understand this, it should be reinforced to managers, and improvements should be made with this concept in mind.

5. *The ROI is only as good as the monetary benefits.* Perhaps the most important part of the calculation is the monetary value of the benefits. This is often the mystery—the part that's entered in the numerator of the formula. Although it is much easier to calculate a program's cost, it is more difficult to capture the actual monetary value of its benefits. The monetary value is developed using an annual value for short-term programs and a conservative number of years for long-term programs.

6. *All the costs should be included.* Although costs are relatively easy to develop, they must be fully loaded in the analysis. "Fully loaded" means they have to include all the costs—both direct and indirect. With this approach, all costs that can be identified and linked to a particular program are included. The philosophy is simple: When in doubt in the denominator, put it in (i.e., if it is questionable whether a cost be included, it is recommended that it be included, even if the cost guidelines for the organization do not require it). This parallels a rule for the numerator, which states, "When in doubt, leave it out" (i.e., if it is questionable whether a benefit should be included in the numerator, it should be omitted from the analysis).

7. *Compare with the objective.* When reviewing the specific ROI calculation and formula, it is helpful to position the ROI calculation in the context of the entire process. The ROI calculation is only one measure generated through the ROI process. Six types of data are developed, five of which are labeled the Five Levels of Evaluation. The process works best when each level of evaluation is driven by a specific objective, as described in Chapter 2. In terms of ROI, specific objectives are often set, creating the expectations of an acceptable ROI calculation. Table 7–2 shows the payoff of a sexual harassment prevention program, as the results at the different levels are clearly linked to the specific objectives of the program (Phillips & Hill, 2001). As objectives are established, data are collected to indicate the extent to which that particular objective was

TABLE 7–2

THE CHAIN OF IMPACT DRIVES ROI

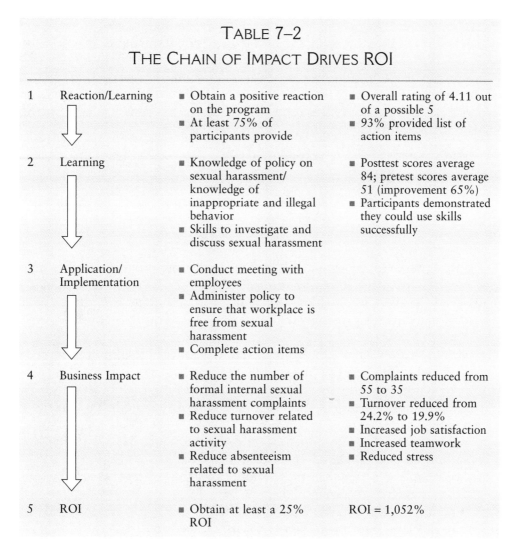

1	Reaction/Learning	■ Obtain a positive reaction on the program ■ At least 75% of participants provide	■ Overall rating of 4.11 out of a possible 5 ■ 93% provided list of action items
2	Learning	■ Knowledge of policy on sexual harassment/ knowledge of inappropriate and illegal behavior ■ Skills to investigate and discuss sexual harassment	■ Posttest scores average 84; pretest scores average 51 (improvement 65%) ■ Participants demonstrated they could use skills successfully
3	Application/ Implementation	■ Conduct meeting with employees ■ Administer policy to ensure that workplace is free from sexual harassment ■ Complete action items	
4	Business Impact	■ Reduce the number of formal internal sexual harassment complaints ■ Reduce turnover related to sexual harassment activity ■ Reduce absenteeism related to sexual harassment	■ Complaints reduced from 55 to 35 ■ Turnover reduced from 24.2% to 19.9% ■ Increased job satisfaction ■ Increased teamwork ■ Reduced stress
5	ROI	■ Obtain at least a 25% ROI	ROI = 1,052%

met. This is the ideal framework that clearly shows the powerful connection between objectives and measurement and evaluation data.

The table also shows the chain of impact as reaction leads to learning, which leads to application, which, in turn, leads to business impact and on to ROI. The intangible data shown in the business impact category consists of items that are purposely not converted to monetary value. Some of those could have been anticipated in the project before it was implemented. Others may not have been anticipated but were indicated as a benefit from those involved in the program. In this example, there was an expectation of 25% for ROI (Level 5). This organization used 25% as a standard for all its ROI projects, and the result of 1,052% clearly exceed the expectation by a huge amount.

8. *Use the data.* These are evaluation data and should be used to drive the changes. The ROI itself may be the hurdle rate for continuing to invest in the program or to implement it in other areas when this calculation is made on a pilot program. Although the hurdle rate may determine the fate of the program, it is important to consider the other measures and to drive improvements or initiate actions for changes based on the totality of the data and not just the single measure of ROI.

POTENTIAL CHALLENGES

Selective Use of ROI

The ROI Methodology should not be applied to every program. It takes time and resources to create a valid and credible ROI study. It is appropriate to underscore the types of programs for which this technique is best suited. It should be reserved for programs that:

- Have a long life cycle. At some point in the life of the program, this level of accountability should be applied to the program.
- Are very important to the organization in meeting its operating goals. These programs are designed to add value and it may be helpful to show that value.
- Are closely linked to the organization's strategic initiatives. Anything this important needs a high level of accountability.
- Are very expensive to implement. A more expensive program should be subjected to this level of accountability.
- Are highly visible and sometimes controversial. These programs often require this level of accountability to satisfy the critics.
- Have a large target audience. If a program is designed for all employees, it may be a candidate for ROI.
- Are commanding the interest of a top executive group. If top executives are interested in knowing the impact, the ROI method should be applied.

These are only guidelines and should be considered in the context of the organization. Other criteria can be used. These can be used in a scheme to sort out those programs that are most likely to be subjected to this level of accountability.

It is also helpful to consider the programs for which the ROI Methodology is not appropriate. It is usually not appropriate for programs that are:

- Very short in duration, such as two-hour briefings. It's difficult to change behavior in such a short time frame unless it is on a very focused issue.
- Legislated or required by regulation. It may be difficult to change anything as a result of this evaluation.
- Required by senior management. It may be that these programs will continue regardless.

- Focused on operator and technical training. It may be more appropriate to measure at Levels 2 and 3 only to ensure that participants know how to do the job and are doing it properly.

This is not meant to imply that the ROI Methodology cannot be implemented for these types of programs. When considering the limited resources for measurement and evaluation, it might not be appropriate to use these resources and time on those types of programs. It is also helpful to think about the programs that would be appropriate for the first one or two ROI studies. Initially, the use of this process will be met with some anxiety and tentativeness. The programs undertaken initially should not only meet the requirements above but should also meet other requirements. These programs should:

1. Be as simple as possible. Reserve the complex programs for later.
2. Be a known commodity. This helps ensure that the first study is not negative.
3. Be void of hidden agendas and political sensitivity. The first study should not be wrapped up in organization politics.

Deciding how many resources to allocate to this process, which programs to pursue for ROI Methodology, and the number of programs to pursue in any given time frame are important issues that are addressed in Chapter 10, Making the Transition.

When the ROI Is Large

The actual ROI value can often be quite large—far exceeding what might be expected from other types of investments in plant, equipment, and companies. It is not unusual for programs involved in leadership, team building, management development, supervisor training, and sales training to generate ROIs in the 100%–700% range. This is not to mean that all ROI studies are positive; many are negative. However, the impact of the training and development can be quite impressive. It is helpful to remember what constitutes the ROI. Consider, for example, the investment in one week of training for a team leader. If that leader's behavior changes as he or she works directly with the team, a series of actions can produce significant improvements. The small amount of behavior change when reflected through the group and spread throughout the team can produce a measurable change in the team's performance. This measure now represents the team's measure. That behavior change, translated into a measurement improvement for the entire year, can be quite significant. When the monetary value of the team's improvement is spread over an entire year and compared to the relatively small investment in that one team leader, it is easy to see why this number can be quite large.

More specifically, as Figure 7–1 shows, there are some very important factors that contribute to high ROI values. The impact can be quite large when a specific need has been identified and a performance gap exists; a new requirement is introduced and the solution is implemented at the right time for the right people at a reasonable cost; the solution is applied and supported in the work

FIGURE 7–1

POTENTIAL MAGNITUDE OF AN ROI FOR A TARGET POPULATION

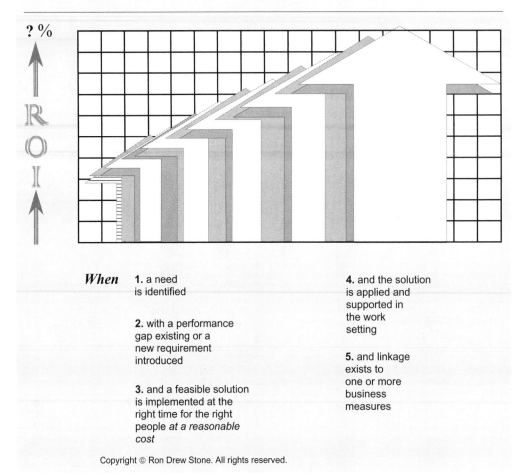

When

1. a need is identified

2. with a performance gap existing or a new requirement introduced

3. and a feasible solution is implemented at the right time for the right people *at a reasonable cost*

4. and the solution is applied and supported in the work setting

5. and linkage exists to one or more business measures

setting; and there's a linkage to one or more business measures. Those factors represent a lot of ifs that must be in place for the training process to be effective. When they are present and functioning as they should, high ROI values can be realized.

It is helpful to remember the context within which the training takes place. For example, a high-impact ROI can be generated in an organization that is losing money (or in bankruptcy) because the impact is restricted to those individuals involved in the training and performance improvement program and the monetary value of their improvement is connected to that program. This does not reflect the entire organization or even a large part of it. At the same time, there can be some disastrous programs generating a very negative ROI in a company that is profitable because the data reflects that the program did not generate enough improvement to overcome the costs.

It is important to understand that a very high ROI value can be communicated and does not necessarily relate directly to the health of the rest of the organization. This is a microlevel activity that evaluates the success of a particular program within a particular time frame.

ROI Do's and Don'ts

Because of the sensitivity of the ROI process, caution is needed when developing, calculating, and communicating the return on investment. The implementation of the ROI process is a very important issue and a goal of many training and development departments. In addition to following the guiding principles, a few do's and don'ts should be addressed to keep the process from going astray. The following cautions are offered when using ROI.

Do Take a Conservative Approach When Developing Both Benefits and Costs

Conservatism in ROI analysis builds accuracy and credibility. What matters most is how the target audience perceives the value of the data. A conservative approach is always recommended for both the numerator of the ROI formula (benefits) and the denominator (program costs). The conservative approach is the basis for the guiding principles.

Do Use Caution When Comparing the ROI in Training with Other Financial Returns

Calculating the return on funds invested or assets employed can be done in many ways. ROI is just one of them. Although the calculation for ROI in training and development uses the same basic formula as in other investment evaluations, the target group may not fully understand it. Its calculation method and meaning should be clearly communicated. More importantly, it should be an item management accepts as an appropriate measure for training program evaluation.

Do Involve Management in Developing the Return

Management ultimately makes the decision if an ROI value is acceptable. To the extent possible, management should be involved in setting the parameters for calculations and establishing targets by which the organization considers programs acceptable.

Do Fully Disclose the Assumptions and Methodology

When discussing the ROI process and communicating data, it is very important to fully disclose the process, steps, and assumptions used in the process. Strengths should be clearly communicated as well as weaknesses and shortcomings. The audience should fully understand what is being presented and the assumptions upon which it is based. Any adjustments made to the data should be highlighted. It should also be clear and there should be no room for doubt that the costs are fully loaded.

Do Approach Sensitive and Controversial Issues with Caution

Occasionally, sensitive and controversial issues arise when discussing an evaluation or an ROI value. It is best to avoid debates over what is measurable and what is not measurable unless there is clear evidence of the issue in question. Also, some programs are so fundamental to the survival of the organization that any attempt to measure them is unnecessary. For example, a program designed to improve customer service in a customer-focused company may escape the scrutiny of an ROI evaluation on the assumption that if the program is well designed, it will improve customer service.

Do Teach Others the Methods for Calculating the Return

Each time an ROI is calculated, the training manager should use this opportunity to educate other managers and colleagues. Even if it is not in their area of responsibility, these individuals will be able to see the value of this approach to training evaluation. Also, when possible, each project should serve as a case study to educate the workplace learning and performance (WLP) staff on specific techniques and methods.

Do Recognize That Not Everyone Will Buy into ROI

Not every audience member will understand, appreciate, or accept the ROI calculation. For a variety of reasons, some individuals will not agree with the values. Attempts to persuade them will be beyond the scope of the task at hand. These individuals may be highly emotional over the concept of showing accountability for training, learning, education, development, and performance improvement. They may feel that these initiatives should represent investments in people and the organization should not be concerned with the return on that investment.

Do Choose the Place for the Debates

The time to debate the ROI Methodology is not *during* a presentation (unless it can't be avoided). There are constructive times to debate the ROI process: in a forum, among the WLP staff, in an education session, in professional literature, on panel discussions, or even during the development of an ROI impact study. The time and place for debate should be carefully selected so as not to detract from the quality and quantity of information presented.

Do Not Show Decimals in the ROI Calculation

Always round the ROI calculation to the nearest whole number. For example, 203.4% becomes 203% and 203.5% becomes 204%. Showing a decimal place gives the impression that the ROI value is exact. This is rarely the case. Usually some estimation is needed to arrive at monetary values, either in the cost (denominator) or the benefits (numerator). Even ROIs developed by engineering, operations, manufacturing, marketing, and finance functions will likely include estimates and are not exact. As stated earlier, the important issues are what caused the results and what methods and assumptions were used to arrive at the conclusions and monetary values that drive the ROI.

Do Not Boast about a High Return

It is not unusual to generate what appears to be a very high return on investment for a workplace learning and performance program. Several examples in this book have illustrated the possibilities. A WLP manager who boasts about a high rate of return will be open to potential criticism from others unless there are indisputable facts on which the calculation is based.

Do Not Communicate Training Outcomes As the Training Department's Results

When follow-up data is collected and reported (Levels 3, 4, and 5), we hope the results come about because we enabled them to happen. However, without the proper job application by the participants (and support by management and others) the results would not occur. We should communicate and discuss ROI in the context of the training process—or, if you prefer, the training and performance process. It is a "we" process, not an "us" process. The training is an enabler; thus, we are in the enabling business. We must promote, communicate, and manage the training process so that others realize the full continuum. As the famous baseball payer Yogi Berra once said, "It ain't over till it's over." Give others credit. Do not say, "And here are the results of the training" or "Here is what the training department accomplished." Say instead, "Here are the results from the training process," "The partnership with our client," or the like.

Do Not Try to Use ROI on Every Program

As discussed earlier, some programs are difficult to quantify, and an ROI calculation may not be feasible. Other methods of presenting the benefits may be more appropriate. As discussed in Chapter 10, training executives are encouraged to set targets for the percent of programs in which ROIs are developed. Also, specific criteria should be established to select programs for ROI analysis, as briefly described.

Do Not Encourage Someone Who Wants to Use the ROI Process for Political Gain

Unfortunately, there are those in the organizations who will misuse tools such as the ROI process to help them get ahead or to get what they want. The ROI process has no place for agendas. It should be considered and applied with objectivity.

How to Deal with a Negative ROI Study

For some, a negative ROI is the ultimate fear. Immediately, they begin to think, "Will this reflect unfavorably on me, on the program, on the function, on the client? Will budgets disappear? Will support diminish? Are there political consequences?" These are all legitimate questions, but most of the fears are unfounded when they realize the potential for improving programs when the ROI is negative. Here are 11 ways to address this issue.

1. *Never fail to recognize the power of the negative study.* Stakeholders can learn much more from a negative ROI than a positive ROI. When the study is negative, an abundance of data always indicates what went wrong. Was it an adverse reaction? Was there a lack of learning? Was there a failure to implement or apply what was learned? Did major barriers prevent success? Or was there a misalignment in the beginning? These are legitimate questions about lack of success, and the answers are always obtained in a comprehensive evaluation study.

2. *Look for red flags.* It is important for the prospects of a negative ROI study to be uncovered early. Indications of problems often pop up in the early stages of initiation—after reaction and learning data have been collected. Many signals can reveal insight into the success or lack of success of the program, such as participants perceiving the program as not relevant to their job, not important to their job success, or containing little or no new information. Perhaps they would not recommend it to others or do not intend to use it on the job. These types of responses can indicate a lack of use on the job, which usually translates into a negative ROI. Connecting this information requires analyzing data beyond the overall satisfaction of the program, instructor ratings, and learning environment. Although important, these types of data and ratings may not reveal the value of the content and its potential use. Also, if an evaluation study is conducted on a program as it is being implemented, low ratings at Levels 1 and 2 may signal the need for adjustments before additional evaluation is conducted.

3. *Lower outcome expectations.* When there is a signal that the study may be negative, or it appears that there could be a danger of less-than-desired success, you should consider lowering expectations about the outcome. The approach "underpromise and overdeliver" is best applied here. Containing your enthusiasm for the results early in the process is important. We're not suggesting gloom and doom throughout the study, but at the same time, we suggest that you manage expectations and keep them on the low side of possibilities.

4. *Look for data everywhere.* As evaluators, it is our challenge to uncover all the data connected to the program—both positive and negative. To that end, it is critical to look everywhere for data that shows value (or the lack of it). This thorough approach will ensure that nothing is left undiscovered—the fear of many individuals when facing a negative ROI.

5. *Never alter the standards.* When the ROI is negative or the results are less than desired, it is tempting to lower the standards or change the

assumptions about collecting, processing, analyzing, and reporting the data. This is not a time to change the measurement process. Changing the standards to make the data more positive renders the study virtually worthless. With weak or no standards there is no credibility.

6. *Remain objective throughout.* Ideally, the evaluator should be completely objective or independent of the program. This objectivity provides an arm's-length evaluation of its success. It is not only important to enter the project from an objective standpoint but to remain objective throughout. Never become an advocate for or against it. This helps alleviate the concern that the results may be biased.

7. *Prepare the team for the bad news.* As red flags pop up and expectations are lowered, it appears that a less-than-desired outcome will be realized. It is best to prepare the team for the bad news early in the process. Part of the preparation is to make sure they don't reveal or discuss the outcome of the program with others until it is time to do so. Even when early data are positive, it is best to keep the data confidential until all data are collected. Also, when it appears that the ROI is going to be negative, an early meeting will help to prepare a strategy to deal with the outcome. This preparation may include how the data will be communicated, the potential actions needed to improve the program, and, of course, explanations as to what caused the lack of success.

8. *Consider different scenarios.* One reason for negative results could be the use of conservative standards. Standards connected with the ROI Methodology are very conservative for a reason: The conservative approach adds credibility, allowing others to buy into the data and the results. However, sometimes it may be helpful to examine what the result might have been if conservative standards had not been used. Other scenarios may actually show a positive ROI. In this case, the standards are not changed, but the presentation shows how different the data would be if other assumptions were made. This approach allows the audience to see how conservative the standards are. For example, on the cost side, including all costs sometimes drives the project to a negative ROI. If other assumptions could be made about the costs, the value could be changed and a different ROI calculation would be made. Also, on the benefit side, sometimes lack of data from a particular group drives this study negative because of the standard, "no data, no improvement." Another assumption could be made about the missing data to calculate another ROI. It is important for these other scenarios to be offered to educate the audience about the value of what is obtained and underscore the conservative approach. It should be clear that the standards are not changed and that the comparisons with other studies would be based on the standards in the original calculation.

9. *Find out what went wrong.* When results are disappointing, the first question usually asked is, "What went wrong?" It is important to uncover the reasons for the lack of success. As the process unfolds, an abundance of data throughout the study often indicates what went wrong. In the follow-up evaluation, specific questions about barriers, inhibitors, impediments, and obstacles are contained. In addition, asking

for suggestions for improvements often underscores how things could be changed to make a difference. Even when collecting enablers and enhancers, clues may arise as to what could be changed to make it much better. In most situations, there is little doubt as to what went wrong and what can be changed. In worse-case scenarios, if the program cannot be modified or enhanced to add value, it may mean that it should be discontinued. Given this situation, it may be helpful to terminate a program that is not adding value and cannot add value in the future.

10. *Adjust the story line.* When communicating data, a negative ROI means the story line needs to change. Instead of saying, "Let's celebrate—we've got great results for this program," the story now reads, "Now we have data that shows how to make this program more successful." The audience must understand that the lack of success had existed previously, but no data were available to know what needed to be changed. Now, the data exist. In an odd sort of way, this becomes a positive spin on less-than-positive data. Additionally, you may discover that the actions required to make this program successful may also have an improvement effect when applied to other programs.

11. *Drive improvement.* Evaluation data are virtually useless unless used to drive action. In a negative ROI study, many areas can usually be changed to make the program more successful. It is important to secure a commitment to make those adjustments so that the program will be successful in the future. Until those actions are approved and implemented, the work is not complete. In worse-case scenarios, if the program cannot be changed to add value, it should be terminated and the important lessons learned communicated to others. This last step underscores that the ROI Methodology is used for process improvement and not for performance evaluation of the staff.

In summary, a negative ROI study does not have to be bad news. It contains much data that can be used not only to explain what happened but also to help improve things for the future. It is important to consider the potential of a negative ROI study and to alter or adjust expectations and strategies throughout the process to keep the negative results from being a surprise. The worse-case situation is for negative data to surprise the key sponsor at the time of presentation.

ROI Myths

ROI for human resource and training programs has been around since the 1980s. During that time professionals have had differing levels of exposure to it. Some understand it very well and use it with success today. Others are learning how to use it. Some are still on the fence trying to decide about learning it and using it. Then there are those who stand afar with some level of curiosity. All of these groups have their own frame of reference and draw their own conclusions about ROI, what it is and what it is not. Many of these conclusions are fed by lack of education and familiarity and have generated various stereotypes and myths about ROI. Complete Exercise 7–1 to see

EXERCISE 7–1. ROI QUIZ

True or False? Please choose the answer you feel is most correct.

		T	F
1.	The ROI Methodology generates just one data item, expressed as a percent.	❑	❑
2.	A program with monetary benefits of $200,000 and costs of $100,000 translates into a 200% ROI.	❑	❑
3.	The ROI methodology is a tool to strengthen/improve the learning/education process.	❑	❑
4.	After reviewing a detailed ROI impact study, senior executives will usually require ROI studies on all programs.	❑	❑
5.	ROI impact studies should be conducted very selectively, usually involving 5%–10% of programs.	❑	❑
6.	For a specific program evaluation, the ROI methodology may be needed, but not the ROI calculation.	❑	❑
7.	A program costing $100 per participant, designed to teach basic skills with job-related software, is an ideal program for an ROI impact study.	❑	❑
8.	Over half of learning/training/development functions are using ROI.	❑	❑
9.	The ROI Methodology contains too many complicated formulas.	❑	❑
10.	The ROI methodology can be implemented for about 3%–5% of my learning/development budget.	❑	❑
11.	ROI is not future oriented; it only reflects past performance.	❑	❑
12.	ROI is not possible for soft skills programs.	❑	❑
13.	If an ROI impact study, conducted on an existing program, shows a negative ROI, the client is usually already aware of the program's weaknesses.	❑	❑
14.	The ROI Methodology is a process improvement tool and not a performance evaluation tool for the learning/development staff.	❑	❑
15.	If senior executives are not asking for ROI, there is no need to pursue the ROI Methodology.	❑	❑

where you stand on these myths. The answers are on the Chapter 7 folder on the CD.

So, How Did You Do?

See how you fared now that the answers to the quiz have been explained (you did visit the answers on the CD, didn't you?). Tally your scores using the scorecard below. Based on the interpretations below, what is your ROI acumen?

No. of Correct Responses	Interpretation
13–15	You could be an ROI consultant
10–12	You could be a speaker at the next ROI Conference
7–9	You need a copy of a thick ROI book
4–6	You need to attend the ASTD two-day ROI workshop
1–3	You need to attend ROI certification

This simple quiz and the explanations have attempted to expose some of the myths and mysteries about ROI. The ROI Methodology is being routinely implemented by many organizations and it is adding tremendous value. It can be an important part of the measurement mix and should at least be considered with an open mind. More importantly, think through the issues and avoid some of the stereotyping or myths about ROI.

ACTION STEPS

The following steps are suggested as the ROI calculation is planned, developed, and used. Follow these steps as you address your impact study.

Practice Calculations

Using the examples in this chapter, practice the calculation so that you can easily understand how it is developed and what it means.

Develop an ROI Objective

An important part of the ROI calculation is to set the target or hurdle rate for an acceptable ROI. Four techniques used were explained earlier in this fieldbook. Perhaps the client, sponsor, or other stakeholders will be able to suggest what an appropriate ROI is. For public-sector nonprofit organizations, this may be zero, which represents a breakeven point.

Compare to Forecast

In some cases, an ROI has been forecasted. If this is the case, it would be helpful to compare the actual ROI with the forecast. In most situations, the actual ROI is less than the forecast—sometimes as much as 50% or more. This is understandable because a forecast is an estimate prior to the skills actually being applied in the work setting.

Prepare for the Presentation

Using the information about dealing with a negative ROI, the information about the presentation, and the tips in Chapter 8, "Telling The Story," prepare for the ROI presentation. Be sure to address the issues of what to do if the ROI is extremely large (or negative) and how to integrate the ROI presentation with other levels of data.

Use the Data

In conjunction with the other measures, bring changes that are needed for the program. Get approval for these changes while the discussion is current. Suggest a time line if necessary. Often times, decisions put off until later have a way of getting lost in the shuffle.

CHAPTER SUMMARY

This chapter explored several key issues around the development and use of ROI, showing how the calculations are developed and how the data are used in the ROI Methodology. This is the most powerful and perhaps explosive data set; yet, ironically, it may not be the most important because it represents only one type in the six types of data that should be presented. Care must be taken to ensure that the ROI is not abused or misused but used in a way that it becomes an important part of the evaluation mix.

REFERENCES

Anthony, R. N., and J. S. Reece. *Accounting: Text and Cases*, 7th ed. Homewood, IL: Irwin, 1983.

Homgren, C. T. *Cost Accounting*, 5th ed. Englewood Cliffs, NJ: Prentice Hall, 1982.

Phillips, Jack J. (Ed.) *In Action: Performance Analysis and Consulting*. Alexandria, VA: ASTD, 1999.

Phillips, Jack J. *HRD Trends Worldwide: Shared Solutions to Compete in a Global Economy*. Woburn, MA: Butterworth Heinemann, 1999.

Phillips, Jack J. *Return on Investment in Training and Performance Improvement Programs*, 2nd ed. Woburn, MA: Butterworth Heinemann, 2003.

Phillips, Jack J., and Dianne Hill. "Sexual Harassment Prevention," in The Human Resources Scorecard: Measuring the Return on Investment by Jack J. Phillips, Ron D. Stone, and Patricia P. Phillips. Boston: Butterworth-Heinemann, 2001.

Phillips, Jack J., and Ron D. Stone. *How to Measure Training Results: A Practical Guide to Tracking the Six Key Indicators.* New York: McGraw-Hill, 2002.

Phillips, Patricia P. *The Bottomline on ROI.* Atlanta, GA: CEP Press, 2002.

CD ⊛

Exercises and Case Study	Tools, Templates, and Job Aids
Exercise 7–1. ROI Quiz	Figure 7–1. Potential Magnitude of an ROI
Exercise 7–1A. Answers to the ROI Quiz	Table 7–1. Misuse of Financial Terms
	Table 7–2. Chain of Impact Drives ROI

TELLING THE STORY

You have collected and analyzed your data. You know the results and you know why these results were achieved. You have developed conclusions and recommendations to address the advantages and the shortcomings. You are faced with clarifying answers to questions such as: Were the objectives met (for both the learning program and the evaluation study)? Does the program need to be modified? Would additional support improve the results? What was learned about the training and performance process that can be used with other programs?

Having developed your conclusions and recommendations, now you are challenged with communicating these results to others in an unbiased and objective way. You must decide what data should be presented, how it should be presented, who should present it, and where it should be presented. To help you in this effort, this chapter examines these and other communication issues. Communicating results is as important as achieving them. This chapter provides useful information to help present evaluation data to the various audiences using both oral and written reporting methods.

In this chapter you will learn

❑ The principles of communicating results.
❑ How to develop your impact study report.
❑ How to communicate the results from your study.

THE FUNDAMENTALS

Why Communication Is Important

People sometimes underestimate the power of communication. To see how communication affects us, we need only be reminded of the informal communication that occurs regarding the training function and process. The training function and its products receive wide exposure in the organization. We are in a fish bowl, so to speak. People participate in our programs and return to their work setting with an opinion (and hopefully new expertise, knowledge, or skills). Our facilitators, process, tools, program content, materials, methods, suppliers—everything—is there to be seen and experienced by the workforce. And that is as it should be.

Perhaps another way to view this is that we are being evaluated on a continuing basis even in our absence. Others are drawing conclusions and often communicating their thoughts to team members and management long after the training is over. This can be a good thing or a bad thing. You can fill in the possible scenarios here. There are many.

Unless we practice some type of formal communication about the contributions of the training process, we are left to the possible demise brought on by the informal communication process. Although it is important to communicate achieved results to interested stakeholders after the project is complete, it is important to communicate throughout the training process as well. This ensures that information is flowing so that adjustments can be made and all stakeholders are aware of the success and issues surrounding the process. There are at least five key reasons for being concerned about communicating results.

Formal Communication Can Initiate Formal Action

Measuring success and collecting evaluation data mean nothing unless the findings are communicated promptly to the appropriate audiences to make them aware of what is occurring so they can take any necessary action. Communication allows a full loop to be made from the program results to necessary actions based on those results. If informal information is floating around the organization about a program or the training process, formal communication can give it context and speak to any issues or corrective actions that need to be addressed.

Communication Is Necessary to Make Improvements

Because information is collected at different points during the process, communication and feedback to the various groups that will take action is the best way for adjustments to be made. Thus, the quality and timeliness of communication become crucial issues for making necessary adjustments or improvements. Even after the project is completed, communication is necessary to make sure the target audience fully understands the results achieved and how the results could either be enhanced in future projects or in the current project, if it is still operational. Communication is the key to making these important adjustments at all phases of the program.

Communication Is Necessary for Explaining Contributions

The different target audiences have different communication needs and a different viewpoint about results and contributions. A communication strategy, including the content of the report, techniques, media, and the overall process, determines the extent to which the audiences understand the contribution. Communicating results, particularly with business impact and ROI, can become confusing for even the most sophisticated target audiences. Communication must be planned and implemented with the goal of making sure the various audiences realize the full contribution of the training process.

Communication About Results Is a Sensitive Issue

Communication about results is one of those important issues that can cause major problems. Because the results of a program can be closely linked to the performance of others and the political issues in an organization, communication can upset some individuals while pleasing others. If certain individuals do not receive the information or it is delivered inconsistently from one group to another, problems can surface. Not only is it an understanding issue, it is also an issue of perceived fairness, quality, and political correctness. Therefore, we must make sure communication is properly constructed and effectively delivered to all key individuals who need the information.

A Variety of Target Audiences Need Different Information

Because there are so many potential target audiences for receiving communication on the results of the training process, it is important for the communication to be tailored directly to their needs. Planning and effort are necessary to make sure the audience receives all the information it needs, in the proper format, and at the proper time. A single report for all audiences may not be appropriate. The scope, size, media, and even information about different types of data and different measurement levels will vary significantly from one group to another, making the target audience the key to determining the appropriate communication process.

Collectively, these reasons make communication an important issue, although it is often overlooked or underestimated in training and performance improvement projects. This chapter builds on this important issue and addresses a variety of techniques for providing all types of communication for various target audiences.

Principles of Communicating Results

Communicating results effectively requires knowing your audience and planning accordingly. Communication style can sometimes be as important as the substance. Regardless of the message, audience, or medium, a few general principles apply and are addressed next.

Communication Must Be Timely

Usually, results should be communicated as soon as they are known. From a practical standpoint, it may be best to delay the communication until a convenient time, such as the publication of the next newsletter or the next general management meeting. Timing issues must be addressed. Is the audience ready for the results in light of other things that may have happened? Are the results going to meet the expectations of the audience? When is the best time for having the maximum effect on the audience? Are there circumstances that dictate a change in the timing of the communication?

Communication Should Be Targeted to Specific Audiences

Communication is more effective if it is designed for a particular target group. The message should be specifically tailored to the interests, needs, and expectations of the target audience.

The results described in this chapter reflect outcomes at all levels, including the six types of data developed in this fieldbook. Some of the data are developed earlier in the project and communicated during the project. Other data are collected after implementation and communicated in a follow-up study. Thus, the results, in their broadest sense, may involve early feedback in qualitative terms to ROI values in varying quantitative terms.

Media Should Be Carefully Selected

For particular groups, some media may be more effective than others. Face-to-face meetings may be better than special bulletins. A memo distributed exclusively to top management may be more effective than the company newsletter. Electronic distance technology (audio and TV broadcasts) will reach a large audience at multiple locations but may have the disadvantage of less personalization and an inability to read audience response. The proper method of communication can help improve the effectiveness of the process.

Communication Should Be Unbiased and Modest

It is important to separate fact from fiction and accurate statements from opinions. Various audiences may accept communication from the workplace learning and performance (WLP) staff with skepticism, anticipating biased opinions. Boastful statements sometimes turn off recipients, and most of the content is lost. Observable, believable facts carry far more weight than extreme or sensational claims. Although such claims may get audience attention, they often detract from the importance of the results. The following tips may help in preparing your presentation.

- Focus on the results from the training process, not the program or the training department. This has three significant advantages. (1) It minimizes the possibility of the training department appearing to be boastful. (2) It seizes an opportunity to reinforce to stakeholders that training is a process, not an event. (3) It plants a seed to reinforce one of the weakest parts of the training process—the need to support transfer strategies to influence implementation in the work setting.
- Give credit to the participants and their supervisors. The results are achieved because of the efforts of many.

- Address the methodology used for the study (data collection and analysis) to help bring credibility to the study's findings.
- Clarify your data sources and why they are credible.
- State any assumptions made during the analysis and reporting and why these assumptions are made.
- Welcome differing points of view and constructive critique. Do not display defensive behavior when issues are raised or questions are asked.
- Make no claims that are not supported by the data. It is okay to speculate as long as it is clear that this is what you are doing.

Communication Must Be Consistent

The timing and content of the communication should be consistent with past practices. A special communication at an unusual time during a training program may provoke suspicion. Also, if a particular group, such as top management, regularly receives communication on outcomes, it should continue receiving communication—even if the results are not positive. If some results are omitted, it might leave the impression that only positive results are reported.

Testimonials Are More Effective Coming from Individuals the Audience Respects

Opinions are strongly influenced by others, particularly those who are respected and trusted. Testimonials about results, when solicited from individuals respected by others in the organization, can influence the effectiveness of the message. This respect may be related to leadership ability, position, special skills, or knowledge. A testimonial from an individual who commands little respect and is regarded as a substandard performer can have a negative impact on the message.

The Audience's Opinion of the Learning Function Will Influence the Communication Strategy

Opinions are difficult to change, and a negative opinion of the WLP group may not change with the mere presentation of facts. However, the presentation of facts alone may strengthen the opinions held by those who already agree with the results. It helps reinforce their position and provides a defense in discussions with others. A WLP group with a high level of credibility and respect may have a relatively easy time communicating results. Low credibility can create problems in efforts to be persuasive. The reputation of the WLP group is an important consideration in developing the overall strategy. It is significantly important to distinguish between who actually provided the data and who is delivering the message. It should be clear that it is not our data, but rather data from credible sources in a position to know about the results and what caused them.

These general principles are important to the overall success of the communication effort. They should serve as a checklist for the WLP team when disseminating program results.

Analyzing the Purpose of the Communication

Because results need to be communicated for many reasons, a list should be tailored to the situation and project. The specific reasons depend on the project, the setting, and the unique needs of the sponsor. The most common purposes are:

- To secure approval for the project and allocate resources of time and money. The initial communication presents a proposal, projected ROI, or other data that are intended to secure the project approval. This communication may not have very much data but rather anticipates what is to come.
- To gain support for the project and its objectives. It is important to have support from a variety of groups. This communication is intended to build the necessary support to make the project work successfully.
- To secure agreement on issues, solutions, and resources. As the program begins, it is important for all those directly involved to have some agreement and understanding of the important elements and requirements surrounding the program.
- To build credibility for the WLP group, its techniques, and the finished products. It is important early in the process to make sure that those involved understand the approach and reputation of the WLP staff, and, based on the approach taken, the commitments made by all parties.
- To reinforce the processes. It is important for key managers to support the program and reinforce the various processes used in design, development, and delivery. This communication is designed to enhance those processes.
- To drive action for improvement in the project. This early communication is designed as a process improvement tool to effect changes and improvements as the needs are uncovered and various individuals make suggestions.
- To prepare participants for the program. Those most directly involved in the program, the participants, must to be prepared for learning, application, and responsibilities that will be required of them as they bring success to the project.
- To enhance results throughout the project and the quality of future feedback. This communication is designed to show the status of the project and to influence decisions, seek support, or communicate events and expectations to key stakeholders. In addition, it will enhance both the quality and quantity of information as stakeholders see the feedback cycle in action.
- To show the complete results of the training process. This is perhaps the most important communication, in which all the results involving all six types of measures are communicated to the appropriate individuals so they have a full understanding of the success or shortcomings of the project.
- To underscore the importance of measuring results. Some individuals need to understand the importance of measurement and evaluation and see the need for having important data on different measures.

- To explain techniques used to measure results. The program sponsor and support staff need to understand the techniques used in measuring results. In some cases, these techniques may be transferred internally to use with other projects. In short, these individuals need to understand the soundness and theoretical framework of the process used.
- To stimulate desire in participants to be involved in the program. Ideally, participants want to be involved in the program. This communication is designed to pique their interest in the program and inform them of its benefits and importance.
- To stimulate interest in the WLP function. From a WLP perspective, some communications are designed to create interest in all the products and services based on the results of current programs. This communication needs to focus on benefits to others and not on the success of the WLP function.
- To demonstrate accountability for expenditures. It is important for a broad group to understand the need for accountability and the approach of the WLP staff. This ensures accountability for expenditures on the project.
- To market future projects. From a WLP perspective, it is important to build a database of successful projects to use in demonstrating to others that the training and performance improvement process can add value.

Although this list is comprehensive, there may be other purposes for communicating results. The situation, context, and audience should be considered when addressing any communication purpose.

Planning the Communication

Any successful activity must be carefully planned for it to produce the maximum results. Planning is a crucial component of communicating the results of major programs. The actual planning of the communications is important to ensure that each audience receives the proper information at the right time and that appropriate actions are taken. Three separate issues are important in planning the communication of results.

Communication Policy Issues

In examining the overall learning process, policy issues need to be developed around the communication of results. These range from providing feedback during a project to communicating the ROI from an impact study. Seven different areas will need some attention as the policies are developed:

- What will actually be communicated? It is important to detail the types of information communicated throughout the project—including the six types of data from the ROI model—but the overall progress with the learning process may be a topic of communications as well. It is also wise to include criteria on communicating around sensitive issues.
- When will the data be communicated? With communications, timing is critical. If adjustments in the program need to be made, the information should be communicated quickly so that swift actions can be taken.

- How will the information be communicated? This addresses the preferences for particular types of communication media. For example, some organizations prefer to have written documents sent out as reports, while others prefer face-to-face meetings, and still others want electronic communications used as much as possible.
- Where should the information be communicated? Some prefer that the face-to-face communication take place close to the sponsor; others prefer the training department offices. The location can be an important issue in terms of convenience and perception.
- Who will communicate the information? Will the WLP staff, an independent consultant, or an individual from the sponsor's office communicate the information? The person communicating must have credibility and must be viewed as objective.
- Who is the target audience? Specific target audiences that should always receive information must be identified, as are others who will receive information when appropriate.
- What specific actions are required or desired? When information is presented, in some cases no action is needed; in others, changes are desired and sometimes even required.

Collectively these seven issues frame the policy around communication as a whole.

Planning the Communication around the Complete Project

When a major project is approved, the communication plan is usually developed. This details how specific information is developed and communicated to various groups and the expected actions. In addition, this plan details how the overall results will be communicated, the time frames for communication, and the appropriate groups to receive information. The WLP team and sponsor need to agree on the extent of detail in the plan. Additional information on this type of planning is provided later.

Planning the Communication of an Impact Study

This planning component is aimed at presenting the results of an impact study. This occurs when a major program is completed and the detailed results are known. One of the major issues is who should receive the results and in what form. When conducting a study, the target audience is identified when developing the Data Collection Plan. The communication plan for an impact study is more specialized than the plan for the entire project because it involves the final study from the project. Table 8–1 shows the communication plan for a major stress reduction program. Teams were experiencing high levels of stress and, through a variety of intervention activities and subsequent behavior changes, stress began to diminish among the teams.

Five different communication pieces were developed for different audiences. The complete report was an ROI impact study, a 75-page report that served as the historical document for the project. It went to the sponsor, the WLP

Table 8–1

Communication Plan for Program Results

Communication Document	Communication Target(s)	Distribution Method
Complete report with appendices (75 pages)	■ Program sponsor ■ WLP staff ■ Intact team manager	Distribute and discuss in a special meeting
Executive summary (eight pages or less)	■ Senior management in the business units ■ Senior corporate management	Distribute and discuss in routine meeting
General interest overview and summary without the actual ROI calculation (10 pages)	■ Participants	Mail with letter
General interest article (one page)	■ All employees	Publish in company publication
Brochure highlighting program, objectives, and specific results	■ Team leaders with an interest in the program ■ Prospective sponsors	Include with other marketing materials

staff, and the manager of each team involved in the study. An executive summary, a much smaller document, went to some of the higher-level executives. A general-interest overview and summary without the ROI calculation went to the participants. A general-interest article was developed for company publications, and a brochure was developed to show the success of the program. That brochure was used in marketing the same process internally to other teams and served as additional marketing material for the WLP staff. This detailed plan may be part of the overall plan for the assignment but may be fine-tuned during the actual process.

Collectively, these two issues and plans underscore the importance of organizing the communication strategy for a particular program or the overall WLP process in an organization.

Analyzing the Audience for Communications

Preliminary Issues

When planning communication for a particular audience, the following questions should be asked about each potential group:

■ Are they interested in the project?
■ Have their expectations been managed, and do I know what they are?
■ Do they really want to receive the information?
■ Has someone already made a commitment to them about communication?
■ Is the timing right for this audience?

- Are they familiar with the project?
- How do they prefer to have results communicated?
- Do they know the team members?
- Are they likely to find the results threatening?
- Which medium will be most receptive and convincing to this group?

For each target audience, several actions are needed:

- To the greatest extent possible, the WLP staff should know and understand the target audience.
- The WLP staff should find out what information is needed and why. Each group will have its own needs relative to the information desired. Some want detailed information while others want brief information. Rely on the input from others to determine audience needs.
- The WLP staff should try to understand audience bias. Each will have a particular bias or opinion. Some will quickly support the results, whereas others may be skeptical or neutral. The staff should be empathetic and try to understand differing views. With this understanding, communications can be tailored to each group. This is especially important when the potential exists for the audience to react negatively to the results.

Basis for Analyzing the Audience

The potential target audiences for information on results vary by job levels and responsibilities. Determining which groups will receive a particular communication piece deserves careful thought, as problems can arise when a particular group receives inappropriate information or when another is omitted altogether. A sound basis for proper communication is to analyze the reason for communication, as discussed earlier. Table 8–2 shows common target audiences and the basis for selecting the communication.

Perhaps the most important audience is the sponsor, the individual or team supporting the ROI study. This group (or individual) initiates the project, reviews data, and weighs the final assessment of its effectiveness. Another important target audience is the top management group. This group is responsible for allocating resources to the program and needs information to help justify expenditures and to gauge the effectiveness and contribution of the efforts.

Selected groups of managers (or all managers) are also important target audiences. Management's support and involvement in the process and the department's credibility are important to success. Effectively communicating program results to management can increase both support and credibility.

Communicating with the participants' team leaders or immediate managers is essential. In many cases, they must encourage participants to implement the project. Also, they often support and reinforce the objectives of the program and encourage implementation.

Occasionally, results are communicated to encourage participation in the program. This is especially true for voluntary programs. Potential participants are important targets for communicating results.

TABLE 8–2

COMMON TARGET AUDIENCES

Reason for Communication	Primary Target Audiences
To secure approval for the project	Sponsor, top executives
To gain support for the project	Immediate managers, team leaders
To secure agreement with the issues	Participants, team leaders
To build credibility for the learning and performance process	Top executives
To enhance reinforcement of the training process	Immediate managers
To drive action for program and process improvement	Sponsor, WLP staff
To prepare participants for the project	Team leaders
To enhance results and quality of future feedback	Participants
To show the complete results of the project	Sponsor
To underscore the importance of measuring results	Sponsor, WLP staff
To explain techniques used to measure results	Sponsor, support staff
To create desire for a participant to be involved	Participants, team leaders
To stimulate interest among the WLP staff	WLP staff
To demonstrate accountability for expenditures	Top executives
To market future projects	Prospective sponsors

Participants need feedback on the overall success of the effort. Some individuals may not have been as successful as others in achieving the desired results. Communicating the results adds additional pressure to effectively implement the program and improve results for the future. For those achieving excellent results, the communication will serve to reinforce the training process. Communicating results to participants is often overlooked, with the assumption that because the program is complete, they do not need to be informed of its success.

The WLP staff must receive information about program results. Whether for small projects where the WLP staff receives an update, or for larger projects where a complete team is involved, those who design, develop, facilitate, and implement the program must be given information on its effectiveness. Evaluation information is necessary so adjustments can be made if the program is not as effective as it could be.

The support staff should receive detailed information about the process to measure results. This group provides support services to the WLP team, usually in the department.

Company employees and stockholders may be less likely targets. General-interest news stories to this group may increase employee respect. Goodwill and positive attitudes toward the organization may also be by-products of communicating results. Stockholders, on the other hand, are more interested in the return on their investment.

While Table 8–2 shows the most common target audiences, there can be others in a particular organization. For instance, management or employees could be subdivided into different departments, divisions, or even subsidiaries. The number of audiences can be large in a complex organization. At a minimum, four target audiences are always recommended: a senior management group, the participants' immediate manager or team leader, the participants, and the WLP staff.

Developing the Information: The Impact Study

The type of formal evaluation report depends on the extent of detailed information presented to the various target audiences. Brief summaries of results with appropriate charts may be sufficient for some communication efforts. For others, particularly those for significant programs requiring extensive funding, the amount of detail in the evaluation report is more extensive. A complete and comprehensive impact study report may be necessary. This report can then be used as the basis of information for specific audiences and various media. The report may contain the following sections.

Executive Summary

The executive summary is a brief overview of the entire report, explaining the basis for the evaluation and significant conclusions and recommendations. It is designed for individuals who are too busy to read a detailed report. It is usually written last but appears first in the report for easy access.

Background Information

The background information section provides a general description of the project. If applicable, it summarizes the needs assessment that led to the implementation of the project. The program is fully described, including the events that led to the intervention. Other specific items necessary to provide a full description of the project are included. The amount of detail depends on the amount of information the audience needs.

Objectives

The objectives for both the impact study and the actual training program are outlined. Sometimes they are the same, but they may be different. The report details the particular objectives of the study itself so that the reader clearly understands the study's rationale and how the data will be used. In addition, the specific objectives of the training program are detailed, as these are the objectives from which the different types or levels of data will be collected.

Evaluation Strategy/Methodology

The evaluation strategy outlines all the components that make up the total evaluation process. This section of the report discusses several components of the results-based model and the ROI Methodology presented in this fieldbook. The specific purposes of evaluation are outlined, and the evaluation design and methodology are explained. The instruments used in data collection are also described and presented as exhibits. Any unusual issues in the evaluation design are discussed. Finally, other useful information related to the design, timing, and execution of the evaluation is included.

Data Collection and Analysis

This section explains the methods used to collect data, as outlined in earlier chapters. The data collected are usually presented in the report in summary form. Next, the methods used to analyze the data are presented with interpretations.

Program Costs

Program costs are presented in this section. A summary of the costs by category is included. For example, analysis, development, implementation, and evaluation costs are recommended categories for cost presentation. The assumptions made in developing and classifying costs are discussed in this section of the report. It should be clear to those reviewing the report that the costs are fully loaded.

Reaction and Satisfaction

This section details the data collected from key stakeholders, particularly the participants in the process, to measure reactions to the program and levels of satisfaction with various issues and parts of the process. Other input from the sponsor or managers may be included to show the levels of satisfaction.

Learning

This section describes the formal and informal methods for measuring learning. It explains how participants have learned new processes, skills, tasks, procedures, and practices.

Application and Implementation

This section shows how the project was actually implemented and the success of the application of new skills and knowledge. Implementation issues are addressed, including any major successes and/or failures.

Business Impact

This section shows the actual business impact measures representing the business needs that initially drove the project. This shows the extent to which performance has changed during the implementation of the program. This data is always shown as a buildup to the ROI calculation.

Return on Investment

This section actually shows the ROI calculation, along with the benefits/cost ratio. It compares the value with what was expected and interprets the actual calculation. A short write-up on the interpretation of the ROI should reinforce how the 12 standards were applied to develop a conservative ROI.

Intangible Measures

This section shows the various intangible measures directly linked to the training program. Intangibles are those measures not converted to monetary values and not included in the actual ROI calculation. The intangibles should be communicated along with the ROI. It should be emphasized that they were not part of the calculation and can only serve to increase the ROI.

Barriers and Enablers

The various problems and obstacles affecting the success of the project are detailed and presented as barriers to implementation. Also, those factors or influences that had a positive effect on the project are included as enablers. Together, they provide tremendous insight into what can hinder or enhance projects in the future.

Conclusions and Recommendations

This section presents conclusions based on all the results. If appropriate, brief explanations are presented on how each conclusion was reached. A list of recommendations or changes in the program or training process, if appropriate, is provided with brief explanations for each recommendation. It is important that the conclusions and recommendations are consistent with one another and with the findings described in the previous sections of the report.

These components make up the major parts of a complete evaluation report.

Developing the Report

Figure 8–1 shows the format of a typical evaluation report for an ROI evaluation. Additionally, Part F of the PMI Case Study is an example of an actual report. It will be useful to review Part F.

Although this format illustrates an effective, professional way to present ROI data, several cautions need to be exercised. Because this document reports the success of a group of employees, complete credit for the success must go to the participants and their immediate leaders. Their performance generated the success. The training process helped to enable the success. Another important caution is to avoid boasting about results. Although the ROI Methodology may be accurate and credible, it still may have some subjective components. Huge claims of success can quickly turn off an audience and interfere with the delivery of the desired message.

FIGURE 8–1
FORMAT OF IMPACT STUDY REPORT

A typical report for the client usually includes the topics outlined next:

- Executive summary
- General information
  - Background
  - Objectives of study
- Methodology for impact study
  - Levels of evaluation
  - ROI process
  - Collecting data
  - Isolating the effects of training
  - Converting data to monetary values
  - Assumptions

  } Builds credibility for the process

- Data analysis issues
- Program costs
- Results: general information
  - Response profile
  - Success with objectives
- Results: reaction and satisfaction
  - Data sources
  - Data summary
  - Key issues
- Results: learning
  - Data sources
  - Data summary
  - Key issues
- Results: application and implementation
  - Data sources
  - Data summary
  - Key issues
- Results: business impact
  - General comments
  - Linkage with business measures
  - Key issues
- Results: ROI and its meaning
- Results: intangible measures

  } The results with six measures: Levels 1, 2, 3, 4, 5, and intangibles

- Barriers and enablers
  - Barriers
  - Enablers
- Conclusions and recommendations
  - Conclusions
  - Recommendations
- Exhibits

A final caution concerns the structure of the report. The methodology should be clearly explained, along with assumptions made in the analysis. The reader should readily see how data were collected from credible sources, how the values were developed, and how the specific steps were followed to make the process more conservative, credible, and accurate. Any detailed statistical analyses required should be placed in the appendix.

Selecting the Communication Media

Many options for communicating program results are available. In addition to the impact study report, the most frequently used media are meetings, interim and progress reports, the organization's publications, e-mail, brochures, and case studies.

Meetings

In addition to the meeting with the sponsor to discuss results, other meetings are fertile opportunities for communicating program results. All organizations have a variety of meetings and, in each, the proper context and consulting results are an important part. A few examples illustrate the variety of meetings.

Staff Meetings
Throughout the chain of command, staff meetings are held to review progress, discuss current problems, and distribute information. These meetings can be an excellent forum for discussing the results achieved in a major training program when it relates to the group's activities. Program results can be sent to executives for use in staff meetings, or a member of the WLP team can attend the meeting to make the presentation.

Manager Meetings
Regular meetings with the first-level management group are quite common. Typically, items that will possibly help their work units are discussed. A discussion of a training program and the subsequent results can be integrated into the regular meeting format.

Best Practices Meetings
Some organizations have best practices meetings or videoconferences to discuss recent successes and best practices. This is an excellent opportunity to learn and share methodologies and results.

Business Update Meetings
A few organizations have initiated a periodic meeting for all members of management, in which the CEO reviews progress and discusses plans for the coming year. A few highlights of major program results can be integrated into the CEO's speech, showing top executive interest, commitment, and support. Results are mentioned along with operating profit, new facilities and equipment, new company acquisitions, and next year's sales forecast.

Interim and Progress Reports

Although usually limited to large projects, a highly visible way to communicate results is through interim and routine memos and reports. Published or disseminated via the intranet on a periodic basis, they usually have several purposes:

- To inform management about the status of the project.
- To communicate the interim results achieved in the program.
- To activate needed changes and improvements.

A more subtle reason for the report is to manage expectations, gain additional support and commitment from the management group, and keep the project intact. This report is produced by the WLP staff and distributed to a select group of managers. Format and scope vary considerably. Common topics are presented here.

Schedule of Activities. A schedule of planned steps/activities should be an integral part of this report. A brief description should be presented.

Reactions from Participants. A brief summary of reaction evaluations may be appropriate to report initial success. Also, brief interviews with participants might be included.

Results. A key focus of this report is progress toward results. Significant results that can be documented should be presented in an easily understood format. The method(s) of evaluation should be briefly outlined, along with the measurement data.

Change in Responsibility. Occasionally, people involved in planning, developing, implementing, or evaluating the program are reassigned, transferred, or promoted. It is important to communicate how these changes affect responsibilities and the program.

Participant Spotlight. A section that highlights a participant can focus additional attention on results. This is an opportunity to recognize outstanding participants responsible for excellent results and bring attention to unusual achievements.

Although this list may not be suited for every report, it represents topics that should be presented to the management group. When produced in a professional manner, the report can improve management support and commitment to the effort.

The Organization's Publications and Standard Communication Tools

To reach a wide audience, the WLP staff can use in-house publications. Whether a newsletter, magazine, newspaper, or electronic file, these types of media usually reach all employees. The information can be quite effective if communicated appropriately. The scope should be limited to general-interest articles, announcements, and interviews. Following are types of issues that should be covered in these publications.

Program Results

Results communicated through these types of media must be significant enough to arouse general interest. For example, a story with the headline "Safety Training Program Helps Produce One Million Hours Without a Lost-Time Accident" will catch the attention of many people because they may have participated in the program and can appreciate the significance of the results. Reports on the accomplishments of a small group of participants may not create interest unless the audience can relate to the accomplishments.

For many training implementations, results are achieved weeks or even months after the project is completed. Participants need reinforcement from many sources. If results are communicated to a general audience, including the participant's subordinates or peers, there is additional pressure to continue the project or similar ones in the future.

Participant Recognition

General-audience communication can bring recognition to participants, particularly those who excel in some aspect of the project. When participants deliver unusual performance, public recognition can enhance their self-esteem. An interesting example of this took place recently in one organization in China. The program coordinator for a soft skill program required 30 participants to write an article four months after program completion to communicate how they had successfully implemented the skills. The top 15 articles were judged on a set of criteria and published in the organization's monthly news magazine.

Human Interest Stories

Many human interest stories can come out of major training programs. A rigorous program with difficult requirements can provide the basis for an interesting story on participants who implement the program.

In one organization, the editor of the company newsletter participated in a very demanding training program and wrote a stimulating article about what it was like to be a participant. The article gave the reader a tour of the entire program and its effectiveness in terms of the results achieved. It was an interesting and effective way to communicate about a challenging activity.

The benefits are many and the opportunities endless for WLP staff to utilize in-house publications and companywide intranets to let others know about the success of programs.

E-mail and Electronic Media

Internal and external Web pages on the Internet, companywide intranets, and e-mail are excellent vehicles for releasing results, promoting ideas, and informing employees and other target groups about results. E-mail, in particular, provides a virtually instantaneous means of communicating and soliciting response from large numbers of people.

Brochures and Pamphlets

A brochure might be appropriate for programs conducted on a continuing basis in which participants have produced excellent results. It should be attractive and present a complete description of the program, with a major section devoted to results obtained with previous participants, if available. Measurable results and reactions from participants, or even direct quotes from individuals, could add spice to an otherwise dull brochure.

Case Studies

Case studies represent an effective way to communicate the results of a training program. Consequently, it is recommended that a few evaluation projects be developed in a case format. A typical case study describes the situation, provides appropriate background information (including the events that led to the intervention), presents the techniques and strategies used to develop the study, and highlights the key issues in the program. Case studies tell an interesting story of how the evaluation was developed and the problems and concerns identified along the way.

Case studies have many useful applications. First, they can be used in group discussions, in which interested individuals can react to the material, offer different perspectives, and draw conclusions about approaches or techniques. Second, the case study can serve as a self-teaching guide for individuals trying to understand how evaluations are developed and used in the organization. Finally, case studies provide appropriate recognition for those involved in the actual case. More important, they recognize the participants who achieved the results, as well as the managers who supported the participants' involvement in the program. The case study format has become one of the most effective ways to learn about project evaluation.

A Case Example

These various methods for communicating program results can be creatively combined to fit any situation. Here is an effective example using three approaches: a case study, management meetings, and a brochure.

The production unit had achieved outstanding results through the efforts of a team of two supervisors. The results were in the form of key bottom-line measures, such as absenteeism, turnover, lost-time accidents, grievances, scrap rate, and unit hour. The unit hour was a basic measure of individual productivity.

These results were achieved through the efforts of the supervisors applying the basic skills taught in a supervisor-training program. This fact was discreetly mentioned at the beginning of a presentation made by the supervisors. In a panel discussion format with a moderator, the two supervisors outlined how they achieved results. It was presented in a question-and-answer session at a monthly meeting for all supervisors. They mentioned that many of the skills were acquired in the training program.

The comments were published in a brochure and distributed to all supervisors through their department managers. The title of the publication was "Getting Results: A Success Story." On the inside cover, specific results were detailed, along with additional information on the supervisors. A close-up photograph of each supervisor, taken during the panel discussion, was included on this page. The next two pages presented a summary of the techniques used to secure the results. The pamphlet was used in staff meetings as a discussion guide to cover the points from the panel discussion. Top executives were also sent copies. In addition, the discussion was videotaped and used in subsequent training programs as a model of application of skills. The pamphlet served as a handout.

The communication effort was a success. Favorable responses were received from all levels of management. Top executives asked the WLP department to prepare and conduct similar meetings. Other supervisors began to use more of the skills and techniques presented by the two supervisors.

Communicating the Information

Perhaps the greatest challenge of communication is the actual delivery of the message. This can be accomplished in a variety of ways and settings based on the target audience and the media selected. Three approaches deserve additional coverage. The first is providing insight into how to give feedback throughout the project to make sure information flows and changes can be made. The second is presenting an impact study to a senior management team. This may be one of the most challenging tasks for the evaluator. The third is communicating regularly and routinely with the executive management group. Each of these three approaches is explored in more detail.

Providing Feedback

One of the most important reasons for collecting reaction, satisfaction, and learning data is to provide feedback so adjustments or changes can be made throughout the program. In most training programs, data is routinely collected and quickly communicated to a variety of groups. Figure 8–2 shows a feedback action plan designed to provide information to several feedback audiences using a variety of media.

As the plan shows, data are collected during the project at four specific time intervals and communicated back to at least four audiences—and sometimes six. Some of these feedback sessions result in identifying specific actions that need to be taken. This process becomes comprehensive and needs to be managed in a very proactive way. The following steps are recommended for providing feedback and managing the feedback process.

- *Communicate quickly*. Whether the news is good or bad, it is important to let individuals involved in the project have the information as soon as possible. The recommended time for providing feedback is usually a matter of days, certainly no longer than a week or two after the results are known.

Figure 8-2
Feedback Action Plan

Data Collection Item	Timing	Feedback Audience	Media	Timing of Feedback	Action Required
1. Pre-program survey ■ Climate/environment ■ Issue identification	Beginning of the project	Participants Team leaders WLP staff	Meeting Survey summary Survey summary Meeting	One week Two weeks Two weeks One week	None None Communicate feedback Adjust approach
2. Implementation survey ■ Reaction to plans ■ Issue identification	Beginning of actual implementation	Participants Team leaders WLP staff	Meeting Survey summary Survey summary Meeting	One week Two weeks Two weeks One week	None None Communicate feedback Adjust approach
3. Implementation reaction survey/interviews ■ Reaction to solution ■ Suggested changes	One month into implementation	Participants Support staff Team leaders Immediate managers WLP staff	Meeting Study summary Study summary Study summary Meeting	One week Two weeks Two weeks Two weeks Three weeks Three days	Comments None None Support changes Support changes Adjust approach
4. Implementation feedback questionnaire ■ Reaction (satisfaction) ■ Barriers ■ Projected success	End of implementation	Participants Support staff Team leaders Immediate managers WLP staff	Meeting Study summary Study summary Study summary Study summary Meeting	One week Two weeks Two weeks Two weeks Three weeks Three days	Comments None None Support changes Support changes Adjust approach

- *Simplify the data.* Condense data into an understandable, concise presentation. This is not the format for detailed explanations and analysis.
- *Examine the role of the WLP staff and the sponsor in the feedback situation.* Sometimes the WLP staff member is the judge, and sometimes the jury, prosecutor, defendant, or witness. On the other hand, sometimes the sponsor is the judge, jury, prosecutor, defendant, or witness. It is important to examine the respective roles in terms of reactions to the data and the actions that need to be taken.
- *Use negative data in a constructive way.* Some of the data will show that things are not going so well, and the fault may rest with the WLP staff or the sponsor. In either case, the story basically changes from "Let's look at the success we've experienced" to "Now we know which areas to change."
- *Use positive data in a cautious way.* Positive data can be misleading, and if they are communicated too enthusiastically, they may create expectations beyond what may materialize later. Positive data should be presented in a cautious way—almost in a discounting mode.
- *Choose the language of the meeting and communication very carefully.* Use language that is descriptive, focused, specific, short, and simple. Avoid language that is too judgmental, macro, stereotypical, lengthy, or complex.
- *Ask the sponsor for reactions to the data.* After all, the sponsor is the customer, and the sponsor's reaction is critical.
- *Ask the sponsor for recommendations.* The sponsor may have some very good recommendations of what needs to be changed to keep a project on track or put it back on track if it derails.
- *Use support and confrontation carefully.* These two issues are not mutually exclusive. There may be times when support and confrontation are needed for the same group. The sponsor may need support and yet be confronted for lack of improvement or sponsorship. The WLP staff may be confronted on the problem areas that are developed but may need support as well.
- *React and act on the data.* Weigh the different alternatives and possibilities to arrive at the necessary adjustments and changes.
- *Secure agreement from all key stakeholders.* This is essential to make sure everyone is willing to make adjustments and changes that seem necessary.
- *Keep the feedback process short.* Don't let it become bogged down in long, drawn-out meetings or lengthy documents. If this occurs, stakeholders will avoid the process instead of being willing to participate in the future.

Following these steps will help move the project forward and provide important feedback, often ensuring that adjustments are supported and made.

Presenting Impact Study Data to Senior Management

Perhaps one of the most challenging and stressful company communications is presenting an impact study to the senior management team when the team also serves as the sponsor on a project. The challenge is convincing this highly skeptical and critical group that outstanding results have been achieved (assuming they have) in a very reasonable time frame, addressing the salient points, and making sure the managers understand the process. Two particular issues can create challenges. First, if the results are very impressive, it may be difficult to convince managers to believe the data. On the other extreme, if the data are negative, it will be a challenge to make sure managers don't overreact to the negative results and look for someone to blame. Following are guidelines that can help make sure this process is planned and executed properly:

- Plan a face-to-face meeting with senior team members for the first one or two major impact studies, as detailed in Figure 8–3. If they are unfamiliar with the ROI Methodology, a face-to-face meeting is necessary to make sure they understand the process. The good news is that they will probably attend the meeting because they have not seen ROI data developed for training or performance improvement. The bad news is that it takes a lot of time, usually an hour for this presentation.
- After a group has had a face-to-face meeting with a couple of presentations, an executive summary may suffice for the next three to five studies. At this point they understand the process, so a shortened version may be appropriate.
- After the target audience is familiar with the process, a brief version may be necessary, which will involve a one- to two-page summary with charts or graphs showing all six types of measures. Figure 8–4 shows a sample of a one-page summary.
- When making the initial presentation, distribute the results at the end of the session. This will allow enough time to present the process and obtain reaction to it before the target audience sees the actual ROI number.
- Present the process step by step, showing how the data were collected, when they were collected, who provided the data, how the data were isolated from other influences, and how they were converted to monetary values. The various assumptions, adjustments, and conservative approaches are presented along with the total cost of the program. The costs are fully loaded

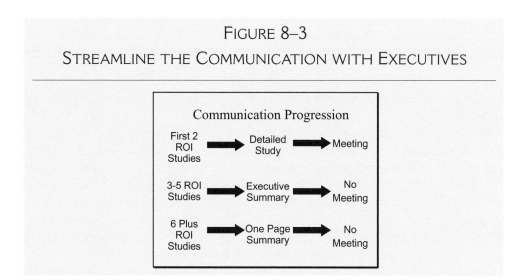

FIGURE 8–3

STREAMLINE THE COMMUNICATION WITH EXECUTIVES

FIGURE 8–4

SAMPLE STREAMLINED REPORT

ROI Impact Study

Program Title: Preventing Sexual Harassment at Healthcare, Inc.

Target Audience: First and Second Level Managers (655); Secondary: All employees through group meetings facilitated by supervisors (6,844).

Duration: 1 day, 17 sessions

Technique to Isolate Effects of Program: Trend analysis; participant estimation

Technique to Convert Data to Monetary Value: Historical costs; internal experts from Legal department and Employee Concerns department

Fully-loaded Program Costs: $277,987 (included participant salaries and benefits)

Results

Level 1: Reaction	Level 2: Learning	Level 3: Application	Level 4: Impact	Level 5: ROI	Intangible Benefits
93% of participants provided action items	65% increase post-test vs. pre-test Skill practice demonstration	96% conducted meetings and completed meeting record 4.1 out of 5 on behavior change survey 68% report all action items complete 92% report some action items complete	Turnover reduction: $2,840,632 Complaint reduction: $360,276 Total improvement: $3,200,908	1,051%	Job satisfaction Reduced absenteeism Stress reduction Better recruiting

so that the target audience will begin to buy into the process of developing the actual ROI.

- When the data are actually presented, the results are presented step by step, starting with Level 1, moving through Level 5, and ending with the intangibles. This allows the audience to see the chain of impact with reaction and satisfaction, learning, application and implementation, business impact, and ROI. After some discussion on the meaning of the ROI, the intangible measures are presented. See Job Aid 8–1 on the Chapter 8 folder on the CD for a template in explaining the conservative approach to calculating the ROI. Allocate time to each level, as appropriate, for the audience. This helps overcome the potentially negative reactions to a very positive or negative ROI.

THE ROI CONSERVATIVE APPROACH

As you finalize your report, include a section (ROI Interpretation) that addresses the conservative nature of the data collection, analysis, and reporting. Consider including statements similar to those in this Job Aid as may be applicable. Placement of this section or these statements in your report should be close to the ROI calculation and results data.

The participants provided the information voluntarily and the questionnaire was anonymous. There was no pressure to provide a certain type of data. In addition, specific guidelines have been followed to produce more realistic and conservative estimates. For example:

A. The total benefits are based only on the data furnished by the participants and other appropriate organization resources.

B. Participants who did not furnish data are assumed to have no improvement and are not included in the benefits portion of the ROI calculation, but they are included in the cost component of the ROI formula.

C. The costs are fully loaded, including estimated salaries and benefits for each participant for the time the participants were in training and, where appropriate, opportunity costs are included.

D. The value of improvements is reduced to reflect the percentage that participants link the results directly to the program.

E. Where estimates are used, the values are adjusted to reflect the confidence level. Each value is reduced by the respective confidence percentage. For example, if a participant reports a $60,000 improvement with an 80% confidence level, the participant is suggesting a potential 20% error in the estimation. The value could be in the range of $48,000 to $72,000. The $48,000 value is used to be conservative.

F. Only the first year values for benefits are used, although there clearly can be second- and third-year benefits.

G. With these adjustments and considerations outlined above, it is highly probable that the ROI is understated.

The formula used for the ROI is the same basic calculation used to evaluate other investments such as investments in equipment and facilities. Thus, the hurdle rates used for other investments could be compared to percentages in this study. However, because this process is not precise, a higher hurdle rate is often suggested. For most organizations involved in calculating return on investments in training programs, a target rate of 25% is established. Thus, if a program is not generating at least a 25% return on investment in the first year, it may be considered to be an undesirable investment, unless the intangible benefits become a strong consideration or there are other compelling mitigating factors.

- Show the consequences of additional accuracy if it is an issue. The trade-off for more accuracy and validity often means more expense and more time dedicated to the evaluation project. Address this issue whenever necessary, agreeing to add more data if required.
- Collect concerns, reactions, and issues for the process and make adjustments accordingly for the next presentation.

Collectively, these steps will help prepare for and present one of the most critical meetings in the ROI process.

Communicating with Executive Management and Sponsors

No group is more important than top executives when it comes to communicating results. In many situations, this group is also the sponsor. Improving communications with this group requires developing an overall strategy, which may include all or part of the actions outlined next.

- Strengthen the relationship with executives. An informal and productive relationship should be established between the WLP manager (responsible for the project evaluation) and the top executive at the location where the project is taking place. Each should feel comfortable discussing needs and project results. One approach is to establish frequent, informal meetings with the executive to review problems with current projects and discuss other performance problems/opportunities in the organization. Frank and open discussions can provide the executive with insight not possible from any other source. Also, it can be very helpful to the WLP manager to determine corrective steps and strategic direction.
- Show how training programs have helped solve major problems. Although hard results from recent projects are comforting to an executive, solutions to immediate problems may be more convincing. This is an excellent opportunity to discuss possible future programs for ROI evaluation.
- Distribute memos on project results. When an intervention has achieved significant results, make appropriate top executives aware of them. This can easily be done with a brief memo or summary outlining what the project was supposed to accomplish, when it was implemented, who was involved, and the results achieved. This should be presented in a for-your-information format that consists of facts rather than opinions. A full report may be presented later.
- All significant communication on training evaluation projects, plans, activities, and results should include the executive group. Frequent information on the projects, as long as it is not boastful, can reinforce credibility and accomplishments.
- Ask the executive to be involved in the review. An effective way to enhance commitment from top executives is to ask them to serve on a training review committee. A review committee provides input and advice to the WLP staff on a variety of issues, including needs, problems with the present project, and project evaluation issues. This committee can be helpful in letting executives know what the projects are achieving.

Analyzing Reactions to Communication

The best indicator of how effectively the results of a training program have been communicated is the level of commitment and support from the management group. The allocation of requested resources and strong commitment from top management are tangible evidence of management's perception of the results. In addition to this macrolevel reaction, there are a few techniques the WLP staff can use to measure the effectiveness of their communication efforts.

Whenever results are communicated, the reaction of the target audiences can be monitored. These reactions may include nonverbal gestures, oral remarks, written comments, or indirect actions that reveal how the communication was received. Usually, when results are presented in a meeting, the presenter will have some indication of how the group received the results. The interest and attitudes of the audience can usually be quickly assessed.

During the presentation, questions may be asked or, in some cases, the information is challenged. A tabulation of these challenges and questions can be useful in evaluating the type of information to include in future communications. Positive comments about the results are desired and, when they are made—formally or informally—they should also be noted and tabulated.

WLP staff meetings are an excellent arena for discussing the reaction to communicating results. Comments can come from many sources depending on the particular target audiences. Input from different members of the staff can be summarized to help judge the overall effectiveness.

When major program results are communicated, a feedback questionnaire may be used for an audience or a sample of the audience. The purpose of this questionnaire is to determine the extent to which the audience understood and/or viewed the information as credible. This is practical only when the effectiveness of the communication has a significant impact on future actions.

Another approach is to survey the management group to determine its perceptions of the results. Specific questions should be asked about results. What does the management group know about the results? How credible are the results? What additional information is desired about the project? This type of survey can help provide guidance in communicating results.

The purpose of analyzing reactions is to make adjustments in the communication process—if adjustments are necessary. Although the reactions may involve intuitive assessments, a more sophisticated analysis will provide more accurate information to make these adjustments. The net result should be a more effective communication process.

POTENTIAL CHALLENGES

Several areas present challenges in reporting results. Sometimes it is difficult to get the time you need to present results to your audience, especially if it is an executive group. Or the meeting may be postponed, which throws off the desired timing. First-time reporting is also a challenge because of the need to explain the methodology and the concern of exploring unknown territory. You must remember that what may seem obvious or simple to you may not be so for your audience.

Another significant challenge occurs when the ROI is a large value (for example 500% or greater). A large ROI can create skeptics and divert attention away from the results and more toward the costs and the evaluation methodology. The guiding principles are your best friend when this occurs along with a needs assessment that indicated a significant performance gap.

ACTION STEPS

- Review and complete Exercise 8–1, National Electric Impact Study Results on the Chapter 8 folder of the CD.
- Review Part F of Premier Motors Case Study on the Chapter 8 folder of CD. This will provide more insight on reporting your results.

EXERCISE 8–1. NATIONAL ELECTRIC IMPACT STUDY RESULTS

Review and critically analyze this report, which was presented to the executive group at National Electric. Is it credible? What type of information is missing that would add to the credibility?

_____

_____

_____

National Electric: Business Impact Report: *Workflow Planning and Management Course*

Background Information

In August 2005, National Electric executives and administrative officers participated in a two-day course, *Workflow Planning and Management*. The purpose of the training was to deliver a planning and execution process to handle the volume of communication, workflow, and projects.

Four months after the program, the training function administered a follow-up questionnaire to the 60 participants to evaluate the success of the training in measurable business contribution to National Electric's overall strategic goals, including a return on investment (ROI).

The participants were asked to indicate their application of what they learned, to evaluate the impact at their worksite, and to estimate time saved daily as a result of the training. Forty-two participants (70%) responded to the questionnaire with both tangible and intangible results.

Intangible Benefits

- Sharing lessons learned from the training with others
- Experiencing less stress about work because of being better organized

Tangible Benefits—Return on Investment (ROI)

- 42 respondents reported 30 minutes saved per person per day (1 person × 240 days per year = 120 hours per year saved)
- 120 hrs/year × $55.00 avg. salary per hour × 42 respondents = $277,200 saved in a year
- Program costs were $92,000

$$ROI = \frac{277,200 - 92,000}{92,000} \times 100 = 201\%$$

- 201% return is a conservative estimate is based on data from only the 42 respondents. The savings would be considerably higher if estimated for all 60 participants.

Conclusion

- The *Workflow Planning and Management* course made a difference in the workplace for the participants and was worth the cost. The return on our investment was excellent.
- The training helped employees save time during their workday, addressing a major problem of inefficiency.
- Respondents reported new skills in the workplace and reported less stress because of being better organized as a result of this training.

CHAPTER SUMMARY

This chapter presented the final step in the ROI model. Communicating results is a crucial step in the overall evaluation process. If this step is not taken seriously, the full impact of the results will not be realized. The general principles presented in this chapter for communicating program results should be followed when developing your study report or other communication. Identifying the target audience and their expectations about the program and the evaluation project should be accomplished early in the process. A suggested format for a detailed evaluation report is provided. Selecting the media for communicating program results is an important step in achieving your communication goals.

REFERENCES AND RESOURCES

Hodges, Toni, ed., and Jack J. Phillips, series ed. *In Action: Measuring Learning and Performance.* Alexandria, VA: ASTD, 1999.

Langdon, Danny G. *The New Language of Work.* Amherst, MA: HRD Press, 1995.

Phillips, Jack J. *Handbook of Training Evaluation and Measurement Methods,* 3rd ed. Woburn, MA: Butterworth-Heinemann, 1997.

Phillips, Jack J., ed. *In Action: Measuring Return on Investment,* Volume 2. Alexandria, VA: ASTD, 1997.

Phillips, Jack J., ed. *In Action: Implementing Evaluation Systems and Processes.* Alexandria, VA: ASTD, 1998.

Phillips, Jack J. *In Action: Performance Analysis and Consulting.* Alexandria, VA: ASTD, 1999.

Phillips, Jack J. *Return on Investment in Training and Performance Improvement Programs,* 2nd ed. Woburn, MA: Butterworth-Heinemann, 2003.

Phillips, Jack J., and Patricia Pulliam Phillips. *ROI at Work: Best-Practice Case Studies from the Real World.* Alexandria, VA: ASTD, 2005.

Phillips, Patricia Pulliam, ed., and Jack J. Phillips, series ed. *In Action: Measuring Return on Investment,* Volume 3. Alexandria, VA: ASTD, 2001.

Phillips, Patricia Pulliam, ed., and Jack J. Phillips, series ed. *In Action: Measuring ROI in the Public Sector.* Alexandria, VA: ASTD, 2002.

Sujansky, J. C. *The Power of Partnering.* San Diego, CA: Pfeiffer & Co., 1991.

Torres, R. T., H. S. Preskill, and M. E. Piontek. *Evaluation Strategies for Communicating and Reporting: Enhancing Learning in Organizations.* Thousand Oaks, CA: Sage Publications, 1996.

Tufte, E. R. *Envisioning Information.* Cheshire, CT: Graphics Press, 1990.

Zelazny, G. *Say It with Charts: The Executive's Guide to Visual Communication,* 3rd ed. New York: McGraw-Hill, 1996.

CD

Exercises and Case Study	Tools, Templates, and Job Aids
Exercise 8–1. National Electric Impact Study Results Case Study—Part F, Premier Motors International (PMI)	Figure 8–1. Format of Impact Study Report Figure 8–2. Feedback Action Plan Figure 8–3. Streamline the Communication with Executives Figure 8–4. Sample Streamlined Report Table 8–1. Communication Plan for Program Results Table 8–2. Common Target Audiences Job Aid 8–1. ROI Conservative Approach

FORECASTING
THE ROI

Forecasting an ROI is becoming essential in the measurement and evaluation scheme. Forecasting is inherently inaccurate, and its limitations need to be clearly understood by those involved. However, with proper attention, resources, and strategies, forecasting provides a credible indication of potential program success. Although forecasting may lack accuracy, it is relatively inexpensive. This chapter explores the four most likely time frames when forecasting can be conducted, as well as the most credible sources of forecast data and the strengths and weaknesses of forecasting.

In this chapter you will learn:

- ❑ The various time frames for creating forecasts.
- ❑ The most credible sources of forecast data.
- ❑ The strengths and weaknesses of forecasting.

THE FUNDAMENTALS

ROI can be developed at different times using different levels of data. Unfortunately, the ease, convenience, and low cost of capturing a forecasted ROI creates trade-offs in accuracy and credibility. Figure 9–1 depicts the trade-offs between preprogram ROI forecasts and postprogram ROI evaluation. The relationship of timing with credibility, accuracy, cost, and level of difficulty are shown. Credibility and accuracy are greater with postprogram ROI evaluation, yet ease and cost effectiveness are greater using the preprogram forecast.

Five distinct time frames are shown during which ROI can be developed. The time intervals are:

1. *A preprogram forecast.* The preprogram forecast can be developed using estimates of the impact of the training program. This approach lacks

FIGURE 9–1

ROI AT DIFFERENT TIMES AND LEVELS

ROI with:	Data Collection Timing (Relative to Program Implementation)	Credibility	Accuracy	Cost to Develop	Difficulty
1. Preprogram data	Before program	Not very credible	Not very accurate	Inexpensive	Not difficult
2. Reaction and satisfaction data	During program				
3. Learning data	During program				
4. Application and implementation	After program				
5. Business impact data	After program	Very credible	Very accurate	Expensive	Very difficult

credibility and accuracy, but it is also the least expensive and least difficult ROI to calculate.

2. *When reaction and satisfaction data are collected.* Level 1 data collection instruments can be extended to develop an anticipated impact, including the ROI. In this case, participants actually anticipate the chain of impact as the knowledge and skills from the program are applied and influence specific business measures. Although the accuracy and credibility of the forecast at this time are greater than for the preprogram forecast, this approach still lacks the credibility and accuracy usually desired.

3. *When learning data are collected.* For some programs, Level 2 data can be used to forecast the ROI. This approach is applicable only when formal testing shows a relationship between acquiring certain skills or knowledge and subsequent business performance. When this correlation is available (it is usually developed to validate the test), test data can be used to forecast subsequent performance. The performance can then be converted to monetary impact and the ROI can be developed. This has less potential as an evaluation tool because of a predictive validation can only infrequently be developed.

4. *When application and implementation data are collected.* When frequency of skills and actual use of skills are crucial, the application and implementation of those skills or knowledge can sometimes be converted to a value using employee compensation as a basis. This is particularly helpful when competencies are being developed and values are placed on improving competencies, even if there is no immediate increase in pay.

5. *When business impact data are converted to monetary value, then compared to the cost of the program.* This is not a forecast. This postprogram evaluation is the principal approach described in this fieldbook. It is the preferred approach. However, because the ROI often has to be forecasted before implementation (or continued implementation), the other approaches are useful.

Preprogram ROI Forecasting

Perhaps one of the most useful steps in convincing a sponsor that a training expenditure is appropriate is to forecast the project's ROI. The process is similar to the postprogram analysis, except that the extent of the impact must be estimated along with the estimated cost.

Basic Preprogram Model

Figure 9–2 shows the basic model for capturing the necessary data for a preprogram forecast. This model is a modification of the postprogram ROI model, except that data are projected instead of being collected during different time frames. In place of the data collection is an estimation of the change in impact data the training program is expected to influence. Isolating the effects of the training becomes a nonissue because the estimation is focused on the

FIGURE 9–2

PRE-PROGRAM ROI FORECAST MODEL

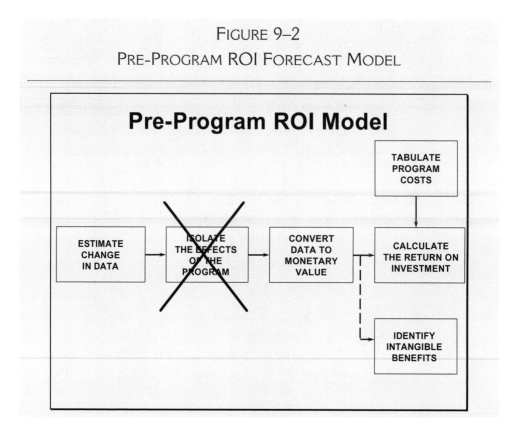

anticipated impact of training only without considering other factors that may come into play.

The method to covert data to monetary values is the same as in postprogram ROI because the data items examined in a pre- and postprogram analysis should be the same. Estimating the program's cost should be an easy step because costs can be anticipated based on previous projects using reasonable assumptions about the current project. The anticipated intangibles are merely speculation in forecasting, but these can be reliable indicators of which measures may be influenced in addition to those included in the ROI calculation. The formula used to calculate the ROI is the same as in the postprogram analysis. The amount of monetary value from the data conversion is included as the numerator, while the estimated cost of the training program is inserted as the denominator.

In a forecasting mode, the problem of isolating the program's effects is not an issue. In this context, the estimates are being made to assess the value of the increased output connected directly to the program. Thus, isolating the effects of the program is not an issue because the estimate itself already isolates the influence of the program only. The projected benefits/costs analysis can be developed along with the actual ROI. The steps to actually develop the process are detailed next.

Steps to Develop the ROI

The detailed steps to develop the preprogram ROI forecast are presented in simplified form below:

1. Develop the Levels 3 and 4 objectives with as many specifics as possible. Ideally, these should be developed from the initial needs analysis and assessment. They detail what will change in the work setting and identify which measures will be influenced. If these are not known, the entire forecasting process is in jeopardy. There must be some assessment of which measures will change as a result of the training, and someone must be able to state the extent to which the measures will change. If not, why is the training even being considered?

2. Estimate or forecast the monthly improvement in the Level 4 business impact data. This is considered to be the amount of change directly related to the intervention and is denoted by ΔP. This is the most difficult step and is examined in more detail in the next section.

3. Convert the business impact data to monetary values using one or more of the methods described in Chapter 5. These are the same techniques, using the same processes as a postprogram analysis; V denotes this value.

4. Develop the estimated annual impact for each measure. In essence, this is the first-year improvement from the training program, showing the value for the change in the business impact measures directly related to the training program. In formula form this is $\Delta I = \Delta P \times V \times 12$, where I is impact, P is performance, and V is value.

5. Factor additional years into the analysis if a program will have a significant useful life beyond the first year. When this is the case, these values may be discounted to reflect a diminished benefit in subsequent years. The sponsor or owner of the program should provide some indication of the amount of the reduction and the values developed for years two, three, and so on. However, it is helpful to be conservative by using the smallest numbers possible.

6. Estimate the fully loaded cost of the program. Using all of the cost categories explained in Chapter 6, the fully loaded cost is estimated and projected for the program. This is denoted as C. Again, all direct and indirect costs should be included in the calculation.

7. Calculate the forecasted ROI using the total projected benefits and the estimated cost in the standard ROI formula:

$$ROI(\%) = \frac{\Delta I - C}{C} \times 100$$

8. Use sensitivity analysis to develop several potential ROI values with different levels of improvement (ΔP). When more than one measure is changing, that analysis would perhaps be performed using a spreadsheet showing different possible scenarios for output and the subsequent ROI.

9. Identify potential intangible benefits by obtaining input from those most knowledgeable about the situation. These are only anticipated and are based on assumptions from previous experience with this type of program.

10. Communicate the ROI projection and anticipated intangibles to stakeholders with caution. Do not allow the projection to be taken out of context. The target audience must clearly understand that this is based on several assumptions (clearly defined), and that the values are the best possible estimates. However, there is still room for error.

These 10 steps enable an individual to forecast the ROI. The most difficult part of the process is the initial estimate of performance improvement. Several sources of data are available for this purpose, as described next.

Sources of Input

When attempting to estimate the actual performance improvement that will be influenced by the training program, multiple sources of input should be considered. The following important possibilities should be explored:

1. Experience in the organization with previous training or similar programs can help form the basis of the estimate. Adapting that breadth of experience can be an important factor as comparisons are rarely, if ever, exact.

2. Data sources may have experience with similar programs in other organizations or in other situations. Here, the experience of the program's designers, developers, and implementers are helpful as they reflect on their experiences with other organizations.

3. The input of external experts who have worked in the field or addressed similar programs in other organizations can be extremely valuable. These may be consultants, suppliers, designers, or others who have earned a reputation as knowledgeable about this type of process in this type of situation.

4. Estimates can be obtained directly from a subject matter expert (SME) in the organization. This is an individual who is very familiar with the internal processes being altered, modified, or improved by the training. Internal SMEs are very knowledgeable and sometimes the most favored source for obtaining conservative estimates.

5. Estimates can be obtained directly from the program sponsor. This is the individual who is ultimately making the purchasing decision and is providing data or input on the anticipated change in a measure linked to the training program. This influential position makes him or her a very credible source.

6. Individuals who are directly involved in the training, often labeled participants, are sometimes in a position to know how much of a measure can be changed or improved with a particular type of program. These individuals understand the processes, procedures, and performance measurements being influenced. Their close proximity to the situation

makes them highly credible and often the most accurate sources for estimating the amount of change.

Collectively, these sources provide an appropriate array of possibilities to help estimate the value of an improvement. This is the weakest link in the ROI forecasting process and deserves the most attention. It is important that the target audience for the forecast understand where the estimates came from, as well as who provided them. Even more important, the target audience must view the sources as credible. Otherwise, the forecasted ROI will have no credibility. Review Exercise 9–1 to help you understand preprogram ROI forecasting.

The obvious strategy requested here is the preprogram forecast. This is not unusual in today's context—executives want some idea of the potential payoff, even if it is only a rough estimate. The groups providing input can vary. The individuals destined for the training, the participants, may be able to provide the input. The manager in the electronics department could provide input. The store manager could provide input. The individual or individuals who conducted the initial analysis and determined that this program may add value could also provide input. A potential supplier of the program is another possibility.

Experienced program designers or organizations that have experienced the same situation may have some input based on previous experience. In this case, the most credible input was from the management group above the store level who wanted to change the current business model and increase customer interaction. Based on their anticipation, combined experience, and initial conversations, they provided estimations of the percent improvement connected to the program. At the same time, the vendor/supplier provided estimates based on their previous work. Also, from the learning and development staff, the analysts who provided the brief needs assessment provided input on the estimate of the sales increase.

Finally, designers who had experience with designing customized sales training programs provided estimates. Collectively, these four inputs created a range from 8% (analysts) to 25% (vendor). The data is presented to the management team with a variety of scenarios that calculate the projected ROI based on the four different estimations. In addition, the breakeven point or zero ROI was developed. Thus, the management team could see the various estimates with their own credibility attached to them and see the point where the program would overcome the cost. This is the preferred way of presenting forecast data. Instead of an absolute estimate, it becomes a range of possibilities with some sensitivity analysis.

Forecasting with a Pilot Program

Although the steps listed above provide a process for estimating the ROI when there is no pilot program, the more favorable forecasting approach is to develop a small-scale pilot project and develop the ROI based on postprogram data. This scenario involves the following five steps:

Situation

Retail Merchandise Company (RMC) is a national chain of 420 stores, located in most major U.S. markets. RMC sells small household items, gifts of all types, electronics, and jewelry, as well as personal accessories. It does not sell clothes or major appliances. RMC executives have been concerned about slow sales growth and were experimenting with several programs to boost sales. One of the concerns focused on the interaction with customers. Sales associates were not actively involved in the sales process, usually waiting for a customer to make a purchasing decision and then proceed with processing the sale. Several store managers had analyzed the situation to determine if more communication with the customer would boost sales. The analysis revealed that the use of very simple techniques to probe and guide the customer to a purchase should boost sales in each store.

The senior executives asked the training and development function to consider a very simple customer interactive skills program for a small group of sales associates. The specific charge from the management team was to forecast the impact and ROI of this proposed program. If the program's forecast showed an increase in sales and represented a significant payoff for RMC, it should be piloted in a small number of stores.

The Proposed Solution

The training and development staff conducted a very brief initial needs assessment and identified five simple skills that would need to be covered in the program. From their analysis, it appeared that the sales associates did not have these skills or were very uncomfortable with using them. A program called "Interactive Selling Skills" was selected—a program with significant use of skill practices. The program included two days of training, in which participants had an opportunity to practice each skill with a fellow classmate, followed by three weeks of on-the-job application. Then, a third and final day of training was planned, including a discussion of problems, issues, barriers, and concerns about using the skills. The program, an existing product from an external training supplier, would be taught by the staff of the training supplier for a predetermined facilitation fee.

1. Which strategy for forecasting should be used?

   _____

   _____

2. Which groups should provide input to the forecast?

   _____

   _____

3. How should the forecast be presented to senior executives?

   _____

   _____

1. As in the previous process, develop Level 3 and 4 objectives.
2. Initiate the program on a very small-scale sample as a pilot program, without all the bells and whistles. This keeps the cost extremely low without sacrificing the fundamentals of the project.
3. Fully implement the program with one or more typical groups of individuals who can benefit from it.
4. Develop the ROI using the ROI model for postprogram analysis. This is the ROI process used in the previous chapters.
5. Finally, decide whether to implement the program throughout the organization based on the results of the pilot program.

Postprogram evaluation of a pilot program provides much more accurate information on which to base decisions about fully implementing the program. Using this scenario, data can be developed using all six types of measures outlined in this fieldbook.

Forecasting with Reaction Data

When reaction data includes participants' planned application of the training, this important data can ultimately be used in forecasting ROI. By detailing how participants plan to use what they have learned and the results they expect to achieve, more valuable evaluation information can be developed. The questions presented in Figure 9–3 illustrate how data are collected with an end-of-program questionnaire for a supervisory training program. Participants are asked to state specifically how they plan to use the knowledge and skills from the program and what results they expect to achieve. They are asked to convert their accomplishments to an annual monetary value and show the basis for developing the values. Participants can moderate their responses with a confidence estimate to make the data more credible while allowing them to reflect their uncertainty with the process.

When tabulating data, the confidence level is multiplied by the annual monetary value, which yields a conservative estimate for use in the data analysis. For example, if a participant estimated that the monetary impact of the program would be $10,000 but is only 50% confident, a $5,000 value is used in the calculations.

To develop a summary of the expected benefits, several steps are taken. First, any data that are incomplete, unusable, extreme, or unrealistic are discarded (Guiding Principle 8).

Next, an adjustment is made for the confidence estimate as previously described. Individual data items are then totaled. Finally, as an optional exercise, the total value is adjusted again by a factor that reflects the subjectivity of the process and the possibility that participants will not achieve the results they anticipate. In many training programs, the participants are very enthusiastic about what they have learned and may be overly optimistic about expected accomplishments. This figure adjusts for this overestimation and can be developed with input from management or established by the training and development staff. In one organization, the benefits are reduced by 50% to develop an even more conservative number to use in the ROI equation. Finally,

FIGURE 9–3

IMPORTANT QUESTIONS TO ASK ON FEEDBACK QUESTIONNAIRES

Planned Improvements

- As a result of this program what specific actions will you take as you apply what you have learned?
  1. _____
  2. _____
  3. _____

- Please indicate what specific measures, outcomes, or projects will change as a result of your actions.
  1. _____
  2. _____
  3. _____

- As a result of the anticipated changes in the above, please estimate (in monetary values) the benefits to your organization over a period of one year.
  $_____

- What is your basis for this estimate?
  _____
  _____

- What confidence, expressed as a percentage, can you put in your estimate? (0% = No Confidence; 100% = Certainty) _____%

the ROI is developed using the net program benefits divided by the program costs. This value, in essence, becomes the expected return on investment, after the two adjustments for accuracy and subjectivity.

Exercise 9–2 helps to illustrate the process of forecasting with Level 1 data. Work the exercise to help clarify any questions about the process.

Only 18 of the 24 participants supplied data (based on the authors' experience, 50–70% of participants will provide usable data on this series of questions). The total cost of the program, including participants' salaries, was $29,000. Prorated development costs were included in the cost figure. The monetary value of the planned improvements is extremely high, reflecting the participants' optimism and enthusiasm at the end of a very effective program. As a first step in the analysis, extreme data items are omitted. Data such as millions, unlimited, and $4 million are discarded, and each remaining value is multiplied by the confidence value and totaled. This adjustment reduces these estimates and increases the credibility of the values. The resulting tabulations yielded a total improvement of $655,125. Because of the subjectivity of the

EXERCISE 9–2. FORECASTING WITH LEVEL 1 DATA

M&H Engineering and Construction Company is involved in the design and construction of large commercial projects such as plants, mills, and municipal water systems. Safety is always a critical issue at M&H and usually commands much management attention. To improve the current level of safety performance, a two-day safety awareness program was initiated. The program focused on safety leadership, safety planning, safety learning programs, safety meetings, accident investigation, policy and procedures, standards, and workers' compensation. Program participants were expected to improve safety performance after completing this learning program. At the end of the two-day program, participants completed a comprehensive reaction questionnaire that asked about specific action items planned as a result of this program and the value of these changes to M&H. In addition, participants were asked to explain the basis for estimates and place a confidence level on them. The first group of participants provided the data shown next.

Participant No.	Estimated Value	Basis	Confidence Level
1	$80,000	Reduction in accidents	90%
2	90,000	OSHA reportable injuries	80%
3	50,000	Accident reduction	100%
4	10,000	First aid visits/visits to doctor	100%
5	50,000	Reduction in lost time injuries	95%
6	Millions	Total accident cost	100%
7	75,000	Workers' compensation	80%
8	7,500	OSHA citations	75%
9	50,000	Reduction in accidents	100%
10	30,000	Workers' compensation	80%
11	150,000	Reduction in total accident costs	90%
12	20,000	OSHA fines/citations	70%
13	40,000	Accident reductions	100%
14	4,000,000	Total cost of safety	95%
15	65,000	Total workers' compensation	50%
16	Unlimited	Accidents	100%
17	45,000	Injuries	90%
18	2,000	Visits to doctor	100%

1. What is your strategy for analyzing this data?

_____

_____

2. How reliable is this data?

_____

_____

3. How could you use this data?

_____

_____

process, the values were adjusted by 50%, an arbitrary discount suggested by the training manager but supported by the program sponsor. This "adjusted" value is $327,563, or $328,000 with rounding. The projected ROI, based on the end-of-program questionnaire, is as follows:

$$\text{ROI} = \frac{\$328,000 - \$29,000}{\$29,000} \times 100 = 1,031\%$$

The training manager communicated these projected values to the CEO but cautioned that the data were very subjective, although they had been adjusted downward twice. The training manager also emphasized that the participants in the program, who should be aware of what they could accomplish, generated the forecasted results. In addition, she mentioned that a follow-up was planned to determine the results that were actually delivered by the group.

A word of caution is in order when using Level 1 ROI data. These calculations are highly subjective and do not reflect the actual extent to which participants apply what they have learned to achieve results. A variety of influences in the work environment can enhance or inhibit the participants' attainment of performance goals. Having high expectations at the end of the program is no guarantee that those expectations will be met. Disappointments are documented regularly in programs throughout the world and are reported in research findings (Kaufman, 2002).

While this process is subjective and possibly unreliable, it does have some usefulness. First, if evaluation must stop at this level, this approach provides more insight into the value of the program than the data from typical reaction questionnaires. Managers will usually find this data more useful than a report stating, "40% of participants rated the program above average." Unfortunately, a high percentage of evaluations stop at this first level of evaluation (Van Buren, 2002). The majority of WLP programs do not enjoy rigorous evaluations at Levels 3 and 4. Reporting Level 1 ROI data is a more useful indication of the potential impact of the program than the alternative of reporting attitudes and feelings about the program and facilitator.

Second, ROI forecast data can form a basis for comparing different presentations of the same program. If one program forecasts an ROI of 300% but another projects 30%, it appears that one program may be more effective than the other. The participants in the first program have more confidence in the planned application of the program material.

Third, collecting this type of data brings increased attention to program outcomes. Participants leave the program with an understanding that specific behavior change is expected, which produces results for the organization. This issue becomes very clear to participants as they anticipate results and convert them to monetary values. Even if this projected improvement is ignored, the exercise is productive because of the important message sent to participants. It helps to change mindsets about the value, impact, and importance of training.

Fourth, if a follow-up is planned to pinpoint postprogram results, the data collected in the Level 1 evaluation can be very helpful for comparison. This

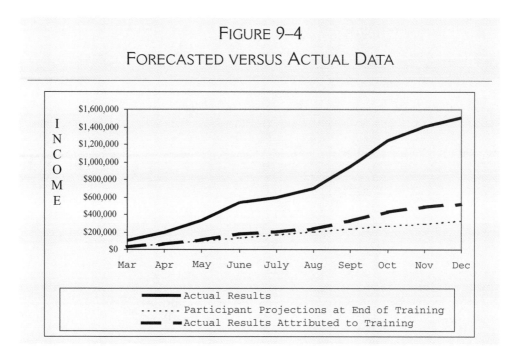

FIGURE 9–4

FORECASTED VERSUS ACTUAL DATA

Legend:
——— Actual Results
······· Participant Projections at End of Training
— — Actual Results Attributed to Training

end-of-program data collection helps participants plan the implementation of what they have learned. For example, in a products training program for Wachovia Bank, the results after training are compared to the forecasted results (Wallace, 2001). Figure 9–4 shows the results of training, the participant's projections at the end of training, and the results attributed to the training. As the figure illustrates, the forecasts are lower than the results attributed to training. This comparison begins to build credibility in a forecasting method and, in this case, revealed that forecasting was actually more conservative than the actual results.

The use of Level 1 ROI is increasing as more organizations base a larger part of ROI calculations on Level 1 data. Although it may be very subjective, it does add value, particularly when it is included as part of a comprehensive evaluation system.

Forecasting ROI with Learning Data

Testing for changes in skills and knowledge in training programs is a very common technique for learning evaluation (Level 2). Participants are often required to demonstrate their knowledge or skills at the end of the program, and their performance is expressed as a numerical value. When this type of test is developed and used, it must be reliable and valid. A reliable test is one that is stable over time with consistent results. A valid test is one that measures what it purports to measure. Because a test should reflect the content of the WLP program, successful mastery of program content should be related to improved job performance. Consequently, there should be a relationship between test scores and subsequent on-the-job performance. Figure 9–5

FIGURE 9-5

RELATIONSHIP BETWEEN TEST SCORES AND PERFORMANCE

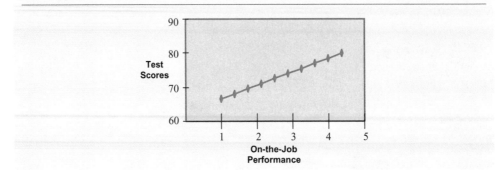

illustrates a perfect correlation between test scores and job performance. This relationship, expressed as a correlation coefficient, is a measure of validity of the test.

This testing situation provides an excellent opportunity for an ROI calculation with Level 2 data using test results. When the relationship between test scores and on-the-job performance is statistically significant, and the performance can be converted to monetary units, then it is possible to use test scores to estimate the ROI from the program, using the following steps:

- Ensure that the program content reflects desired on-the-job performance.
- Develop an end-of-program test that reflects program content.
- Establish a statistical relationship between test score data and output performance for participants.
- Predict performance levels of each participant with given test scores.
- Convert performance data to monetary value.
- Compare total predicted value of program with program costs.

Exercise 9-3 helps to illustrate the process of forecasting with Level 2 data. Work the Exercise to help clarify any questions about the process.

This is a forecast of the ROI and not the actual value. Although participants acquired the skills and knowledge from the program, there is no guarantee that they will apply the techniques and processes successfully and that the results will be achieved. This process assumes that the current group of participants has the same relationship to output performance as previous groups. It ignores a variety of environmental influences, which can alter the situation entirely. Finally, the process requires calculating the initial correlation coefficient, which may be difficult to develop for most tests.

Although this approach develops an estimate based on historical relationships, it can be useful in a comprehensive evaluation strategy, and it has several advantages. First, if postprogram evaluations (Level 4) are not planned, this process will yield more information about the projected value of the program than what would be obtained from the raw test scores. This process represents

Consumer Products Marketing (CPM) is the marketing division of a consumer products company. Sales representatives for CPM make frequent calls on large retail food and drug companies with the goal of increasing sales and market share of CPM products. Sales representatives must ensure that retailers understand the advantages of CPM products, provide adequate space for their products, and assist in promotional and advertising efforts.

CPM has developed a very strong sales culture and recruits highly capable individuals for sales representative positions. Newly recruited representatives rotate through different divisions of the company in a two-month assignment to learn where and how the products are made, their features and benefits, and specific product marketing strategies. This initial assignment is topped off with an intensive one-week Professional Marketing Learning Program, which focuses on sales techniques, marketing strategies, and customer service skills. At the end of the program, participants take a comprehensive test based on the knowledge and skills taught in the program. As part of the test, participants analyze customer service and sales situations and decide on specific actions. The test also covers product features, policies, and marketing practices.

To validate the test, CPM developed correlations between test scores and actual sales volumes, sales growth, and market share for sales representatives. The correlation was very strong and statistically significant, enabling program coordinators to use test scores to predict the level of sales, market share, and sales growth for each participant. As a quick way of calculating the return for a program, CPM estimates output levels for each item, converts them to monetary values, and calculates the ROI forecast.

1. How reliable is this estimate of ROI at Level 2?

_____

_____

2. What other issues might need to be considered in this process?

_____

_____

3. Is this information useful? If so, how should the information be used?

_____

_____

an expected return on investment based on the historical relationships involved. Second, by developing individual ROI measurements and communicating them to participants, the process has reinforcement potential. It communicates to participants that increased sales and market share are expected through the application of what was learned in the program. Third, this process can have considerable credibility with management and can preclude expensive follow-ups and postprogram monitoring. If these relationships are statistically sound, the estimate should have credibility with the target group.

Forecasting ROI with Application and Implementation Data

In almost every training program, participants are expected to change their on-the-job behaviors by applying the knowledge and skills learned. On-the-job application is essential to program success. Although the use of the skills on the job is no guarantee that results will follow, it is an underlying assumption for most programs that if the knowledge and skills are applied, then results will follow. Some of the most prestigious training organizations, such as Motorola University, base their ultimate evaluation on this assumption. A few organizations attempt to take this process a step further and measure the value of on-the-job behavior change and calculate the ROI. In these situations, estimates are taken from individual participants, their supervisors, the management group, or experts in the field. This is a forecast of the impact, based on the change in behavior on the job immediately after the program. The following steps are used to develop the ROI:

1. Develop competencies for the target job.
2. Indicate the percentage of job success that is covered in the training program.
3. Determine the monetary value of competencies using salaries and employee benefits of participants.
4. Compute the worth of pre- and postprogram skill levels.
5. Subtract postprogram values from preprogram values.
6. Compare the total added benefits with the program costs.

This is called a utility analysis. It attempts to place a value on an individual's improvement. The concept ignores the consequence of this improvement (Level 4), but examines the behavior change (Level 3) and factors the monetary value relative to the individual's salary. This is referred to as a Level 3 ROI forecast because it takes the change in behavior and converts it to monetary value using salaries of participants as a base. Exercise 9–4 includes an example of forecasting with Level 3 data.

Calculations yield the following ROI.

$$\text{ROI} = \frac{\$3,418 - \$1,368}{\$1,368} = \frac{2,050}{1,368} \times 100 = 150\%$$

As with other estimates, a word of caution is in order. These results are subjective because the rating systems used are subjective and may not necessarily reflect an accurate assessment of the value of the program. This is a Level 3 ROI forecast. Since training is usually implemented to help the organization achieve its objectives, some managers insist on tangible changes in business

Exercise 9–4. Forecasting with Level 3 Data

The U.S. federal government recently redesigned its Introduction to Supervision course, a five-day learning program for newly appointed supervisors. The program focuses on eight competencies:

- Role and responsibilities of the supervisor
- Communications
- Planning, assigning, controlling, and evaluating work
- Ethics

- Leadership and motivation
- Analyzing performance problems
- Customer service
- Managing diversity

The immediate managers of the new supervisors indicated that the competencies accounted for 81% of the first-level supervisors' job. In the target group being evaluated, the average annual salary (plus benefits) for the newly appointed supervisors was $42,202. Thus, multiplying this figure by the amount of job success accounted for by the competencies (81%) yielded a dollar value of $34,184 per participant. If a person were to perform successfully in these competencies for one year, the value to the agency would be $34,184.

Managers rated the skills for each of the competencies before the program was conducted using a scale of 0–9. The average level of skills required to be successful in the job was determined to be 6.44. The skill ratings, prior to the job, were 4.96, which represented 77% of the 6.44 (i.e., participants were performing at 77% of the level to be successful in the competencies). After the program, the skill rating was 5.59, representing 87% of the level to be successful.

Dollar values were assigned based on the participants' salaries. Performance at the required level was worth $34,184. At a 77% proficiency level, the new supervisors were performing at a contribution value of $26,322. After learning, this value had reached 87%, representing a contribution of $29,740. The difference in these values ($3,418) represents the gain per participant attributable to learning. The program cost $1,368 per participant.

1. What is the ROI for this program?

2. How credible is this approach to calculating ROI?

3. Could this same approach be used to forecast the value prior to the implementation of the program?

impact data such as output, quality, cost, and time. For them, a Level 3 ROI forecast is not always an acceptable substitute for business impact (Level 4) data.

Although this process is subjective, it has several useful advantages. First, if there are no plans to track the actual impact of the program in terms of specific measurable business impact (Level 4), this approach represents a credible substitute. In many programs—particularly skill-building and competency programs for supervisors—it may be difficult to identify tangible changes on the job. Therefore, alternative approaches to determine the worth of a program are needed. Second, this approach has been developed in the literature as utility analysis. Third, this approach develops data that may be credible with management if they understand how it is developed and the assumptions behind it. An important point is that the data on the changes in competence level came from the managers who have rated their supervisors. In this specific project, the numbers were large enough to make the process statistically significant.

Forecasting Guidelines

With the four different time frames for forecasting outlined in this chapter, a few guidelines may help drive an organization's forecasting possibilities. These guidelines are based on experience in forecasting a variety of processes along with training and performance improvement (Bowers, 1997).

1. *If you must forecast, forecast frequently.* Forecasting is a process that is both an art and a science, and it needs to be pursued regularly to build confidence, experience, and history with the process. Also, those who use the data need to see forecasting frequently, to further integrate it as part of the training evaluation mix.
2. *Consider forecasting an essential part of the evaluation mix.* This chapter began with a list of reasons why forecasting is essential. The concept is growing in use, and many executives are demanding it. It can be an effective and useful tool when used properly and in conjunction with other types of evaluation data. Some organizations have targets for the use of forecasting (for example, if a project exceeds a certain cost, it will always require a preprogram forecast). Others target a certain number of programs for a forecast based on reaction data and use that data in the manner described in this chapter. Others have some low-level targets for forecasting at Levels 2 and 3. The important point is to plan for the forecast and let it be a part of the evaluation mix, working it regularly.
3. *Forecast different types of data.* Although most of this chapter focuses on how to develop a forecasted ROI using the standard ROI formula, it is helpful to forecast the value of other data. A useable, helpful forecast includes predictions about reaction and satisfaction, the extent of learning, and the extent of application and implementation. These types of data are very important in anticipating movements and shifts based on the planned program. It is not only helpful in developing the overall

forecast but important in understanding the total anticipated impact of the project.

4. *Secure input from those who know the process best.* As forecasts are developed, it is essential to secure input from individuals who understand the dynamics of the workplace and the measures being influenced by the training project. Sometimes the participants in training or their immediate managers are the best sources. In other situations, it is the variety of analysts who are aware of the major influences in the workplace and the dynamics of those changes. The important point is to go to the experts. This will increase not only the accuracy of the forecast but also the credibility of the final results.

5. *Long-term forecasts are usually inaccurate.* Forecasting works much better in a short time frame. For most short-term scenarios, it is possible to have a better grasp of the influences that might drive the measure. On a long-term basis, a variety of new influences, unforeseen now, could enter the process and drastically change the impact measures. If a long-term forecast is needed, it should be updated regularly to become a continuously improving process.

6. *Expect forecasts to be biased.* Forecasts consist of data coming from those who have an interest in the issue. Some want the forecast to be optimistic; others have a pessimistic view. Almost all input is biased in one way or another. Every attempt should be made to minimize the bias, adjust for the bias, or adjust for the uncertainty in the process. Still, the audience should recognize that it is a biased prediction.

7. *Serious forecasting is hard work.* The value of forecasting often depends on the amount of effort put into the process. High-stakes programs need to have a serious approach, collecting all possible data, examining different scenarios, and making the best prediction available. It is in these situations that mathematical tools can be most valuable.

8. *Review the success of forecasting routinely.* As forecasts are made, it is imperative to revisit the forecast with actual postprogram data to check the success of the forecast. This can aid in the continuous improvement of the processes. Sources could prove to be more credible or less credible, specific inputs may be more biased or less biased, and certain analyses may be more appropriate than others. It is important to constantly improve the organization's ideal methods and approaches for forecasting.

9. *The assumptions are the most serious error in forecasting.* Of all the variables that can enter into the process, the one with the greatest opportunity for error is the assumptions made by the individual providing the forecast. It is important for the assumptions to be clearly understood and communicated. When there are multiple inputs, each forecaster should use the same set of assumptions, if possible.

10. *Utility is the most important characteristic of forecasting.* The most important use of forecasting is that it provides information and input for the decision maker. Forecasting is a tool for those attempting to make a decision about training or performance improvement. It is not a process used to try to maximize the output or minimize any

particular variable, nor to attempt to dramatically change the way in which the program is implemented. The greatest utility of forecasting is as a process to provide data for decisions.

POTENTIAL CHALLENGES

The biggest challenge of forecasting is estimating the business impact (Level 4). Assumptions are the basis of this estimation no matter who the source is. As stated earlier, and as would be expected, this affects the credibility of the ROI.

The next challenge is actually estimating the extent to which participants will apply/implement the knowledge and skills. Many variables surround the performance of participants when they return to the work setting. Identifying these variables and their influence on application/implementation can be difficult.

Another challenge is changing the mindset of those closest to the program. ROI forecasting may not be on the radar screen for program designers, developers, facilitators, and others. They may be satisfied with traditional Level 1 and Level 2 data. Gaining sponsorship in the WLP organization and perhaps in other parts of the organization is an important part of changing this mindset.

ACTION STEPS

- Review the objectives from one of your programs and consider the context in which the program will be delivered. Select one of the forecasting methods described in this chapter and take a stab at forecasting the ROI. You may be surprised at how much you learn.
- Seek out a sponsor in your WLP organization who has an interest in seeing ROI data. Brief this individual on the five time frames and approaches to forecasting. Present the benefits you perceive from forecasting and ask for support to implement one of the approaches.

CHAPTER SUMMARY

This chapter illustrates that ROI forecasts can be developed within different time frames. Most practitioners and researchers use actual application and impact data for ROI calculations, but sometimes Level 3 and Level 4 data are not available or evaluations at those levels are not attempted or planned. ROI forecasts, developed before the program is implemented, can be very useful and helpful to management and the WLP staff, while at the same time they focus attention on the potential economic impact of training. Forecasts are also possible with reaction and learning data. Be aware that using ROI forecasts may provide a false sense of accuracy. As would be expected, ROI forecasts on a preprogram basis are the lowest in credibility and accuracy but have the advantage of being inexpensive and relatively easy to conduct. On the other hand, ROI calculations using Level 4 data are highest in credibility and accuracy but are more expensive and difficult to develop.

Although ROI calculations with business impact data (Level 4) are preferred, ROI forecasts at other times are an important part of a comprehensive and systematic evaluation process. This usually means that targets for evaluation should be established to include forecasting.

REFERENCES AND RESOURCES

Bowers, D. A. *Forecasting for Control and Profit,* Menlo Park, CA: Crisp Publications, 1997.

Kaufman, R. "Resolving the (Often-Deserved) Attacks on Training." *Performance Improvement,* 5, no. 6, 2002.

Phillips, Jack J. *Handbook of Training Evaluation and Measurement Methods,* 3rd ed. Woburn, MA: Butterworth-Heinemann, 1997.

Phillips, Jack J. *Return on Investment in Training and Performance Improvement Programs,* 2nd ed. Woburn, MA: Butterworth-Heinemann, 2003.

Van Buren, M. *ASTD Report,* Alexandria, VA: American Society for Training and Development, 2004.

Wallace, D. "Partnering to Achieve Measurable Results in the New Economy," *In Action: Measuring Return on Investment, Volume 3,* Jack J. Phillips, ed. Alexandria, VA: American Society for Training and Development, 2001, pp. 81–104.

CD ⊛

Exercises and Case Study	Tools, Templates, and Job Aids
Exercise 9–1. Retail Merchandise Company—Pre-Program Forecasting	Figure 9–1. ROI at Different Times and Levels
Exercise 9–2. Forecasting with Level 1 Data	Figure 9–2. Pre-Program ROI Forecast Model
Exercise 9–3. Forecasting with Level 2 Data	Figure 9–3. Important Questions to Ask on Feedback Questionnaires
Exercise 9–4. Forecasting with Level 3 Data	Figure 9–4. Forecasted versus Actual Data
	Figure 9–5. Relationship between Test Scores and Performance

Part Three
Implementation Issues

MAKING THE TRANSITION

In Part One, you learned how to get started with ROI measurement and evaluation. In Part Two, you learned how to put the respective pieces of the evaluation puzzle together to implement the process. Now in Part Three, Implementation Issues, you'll learn about common implementation issues that can help or hurt your efforts. It's important to remember that integrating and implementing a results-based training process doesn't happen overnight. On both an individual and organizational level, this additional effort typically involves changing old habits and daily practices of conceiving, designing, developing, and delivering training or performance improvement solutions. To achieve optimal support for this type of paradigm shift, you'll need an organizational culture that supports it. Transition planning provides the foundation and the framework for developing that culture.

In this chapter you will learn to:

- Assess individual and organizational readiness issues.
- Identify transition planning steps, tools, and strategies.
- Address common myths, fears, or false assumptions about the ROI process.
- Integrate transition planning elements with your own evaluation efforts.

THE FUNDAMENTALS

The best-designed process model or technique is meaningless unless it is integrated efficiently and effectively in the organization. Effective integration means that the ROI process is blended into the routine of an organization and is fully endorsed, at all levels, by those who must make it work. The move from initial, start-up impact projects to an integrated evaluation culture begins with transition planning. The tips and tools in this chapter will guide you in assessing individual and organizational readiness issues and in developing effective transition management strategies for moving towards a results-based performance improvement function that will stand the test of time.

Transition Issues

Once you've decided to introduce the ROI process into your existing training or performance improvement work, it's important to step back and take a look at where you're planning to go, what issues may arise over resulting changes, and how you plan to address those issues. Individuals frequently have different views on whether a change is needed, what is driving it, and how much impact it will have. It's important to remember that no one in the organization will support a results-based change effort without some understanding of why the change is needed and what benefits it may produce.

As you've learned in your case study work so far, implementing strategies to measure learning, collect postprogram data, isolate the effects of training, and calculate cost-benefit ratios requires a significant level of commitment, knowledge, and support across *all* organizational levels. Unless your desired purposes and outcomes are clear, it's unrealistic to expect that others will be willing to invest time and effort in the process.

To address these challenges, we've found that treating long-term ROI process implementation as a change effort improves the likelihood of its success. Most executives, managers, or employees think of major organizational change in terms of reengineering, restructuring, or culture change. For purposes of this chapter, we're describing change as the fundamental shift from an old state (activity-based measurement and evaluation) to another, transformed, state (result-based measurement and evaluation). This shift will encompass reengineering the training function; restructuring workplace learning policy, procedures, and practices; and influencing organization culture around the value of the WLP function and the role that executives, managers, and employees play in achieving performance results. In fact, most change efforts typically involve more than one type of change. Given that context and scope then, getting from an old to a new state is more successful when incremental transition-planning steps are applied.

Proven common steps to transition planning are illustrated in Figure 10–1. Each step comprises specific activities that serve to:

- surface potential barriers to ROI readiness and
- help you and your organization identify areas of both strength and opportunity in the implementation process.

Transition Planning Steps

Step 1: Assess Readiness

By some estimates, 70% to 75% of major organizational change efforts fail. Imagine the time, money, and human effort wasted with that dismal figure. If

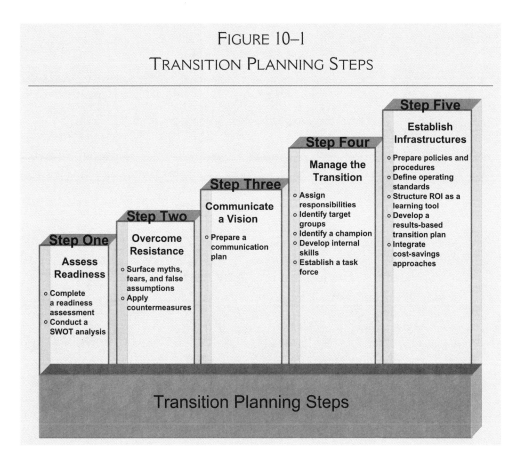

FIGURE 10–1
TRANSITION PLANNING STEPS

Step One

Assess Readiness

○ Complete a readiness assessment
○ Conduct a SWOT analysis

Step Two

Overcome Resistance

○ Surface myths, fears, and false assumptions
○ Apply countermeasures

Step Three

Communicate a Vision

○ Prepare a communication plan

Step Four

Manage the Transition

○ Assign responsibilities
○ Identify target groups
○ Identify a champion
○ Develop internal skills
○ Establish a task force

Step Five

Establish Infrastructures

○ Prepare policies and procedures
○ Define operating standards
○ Structure ROI as a learning tool
○ Develop a results-based transition plan
○ Integrate cost-savings approaches

Transition Planning Steps

implementing organizational change is truly that difficult, then it's clear that planning, resource, and management needs have to be addressed from the very beginning. For that reason, it's important for you to take time upfront to assess the kinds of planning, resource, and management activities needed to support current or ongoing ROI efforts. Remember, proper prior planning on the front end will save you time on the back end! Make sure to assess your organization's perceptions and mind-sets about evaluation, along with its readiness for the ROI process, before undertaking a time-consuming, labor-intensive measurement ROI project.

Reference the readiness assessment, "Is Your Organization a Candidate for ROI Implementation" (Exercise 10–1), that you completed in Chapter 1, to determine how to best focus your organizational readiness activities.

At this point of implementation, each of these statements should be examined or re-examined for its potential influence upon your results-based measurement effort. For instance, if there is a strong agreement with item 11, then an immediate need or opportunity is present to position ROI as a compelling piece of organizational strategy and to then define the readiness conditions required to support it.

Using your responses from the readiness assessment, identify and prioritize key focus areas for readiness activities. In particular, consider the following:

EXERCISE 10–1. IS YOUR ORGANIZATION A CANDIDATE FOR ROI IMPLEMENTATION?

Check the most appropriate level of agreement for each statement:

1 = Strongly Disagree; 5 = Strongly Agree

	Disagree			Agree	
	1	2	3	4	5
1. My organization is considered a large organization with a wide variety of programs.	❏	❏	❏	❏	❏
2. We have a large budget that attracts the interest of senior management.	❏	❏	❏	❏	❏
3. Our organization has a culture of measurement and is focused on establishing a variety of measures in all functions and departments.	❏	❏	❏	❏	❏
4. My organization is undergoing significant change.	❏	❏	❏	❏	❏
5. There is pressure from senior management to measure results of our programs.	❏	❏	❏	❏	❏
6. My function currently has a very low investment in measurement and evaluation.	❏	❏	❏	❏	❏
7. My organization has experienced more than one program disaster in the past.	❏	❏	❏	❏	❏
8. My department has a new leader.	❏	❏	❏	❏	❏
9. My team would like to be the leaders in our field.	❏	❏	❏	❏	❏
10. The image of our department is less than satisfactory.	❏	❏	❏	❏	❏
11. My clients are demanding that our processes show bottom-line results.	❏	❏	❏	❏	❏
12. My function competes with other functions within our organization for resources.	❏	❏	❏	❏	❏
13. There is increased focus on linking our process to the strategic direction of the organization.	❏	❏	❏	❏	❏
14. My function is a key player in change initiatives currently taking place in the organization.	❏	❏	❏	❏	❏
15. Our overall budget is growing and we are required to prove the bottom line of value of our processes.	❏	❏	❏	❏	❏

EXERCISE 10–1. IS YOUR ORGANIZATION A CANDIDATE FOR ROI IMPLEMENTATION?—*Continued*

Scoring

If you scored:

15–30	You are not yet a candidate for ROI. Reading this fieldbook will help prepare you.
31–45	You are not a strong candidate for ROI; however, it is time to start pursuing some type of measurement process.
46–60	You are a candidate for building skills to implement the ROI process. At this point there is no real pressure to show the ROI, which is the perfect opportunity to perfect the process within the organization.
61–75	You should already be implementing a comprehensive measurement and evaluation process, including ROI.

Are you a candidate? _____

- What programs, processes, and/or persons exist in the organization that support your desired future state of measurement focus? *(Strengths)*
- What gaps are there between where you are and where you want to be with respect to a result-based WLP function? *(Weaknesses)*
- What processes or programs may have to be changed or reconfigured? *(Opportunities)*
- To what extent do managers and WLP staff perceive current training and development efforts to be effective? *(Opportunities)*
- What resource constraints may impede implementation support? *(Threats)*
- What processes may have to be created from scratch? *(Opportunities)*
- What particular areas need immediate implementation support? *(Weaknesses)*
- What metrics, milestones, and/or status reports are needed to track and monitor implementation progress? *(Opportunities)*

Based upon your readiness assessment review and deliberation of the above factors, complete a strengths, weaknesses, opportunities, and threats (SWOT) analysis of your organization's readiness state.

Strengths	Weaknesses
✓	✓
✓	✓
✓	✓
✓	✓
Opportunities	**Threats**
✓	✓
✓	✓
✓	✓
✓	✓

MAKING THE TRANSITION   275

Once you've populated your SWOT analysis to identify and prioritize key focus areas, then it may be helpful to develop a readiness plan to address specific areas needing attention or action during implementation.

Figure 10–1 shows how one organization created a Readiness Action Plan to address company-specific issues in the ROI implementation effort.

Step 2: Overcome Resistance

With any new process or change, there is typically some form of resistance. Resistance can occur within any target audience, including managers, participants, and WLP staff. One group that most often resists the ROI Methodology is the WLP staff, who are tasked with the design, development, delivery, and coordination of the learning solution and its evaluation effort.

These individuals may perceive implementation of the process as threatening, time-consuming, or an unwelcome intrusion on an already overloaded plate of looming deadlines, multiple requests for service, and never-ending client demands. Many practitioners are also deterred from pursuing systematic evaluation efforts because of false assumptions about the cost and complexity of implementing evaluation at the ROI level. Compounding these issues is the occasional misuse of measurement data as a corrective or fault-finding tool instead of as a source of continuous improvement. Furthermore, environmental barriers are typically present because most WLP departments do not have the infrastructure and success criteria in place to support a results focus.

As discussed in Chapter 1, there are common myths, fears, and false assumptions about implementing evaluation at the ROI level. Some of the more prevalent ones are noted in Table 10–1, along with reality-based countermeasures for eliminating resistance associated with these assumptions. Each countermeasure approach is detailed in this fieldbook.

Exercise 10–2 provides a checklist of common myths, fears, or false assumptions associated with implementing the ROI process. Complete this exercise to determine how you can overcome resistance in your organization.

Step 3: Communicate a Vision

You and your WLP team can enhance organizational readiness by actively communicating the vision, mission, and desired outcomes of a results-focused evaluation and measurement strategy. Your vision, by definition, is the difference between the current reality of where you are with your measurement focus and where you want to be. By using communication forums or briefings with senior, mid-, and line managers you can paint a picture about the value of moving from an activity-based measurement focus to a results-based one and gather input about how others view the change. These initial communications should assist organizational leaders in understanding:

- Why the paradigm shift to a results-based measurement focus is needed.
- What the desired outcomes will be.
- Who the targets for change are and who the resources needed to make it work are.

TABLE 10–1

OVERCOMING MYTHS, FEARS, AND FALSE ASSUMPTIONS

Myth, Fear, or False Assumption	Reality-Based Countermeasure
1. Measurement and evaluation is too expensive.	■ A comprehensive measurement and evaluation system can typically be implemented for less than 5 percent of the direct training and development budget. ■ Benchmark with other organizations to determine the extent of your evaluation costs. Learning and application data is often sufficient for some organizations, with the cost of a detailed impact study being infrequent.
2. Evaluation takes too much time.	Use automated techniques and templates, including these proven shortcuts and cost-savings approaches. 1. Build evaluation into the performance improvement process 2. Develop criteria for selecting program measurement levels 3. Plan for evaluation early in the process 4. Share the responsibilities for evaluation 5. Require participants to conduct major steps 6. Use short-cut methods for major steps 7. Use estimates in the data collection and analysis 8. Develop internal capability in the ROI process 9. Streamline the reporting process 10. Use Web-based technology
3. If senior management does not require additional measurement, there is no need to pursue it.	■ Leadership is demanding more and more accountability. ■ If there is no evidence of results, the WLP function becomes an easy target for staff reductions. ■ When senior leaders suddenly ask for results, they expect a quick response. ■ It is better to have results available and not need them than need results and not have them. ■ Developing ROI information is one of the best ways to garner the respect of senior management and show the business value of the WLP function.
4. Measurement and evaluation is a passing fad.	■ Increased accountability and measurement are among the most critical issues in the WLP field today. ■ Although the status of ROI practice among professionals is mixed, there is a persistent trend to show bottom-line value of training investments.
5. Evaluation generates only one or two types of data.	■ The ROI process has the potential to generate up to six different types of qualitative and quantitative data.
6. Evaluation cannot be easily replicated.	■ Follow the guiding principles and adopt operating standards to ensure consistency in the ROI process and the approach.
7. Evaluation is too subjective.	■ The use of estimates is extremely reliable when used in concert with sound operating standards. ■ Accounting, engineering, and technology fields routinely use estimates.
8. Impact evaluation is not possible with soft skills programs, only for technical and hard skills programs.	■ Hundreds of case studies have been conducted showing the successful application of the ROI Methodology to soft skills programs. ■ Link needs, objectives, and impact measures to identify performance improvement at Levels 3, 4, and 5.

Continued

TABLE 10-1—*Continued*

OVERCOMING MYTHS, FEARS, AND FALSE ASSUMPTIONS

9. Evaluation is more appropriate for certain types of organizations.	■ The ROI process methodology has been successfully used by diverse organizations of multiple sizes around the globe. ■ Impact measures of program success exist in any organizational setting.
10. It is not always possible to isolate the effects of learning and development.	■ Several methods are available to isolate the effects of a given program or intervention. ■ The challenge is in selecting the appropriate method for any given situation. ■ Ignoring the isolation issue creates poor credibility for the WLP function and makes it difficult to know the linkage between the learning program and key business measures.
11. Because learning and development staff have no control over participants after they complete a program, evaluating the on-the-job improvement is not appropriate.	■ Although WLP staff may not have direct control over what happens to participants in the workplace, they do have influence on the transfer process. ■ Objectives must be developed that focus on application of learning and expected consequences. ■ Partnerships between key managers and the WLP help ensure that learning transfer takes place.
12. A participant is rarely responsible for the failure of a program.	■ Participants need to be held accountable for their own learning and are a credible source of information about the actual consequences of learning. ■ Training and development programs need to be positioned with results-based expectations for participants. ■ Participants have the ultimate responsibility to learn and apply new skills and knowledge and to identify enablers and barriers to their success in doing so.
13. Evaluation is the evaluator's responsibility.	Evaluation must be a shared responsibility: ■ Managers and performers provide input on performance and skill deficits. ■ WLP team members design, develop, and deliver the program. ■ Managers and stakeholders review and approve the evaluation plan. ■ Participants and key stakeholder provide data about success after the program.
14. Successful evaluation implementation requires a university degree in statistics or evaluation.	■ An effective, credible evaluation process can be implemented with a simple, step-by-step process and without a complicated set of formulas. ■ Many evaluation studies do not require the use of statistics.
15. Negative data is always bad news.	■ Communicate purpose and scope of ROI process as a continuous learning tool that will help assess program priorities and areas of impact. Develop staff capability, share ownership.

EXERCISE 10–2. OVERCOMING RESISTANCE TO MYTHS, FEARS, AND FALSE ASSUMPTIONS

The following table provides a checklist of common myths, fears, or false assumptions associated with implementing the ROI process.

Myth, Fear, or False Assumption	Yes	No
1. Measurement and evaluation is too expensive.	❑	❑
2. Evaluation takes too much time.	❑	❑
3. If senior management does not require additional measurement, there is no need to pursue it.	❑	❑
4. Measurement and evaluation is a passing fad.	❑	❑
5. Evaluation generates only one or two types of data.	❑	❑
6. Evaluation cannot be easily replicated.	❑	❑
7. Evaluation is too subjective.	❑	❑
8. Impact evaluation is not possible with soft skills programs, only for technical and hard skills programs.	❑	❑
9. Evaluation is more appropriate for certain types of organizations.	❑	❑
10. It is not always possible to isolate the effects of learning and development.	❑	❑
11. Because learning and development staff have no control over participants after they complete a program, evaluating the on-the-job improvement is not appropriate.	❑	❑
12. A participant is rarely responsible for the failure of a program.	❑	❑
13. Evaluation is the evaluator's responsibility.	❑	❑
14. Successful evaluation implementation requires a university degree in statistics or evaluation.	❑	❑
15. Negative data is always bad news.	❑	❑

For this exercise:

1. Review the list of objections associated with the ROI process and identify the three that *most* reflect your organization's current mindset around measurement and evaluation.
   1.
   2.
   3.
2. Using the reality-based countermeasures noted in Table 10–1 as a guide, identify an action, strategy, or approach you will use as a countermeasure during completion of your current impact study.
   1.
   2.
   3.

By when:

_____

_____

_____

Review date: (identify person with whom you will share progress)

_____

_____

_____

- When the impact will occur.
- How a results-based WLP function will align with company performance goals, vision, mission, values.
- How the organization, its internal processes, and its key people will be developed to manage the change effort.
- Where the checkpoints, process documents, and project plans are that detail the scope of the effort and its impact to the business.

Communication should also include education about the components of a results-based measurement strategy including:

- How evaluation data can be used to uncover barriers to successful application of skills or knowledge.
- How the data can be used to manage and correct barriers.
- The role of management in ensuring training's success.
- The role of top management in supporting data collection.
- How a results focus can save money and enhance business performance.

Chapter 11 discusses the role of management in ROI process implementation in more detail and provides additional tools for developing and strengthening partnerships with management groups. In communicating the vision for a results-based effort, however, it's important to emphasize that it is not a quick fix and that successful implementation requires sustained support and participation across all organizational levels. Communication with stakeholders, then, typically acknowledges that getting from point A to point B with a results-based evaluation framework is a gradual, iterative process.

Developing and/or maintaining a communication plan to promote shared awareness and commitment for a results-based evaluation focus is critical, not only for your current impact study but for future ROI efforts. Figure 10–3 is an example of a communication plan. Exercise 10–3 helps you identify areas of strength and opportunities for improving your existing communication work.

Step 4: Manage the Transition

As with many change efforts, it's natural for people to underestimate the time, energy, and resources required to achieve evaluation goals. In fact, one of the most common errors made in any change effort is to inaccurately define scope, typically making it too narrow and overlooking internal dynamics of day-to-day communications and working relationships. Imagine the time and productivity loss that occurs when those tasked with supporting and participating in a new evaluation strategy are unclear about their role and the resources needed to support it. That's why defining roles and responsibilities is such an important part of ROI transition planning and change management. The following key tasks are critical components of managing this transition.

EXERCISE 10–3. COMMUNICATION PLANNING

1. Using Figure 10–2 as a guide, complete a communication plan for your current impact study.
2. Next, use the checklist below to identify areas of strength and opportunities for improvement in your existing communication plan.

Communication Planning Checklist	Yes	No
Have I checked with members of my target audience to assess communication needs, concerns, or questions?	❏	❏
Have I considered the organizational impact of a results-based WLP focus?	❏	❏
Have I engaged the support of a credible sponsor at the senior leadership level?	❏	❏
Have I clarified the purpose of the results-based evaluation, what outcomes are desired, and what decisions will be made based upon results information?	❏	❏
Have I used baseline data to support the effort?	❏	❏
Have I positioned this effort as a compelling piece of company strategy?	❏	❏
Have I assessed external factors that may be out of WLP staff or individual client's control?	❏	❏
Have I developed an evaluation plan with targeted program objectives across multiple levels?	❏	❏
Have I included communications about timelines and resource requirements?	❏	❏
Have I communicated evaluation roles and responsibilities across all organization levels?	❏	❏
Have I communicated how a results-based evaluation process will be integrated with existing policy and purpose statements?	❏	❏
Have I communicated a transition plan with realistic milestones?	❏	❏
Have I communicated about the data collection instruments to be used for measuring results in targeted areas?	❏	❏
Have I clearly communicated the resource requirements for stakeholders who participate in the evaluation process?	❏	❏
Have I communicated accountability measures for stakeholders who commit to participate in the evaluation process?	❏	❏

Continued

Communication Planning Checklist	Yes	No
Have I provided adequate communication about how participants will be trained to provide data?	❏	❏
Have I communicated how results will be used for continuous improvement and WLP action planning?	❏	❏

Areas of strength:

_____

_____

_____

Opportunities for improvement:

_____

_____

_____

3. Identify actions to maintain strengths and enhance communication efforts in those areas needing improvement.

Sustaining actions:

_____

_____

_____

Enhancing actions:

_____

_____

_____

Assign and Share Responsibilities

Peter Drucker has said that "sooner or later all plans degenerate into work." Therefore, a well-designed transition plan is one that accurately identifies the breadth and depth of evaluation responsibilities, as well as the target groups who are both impacted by the change and required to carry it out. Establishing a foundation of shared ownership for results-based responsibilities increases the likelihood of your success with short- and long-term ROI implementation. Job Aid 10–1, "Roles and Responsibilities," which is found on the CD provides guidance for assigning and sharing responsibilities for key target group members.

FIGURE 10-2
READINESS ACTION PLAN

Sample Readiness Plan		
Operational Process: Results-Based Measurement and Evaluation		

Instructions:

This plan helps identify key areas that need attention and action when implementing an enterprise-wide, results-based measurement and evaluation focus. Use this tool to support implementation efforts and to identify any gaps between your current organizational processes for measurement and evaluation and your desired measurement processes. The following planning tools are recommended as supporting documents: "Is Your Organization a Candidate for ROI Implementation?," SWOT Analysis, Stakeholder Engagement Tool, Communication Plan, Results-Based Transition Plan, Policy Statement, Guidelines for Existing Workplace Learning and Training Programs, and WLP Standardization Process. To complete these tools, you may need to work with other functional or subject matter experts.

1. Use the information required from the tools above to help you populate this Readiness Plan.
2. Review your findings with your process sponsor and process champion to ensure that he or she is informed of possible gaps and can contribute to solutions.

1. Stakeholder Support	Gaps/Comments	Actions to Close Gap
Have all stakeholders been identified?		
Have stakeholder engagement opportunities been assessed?		
Have stakeholders' business needs and objectives been identified?		
2. Communication	Gaps/Comments	Actions to Close Gap
Have target audiences been identified?		
Has a communication plan been completed?		
Have stakeholders endorsed the communication plan?		
Are communication materials available?		
Are persons in charge for delivering the communication available?		
Have communication resources, facilities and logistics support been made available?		

FIGURE 10–2—*Continued*
READINESS ACTION PLAN

	Gaps/Comments	Actions to Close Gap
3. Workplace Learning Professionals (internal WLP staff)		
Have purpose and importance of a results-based effort been identified?		
Have staff been trained in ROI process methodology?		
Has a training timeline been prepared?		
Has an ROI leader or champion been identified?		
4. Performance Measurement and Recognition	**Gaps/Comments**	**Actions to Close Gap**
Has a plan to track and report implementation progress been developed? (leading/lagging indicators identified)		
Has a plan been developed to motivate users/stakeholders with supporting the implementation and building accountability?		
5. Organizational Resources	**Gaps/Comments**	**Actions to Close Gap**
Human resources: Links to current systems/processes (i.e., performance management, incentive plans or bonus pay structures, succession planning, leadership development, career development or individual development plans [IDPs], job rotations, mentoring programs)		
Materials: Supporting policy/procedures/guidelines; Process Development Plan; Project Plan		
Technology: Database administration, data collection, analysis, reporting mechanisms		
6. Process Specific	**Gaps/Comments**	**Actions to Close Gap**
Has a process sponsor been identified/trained?		
Has a process champion or ROI leader been identified/trained?		
Has a process development team been identified/trained?		
Have supporting policies, procedures, guidelines, standards, and governance processes been developed and approved?		
7. Other Areas Requiring Consideration	**Gaps/Comments**	**Actions to Close Gap**
Has the selection process for external vendors been revised, updated?		
Have vendors been educated about the transition to a results-based learning approach?		
Have internal, vendor-based programs been modified to fit desired standards for results?		

FIGURE 10–3
SAMPLE COMMUNICATION PLAN

Process: Results-Based Measurement and Evaluation

Key Message	Stakeholder	Objective	Approach	Frequency	Responsibility	Delivery	Considerations
What is the primary message to be conveyed or issue to be addressed?	*Target audience*	*Info only, seeking support, requesting review or action?*	*Web, newsletter, e-mail, face to face, hardcopy, town hall, Intranet, etc.*	*Timing or other milestone date*	*Who will develop content?*	*Who will deliver the communication?*	*Potential obstacles, time availability, stakeholder issues/concerns with message*
Stage 1—Initial Rollout							
Value proposition of ROI and results-based measurement processes. Why, what, who, when, how evaluation data will be used. Communicate best practices, industry, and WLP profession.	Senior leadership	Solicit support, resources for Initial impact study.	Face to face, powerpoint presentation with benchmarking data	One time by (date), ongoing as determined	Process sponsor or WLP lead/ advisor	Process sponsor or WLP lead/advisor	Why ROI? Why now? How to manage with limited resources? Should we do ROI for all programs? What will we do with the results? How can results with soft skills programs be measured? How can we know it was the training that got the result?
Emphasize process vs. project nature of focus. Not a one-time-only initiative. Sponsorship roles and responsibilities—shared accountabilities for creating a learning environment and a results-based WLP culture.	Senior leadership	Request technical review of revised WLP policies/ procedures to support results-based process infrastructure. Request commitment to action with sponsorship roles/ responsibilities in all evaluation phases.	Face to face, powerpoint presentation with benchmarking data	One time, ongoing as determined	WLP lead/ advisor	Process sponsor or WLP lead/ advisor and initial evaluation team	Any conflict with existing critical business issues? Compatibility, synergies? Accountability measures?
Summary of current impact study. Show how ROI can be used to solve real business problems. High level project plan, roles/responsibilities, resource requirements, expected outcomes/results, communication strategy	Senior leadership	Seek support for implementation plan. Generate accountability for mid-managers'/line supervisors'/ employees' participation. Request documented support with sign-off on Data Collection Plan.	Face to face, powerpoint presentation with benchmarking data. Data Collection Plan.	As above	Process sponsor or WLP lead/ advisor	Process sponsor or advisor	Amount of resources needed; confidentiality of results. What will happen with negative or less than desirable data?

FIGURE 10–3—*Continued*
SAMPLE COMMUNICATION PLAN

Process: Results-Based Measurement and Evaluation

Key Message	Stakeholder	Objective	Approach	Frequency	Responsibility	Delivery	Considerations
Value proposition. How results-based measurement processes can solve real business problems. Specific roles and responsibilities for achieving desired results—shared accountabilities for learning transfer and application of learned skills/knowledge.	Line supervisors	Seek support for implementation plan. Request task force involvement. Request documented support with sign-off on Data Collection Plan. Request commitment to action with supervisor roles/responsibilities in all evaluation phases.	Face to face, powerpoint presentation with benchmarking data. Data Collection Plan. Transfer Strategy Matrix.	As above	As above	As above	Resource constraints? What will we do with the results? What about negative results? How do we manage feedback about management support? What accountability is there for managers/supervisors/trainees to apply learning and achieve results? How will performance tracking be conducted? What impact upon performance management processes? What's in it for me? Organizational/management barriers—how addressed?
Value proposition. How results-based measurement processes can solve real business problems. Specific roles and responsibilities for achieving desired results—shared accountabilities for learning transfer and application of learned skills/knowledge.	Employees/training participants	Seek support for implementation plan. Request documented support with sign-off on Data Collection Plan. Request commitment to action with trainee roles/responsibilities in all evaluation phases.	Face to face, powerpoint presentation with benchmarking data. Data Collection Plan. Transfer Strategy Matrix.	As above	As above	As above	Resource constraints? What will we do with the results? What about negative results? How can we know it was the training that got the result? How do we manage feedback about management support? What accountability is there for managers/supervisors/trainees to support learning transfer? How will performance tracking be conducted? What's in it for me? How will organizational barriers be identified/addressed?

Stage 2—Evaluation Planning

Key Message	Stakeholder	Objective	Approach	Frequency	Responsibility	Delivery	Considerations
What business needs or gaps are we trying to address? What are the current and desired performance levels? What performance measures are available to track progress with objectives?	Line supervisors	Review extant, baseline data. Collect input on cause analysis, proposed performance improvement solution. Establish evaluation targets with corresponding measures.	Face to face, powerpoint presentation with benchmarking data. Data Collection Plan. Transfer Strategy Matrix.	Weekly as needed. Evaluation Plan to be completed, with SME input, by (date)	Evaluation lead, task force members, instructional design team rep, designated subject matter experts, participants.	Evaluation lead, task force members, instructional design team rep, designated subject matter experts, participants.	What about conflicting priorities? Moving targets?

Stage 3—Data Collection

Objectives	Audience	Strategy	Instruments/Method	Timing	Responsibility	Responsibility	Considerations
Solicit feedback about success with satisfaction, planned action, learning, performance, and impact objectives. Collect application and business measures of program impact.	Line Supervisors	Request feedback during and after solution implementation. Instruct participants on how to provide feedback. Gather input to convert data to monetary value and calculate ROI (as indicated).		Per Data Collection Plan, by (date)	Evaluation lead, task force members, instructional design team rep, designated subject matter experts, participants.	Evaluation lead, task force members, instructional design team rep, designated subject matter experts, participants.	What about extreme data? What about missing data? Standards for converting data and ensuring credibility? Confidential? Annualized?
Solicit feedback about success with satisfaction, planned action, learning, performance, and impact objectives. Collect application and business measures of program impact.	Training participants	Request feedback during and after solution implementation. Instruct participants on how to provide feedback. Gather input to convert data to monetary value and calculate ROI (as indicated).	Level 1 Feedback completion. Pre/Post Assessments after training event. Action plan and Impact Survey completion 60 days after training.	Per Data Collection Plan, by (date)	Evaluation lead, task force members, instructional design team rep, designated subject matter experts, participants.	Evaluation lead, task force members, instructional design team rep, designated subject matter experts, participants.	What about extreme data? What about missing data? Standards for converting data and ensuring credibility? Confidentiality? (How to report barriers with management support?) Annualized?

Stage 4—Reporting Results

Objectives	Audience	Strategy	Instruments/Method	Timing	Responsibility	Responsibility	Considerations
Success with program objectives? Enablers/barriers?	Senior/mid-managers	Communicate results. Seek support for action planning, program revisions, enhancement as needed.	Town hall meetings. Impact Study report. Lessons Learned report.	Select senior/mid-management briefings. Two town hall forums by (date)	Sponsor, evaluation lead, task force members, designated subject matter experts, participants.	Sponsor, evaluation lead, task force members, designated subject matter experts, participants.	How will results be used for continuous improvement and WLP action planning? How will issues around management support (or lack of it) be addressed going forward?
Success with program objectives? Enablers/barriers?	Line supervisors	Communicate results. Seek support for future impact study participation, task force involvement. Generate enthusiasm for process.	Select briefings. Intranet communications, poster boards. Lessons Learned report.	Ongoing as needed	Sponsor, evaluation lead, task force members, designated subject matter experts, participants.	Sponsor, evaluation lead, task force members, designated subject matter experts, participants.	How will results be used for continuous improvement and WLP action planning? How will issues around management support (or lack of it) be addressed going forward?

Job Aid 10–1
Roles and Responsibilities Matrix

Transition Planning

Key Tasks/ Actions	Responsible Party	Key Outputs/Deliverables	Milestone or Due Dates	Success Indicators

Evaluation Planning

Key Tasks/ Actions	Responsible Party	Key Outputs/Deliverables	Milestone or Due Dates	Success Indicators

Data Collection

Key Tasks/ Actions	Responsible Party	Key Outputs/Deliverables	Milestone or Due Dates	Success Indicators

Data Analysis

Key Tasks/ Actions	Responsible Party	Key Outputs/Deliverables	Milestone or Due Dates	Success Indicators

Reporting Results

Key Tasks/ Actions	Responsible Party	Key Outputs/Deliverables	Milestone or Due Dates	Success Indicators

Identify Target Groups

For an ROI process to be fully integrated into the organization, major target audiences must be identified and involved in carrying out the planning and implementation process. These typically include: WLP practitioners, senior managers/sponsors/clients, midlevel managers, instructional designers, and researchers. Engaging primary stakeholders in the process is one of the most effective ways to create organizational support and readiness for a results-based effort. In fact, one of the most common questions of target groups in any change effort is "How does this affect my job on a daily basis?"

Ways to define target groups and potential job impact include the following:

- by customer requirement
- by function
- across specific functions
- between stakeholder groups
- by business line
- between specific levels of the organization
- by geography
- by specialty
- by technical training needs
- by management development training needs
- by human resource needs

Exercise 10–4 will help you to assign responsibilities and identify target groups.

Identify a Champion

A designated champion should be assigned to lead the internal change effort and to take responsibility for ensuring that the process is successfully planned and implemented. Typically, this individual is one who is most familiar with the ROI process, understands its value and place in the organization, and is willing to share this knowledge with others. Some companies opt to assign this responsibility to a manager of measurement and evaluation, while others may designate a team to lead the ROI effort. If the change is already underway without a designated champion, you can help clarify leadership roles and ensure that everyone working on the effort is "on the same page" and clearly aligned.

Develop Internal Skills

Developing internal capabilities for short- and long-term ROI process implementation starts with the WLP staff leading the charge, but it doesn't end there. Every successful impact study has a powerful team of key staff members, helpers, and internal resources who handle everyday tasks and do the bulk of

1. How have you defined roles and responsibilities for your current or future evaluation work?

   _____

   _____

   _____

2. How will you determine which groups should be targeted for carrying out and implementing the ROI evaluation process?

   _____

   _____

   _____

3. How will you position these roles and responsibilities so that they're acceptable and relevant to those involved?

   _____

   _____

   _____

the work. Providing stakeholders and responsible parties with education and a thorough understanding of each step in the evaluation process will help promote consistency in the use and practice of measurement and evaluation strategies and will help ensure a common organizational language around its application.

As shown in previous chapters, involvement from subject matter experts, participants, and line managers helps provide technical expertise in defining standard units of measure for converting data to monetary value. These individuals also serve as a key resource in defining barriers to on-the-job application of learned skills and knowledge. More tips and tools for developing internal capability will be provided in the next chapter.

Establish an Internal ROI Task Force or Steering Committee

An ROI task force or steering committee can help establish evaluation targets and implement core elements of transition planning. This committee typically consists of 6 to 12 members from functional groups across all levels of the organization. Some organizations rotate membership on a quarterly basis or establish teams that are committed to overseeing one particular project or initiative. For best results, the team must be clear about their purpose. Recommended questions to consider before convening this group include:

- What is the group's charter, purpose, and scope?
- How will roles and responsibilities be defined?
- What must be accomplished (goals, objectives, time lines, deliverables)?

- What kind of authority and resources are needed to ensure completion of assigned tasks?
- What are the established ground rules and team commitments?
- How will the group engage the whole organization and report on its activities?

The following case scenario (McCoy, 1998, pp. 171–175) shows an example of how one organization successfully used an internal task force to support readiness efforts for ROI implementation.

A large assembly plant built credibility and shared ownership through a training advisory board. They created a Progressive Education Council (PEC) consisting of both management and union employees that helped set the direction and ultimately improve the effectiveness of their Interactive Learning Center.

At monthly meetings, the Progressive Education Council reported and reviewed training issues, analyzed corporate-initiated training, and assisted in change management efforts such as improving culture and communications. Most of the initial meetings were spent formulating a mission statement. The mission was to facilitate the training and educational development of all employees to deliver high-quality products to satisfy customers. To accomplish this mission, the following goals were established:

- Monitor the use of training resources.
- Increase employee awareness.
- Enhance skills development and ability to work together more effectively.
- Serve constituents by gathering and disseminating training-related information.
- Increase awareness of the role training plays at Navistar.
- Make recommendations that would address current, short-term, and long-term training needs for union and nonunion leadership.

Based on the mission and goals, a short-term action plan was developed. This helped focus efforts and enabled the team to identify critical steps. The plan was presented to senior management for review and approval.

Part of the review included action planning about how to avoid real and potential pitfalls experienced by the task force, such as:

- An advisory group can only be effective if empowered to be so.
- A well-structured selection process is critical to the success of this group—especially when the organization does not view training as a strategic business partner (i.e., if appropriate, have members from both labor and management).
- Ensure that recognized team or peer leaders list core competencies and characteristics required for participation in the group.
- Be willing to stand up for your selection requirements.
- Avoid dictating what this group can and cannot do.
- Don't give too many limitations.
- Focus on issues of concern to the whole organization instead of each member's area of responsibility.

- Encourage members to set an example of how groups can work together toward a common goal.
- Set clear and consistent goals to maintain momentum and show progress.

Step 5: Establish Management Infrastructures to Support the Process

The operational structures and guidelines described in Chapter 1 are the types of system infrastructure needed in this step. These systems ensure consistency in application of the ROI process and replication of its use. They also keep the process focused, consistent, and credible by communicating how new approaches for measuring performance will be aligned with existing business processes and structures. Developing the proper infrastructure requires the following actions:

Prepare Policy, Procedures, and Guidelines

As part of the integration process, operating policies, procedures, and/or standards concerning measurement and evaluation should be established or revised.

Figure 10–4 shows a sample policy statement used to frame the purpose of results-based WLP initiatives in one organization.

Policy statements should also address critical issues that will influence the effectiveness of the measurement and evaluation process and are best developed with input from WLP staff and key stakeholders or clients of WLP products, programs, and services. Typical topics include:

- The adoption of an evaluation framework (such as the five-level model presented here).
- Requiring performance and business impact objective of some or all WLP programs.
- Defining roles and responsibilities.

Policy statements provide an excellent opportunity to communicate basic evaluation requirements, including the accountability requirements of those

---

FIGURE 10–4

SAMPLE POLICY STATEMENT

Topic: Evaluation Purpose

The purpose of workplace learning initiatives at Company X is to increase organizational, operational, and individual effectiveness. Initiatives will offer tangible and intangible returns to customers and will assist Company X in addressing all factors influencing organizational, operational, and individual performance.

FIGURE 10–5
POLICY STATEMENT CHECKLIST

	Yes	No
Purpose of results-based measurement and evaluation strategy stated?	❑	❑
Purpose aligned with compelling business strategy?	❑	❑
Evaluation framework stated?	❑	❑
Evaluation process clearly linked with entire performance improvement cycle, beginning with needs analysis and ending with communicating results?	❑	❑
Evaluation targets stated (i.e., percentage of programs to be evaluated at Level 3 or above)?	❑	❑
Evaluation responsibilities stated for participants, managers, WLP staff, and stakeholders?	❑	❑
Standards for developing, applying, and ensuring credibility of data collection instruments addressed?	❑	❑
Required capabilities for internal and external measurement staff stated?	❑	❑
Administrative or database issues addressed?	❑	❑
Criteria for communicating evaluation results stated?	❑	❑
Continuous improvement review process of evaluation data stated?	❑	❑

responsible for carrying out the process. Figure 10–5 shows a recommended checklist of items to include when updating organizational policy statements to better reflect a results-based WLP strategy.

Exercise 10–5 will help you address strengths and gaps in your current policy statements.

Guidelines tend to be more technical and detailed than policy statements and are meant to show how aspects of a results-based policy are actually undertaken and put into practice. They often include specific forms, instruments, and tools necessary to facilitate the process. Figure 10–6 illustrates sample guidelines for existing programs. Additional guidelines are provided on the CD.

Figure 10–7 shows how one training department applied a corporate template for business process development towards their efforts to standardize results-based WLP processes as credible, value-added business practices throughout the organization. In this example, policy statements are referenced as supporting documentation.

Because of heightened skepticism, it is more important than ever to define operating standards for ROI Methodology that will stand up under scrutiny. Once again, operating standards are needed to ensure that the practice is consistent and conservative from one staff member and one impact study to the next. When developing and communicating operating standards for ROI, here is a review of some guiding principles:

1. If you have not done so already, write a policy statement to describe the purpose of your results-based evaluation focus. If policy statements are already in place in your organization, describe how your impact study supports this statement of purpose. Write this as a 3–4 minute "elevator speech" you would give to orient a senior leader or manager who was unfamiliar with your impact study.

   _____

   _____

   _____

   _____

2. Compare your current evaluation policy statements with the additional recommended policy items found in Figure 10–6. Identify 2–3 areas of strength or compatibility.

   _____

   _____

   _____

3. Identify 2–3 areas where your current evaluation policies can be enhanced to better reflect a results-based approach.

   _____

   _____

   _____

4. What actions will you take to position and integrate these policy statements so that they are acceptable and relevant to key stakeholders?

   _____

   _____

   _____

FIGURE 10–6

SAMPLE GUIDELINES FOR EXISTING TRAINING PROGRAMS

- The results-based approach will affect existing training programs in several ways. First, a few training programs will be selected for increased evaluation activity at Levels 3, 4, and 5. Based on the results from evaluation data, the training program could be enhanced, modified, changed, or discontinued.

- Facilitators for ongoing programs will be asked to relate learning activities more closely to output measures. In some training programs, specific action plans will be developed to link programs to output variables.

- When a training program is being revised or redesigned, the needs assessment will be revisited and Level 3 and 4 objectives will be established. The results-based philosophy will be integrated into the existing programs on a gradual basis, and ultimately all training programs will have the results-based approach fully in place.

FIGURE 10–7

WORKPLACE LEARNING AND PERFORMANCE STANDARDIZATION PROCESS

Contents

1.0 Process Overview

1.1 Purpose and Objective

Develop, approve and deploy standardized Workplace Learning and Performance (WLP) processes that are capable of enhancing and improving operational performance.

1.2 Scope

These WLP Standardization processes will establish specific, mandatory requirements related to workplace learning throughout the organization, and will also contain additional guidelines to help business units meet the intent of the WLP Standardization Expectations. The process includes:

- Governance
- OE process development
- Training for governance team members and key WLP process implementers

1.3 Linkage to Operational Goals

This process facilitates meeting Operational goals of Excellence throughout the organization.

1.4 Process Requirements

1. All WLP processes will be consistent with:
   - The Company X Way
   - Company X Mission, Vision, Values
2. A Development Team will manage the creation of the initial set of WLP Standardized processes.
3. WLP Standardized processes will be developed using a team approach, with membership that includes subject matter experts and representatives from select business units.
4. WLP Standardized processes will be benchmarked against recognized best practices and industry leaders in workplace learning and performance to ensure that Company X processes are capable of delivering intended objectives.
5. WLP Standardized processes will be reviewed and approved by critical stakeholders before finalization.
6. A Review Council will examine final WLP Standardized processes for business alignment and fitness for purpose.

7. An Approval Board will ensure that WLP Standardized processes align with the Company X's strategic plan and that significant implementation issues and business impacts have been accounted for.
8. Each WLP Standardized process will be deployed with an implementation plan that identifies and gives guidance on significant implementation issues, such as communication, resource planning, and alignment with operational excellence (OE) strategies.
9. An exception procedure will be available for use by business units and departments in cases where they feel they cannot comply with a specific WLP process requirement or compliance would not make business sense.

1.5 Links to Other Operational Processes

WLP Standardization supports all other appropriate business processes, such as annual business planning, performance appraisal cycles, and individual development planning processes.

2.0 Procedures

2.1 Overview

A governance model will be used to develop, review, and approve WLP processes. The governance model has four representative components, including a:

- Process Sponsor to provide executive leadership and allocate resources for process implementation
- Process Champion to provide WLP technical expertise, mentoring, and training for process development team members and organizational stakeholders
- Process Development Team to revise, write, and implement WLP processes. This plan will identify significant implementation issues and give guidance on approaches and timing.
- Process Review Council to examine processes to ensure fitness for purpose and alignment with business plans and give final approval

2.2 Details of Governance

2.2.1 Governance—Process Sponsor Charter

Description: This charter describes process Sponsorship roles and responsibilities and procedures used for scheduling, resourcing, and soliciting stakeholder engagement in WLP Standardized process development.

2.2.2 Governance—Process Champion Charter

Description: This charter describes process Champion roles and responsibilities and procedures used for advising, resourcing, and training process Development team members and organizational stakeholders.

2.2.3 Governance—Process Development Team Charter
Description: This charter describes team membership, roles and responsibilities, and procedures used for scheduling, resourcing,
writing, and soliciting input and approval for WLP Standardized processes.
2.2.4 Governance—Review Council Charter
Description: This charter describes team membership, roles and responsibilities, and procedures used for advising on overall priorities and reviewing and approving for WLP Standardized
processes.

2.3 Components of Process Development
  2.3.1 WLP Processes—Terms and Definitions
  2.3.2 Purpose and Scope Statements
  2.3.3 Process Development Procedures
  2.3.4 Process Development Flowchart
  2.3.5 Process Approval Procedure

3.0 Resources, Roles, and Responsibilities

WLP Standardization
                              Name(s), Title
Process Sponsor:
WLP Standardization
                              Name(s), Title
Process Champion:
WLP Standardization
                              Name(s), Title
Process Development Team
WLP Standardization
                              Name(s), Title
Process Review Council

The following table outlines the roles and responsibilities associated
with this process.

Role	Responsibilities	Competencies
WLP Standardization Process Sponsor	■ Provide executive leadership for the WLP Standardization Process integration ■ Ensure that this process is kept current ■ Allocate personnel, funding, and other resources to support process execution ■ Review Standardization Process documentation and records ■ Participate in an annual review of process effectiveness and efficiency	■ Fluency in Operational Excellence ■ Comprehensive knowledge of all elements of a results-based WLP focus, including understanding of the five-level measurement and evaluation framework ■ Ability to provide vision and strategic direction

FIGURE 10–7—*Continued*

WORKPLACE LEARNING AND PERFORMANCE
STANDARDIZATION PROCESS

Role	Responsibilities	Competencies
WLP Standardization Process Champion	▪ Provide subject matter expertise and technical assistance for process development and execution ▪ Ensure that processes adhere to operating standards, policies, and guidelines ▪ Conduct performance reporting and trend analysis company-wide ▪ Facilitate organization-wide changes in WLP process methodology ▪ Mentor, train, and manage the internal WLP and/or ROI community of practice	▪ Extensive experience and comprehensive knowledge of best practice WLP processes, including results-based learning and ROI process models ▪ Facilitative skills ▪ Ability to evaluate results against organizational goals ▪ Data analysis/ interpretation skills ▪ Strong business acumen, including understanding of Operational Excellence (OE) components ▪ Demonstrated performance consulting skills ▪ Influencing skills
WLP Standardization Process Development Team Members	▪ Described in the Development Team Charter	▪ Influencing skills ▪ Technical subject matter expertise ▪ Understanding of internal business unit networks ▪ Understanding of continual improvement ▪ Understanding of OE components ▪ Strong communication skills
Review Council Members	▪ Described in the Review Council Charter	▪ Fluency in OE components ▪ Ability to provide vision and strategic direction ▪ Understanding of the WLP Standardization Process ▪ Understanding of business impacts of deploying WLP Standardization processes

4.0 Measurement and Verification

4.1 Measurement of WLP Effectiveness

Phillip's five-level framework and ROI process model will be used to measure WLP effectiveness across multiple levels of results. The following metrics will be tracked to determine that the WLP Standardization process is effective in meeting its stated purpose. Measures will include:

4.1.1 Leading Measures

4.1.2 Lagging Measures

FIGURE 10–7—*Continued*

WORKPLACE LEARNING AND PERFORMANCE STANDARDIZATION PROCESS

4.2 Verification

The following steps will be conducted to measure and verify that WLP processes, services, and products operate within defined standards of performance.

4.2.1 Review of Process Effectiveness

The WLP Standardization Process Sponsor and Process Champion shall review and verify that all parts of the WLP processes are effective in fulfilling the OE Expectations and results-based process purpose. The review will be performed at least annually.

4.2.2 Audit of Performance

The WLP Standardization Process Sponsor and Process Champion shall verify adherence and identify nonconformance to WLP processes as designed and documented. A documented audit of the processes shall occur at least annually and shall be based upon the following:

- Documents and records
- Demonstrated competence across five levels of WLP performance measures
- Process leading and lagging metrics
- Benchmarking data, if applicable

4.2.3 Governance Body Reviews

Governance bodies shall perform the following reviews:

- Under the direction and guidance of the WLP Standardization Process Sponsor and the Process Champion, the Review Council shall evaluate the performance of the Process Development Team annually.

5.0 Continual Improvement

The following steps will be conducted to assess and improve process performance.

5.1.1 Review of Process Effectiveness

The WLP Standardization Process Sponsor and Process Champion shall review and verify that all parts of the WLP processes are effective in fulfilling the Operational Expectations and results-based process purpose. The review will be performed at least annually.

5.1.2 Audit of Performance

The WLP Standardization Process Sponsor and Standardization Process Champion shall verify adherence and identify non-conformance to WLP processes as designed and documented. A documented audit of these processes shall occur at least annually and shall be based upon the following:

- Documents and records
- Adherence to documented operating standards, policies, and guidelines
- Demonstrated competence across five levels of WLP performance measures
- Process leading and lagging metrics
- Benchmarking data, if applicable

5.1.3 Governance Body Reviews

Governance bodies shall perform the following reviews:

- The Review Council shall perform annual reviews to ensure appropriate progress toward implementation of the WLP processes throughout the organization.
- The Review Council shall evaluate the performance of the Process Development Team annually.
- The Process Sponsor shall evaluate the performance of the Review Council annually.

5.1.4 Gap Analysis

The WLP Standardization Process Sponsor, Standardization Process Champion, and Development Team shall prioritize performance gaps and nonconformities that are identified as part of the process improvement step. Considerations will include operational directives, deviations from standard operating procedures, risk issues, and resource enablers/barriers.

5.1.5 Continual Improvement Plans

Process gaps, nonconformance, and improvement opportunities identified from 5.1.4 shall be summarized and used to assist in building Continual Improvement Plans.

5.1.6 Linkage to Annual Business Plan

The WLP Standardization Process Champion and Development Team shall use the prioritized performance gaps and non-conformities to develop a Continual Improvement Plan that is linked with annual business plans. In some circumstances, improvement activities may extend over several years.

5.1.7 Contents

The Continual Improvement Plan for OE processes will identify the following:

- Improvement opportunities and gaps to be closed
- Resources required
- Responsible person(s)
- Timing and milestones for improvements

6.0 Document Control Information

Description	Policy and Procedure Statement
Revision Date	
Revision Frequency	Every 3 years
Control Number	

7.0 Document List
This is a complete list of the documents referenced in this process.

- Five-Level Framework for Measuring WLP Results
- ROI Process Model
  - Selection Matrix
  - Sample Data Collection Plan
  - Sample ROI Analysis Plan
- Sample Client Engagement and Service Level Agreement
- WLP Policy, Procedures, and Guidelines, including Operating Standards for WLP measurement and evaluation
- WLP Standardization Process Sponsor Charter
- WLP Standardization Process Champion Charter
- WLP Standardization Process Development Team Charter
- WLP Standardization Process Review Council Charter
- Glossary of Terms and Definitions

Report the Complete Story

ROI is a critical measure, but it is only one of many levels. Once the program is implemented, evaluate participant reaction (including the perceived ability to put the training into action), the extent to which participants improved their knowledge, how well people apply the skills, and the business impact. If measurements are not taken, it is difficult to conclude that the results are due to the training.

Enhance Credibility

Using the most credible source (often the participants) will enhance the perception of the quality and accuracy of the data analysis and results.

Be Conservative

Select the most conservative calculation. This lowers the ROI but helps build credibility.

Account for Other Factors

Because the ROI process is implemented as a systems approach, you must account for other factors in the work environment that helped or hindered results. Plan to use at least one method of those discussed in Chapter 4 to isolate the program effects. Without some method of isolation, the evaluation results will be inaccurate and overstated. Isolation strategies include:

- Comparing a pilot group in a training program to a control group not in the program.
- Forecasting results without the training and then comparing to postintervention results.
- Using participants' estimates of the influence of a training program on key measures.

Account for Missing Data

Sometimes training participants leave the organization or change their job function. If training participants cannot provide postintervention improvement data, assume that little or no improvement has occurred. It damages the credibility of the evaluation to make assumptions about improvements for which no substantiating data exists.

Adjust Estimates for Error

It's common to use estimates in reporting financial and cost-benefit information. To enhance the credibility of estimated data, weigh the estimates based on the level of confidence you have in the data and adjust accordingly.

Omit the Extremes

Extreme data items can skew results, so omit them.

Capture Annual Benefits

Only use the first year of benefits of short-term programs. If benefits are not quickly realized, they are probably not worth the cost. Reserve multiple-year ROI analysis for more extensive programs.

Tabulate All Program Costs

The ROI must include all costs associated with training. Omitting or understating costs will destroy the credibility of ROI results.

Collectively, these principles will do much to overcome resistance and influence stakeholders that the ROI process is credible and produces accurate values and consistent outcomes.

Structure ROI as a Learning Tool—Not a Performance Evaluation Tool

A common reason that internal staff may resist the ROI process is because they fear that evaluation results will be used to highlight personal or programmatic failures. For this reason, it's important to use your policies and guidelines as a framework for positioning ROI as a continuous improvement tool that can help assess whether programs are meeting their objectives and proving their worth.

Develop a Transition Project Plan

An important part of transition planning is to establish a project plan, as shown in Figure 10–8. This is helpful for tracking progress towards goals and for identifying specific individuals, timetables, milestones, and deliverables required to initiate and implement the process. This becomes a fluid document and the master project plan for the completion of the various actions presented in this and subsequent chapters. Figure 10–9 presents a results-based transition plan.

FIGURE 10–8
PROJECT PLAN

Program: _____

Description: _____

Duration: _____   No. Participants: _____   Begin Date: _____   End Date: _____

	J	F	M	A	M	J	J	A	S	O	N	D
Form Evaluation Team												
Team Member 1												
Team Member 2												
Evaluation Planning												
Develop Data Collection Plan												
Develop Data Collection Instruments												
Design												
Test												
Redesign												
Data Collection Administration Plan												
Data Collection												
Implement Data Collection Plan												
Collect Responses												
*Distribute Incentives *see DC Admin Plan*												
Data Analysis												
Develop ROI Analysis Plan												
Develop Cost Profile												
Analyze Data												
Communication of Results												
Develop Communication Report												
Report Results—Stakeholder Group 1												
Report Results—Stakeholder Group 2												
Report Results—Stakeholder Group 4												
Evaluation Follow-up												
Steps to be taken to improve program												
Respond to questions from stakeholders												

FIGURE 10–9

RESULTS-BASED TRANSITION PLAN

2006 Transition Plan	Activity		Q1											
	Milestone	Jan-9	Jan-16	Jan-23	Jan-30	Feb-6	Feb-13	Feb-20	Feb-27	Mar-1	Mar-13	Mar-20	Mar-27
Key Tasks													
Form Measurement Team													
Recruit Process Sponsor													
Deliver Internal Awareness Presentations													
Develop Measurement Policy, Guidelines													
Conduct Internal Readiness Assessment													
Set Evaluation Targets, with Stakeholder Input													
Define Roles/Responsibilities													
Identify Business Critical Priorities and/or "Quick Wins" —Identify ROI Project #1 —Identify ROI Project #2													

Develop Scorecard Framework								
Develop Communication Plan								
Provide Professional Development Training for Internal Staff								
Train Supplier Partners								
Revise RFP Guidelines								
Provide Management, Executive Briefings								
Develop, Acquire Support Tools								
Develop Sustaining Mechanisms								
Present Impact Study Results (internally and externally)								

Integrate Cost-Savings Approaches

Some of the more common organizational concerns about ROI implementation focus on the cost, time, and human resources necessary to fully implement the process. A department with limited time and resources can use proven short-cut methods for major steps in the evaluation process. This provides a practical means to transition into ROI implementation and addresses any resistance that might be due to concerns about resource requirements.

Figure 10–10 depicts a flow chart showing how these cost-savings approaches can be used in specific phases of transition and implementation planning. These approaches are also shown more fully, with corresponding guidelines and tools, in Table 10–2.

As an example, a tool associated with the cost-savings approach of "Using Short-cut Methods for Major Steps" is the Just-in-Time Gap Analysis. This short-cut tool can be used to assess and prioritize needs and gaps, in lieu of a comprehensive needs assessment. Because cause analysis is often one of the most time-consuming phases of evaluation planning, a Just-in-Time approach conserves resources by making assumptions about gaps and checking them out with reliable sources through a focus group format. Targeted questions to this group may include:

- What are some other assumptions we can make about this issue?
- What other information is needed to tell a better story or give a bigger picture?
- What are the driving and restraining forces with the proposed solution?
- Can gaps be closed by redesigning a work process instead of creating a training event or a training solution?

Figure 10–11 depicts a tool showing how this process was applied to an operational performance gap, in which poor job performance by operators was first identified as the cause and operator training was first considered the only solution. In this case example, the Just-in-Time Gap Analysis process gathered input from eight subject matter experts in a 60-minute session to "drill down" the issue and identify other contributing factors and potential solutions. This approach can also be used to check out assumptions or interpretations in the data analysis step of ROI calculations.

LESSON LEARNED

It is important to integrate just-in-time solutions with existing systems and to caution against an overreliance on a "quick fix" performance improvement mentality. While just-in-time solutions are a practical way to shave time and provide direction, they are most effective when provided in the context of established client relationships based upon trust and support. In other words, short-term techniques are no substitute for long-term business relationships, which ultimately drive the evaluation purpose, scope, and process.

A blank worksheet for you to use when conducting your own Just-in-Time Gap Analysis is provided on the CD. When using this approach, remember to

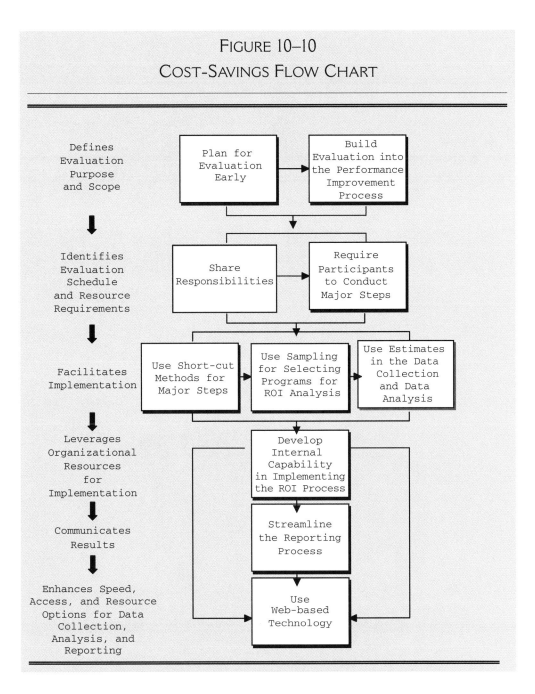

FIGURE 10–10
COST-SAVINGS FLOW CHART

Defines Evaluation Purpose and Scope	Plan for Evaluation Early	Build Evaluation into the Performance Improvement Process
Identifies Evaluation Schedule and Resource Requirements	Share Responsibilities	Require Participants to Conduct Major Steps
Facilitates Implementation	Use Short-cut Methods for Major Steps	Use Sampling for Selecting Programs for ROI Analysis

Use Estimates in the Data Collection and Data Analysis

Leverages Organizational Resources for Implementation

Develop Internal Capability in Implementing the ROI Process

Communicates Results

Streamline the Reporting Process

Enhances Speed, Access, and Resource Options for Data Collection, Analysis, and Reporting

Use Web-based Technology

position the ROI process as something more than a "quick fix" or "flavor-of-the-month" practice.

POTENTIAL CHALLENGES

As we've discussed, typical challenges in transitional planning include:

- False assumptions, myths, or fears about the process.
- Resistance to change.

FIGURE 10–11

JUST-IN-TIME GAP ANALYSIS: CASE EXAMPLE

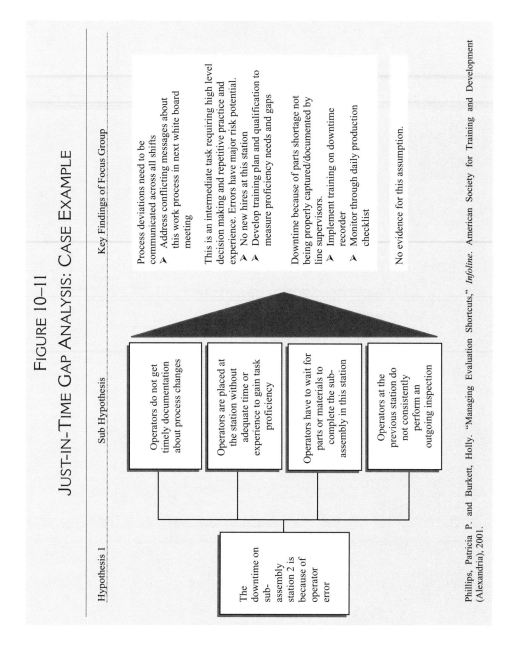

Phillips, Patricia P. and Burkett, Holly. "Managing Evaluation Shortcuts," *Infoline*. American Society for Training and Development (Alexandria), 2001.

- Real or imagined resource constraints.
- Limited infrastructures to support a results-based focus.

Since it's estimated that one-fourth of all training departments in the United States consist of only one trainer with a broad range of responsibilities, concerns about the cost, time, and resources required to show results certainly have merit. In business climates that increasingly demand more results with fewer resources, many of you may be challenged to leverage and compete for needed resources to demonstrate training's bottom-line value.

One way to address these challenges is to use the broad range of cost-savings approaches highlighted in Table 10–2. These 10 "tried-and-true" strategies significantly decrease resource requirements and address readiness, resistance, and infrastructure issues while still providing sound, credible data. These approaches can be easily adapted to training organizations of any size or scope and can be modified to meet evolving business needs.

ACTION PLANNING

Now that we've outlined the steps and activities involved in transition planning and identified ways to counter potential challenges in the process, it's time for you to take action. Exercise 10–6 will help you plan that action.

CHAPTER SUMMARY

Achieving a results-oriented evaluation strategy can be time consuming, labor intensive, and sometimes perceived as threatening. Yet with proper transitional planning and clearly defined, shared responsibilities, the ROI process can be implemented in a proactive, systemic manner. Transition planning allows for the assumption that linking training to business results is still generally a new process for most managers and WLP staff and that the implementation of a results-based culture evolves over time. Assessing and creating individual and organizational readiness for ROI implementation is a vital step towards establishing business partnerships that will enhance commitment for WLP or human performance improvement initiatives going forward.

What?

In this chapter, we looked at ROI implementation as an iterative change process and emphasized the importance of transition planning as a way of moving towards long-term integration of the process into the mainstream. Transition planning steps, guidelines, and tools were provided to facilitate this effort.

TABLE 10–2

COST-SAVING APPROACHES

Approach 1. Plan for evaluation early in the process.
Guideline: Define business needs, establish evaluation purposes, determine target evaluation levels, develop project objectives, and determine evaluation timing.
Tools: Data Collection Plan, ROI Analysis Plan.

Approach 2. Build evaluation into the training process.
Guideline: Link business needs, program objectives, and evaluation targets throughout the entire cycle of training needs assessment, instructional design, delivery, and evaluation. Establish an infrastructure of evaluation policies, procedures, guidelines, and operating standards.
Tools: Linking Needs to Objectives and Evaluation (Reliance Insurance example), Sample Policy and Procedure.

Approach 3. Share responsibilities for evaluation.
Guideline: Invite managers and performers to provide input on performance and skill deficits; ask stakeholders to review and approve evaluation plans; and collect participant and key stakeholder feedback data after the program.
Tools: Transfer Strategy Matrix, Management Involvement Checklist.

Approach 4. Require participants to conduct major steps.
Guideline: Hold participants accountable for learning and applying new skills and knowledge and for identifying enablers and barriers to planned application.
Tool: Action Plan.

Approach 5. Use shortcut methods for major steps.
Guideline: Use just-in-time solutions for gap analysis, solution design, and data collection. Caution against an overreliance on short-cut methods and a "quick-fix" mentality.
Tools: Just-in-Time Gap Analysis, Impact Questionnaire.

Approach 6. Use sampling to select the most appropriate programs for ROI.
Guideline: Only specific types of programs should be selected for a comprehensive, detailed analysis. Set targets for the number of programs to be evaluated at each level.
Tool: Selection Criteria Matrix.

Approach 7. Use estimates in data analysis and collection.
Guideline: Estimates can save a great deal of resources in the isolation and data conversion steps. Use the most credible and reliable sources for estimates, take a conservative approach, and develop a culture for the estimation process.
Tools: Level 1 and Impact Questionnaires, Action plans.

Approach 8. Develop internal capability.
Guideline: Communicate purpose and scope of ROI process as a continuous learning tool that will help assess program priorities and areas of impact. Develop staff capability and shared ownership through education and training and targeted development plans.
Tools: Management Briefing Outline, Individual Development Plan.

Approach 9. Streamline the reporting process.
Guideline: Once management is comfortable with the process of ROI evaluation and a results-based measurement focus has integrated into the organization, a streamlined approach to reporting results may be more appropriate and cost effective.
Tool: Streamlined Impact Study template.

Approach 10. Use technology.
Guideline: Use suitable software packages to speed up various aspects of ROI analysis, design, evaluation, and reporting. Use technology to enhance internal capability by offering on-line needs assessment, self-assessments, or evaluation templates for key stakeholders.
Tools: Knowledge Advisors, Survey Pro.

EXERCISE 10–6. MANAGING THE TRANSITION

Review the transition planning steps and activities associated with each step shown in Figure 10–1.

Identify 1–3 actions that will help you, your staff, or your organization in its current transition to a results-based WLP focus. Examples of actions you may decide to take include:

- Completing a readiness assessment.
- Conducting a communication meeting regarding the vision for a results-based measurement focus.
- Establishing an evaluation advisory committee.
- Updating policy statements.
- Developing a transition project plan.
- Completing a roles and responsibilities matrix for an existing or future evaluation effort.
- Integrating a cost-savings approach into existing evaluation efforts.

Action(s) you will take:

_____
_____
_____

By when:

_____
_____
_____

Review date: (identify person with whom you will share progress)

_____
_____
_____
_____
_____

So What?

The best designed tools and techniques for ROI process implementation are meaningless unless they are integrated into the fabric of the organization and accepted by those responsible for making it work.

Now What?

Recognize your own role as an evaluation champion and change agent. Routinely assess system readiness and resistance to change. Take the time to address objections, assign responsibilities for results, and develop a transition plan for measuring progress. Commit to teaching others.

REFERENCES

Broad, Mary L., and John W. Newstrom. *Transfer of Training.* New York: Addison-Wesley, 1992.

Burkett, Holly. "Transition Planning Tips for Implementing the ROI Methodology." ASTD ROI Network Newsletter, Alexandria, VA: American Society for Training and Development, April 2004.

Burkett, Holly. "An ROI Shortcut for Budget Challenged Training Departments." Interview by Institute of Management and Administration (IOMA). *Report on Managing Training and Development,* August 2004.

Burkett, Holly. "ROI on a Shoestring: Measuring More with Less." *Industrial & Commercial Training,* 5, nos. 1 & 2 (January and March 2005).

Kirkpatrick, Donald L. *Evaluating Training Programs: The Four Levels,* 2nd ed. San Francisco: Berrett-Koehler, 1998.

McCoy, Carol. *In Action: Managing the Small Training Staff,* ed. J. J. Phillips. Alexandria, VA: American Society for Training and Development, 1998.

Phillips, J. J. *Return on Investment in Training and Performance Improvement Program.* Boston: Butterworth-Heinemann, 1997.

Phillips, Patricia P., and Holly Burkett. "Managing Evaluation Shortcuts." *Infoline.* Alexandria, VA: American Society for Training and Development, 2001.

Rossett, A. *First Things Fast.* San Francisco: Jossey-Bass, 1999.

Stamp, Pauline L., Michele Sisto, Roberta Sabitus, Christine Burt, Richard Rava, William Muth, Susan Hall, and Bonnie Onofre. "The Role of ROI in a High Performance Learning Organization." In *In Action: Implementing Evaluation Systems and Processes,* ed. J. J. Phillips. Alexandria, VA: American Society for Training and Development, 1998, pp. 55–79.

CD 🜨

Exercises	Tools, Templates, and Job Aids
Exercise 10–1. Is Your Organization a Candidate for ROI Implementation?	Figure 10–1. Transition Planning Steps
Exercise 10–2. Overcoming Resistance to Myths, Fears, and False Assumptions	Figure 10–2. Readiness Action Plan
Exercise 10–3. Communication Planning	Figure 10–3. Sample Communication Plan
Exercise 10–4. Assigning Responsibilities and Identifying Target Groups	Figure 10–4. Sample Policy Statement
Exercise 10–5. Preparing Evaluation Policies	Figure 10–5. Policy Statement Checklist
Exercise 10–6. Managing the Transition	Figure 10–6. Sample Guidelines for Existing Training Programs
	Figure 10–7. Workplace Learning and Standardization Process
	Figure 10–8. Performance Project Plan
	Figure 10–9. Results-Based Transition Plan
	Figure 10–10. Cost-Savings Flow Chart
	Figure 10–11. Just-In-Time Gap Analysis: Case Example
	Table 10–1. Overcoming Myths, Fears, and False Assumptions
	Table 10–2. Cost-Savings Approaches
	Job Aid 10–1. Roles and Responsibilities

BUILDING INTERNAL CAPABILITY AND MANAGEMENT SUPPORT

In our last chapter, we looked at ROI implementation as a transitional change process and emphasized the importance of addressing objections, assigning responsibilities for results, and teaching others as part of effective transition planning. What we know for sure is that implementing results-based evaluation strategies requires support from an infrastructure of diverse stakeholders with complex interactions and an array of reporting relationships. Since many individuals assume multiple or shifting roles in an evaluation effort, a major implementation challenge is to identify the right people, get them involved, foster their commitment, and keep them well informed at all stages of the process.

Engaging the participation and commitment of different management groups is also a critical component of building internal capability and support for the ROI process. Because managers must approve time and resource allocations for all phases of ROI implementation—including planning, data collection and analysis, and communication of results—addressing their unique needs and concerns poses special challenges.

Few initiatives will be successful without the support and commitment of those involved in making it happen, and implementing the ROI process is no different. This chapter outlines approaches for creating shared ownership for ROI process implementation in both the short and long haul.

In this chapter you will learn to:

- Identify strategies for building internal capabilities in ROI process implementation.
- Create an individual development plan for enhancing your own evaluation capabilities.
- Identify the role of management in successful implementation of the ROI process.

❑ Engage managers' participation in various aspects of ROI process implementation.

❑ Identify implementation risk issues that may hinder organizational support.

THE FUNDAMENTALS

Providing stakeholders, managers, and responsible internal parties with education and a thorough understanding of the ROI evaluation process will help promote consistency in its use and ensure a common organizational language around its application. Consistency is needed in implementation. With consistency comes accuracy and credibility from one impact study and from one practitioner to the next. In environments where training has become decentralized and distributed more and more to line managers, it's even more important to provide internal staff members with consistent education and training on each step of the ROI process.

Preparing internal staff for ROI implementation is a critical issue and must be addressed as part of implementation planning for the following reasons:

▪ Effective and consistent implementation requires capable and knowledgeable practitioners who can deliver on the promise and practice of the ROI process.

▪ Skill development in measurement and evaluation is not always a formal part of learning to become a facilitator, instructional designer, performance improvement specialist, organizational effectiveness consultant, or manager.

▪ Effective development planning around ROI process implementation is a key to enhancing internal capability.

Given the need for implementation support across all organizational levels, it may be helpful to identify key gaps and engagement opportunities as a first step toward developing internal capability in the ROI process. Figure 11–1 shows a sample tool that internal WLP staff can apply towards this purpose.

The perceived gaps and engagement opportunities identified from this assessment can help you pinpoint critical business partners with whom to apply the engagement and skill-building tactics described in this chapter. It can also help you and your team identify where to leverage internal resources for the purpose of:

▪ Promoting results-based measurement objectives
▪ Developing organizational understanding about the business value of a results-based process
▪ Creating support for resource allocation
▪ Building organizational commitment to ensure implementation success.

The Role of Internal WLP Staff

Because internal WLP staff are typically responsible for assessing stakeholder needs and gaps and engaging stakeholders in all aspects of ROI process imple-

FIGURE 11-1

STAKEHOLDER ENGAGEMENT TOOL

Stakeholder Engagement Tool for WLP Staff

Rating Scale: Use the following scale to assess individual stakeholders, as well as stakeholder categories, in terms of their perceived influence within the organization and their perceived level of support with a results-based measurement and evaluation focus. When assessing degree of support, consider the extent to which individuals and/or groups will actually *participate* in implementation activities (i.e., communication briefings, transition planning, data gathering, and impact analysis).

5 = Consistently influential; consistently supportive
4 = Mostly influential; mostly supportive
3 = Adequate influence; adequate support
2 = Some influence; some support
1 = Little to no influence; little to no support

Stakeholder Category	Perceived Degree of Influence	Perceived Degree of Support	Perceived Gap	Stakeholder Engagement Opportunities Targeted Actions (If Influence 3 or greater and support less than 3)
Executive Management (Names/Titles)				
1.				
2.				
3.				
Middle Management (Names/Titles)				
1.				
2.				
3.				
4.				

FIGURE 11-1—*Continued*

STAKEHOLDER ENGAGEMENT TOOL

Stakeholder Category	Perceived Degree of Influence	Perceived Degree of Support	Perceived Gap	Stakeholder Engagement Opportunities Targeted Actions (If Influence 3 or greater and support less than 3)
Line Supervisors (Names/Titles)				
1.				
2.				
3.				
Internal WLP Staff (Names/Titles)				
1.				
2.				
3.				
Employees/Participants				
1.				
2.				
3.				
Other:				
1.				
2.				

mentation (coordination, execution, and logistics), they need proper training and resources to step up to these expanded roles and responsibilities. Although some professionals have measurement and evaluation formal preparation, few are prepared to meet the challenges of today's organizational evaluation needs. For those with no formal training at all, there is much to learn.

One financial institution addressed this issue in its "strategic shift to a results-oriented paradigm." The education and training staff had to execute and champion the process if implementation of the ROI program evaluation process was to be successful. Training was provided to all employees of the group. The issues covered included:

- How mapping specific business objectives and performance objectives down to the skills and knowledge required permitted a tighter definition of the training requirements.
- Why each training and performance objective needed to have a specific method of evaluation.
- The value of incorporating these measures into the training for easier data collection.
- The need for the training to include discussions with the participants of their training, on-the-job performance, and business goals. This ensured that participants knew what results they were expected to achieve.
- The role of the training group in the process and the roles of other stakeholders.
- How the measurement process assisted in the achievement of the overall business strategy.

Potential Challenges—Internal WLP Staff

Although there are many compelling reasons to enhance internal capability in training evaluation, establishing an evaluation culture is no easy task. On many organizational levels, objections may arise about the real or imagined time, cost, and complexity involved in applying the process. WLP staff, in particular, might be concerned that ROI results will lead to criticism. Building internal capability in the ROI process is one of the best ways to overcome these challenges. Building capability is not just about providing people with the right skills—it's also about providing the right skills to the right people at the right time.

The following tactics will help with that effort.

1. Build a business case for skill development. First, evaluation makes good economic sense and should be required of any program representing a significant expenditure of funds. Second, managers and stakeholders need evidence that investments of time, money, and resources are worthwhile, particularly as competition for resources intensifies. Who's going to invest in a training and performance improvement effort that can't show its value? Trends show that increased pressure from stakeholders to show value-added contributions will remain a driving force in WLP practice. Figure 11–2 shows an example of how one public-sector

FIGURE 11–2

SAMPLE BUSINESS CASE OUTLINE

Project Business Case

Version: Draft v.02
Date: October 23, 2005
Author: Jane Doe
Owner: Project Management Competency

Table of Contents

About This Document
This document defines the Business Case for the

Related documents
This document should be used in conjunction with:

FIGURE 11–2—*Continued*
SAMPLE BUSINESS CASE OUTLINE

Summary of changes

This section records the history of changes to this document.

Version	Date	Author	Description of change
.01			Initial Draft

When significant changes are made to this document, the version number will be incremented by 1.0. When changes are made for clarity and reading ease only and no change is made to the meaning or intention of this document, the version number will be increased by 0.1.

Reviews and approvals

This document requires review and approval.

Approval

This document was approved by:

Name	Role	Date
	Project Sponsor	

Reviewers

This section lists persons or areas that have specific, formal roles in the project.

This document was reviewed by:

Name	Role	Date

FIGURE 11–2—*Continued*
SAMPLE BUSINESS CASE OUTLINE

Distribution
This section lists all the persons or areas that will receive a copy of this document after it has been finalized.

Name	Area	Date

Business Case
END OF DOCUMENT

Chapter 1 Business Case

1.1 Purpose of this Document

1.2 Description of Requirement or Initiative

1.3 Is this request related to or associated with any existing request or projects?

1.4 Who will benefit from the successful outcome and what is the benefit?

1.5 Benefits Realization

1.6 How long should it take or is there an important delivery date?

1.7 How much is it expected to cost?

1.8 Are there any known risks or impediments in achieving an outcome?

Business Case
END OF DOCUMENT

organization framed a business case with potential sponsors when requesting formal support for an ROI impact study.

2. Stress the need for business linkage. If your services don't align with what management is measuring, how can you expect to impact it? Emphasize that the purpose of ROI implementation is to continuously improve WLP programs and services, to measure the effectiveness of WLP efforts against business measures, and not to be a source of performance measurement for staff.

3. Point to rising standards. Peer pressure from other WLP professionals who have contributed to the growing literature of ROI case study and research has continued to "raise the bar" in evaluating best practice. The more a WLP knows about and adheres to evaluation standards, the more effective their WLP time and resource management will be.

4. Stress self-satisfaction. Most professionals want to know if their solutions solved a problem, addressed root causes, and made a valuable difference to the organization and the people involved. How can you know if you've matched the right solution to the right problem without some form of evaluation and measurement?

5. Develop an ROI leader. An important step in successful ROI implementation is the designation of an internal leader or champion for the ROI process. As with most change efforts, someone must take responsibility for ensuring that the process is implemented in a way that adds value to the whole organization. In preparation of this role, some individuals obtain special training to build specific skills and knowledge in the ROI process.

   Table 11–1 illustrates how one financial organization defined the role of its internal ROI champion and blended performance consulting and evaluation skill sets into a required competency profile. The profile was then used as a guide for selecting appropriate Assessment, Measurement, and Evaluation (AME) Champions and fostering their continued professional development through specialized training and/or certifications.

   Many training programs are available, ranging from two-day to five-day intensive workshops to provide help with this challenging assignment. Some are sponsored by professional associations like ASTD and ISPI. Others are offered by vendors. One of the most comprehensive and rigorous is Phillips' ROI certification program designed for those tasked with implementing the ROI Methodology in their organization. To date, over 3,000 individuals have attended a certification workshop, representing 500 organizations in 35 countries.

6. Commit to teaching others. One of the best ways to deepen learning about a subject is to have to teach it to someone else. This step challenges internal staff to continually hone their own evaluation competencies and skill sets. Developing the evaluation skills of others outside the WLP function not only increases the number of people who can deliver the right message but also allows the resource-constrained department to reach more people faster. In addition, subject-matter experts or line managers who are closest to the business have the credibility and capacity to tailor evaluation data to real-time business needs.

TABLE 11–1

AME CHAMPION PROFILE

Role	Required Skills and Competencies	Activities
Assessment Expert	<ul><li>Strong performance consulting skills.</li><li>Strong HR and L&D consulting skills.</li><li>Strong analytical and problem-solving skills.</li><li>Strong influencing skills.</li><li>Strong collaboration skills.</li><li>Strong business acumen.</li></ul>	<ul><li>Analyze multiple factors that impact cause and effect relationships.</li><li>Consult with LOB Learning Team members to develop effective AME strategies.</li></ul>
Measurement and Evaluation Expert	<ul><li>Strong performance consulting skills.</li><li>Strong HR and L&D consulting skills.</li><li>Strong expertise in ROI methodologies.</li><li>Working knowledge of instructional design.</li><li>Strong influencing skills.</li><li>Strong collaboration skills.</li></ul>	<ul><li>Implement comprehensive measurement and evaluation systems, processes, and tools (level 1–5) on each LOB Learning Team to determine the impact of training and to provide program effectiveness information to designers.</li><li>Lead and document impact studies that show the business impact of individual learning interventions and ensure managers have the information they need to improve performance.</li><li>Develop a "dashboard" of performance indicators that will be regularly monitored to ensure the effectiveness of learning interventions and show the impact of learning.</li></ul>
Project Manager	<ul><li>Strong organization skills.</li><li>Strong communication skills with all levels of the organization.</li></ul>	<ul><li>Coordinate technology required to support AME work.</li><li>Must be comfortable in a role where they do not always "get credit" visibly for the work they produce as they will rarely be the one communicating with the client on a specific initiative, but rather prepare others for such interactions.</li><li>Implement cost effective and efficient processes that add value to the organization.</li></ul>
AME Coach and Mentor	<ul><li>Strong influencing skills.</li><li>Strong listening skills.</li></ul>	<ul><li>Mentor, educate, and coach training staff and other affected HR team members on AME methodologies and tools.</li></ul>

Note: "LOB" denotes Line of Business.
Source: Wallace, Debi. *Keeping on Track: Sustaining Strategies for ROI Implementation.* Irvine, CA: ASTD ROI Network Conference, 2004.

7. Educate vendors. The idea of presenting with the end in mind should not be limited to in-house facilitators or staff. Training suppliers who deliver internal WLP programs should also be aware of the organization's evaluation targets and should be able to articulate the business and performance objectives of their products. Internal staff need the capability to communicate the organization's evaluation framework and strategy to training suppliers. Working with training suppliers to develop appropriate objectives and data collection tools not only ensures that the training supplier is providing a program that directly affects the business of the organization but also prevents costly backtracking by internal staff when evaluating the program and justifying the expense.

8. Network with others. Joining an established network is a helpful development activity. Many communities have local chapters of ASTD or ISPI, in which performance measurement resources, ideas, and support can be gained for those at any stage of implementation. Additional resources include the following:

   - *The ASTD ROI Network (www.astd.org)*. An affiliation of about 600 that was specifically created as a community of practice for professionals to exchange information and evaluation best practices, particularly around the ROI process.

   - *The American Evaluation Association (www.eval.org)*. Primarily for those involved in evaluation education, government health care, and nonprofit organizations. Although membership is across all segments, most of the members are in the education and public sector. In 2004, there were 2,000 members.

   - *The ROI Institute (www.roiinstitute.net)*. Available for those who have completed certification on the ROI methodology. The ROI Institute is a research, information, and benchmarking organization designed to provide workshops, research, and advice in the area of measurement and evaluation, including the ROI Methodology. The individuals who complete certification in the ROI Methodology become members of the institute. Others may visit the Website to obtain additional information. The ROI Institute conducts a variety of educational program, including workshops and certification. In 2006, the institute had approximately 3,000 members.

   - *The Evaluation Consortium*. A group of evaluation professionals from various organizations throughout the United States. Memberships are usually in the range of 10 to 15 organizations that meet to exchange information. There is no Website or e-mail for the consortium. For additional information on this group, contact the authors.

   - *The Society for Human Resource Management (www.SHRM.org)*. Provides a variety of services for individuals involved in the human resource management field. Although there is no membership option for those involved in evaluation, many of their programs and conferences address evaluation topics. Books and workshops are offered through SHRM and focus on the evaluation process as well.

   - *The International Society for Performance Improvement (www.ISPI .org)*. This organization is composed of those individuals improving human performance in the workplace. Members work for all kinds of organizations, including industry, government, education, and military. Although there is no particular evaluation membership option for ISPI, multiple products and services focus on aspects of performance management and measurment for both individuals and organizations. ISPI's Performance Technology Standards (2002) emphasize a "focus on outcomes," a "systems view," and a systematic "evaluation," among others, as standards of practice guiding the profession.

9. Emphasize professionalism. Evaluation skill sets are a professional, core competency associated with both the evaluator role in human performance improvement work and the emerging role of the performance consultant.

Professional associations, such as ASTD, have identified several potential roles of an implementation leader. For example, the following roles emerged from the 2004 Workplace Learning and Performance Competency study by ASTD:

- Technical expert
- Consultant
- Problem solver
- Initiator
- Designer
- Developer
- Coordinator

- Cheerleader
- Communicator
- Process monitor
- Planner
- Analyst
- Interpreter
- Teacher

Other associations, such as ISPI and the Evaluation Consortium, have identified key roles and competencies for professionals who perform evaluation functions. A sample listing of evaluator knowledge, skills, and competencies are noted below:

Function	Role of the Evaluator	Sample Competencies
Workplace Learning and Performance Area of Expertise: *Measuring and Evaluating* (ASTD 2004 Competency Study)	Serve as business partner. Gather data to answer specific questions regarding the value or impact of learning and performance solutions; focus on the impact of individual programs and create overall measures of system effectiveness; leverage findings to increase effectiveness and provide recommendations for change.	▪ Knowledge of analysis methods, such as cost-benefit analysis, ROI, etc. ▪ Knowledge of data interpretation and reporting ▪ Performance gap evaluation skills ▪ Ability to evaluate results against organizational goals ▪ Standard setting skills ▪ Ability to assess impact on culture ▪ Human performance improvement intervention reviewing skills ▪ Feedback skills

Continued

Function	Role of the Evaluator	Sample Competencies
Human Performance Technologist (Rothwell, 1996).	Identify the impact of an intervention on individual or organizational effectiveness. Assess the impact of non-training interventions (reengineering initiatives, reward or incentive systems, recruitment efforts, job design, and implementation of new technology, equipment or tools).	■ Performance gap evaluation skills ■ Ability to evaluate results against organizational goals ■ Standard setting skills ■ Ability to assess impact on cultures ■ Human performance improvement intervention reviewing skills ■ Feedback skills
Performance Consultant (Robinson, 2002).	Achieve results in such key areas as: forming business partnerships; conducting performance analysis; managing change projects; and measuring the impact of solutions.	■ Analysis skills ■ Business knowledge ■ Change management skills ■ Facilitation skills ■ Human performance ■ Improvement understanding ■ Influencing skills ■ Project management skills ■ Questioning skills ■ Relationship building skills ■ Systematic thinking skills

A common theme is the focus on a systems view of the organization and a business perspective with desired learning or performance results. In other words, to gain credibility as an evaluation leader, it's important to evaluate factors of organizational as well as learner performance when measuring the impact of a single program or process. Being able to understand the role that environmental enablers and barriers play in individual and business performance will help you identify the key leverage points for applying your influencing, change management, and project management skills—as well as evaluation technical skills—when implementing a results-based measurement effort.

10. Review evaluation targets. As previously discussed, it's important to establish specific evaluation targets in order to track progress and keep the process within a manageable scope for internal staff and the organization as a whole. These targets should be periodically reviewed and approved by both internal and management staff to ensure that the targets are realistic and achievable. Endorsement by the senior management team is especially important.

Table 11–2 shows an example of a management plan for implementing evaluating targets over time.

The Role of Managers

The role of managers can be examined in different ways. First are the lower-level managers who supervise the participants involved in programs or who are in powerful roles of ensuring that the WLP function continues to provide accountability. When they see data that represent the value of this process and react to it, the process is perceived to be necessary and adding value. They will

TABLE 11–2

MANAGEMENT PLAN FOR EVALUATING TARGETS OVER TIME

	Percent of Courses Evaluated at Each Level					
	Year 0	Year 1	Year 2	Year 3	Year 4	Year 5
Reaction and planned action	85%	90%	95%	100%	100%	100%
Learning	30%	35%	40%	45%	50%	60%
Job application	5%	10%	15%	20%	25%	30%
Business results	2%	4%	5%	9%	12%	15%
ROI	0%	2%	4%	6%	8%	10%

request additional measurement processes in the future and will support the efforts necessary to provide the data. More important, they will support the decisions made to correct situations based on the data.

The next key group is middle management. This group often sets the tone for the organization's acceptance of the data processes through one or more of the following actions:

- Active participation in a WLP initiative (or lack of participation).
- Demonstrated support for the ROI evaluation process (or lack of support).
- Allowing subordinates the time to be involved in ROI process activities (or not).
- Taking the time to review initial analyses or data (or not).
- Implementing actions to drive improvements (or not).

The point is that the tone set for this group is very important for the first-level managers, who often look to the middle manager for leadership.

The upper-level managers are also critical. They must be actively involved and show that they support the process. They have to take time to review the data and react to it. They have to attend meetings, make assignments, and reinforce actions and support. Most importantly, they must approve budgets, particularly the budget for the measurement and evaluation funding. Funding will likely be based upon how the WLP function is viewed in terms of its business value to the organizations. Subsequently, each of these three groups—lower-, mid-, and upper-level managers—need attention for long-term commitment and viability of the ROI process.

Potential Challenges—Management Staff

Management support is critical to successful implementation and integration of the ROI process. As previously stated, managers' involvement is needed to approve time, money, and resources for all phases of ROI implementation.

Inadequate management support is also a frequent cause of learning and performance failure. Typical management concerns that impede full support of ROI process implementation include those about:

- Conflicting priorities or moving targets.
- Time, cost, or resource requirements of the ROI process.
- Credibility of WLP's role as a business partner.
- Expectations about use of the process.
- How negative results will be used.

These concerns must be addressed across three levels of lower, middle, and upper management in order to secure support and commitment for the process. The following tactics will help to enlist managers' involvement and enhance the credibility and perceived value of the WLP function as a strategic business partner.

1. Provide ongoing and new-hire manager workshops. One effective approach for engaging management support is to conduct a workshop along the lines of "Manager's Role in Learning and Performance." Use this opportunity to discuss and illustrate the consequence of inadequate management support for training, learning, and performance as well as to show how the ROI process can improve WLP results and save money.
   Typical workshop content includes the following:

   - The strategic importance of a results-based learning and performance effort
   - The organizational impact of a results-based WLP effort
   - A results-based workplace learning and performance framework (i.e., the five-level ROI process methodology)
   - Internal WLP staff responsibilities for achieving desired results
   - Manager's role in achieving desired results

   These sessions can be an expansion of the communication briefings held during transition planning and should be routinely incorporated into new-hire orientation for middle-management groups.
2. Ask for management involvement. An effective way to enhance commitment to the ROI process is to invite managers to serve on an executive steering committee, an internal advisory committee, or on an impact study review team. The role of managers in these groups is to provide input and advice to the project staff on a variety of issues, including needs, implementation problems, and evaluation issues. Table 11–3 illustrates a checklist that can used to invite management involvement. This can also be used as a catalyst for discussion during the manager workshops described previously.
3. Show how projects have helped solve major problems. It's not always about showing hard numbers or a financial return on investment. Most managers simply want to know whether the implementation is on track, meeting targets, and solving problems. Providing information about

TABLE 11–3

MANAGEMENT INVOLVEMENT CHECKLIST

The following are areas for present or future involvement in the WLP process. Please check your areas of planned involvement.

Involvement	Inside Your Area	Outside Your Area
Attend a program designed for your staff	❏	❏
Provide input for WLP need or gap analysis	❏	❏
Serve on a WLP or evaluation advisory committee	❏	❏
Provide input on WLP program design	❏	❏
Serve as a subject matter expert	❏	❏
Volunteer to evaluate an external WLP program	❏	❏
Assist in the selection of a vendor-supplied WLP program	❏	❏
Participate in briefings to communicate purpose and importance of select WLP programs	❏	❏
Provide reinforcement to employees as they become involved in an WLP program	❏	❏
Remove barriers to attendance of WLP programs	❏	❏
Remove barriers to application of WLP performance objectives	❏	❏
Assist in program evaluation and follow-up	❏	❏

how a training or nontraining solution has added value to individual and departmental performance is a convincing way to secure commitment to the process and negotiate for measuring select solutions at an ROI level down the road.

Figure 11–3 shows how one manufacturing organization used a streamlined scorecard template to compare and contrast results between a results-based pilot effort and a high-profile activity-based WLP program. This template provided a powerful visual about the business value of a results-based WLP focus and was successfully used during management briefings to generate management buy-in for continued ROI implementation beyond the pilot group offering.

4. Strengthen relationships. Although it's important to actively collaborate with managers before, during, and after solution planning and implementation, the best time to establish support is before you need it. Take time to build allies, develop partnerships, and understand the needs of your business and its stakeholders.

5. Leverage standard communication tools to promote results. When an impact study has achieved significant results, increase managers' awareness by creating a brief memo or summary statement outlining the goals of the evaluation effort, when it was implemented and by whom, and the results achieved. Use existing communication forums such as newsletters, internal Websites or intranets, business update or staff meetings, brochures, and quarterly reports. Frequent, targeted communications to the management group on evaluation projects, plans, and

FIGURE 11–3

CASE EXAMPLE: COMPARING THE PERFORMANCE VALUE OF A RESULTS-BASED WLP PROGRAM TO AN ACTIVITY-BASED WLP PROGRAM

Results-Based WLP Program (Pilot)	Select Reaction/Planned Action Results	Select Learning Results	Select Application Results	Select Impact Results (*directly attributable to training*)	Return on Investment	Select Intangible Benefits
Career Development Program Business Objective: Increased Operational Capacity	Overall satisfaction rating: 4.8 I would recommend this program to others: 4.8 Program was relevant to my daily job: 4.5 92% reported intention to conduct a development discussion with their manager within 30 days of the workshop	I have a better understanding of my Performance Priorities for the next 6–12 months: 4.48 I have a better understanding of my development needs as they relate to my current position: 4.37 I having a better understanding of my talents as they relate to my current position: 4.26	94% conducted a development discussion with their manager within 60 days of workshop 76% apply critical skills from development discussion plan 52% are enhancing development through development plans approved by their manager	Monetary benefits of increased productivity: $187,000 Monetary benefits from increased efficiencies: $92,000	ROI (%) = Net Program Benefits / Costs $195,700 / $83,300 = 235% ROI	Improved relationship with immediate manager Increased perception that employer cares about employee's career growth Improved ability to view performance priorities in relation to "big picture" Anticipated plan to stay with employer for next 12 months

FIGURE 11-3—*Continued*

CASE EXAMPLE: COMPARING THE PERFORMANCE VALUE OF A RESULTS-BASED WLP PROGRAM TO AN ACTIVITY-BASED WLP PROGRAM

Activity-Based WLP Program (Pilot)	Select Reaction/ Planned Action Results	Select Learning Results	Select Application Results	Select Impact Results (*directly attributable to training*)	Return on Investment	Select Intangible Benefits
Front-Line Leadership Program *"Management Essentials"* Business Objective: Improved Operational Efficiencies	Overall satisfaction rating: 3.7 I would recommend this program to others: 3.0 Program was relevant to my daily job: No data captured Reported intention to apply leadership skills/knowledge: No data captured	Participants participated in role play and skill practice scenarios No data captured on learning gains	Focus Group follow up: ✓ 20% used Front Line Leadership skills on daily job ✓ 60% reported organizational barriers to use (limited management support, conflicting priorities, mixed messages)	No data captured on progress with business objectives Efficiency Indicators (cycle time, labor efficiency index) continued to be below standard 90 days after program completion	Estimated program costs: $92,500 No data captured on cost benefits	Antidotal evidence suggests that: ✓ Front-line leaders have not consistently applied program skills/knowledge ✓ There was little reinforcement, incentive, or organizational support to apply skills

activities will bolster the visibility and influence of WLP as a business partner. Just be cautious about inundating managers with superfluous papers, forms, or e-mails.

6. Use technology. Use technology to increase evaluation literacy and management understanding of the ROI process. For instance, you can use technology to:

   ■ Offer on-line needs assessment, self-assessments, or evaluation templates for key managers or leaders.
   ■ Create an internal listserv to exchange information about training needs, business issues, and evaluation trends.
   ■ Provide regular briefing sessions (managers/employees/sponsors).
   ■ Market train-the-trainer services for project sponsors, ROI advisory groups, or site ROI champions.
   ■ Publish testimonials using newsletters, e-mail, Web pages, or online discussion groups.
   ■ Involve multiple stakeholders in project action plans.

   For example, a technical education center used existing technology to support a new evaluation culture after laying much of the groundwork through the development of an enterprisewide evaluation strategy and philosophy. The next step was education in training evaluation for managers and staff. The organization framed the purpose of the training in terms of providing stakeholders with a consistent message and approach to implementing an evaluation system and promoting a shared understanding of the benefits of training evaluation.

   Upon formulating a strategy and philosophy of evaluation and providing an educational foundation, the education center developed a process to incorporate evaluation into the existing course development and delivery process. It used a milestone process that reflected the stages of instructional systems design (ISD) within a project management framework. The milestone process included six distinct project milestones: mile 0 (initiation), mile 1 (planning), mile 1a (design), mile 2 (development), mile 3 (implementation), and mile 4 (evaluation). It allowed the center to operate in a competitive business environment by providing structure in the management of project resources.

7. Put a face to the numbers. Some of the most compelling elements of a results-based effort are the human-interest stories that emerge from the process. A rigorous program with difficult requirements can be a source of accomplishment and public recognition for participants, who are usually more than willing to share their experience. Consider inviting a select group of participants into a management review meeting, perhaps one dealing with a project that met some resistance.

   Such a face-to-face testimonial typically has powerful results:

   ■ It reinforces to participants that their WLP involvement makes a difference to the business.
   ■ It reinforces to managers that most participants genuinely care about making a difference.

- It allows participants the opportunity to share how application of learned skills or knowledge improved their job performance and/or work climate.
- It allows participants the opportunity to reinforce the consequence of inadequate management support for training, learning, and performance.

If your participant group is one that has infrequent contact with managers, it may be helpful to provide some advance coaching so that they stay focused on the meeting purpose and manage their meeting time properly.

8. Use project management skills with executive managers and sponsors. *Sponsor* is the term used to describe senior managers who are responsible for allocating an organization's limited resources to accomplish organizational goals. A sponsor is not considered the same as an advocate. Although an advocate may persuasively communicate the need for people, money, and materials, it takes the support of an executive sponsor to provide the resources needed to initiate and sustain evaluation projects. WLP specialists cannot assume a sponsorship role. Only those with legitimate authority and influence to secure major changes can be sponsors.

One of the costliest mistakes evaluation project managers make is not identifying and dealing with the sponsorship component early on. Impact studies happen because a sponsor chooses to commit resources to it and he or she believes that it will achieve a beneficial result for the organization. Sponsors play a pivotal part in jump-starting an evaluation project, identifying people to assume needed roles, and assigning people to fill potential "black holes" in the effort. Effective sponsors also recognize that a well-managed evaluation process may entail personal, political, and organizational costs and are willing to pay them. For example, when managers who should be acting as advocates do not do their job well, a sponsor must communicate a resolve for immediate resolution and corrective action.

Given the infinite number of possible projects in an organization and the finite nature of resources available, evaluation leaders must think like project managers and position their ROI strategy and resource requirements in a meaningful organizational context.

Once the business case has been made and leadership support has been generated, Figure 11–4 provides a checklist of implementation questions to be used as a context for building and sustaining sponsorship support on an ongoing basis throughout all phases of ROI implementation.

These questions get to the heart of the sponsor's business orientation. The sponsor must continually determine whether a project warrants continued investment based on current progress and expected value.

9. Provide progress or status reports. A well-managed implementation process has regular status reviews to update both sponsors and managers on the health of the project, its performance against its goals,

FIGURE 11–4

IMPLEMENTATION CHECKLIST FOR PLANNING AND MANAGING EVALUATION PROJECTS

Implementation Issues to Address with Your Sponsor	Yes	No
Are the resource estimates for data collection, data analysis, and calculating cost/benefits credible?	❏	❏
Is the evaluation project the best use of organizational resources?	❏	❏
Is the projected evaluation plan realistically aligned with organizational capacity and constraints?	❏	❏
Are the schedule, scope, and quality of project deliverables clear?	❏	❏
Have the business imperatives for initial, start-up evaluation targets changed?	❏	❏
Does the currently projected completion date for the evaluation project affect the project's immediate or short-term value?	❏	❏
Have risk management issues been identified: ▪ Key players changing	❏	❏
▪ Conflicting units of value for business improvement measures	❏	❏
▪ Incomplete or missing data	❏	❏
▪ Credibility of data sources	❏	❏
▪ Barriers to management or participant involvement	❏	❏
▪ Shifting priorities, moving targets, and organizational competition for resources	❏	❏
▪ Hard-to-get or large amounts of resources	❏	❏
Is there a milestone point in the evaluation life-cycle where identified risks warrant a reassessment of project continuation?	❏	❏
Is there a business case for continuing the evaluation project through its identified phases and process life-cycle?	❏	❏

resources expended to date, and predictions of the schedule and resources required for completion. The review also provides an opportunity to review and reflect on:

- Initial assumptions about results.
- Interim results.
- Needed changes or improvements.
- Changes in responsible parties.
- Risk events that may have occurred, become less likely, or recently emerged.

Although these topics may not be suitable for every meeting, they represent typical areas of interest and concern to management.

10. Proactively manage risks. To gain and maintain executive sponsorship support, the ROI leader must also convey a desire to consciously manage risk or "hot spots." This is a facet of implementation that WLP professionals often underestimate or misjudge. However, tackling risk management yields the following benefits:

- It provides an opportunity to remind sponsors that there are risks.
- It establishes a foundation for later sponsor discussion of possible responses to risks.
- It gives your team a chance to talk openly about risk issues or concerns.
- It legitimizes risk management as a standard practice in evaluation or ROI implementation.
- It positions you as being a proactive business partner.
- It positions ROI implementation as a change management strategy.

Sponsors use risk management information to assess:

- whether the process remains viable,
- is consistent with the organization's goals, and
- is worth the risk of continued investment.

It is not unusual for sponsors to cancel or redefine evaluation projects in response to emerging news and in response to changes in the organizational environment. Electing to continue an evaluation project should be a considered and conscious choice. There is a myth that well-managed evaluation projects always meet their goals, finish on schedule and on budget, and show bottom-line impact with a positive ROI. In the real world, some evaluation projects fail to realize their expected value. When this happens, the evaluation project manager must address hard issues with the sponsor:

- *When did we know this project was in trouble?* A data trail should exist to answer this question, and the information should have been promptly relayed to the project's sponsors.
- *Was continuing the project an informed decision?* If the sponsor had timely and accurate status information, the answer to this question should be "yes."

Building Management Support as an Outside Consultant

The principles of enlisting management involvement through relationship building, effective project management, and proactive, streamlined communications have broad application to both the internal and external ROI professional.

However, external consultants face special challenges if they do not have the inside track on organizational culture, climate, and formal and informal decision makers. Although some consultants attain immediate status and influence as an outsider to the system, they still have to overcome obstacles and biases when engaging managers. For instance, an internal director or consultant can market his or her own programs and even mandate training. As an external consultant or contractor, building strong relationships, meeting customer expectations, and adapting solutions to fit an organization's unique needs and culture are keys to ensuring project and solution success.

One outsourced director of training and development had to build ownership for the evaluation of a project that was the biggest consulting job in the company's history. She had to depend upon internal champions—such as the vice president of quality and the vice president of human resources—to sell the evaluation plan internally and ensure that support was available from upper and mid-management through the year of the contract. Cultivating strong relationship with top decision makers, being flexible with plans and targets, and building the schedules of other clients around this particular client—who was her biggest client—were all important factors in receiving ongoing support for the evaluation effort. Exercise 11–1 provides a list of the 10 tactics described for building management support. Review these now and determine which ones you will apply to improve management support for your impact study.

ACTION PLANNING

Building Internal Capability with Internal Staff by Using Individual Development Plans

As with other comprehensive professions, evaluation work has many "layers of knowledge." Regardless of the knowledge or skills acquired, there is always more to learn. The necessary competencies are constantly changing. Suffice to say that ROI implementation encompasses an ever-expanding range of roles and skill sets, most of which are learned through trial and error. Given the variety and complexity of these roles and skills, it's important to routinely assess individual strengths and opportunities for improvement. Completing an impact project or two is typically not enough to build internal capabilities in ROI process implementation. Remember that credibility is always an issue when developing management support and communicating program results. Build credibility by continually developing your own evaluation skill sets.

EXERCISE 11–1. TEN TACTICS FOR BUILDING MANAGEMENT SUPPORT

1. Review the list of tactics provided for building management support.

   Tactics

   1. Provide ongoing and new-hire manager workshops.
   2. Ask for management involvement.
   3. Show how projects have helped solve major problems.
   4. Strengthen relationships.
   5. Leverage standard communication tools to promote results.
   6. Use technology.
   7. Put a face to the numbers.
   8. Use project management skills with executive managers and sponsors.
   9. Provide progress or status reports.
   10. Proactively manage risks.

2. Identify 1–3 tactics that you will apply in order to improve management support with your current impact study.

   _____

   _____

3. Identify one tactic that if proactively applied now would ***most positively*** impact the success of your current evaluation effort.

   _____

   _____

4. Commit to apply this tactic to facilitate a positive outcome.

   Action(s) you will take:

   _____

   _____

   _____

   By when:

   _____

   _____

   _____

   Review date: (identify person with whom you will share progress)

   _____

   _____

   _____

Assess the Gap Between Current and Desired Capabilities

To get started, it might help to assess your immediate goals and roles in relation to your current impact study. The Evaluation Consortium suggests that implementing an effective evaluation effort requires skills in one or more of the following areas:

- *Positioning.* ROI implementation must be positioned correctly within an organization in order to accomplish its tasks and ensure that it brings meaning and value to the organization.
- *Leading.* ROI implementation has the opportunity to both *prove* value and *improve* worth. The evaluator should serve as a partner to other organizational areas, demonstrate leadership in meeting organizational goals, and provide innovation in using the best concepts and technology available.
- *Executing.* This is the nuts-and-bolts, roll-up-your-sleeves part of ROI implementation. Once it is positioned correctly and leadership is established, the focus is on accelerating and driving performance. As an evaluator, you must take action and conduct evaluations.

Determine which overarching role, from those above, requires further development. For instance, in the *Positioning* space you may be relatively adept at defining how an evaluation project links to strategic business needs when completing a data collection plan but have trouble communicating that linkage to senior management from a facilitative standpoint.

Similarly, with the *Leading* role and corresponding skill sets, you may be proficient in providing leadership around evaluation concepts and technology to internal WLP staff but need some development work in doing the same activities in partnership with organizational stakeholders.

Finally, in the *Executing* role, you may be more proficient in start-up activities like gap and cause analysis than the actual implementation of the recommended solution. Or maybe detailed data analysis or project plans are not in your skill set for *Execution.*

Overall, when assessing your current and desired capabilities in any of the three roles, consider the primary technical skills needed for effective ROI implementation:

- Designing data collection instruments.
- Providing assistance for developing an evaluation strategy.
- Analyzing data, including specialized statistical analyses.
- Interpreting results and making specific recommendations.
- Developing an evaluation report or case study to communicate overall results.
- Providing technical support in any phase of the ROI evaluation.

Once you've identified specific areas for development, you can make a decision about the kinds of development activities and resources you'll need to "sharpen the saw" in those areas. The multitude of development activities available include:

- Active networking with professional associations.
- Attending conferences, workshops, or certifications.
- Continuing education through graduate school.
- Challenging job rotations, assignments, or task forces.
- Job shadowing or mentoring.
- Impact or case study applications.
- Publishing articles in company and/or professional newsletters, journals.
- Publishing case studies.
- Presenting or copresenting at professional conferences.
- Serving on an expert panel.

An example of a development planning tool for documenting a plan to enhance ROI leadership skills is provided in Figure 11–5.

Exercise 11–1 will help you assess individual strengths and gaps in the areas of positioning, leading, and executing.

We recommend that you share your development plan with your manager and assign completion dates for each activity. If you are an ROI leader or manager, be sure to select individuals with those skills that can best round out the existing talents of your WLP team.

CHAPTER SUMMARY

One of the key tasks of an ROI leader is to teach others and build internal capabilities for the process. Providing stakeholders, managers, and responsible internal parties with education and a thorough understanding of the ROI evaluation process will help promote consistency in its use and ensure a common organizational language around its application. Routinely examine personal beliefs and attitudes that may hinder progress. Remember, achieving a results-oriented evaluation approach begins with the mind-set and philosophy of those leading the charge. This mind-set includes:

- How you think about evaluation.
- How you plan for it, implement it, use it.
- How much time you're willing to spend on it.
- How you prioritize it.

Key Principles for Building Internal Capability

In business environments where employees are increasingly being tasked to do more with less, keep the following principles in mind when attempting to partner with internal staff around the administration, support, and execution of an ROI implementation effort.

- Have patience and persistence throughout the process.
- Follow win-win opportunities.
- Deal with problems and conflicts quickly.
- Share information regularly and purposefully.

FIGURE 11–5

SAMPLE INDIVIDUAL DEVELOPMENT PLAN FOR ROI LEADER

Core Function	Job/Task	Knowledge, Skills, Abilities	Development Activity
1. Provide strategic consultation for results-based WLP initiatives by serving as an evaluation leader and primary business partner for key stakeholders	■ Provide stakeholders with data-driven indicators of WLP effectiveness, regarding both training and nontraining performance solutions ■ Collaborate with managers to resolve issues or concerns about evaluation resource requirements ■ Execute to, and integrate with, organizational and departmental strategic plan(s) ■ Provide leadership and oversight for all WLP cost centers ■ Oversee vendor contracts for WLP support	■ Broad-based business and industry knowledge ■ Relationship building skills ■ Systems thinking; ability to view the organization holistically for effective integration of the ROI process ■ Analytical skills ■ Strong consulting skills with demonstrated ability to effectively translate desired client results into practical, measurable solutions ■ Proficiency in project management ■ Coaching and feedback skills ■ Demonstrated ability to function effectively in a high-growth, fast-paced, dynamic environment	■ Successful completion of *one of the following:* 　■ 2-day intensive evaluation workshop 　■ 5-day intensive evaluation workshop 　■ ROI certification 　■ CPT certification ■ Active networking with ASTD ROI Network for benchmarking and identification of best practices ■ Conduct 2–4 manager and/or employee workshops for capacity-building purposes by Q3 ■ Identify 3–5 engagement opportunities and subsequent engagement actions to increase management involvement in results-based WLP efforts ■ Completion of one impact study to measure on-the-job application with Q4 Customer Service initiative

FIGURE 11–5—Continued
SAMPLE INDIVIDUAL DEVELOPMENT PLAN FOR ROI LEADER

Core Function	Job/Task	Knowledge, Skills, Abilities	Development Activity

2. Provide leadership to ensure standards are in place for all levels of evaluation	■ Provide internal coaching and training on evaluation tools and best practice processes, particularly at the ROI level
	■ Ensure consistency among internal WLP staff with evaluation practices and communications
	■ Collaborate with organizational lines of business and WLP communities of practices to develop appropriate benchmarks and metrics; performance improvement cycle times; staff ratios; and program evaluation costs
	■ Coach instructional designers on the design, development, and administration of data collection instruments to measure WLP results
		■ Comprehensive, working knowledge of best practice evaluation models, (i.e. the Kirkpatrick four-level measurement framework and Phillips' five-level evaluation framework and ROI process methodology)
		■ High personal performance standards and a business results-orientation
		■ Able to prioritize multiple tasks and goals
		■ Excellent verbal and written communication skills
		■ Knowledge of data interpretation and reporting
		■ Experience in budget preparation and forecasting
		■ Performance gap evaluation skills
		■ Ability to assess impact on culture
			■ Establish policies, procedures, guidelines, and/or operating standards for WLP processes and practices
			■ Successfully engage internal staff in development of a results-based Transition Plan
			■ Engage management staff in developing a plan for establishing evaluating targets over the next fiscal year
			Optional Stretch Goals:
			■ One or more of the following
			  1. Case study poster submission for annual ISPI "Got Results" campaign
			  2. Article submission for ASTD ROI Links or ISPI's Performance Express electronic newsletters
			  3. Conference presentation at annual ISPI or ASTD International Conference(s)

EXERCISE 11-2. INDIVIDUAL DEVELOPMENT PLANNING (SELF-ASSESSMENT)

1. Assess individual strengths and gaps in one or more of the following areas:
   (a) Implementation Role with Current Impact Study:
      - Positioning
      - Leading
      - Executing
   (b) Technical Skills with Current Impact Study:
      - Designing data collection instruments
      - Providing assistance for developing an evaluation strategy
      - Analyzing data, including specialized statistical analyses
      - Interpreting results and making specific recommendations
      - Developing an evaluation report or case study to communicate overall results
      - Providing technical support in any phase of the ROI evaluation
2. Identify any or all areas where you perceive your *current* level of proficiency to be *less* than your impact study requires. For purposes of this exercise, we'll identify those areas as skill gaps.

   Identified skill gap(s):

   _____

   _____

   _____

3. Next, identify 1–3 skill gaps where you're willing to take action for continuous improvement. We'll consider those areas to be development opportunities.

   Development opportunities:

   _____

   _____

   _____

4. Using the development activities recommended in this chapter as a guide, along with the resources listed in the appendix, identify 1–3 actions and/or resources you will pursue to foster your own development.

   Actions you will take, by when:

   _____

   _____

   _____

5. Identify a person with whom you will share your plan and select a review date where you both will review your progress (30 months from initiation)

   Development plan partner:

   _____

   Review date:

   _____

- Take every opportunity to explain, inform, and educate.
- Give credit where credit is due.
- Display honesty and integrity in all interactions.
- Keep high standards of professionalism in each interaction.
- Involve others in as many activities as possible.

What?

In this chapter, we looked at the importance of building internal capability as a means of creating and sustaining short- and long-term support for the ROI process. Specific approaches for educating WLP staff and other stakeholders within the organization were provided, along with strategies for enhancing the individual capabilities of ROI leaders.

So What?

The best designed tools and techniques for ROI process implementation are meaningless unless they are perceived as valuable to the organization and the internal groups that must provide and approve the resources to make it happen.

Now What?

Recognize your role as an educator, project manager, and business partner. Build allies, strengthen relationships, and anticipate the business needs of your stakeholders. Promote skill building as a continuous improvement opportunity. Maintain a spirit of continuous improvement about your own development. Provide education and training and invite involvement by stakeholders throughout the organization. Leverage information, best practices, and tools and templates from the growing network of evaluation experts in the WLP field.

REFERENCES

Broad, Mary L., and John W. Newstrom. *Transfer of Training*. New York: Addison-Wesley, 1992.

Burkett, H. "Evaluation: Was Your HPI Project Worth the Effort?" In *HPI Essentials*, Alexandria, VA: ASTD, 2002.

Burkett, H., and P. Hall. "Take Me to Your Leader: The Value of Sponsorship in Managing Evaluation Projects." In *ASTD Links*, Alexandria, VA: American Society for Training and Development, 2003.

Phillips, Jack J., Patti P. Phillips, and Toni Hodges. *Making Training Evaluation Work*. Alexandria, VA: ASTD, 2004.

Robinson, Dana, and James Robinson. *Performance Consulting, Moving Beyond Training*. San Francisco: Berrett-Koehler, 1996.

Exercises	Tools and Templates
Exercise 11–1. Ten Tactics for Building Management Support	Figure 11–1. Stakeholder Engagement Tool
Exercise 11–2. Individual Development Planning (Self Assessment)	Figure 11–2. Sample Business Case Outline
	Figure 11–3. Case Example: Comparing the Performance Value of Results-Based WLP Program to an Activity-Based Program
	Figure 11–4. Implementation Checklist for Planning and Managing Evaluation Projects
	Figure 11–5. Sample Individual Development Plan for ROI Leader
	Table 11–1. AME Champion Profile
	Table 11–2. Management Plan for Evaluating Targets over Time
	Table 11–3. Management Involvement Checklist

Part Four
Staying on Track

MAINTAINING MOMENTUM: KEEPING THE PROCESS ON TRACK

Keeping the process on track is one of the biggest challenges in ROI process implementation. In many ways, it's equivalent to training for a marathon. You start small with manageable goals, keep stretching your muscles, change your habits, celebrate milestone events, and then wait for the training and preparation to kick in so you can go the distance. Then, if you're like most people hooked on running, you feel so great about the accomplishment that you know you have to maintain the habits and mind-sets to keep yourself from atrophying.

Preparing and sustaining a results-based measurement change effort isn't any different. Making the distance is only half the journey. Staying on track in the face of continuous change and maintaining the health and integrity of the ROI process over time will typically pose the most formidable obstacles on your path to creating an enduring, systemwide results-based measurement focus.

In this chapter you will learn to:

- Identify stages of ROI implementation.
- Identify inhibitors and enablers to successful integration of the ROI process.
- Apply strategies to facilitate integration of the ROI process over time.

THE FUNDAMENTALS

As with any change effort, consistent attention and focus must be maintained to build and sustain a process over time. In our last chapter, we looked at the importance of building internal capability and skill sets to help maintain a results-based measurement focus. Without this kind of attention, there's a risk that your organization's "line of sight" on ROI will fade and be labeled as another "flavor of the month." Long-term, effective evaluation solutions need to stand the test of time. This is an aspect of ROI implementation that is often overlooked and underestimated. After all, there is not a block in the model that suggests that the process should be implemented to focus on the long term. Yet emphasizing the ROI process as a long-term process-improvement tool adds tremendous value and keeps it from becoming a passing fad or short-term phenomenon.

Motivation for long-term viability could come initially from the results of your current impact study. Motivation can also be maintained as WLP programs continue to be adjusted, modified, enhanced, or eliminated in order to add value. To best ensure complete integration of the ROI Methodology as a mainstream, workplace learning approach, critical stages in ROI process implementation must be addressed. This final chapter will help you anticipate predictable implementation stages, identify various signs and symptoms of implementation trouble spots that may require action, and move past trouble spots by taking actions to keep on track.

POTENTIAL CHALLENGES

Why does ROI process implementation typically fail to take hold in an organization? Here are the top reasons individuals from all types of business environments give for ineffective implementation:

- Lack of a clear vision or goal.
- Changing directions in midstream.
- Conflicting priorities.
- Poor communication.
- Unmet customer expectations.
- No buy-in or support from key stakeholders.
- Poor leadership.
- Poor planning or no planning.
- No clear methodology.
- No clear understanding of what needs to be done (who is going to do what by when).
- Scope change.
- Not enough resources.
- Unrealistic expectations.

Each of these issues needs to be addressed in both short- and long-term implementation. From a short-term perspective, applying tips, tools, and strategies from Chapter 10, "Making the Transition," will help mitigate many of these issues. High-level strategies for addressing each challenge are shown in Table 12–1, "Reasons for Ineffective Implementation."

Exercise 12–1 will help you identify implementation issues that pose a threat to the success of your impact study.

TABLE 12-1
REASONS FOR INEFFECTIVE IMPLEMENTATION

If This	Then . . .	Tactic or Fieldbook Support Tool(s)
Lack of a clear vision or goal	1. Initiate goal setting, stakeholder communication, and action planning around the value of result-based measurement focus. 2. Position ROI process implementation as a compelling piece of organizational strategy. 3. Partner with key stakeholders. 4. Engage a credible sponsor at the executive level.	1. Communication briefings 2. Communication plan 3. Business case outline 4. Linking needs to objectives and evaluations 5. Writing objectives that focus on results 6. Readiness action plan 7. Stakeholder engagement tool
Changing directions in midstream	1. Review project schedule/scope change and related risk factors with sponsors, key stakeholders, and client groups. 2. Integrate training and workplace learning change efforts into existing management systems/cycles, such as: ■ Business planning ■ Budget development ■ Corporate and departmental measurement plans ■ Compensation planning ■ Succession planning	1. Implementation issues to address with your sponsor 2. Results-based transition plan 3. Readiness action plan 4. SWOT analysis 5. WLP roles during stages of ROI process implementation
Conflicting priorities	1. Balance organizational priorities to protect resources dedicated to ROI implementation efforts. 2. Make necessary compromises or adjustments in the implementation schedule to meet organizational needs. 3. Identify current stage of ROI process implementation and implement appropriate WLP actions/tasks.	1. Results-based transition plan 2. Project plan 3. Implementation issues to address with your sponsor 4. SWOT analysis 5. WLP roles during stages of ROI process implementation
Poor communication	1. Commit to regular review meetings to assess progress. 2. Make performance data available to implementation members or stakeholders. 3. Use technology. 4. Follow up relentlessly.	1. Communication plan 2. Communication planning checklist 3. Stakeholder engagement tool 4. Management involvement checklist 5. Transfer strategy matrix 6. Action planning 7. Project status report 8. Impact study report

TABLE 12–1—Continued

REASONS FOR INEFFECTIVE IMPLEMENTATION

If This	Then . . .	Tactic or Fieldbook Support Tool(s)
Unmet customer expectations	1. Develop metrics and communication methods to routinely track progress and productivity. 2. Define objectives across all evaluation levels. 3. Establish partnerships for achieving desired results. 4. Speak the language of the business.	1. Business case outline 2. Linking needs to objectives and evaluations 3. Matching objectives with needs 4. Stakeholder engagement tool 5. Communication plan 6. Myths, fears, and countermeasures worksheet
No buy-in or support from key stakeholders	1. Meet with key stakeholders from client organizations to define the value proposition of a results-based measurement focus. 2. Establish business partnerships. 3. Show the payback of WLP efforts.	1. Stakeholder identification 2. Stakeholder engagement 3. Management involvement checklist 4. Communication briefings 5. Annual reviews 6. Show the ROI on the ROI
Poor leadership	1. Solicit a credible sponsor. 2. Use a credible, competent evaluation lead. 3. Follow up on established consequences if desired performance levels are not being met. 4. Identify tactics to build project team strengths and minimize weaknesses.	1. Senior/mid-management briefings 2. Professional development, training, ROI certification for internal WLP staff 3. Individual development plans 4. Best practice benchmarking
Poor planning or no planning	1. Use a credible, consistent evaluation methodology. 2. Work from an implementation plan. 3. Initiate a task force to address and remove inhibitors. 4. Identify current stage of ROI process implementation and implement appropriate WLP actions/tasks.	1. Five-level framework 2. Project plan 3. Results-based transition plan 4. Data collection plan 5. Roles/responsibilities matrix 6. Identify a champion 7. Evaluation team charter 8. Transfer strategy matrix

No clear methodology	1. Use a credible, consistent evaluation methodology. 2. Define where information for each metric is coming from, who will obtain the information, and in what manner results toward goals will be reported.	1. Operating standards 2. Guiding principles 3. Policy, procedures 4. Standardized evaluation processes 5. Cost estimating worksheet
No clear understanding of what needs to be done (who is going to do what by when)	1. Plan and deploy well. 2. Break implementation tasks down into manageable, meaningful activities. 3. Establish specific accountabilities for project team members. 4. Define clear milestones. 5. Ensure adequate staffing and funding to support the implementation plan.	1. Project plan 2. Results-based transition plan 3. Data collection plan 4. ROI analysis plan 5. Readiness action plan 6. Roles/responsibilities matrix 7. Transfer strategy matrix 8. Action planning 9. WLP roles during stages of ROI process implementation 10. Implementation checklist 11. Management involvement checklist 12. Job Aid: Five Steps to Convert Data
Scope change	1. Communicate implementation plan, scope, schedule, and resource requirements to appropriate executives or stakeholders. 2. Develop contingency plans.	1. Management plan for evaluating targets over time 2. Implementation issues to address with your sponsor
Not enough resources	1. Acknowledge legitimate organizational issues around capacity and resource constraints. 2. Use cost-savings approaches to consolidate steps and conserve resources. 3. Replicate, leverage existing tools and resources. 4. Conduct ROI impact studies on a selective basis. 5. Develop contingency plans for team attrition.	1. 10 cost-savings approaches 2. Just-in-time gap analysis 3. Selection criteria matrix 4. Sample L1 questionnaire 5. Sample L2 performance observation 6. Sample L3 before and after questionnaire 7. Template L2 performance observation 8. Sample isolation impact questions and adjustments 9. Sample streamlined impact report
Unrealistic expectations	1. Continuously ensure that results are related to business and strategic goals. 2. Address organizational myths, fears, concerns.	1. Business case outline 2. Linking needs to objectives and evaluations 3. Matching objectives with needs 4. Stakeholder engagement tool 5. Communication plan 6. Myths, fears, and countermeasures worksheet

To put more context around the appropriate time, place, and use of these implementation issues and approaches, it's important to understand the common stages of ROI process implementation.

Stages of Implementation

You may have already discovered from your own experience that there are predictable obstacles to progress as the ROI process gets introduced and integrated to a workplace. Large or small, public or private, we've found that most training and workplace learning or performance improvement organizations undergo distinct stages on their journey toward increased accountability. As Figure 12–1 shows, these stages are part of a naturally evolving process that can be compared to the analogy of walking before you run.

Stage One: Recognition

In this early stage, the organization realizes that evaluation accountability is an issue, a "wake-up call" is generated, and preliminary action is taken. This stage is usually initiated by a single person or small group, and at this point ROI is not necessarily viewed as a strategic imperative by senior management. For these reasons, commitment may be limited or marginal, and long-lasting evaluation processes are obviously not yet in place.

Indicators of the recognition stage were noted as readiness issues in Chapter 1, Exercise 1–1, "Is Your Organization a Candidate for ROI Implementation?", and include such factors as:

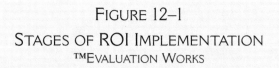

FIGURE 12–1
STAGES OF ROI IMPLEMENTATION
™EVALUATION WORKS

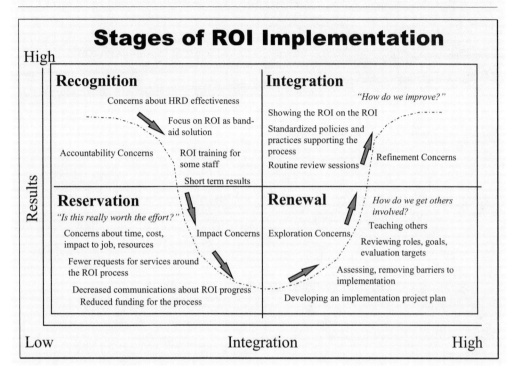

Adapted from Scott, Cynthia, and Dennis Jaffe. *Getting Your Organization to Change.* Menlo Park, CA: Crisp Publications, 1999.

- Training and workplace learning expenditures are identified as significant.
- The organization is undergoing significant change.
- Client complaints or concerns about the value of training and workplace learning services.
- The program has a history of more than one disaster.
- Clients are demanding that the training and workplace learning and performance improvement function show bottom line results.
- Focus on linking training and workplace learning and performance improvement to strategic directions of the organization has increased.
- The training and workplace learning and performance improvement function has a low investment in measurement and evaluation.
- Nonintegrated, disparate data and measurement processes have been created.
- Commitment of funding and resources is provisional.
- Evaluation skill sets among internal staff have gaps, and there is some disconnect regarding evaluation focus.

TABLE 12–2

TRAINING AND WORKPLACE LEARNING TASKS AT STAGE ONE

WLP Role in this Stage: Solution Generator

Key Tasks
- Remove barriers to implementation, facilitate problem solving
- Initiate goal setting, stakeholder communication, and action planning around the value proposition of a results-based measurement focus
- Install short-term solutions
- Evaluate solutions to determine whether they are meeting organizational goals

The role of WLP at this stage is that of finding solutions. Table 12–2 indicates the key tasks at this stage.

Stage One: Key Tasks

Remove barriers to implementation, facilitate problem solving.

Do . . .	Don't . . .
Consider yourself a change agent and ROI champion	Neglect the need to assess your organization's readiness for a major change effort
Partner with key stakeholders from client organizations to define the ROI effort	Neglect the need for executive sponsorship with systemic change
Prepare the organization for changes in training and workplace learning focus	Promote ROI implementation as a panacea

Initiate goal setting, stakeholder communication, and action planning around the value proposition of a results-based measurement focus.

Do . . .	Don't . . .
Relate the effort to organizational strategies	Neglect to research the factors that affect training and workplace learning change in your organization
Plan, communicate, and deploy well	Neglect the need for consistent education and awareness building, along with adequate staffing and funding to deploy the implementation plan
Ensure that time and resources are available for people to develop the skills they need	Neglect legitimate organizational issues around capacity and resource constraints

Install short-term solutions.

Do ...	Don't ...
Determine the infrastructure of an ROI implementation team (members, selection process)	Neglect the need to orient and educate project team members about ROI implementation requirements
Institute a reward system for involved parties and communicate it prior to their involvement	Neglect to link rewards to desired outcomes and to follow up with promised incentives
Identify 1–3 "quick hit" opportunities to show training and workplace learning's value	Neglect to define how these scenarios will be generated, evaluated, and used to guide future evaluation work

Evaluate solutions to determine whether they are meeting organizational goals.

Do ...	Don't ...
Commit to regular review meetings (at least monthly) to assess progress	Neglect to assign responsibilities for specific deliverables
Develop metrics to track progress and productivity	Neglect to define consequences for exceptional and poor performance with respect to milestone achievements

Stage Two: Reservation

In this stage, clear symptoms that the ROI process is no longer achieving its intended objectives emerge. For instance, there may be renewed objections about the impact of the process on time and resources and the organization becomes preoccupied with new business demands that compete for time and resources. There's a prevailing sense of impatience and concern that the investment of time and effort needed to move toward a results-based HRD focus is not worth the effort. The initial support and goodwill from preliminary successes with the process have waned. It's not uncommon at this stage for the organization to either abandon the effort or to significantly decrease its original commitment of support. If you go back to our marathon analogy, this is the point in your training and workplace learning in which you might find yourself at the breakfast table with cigarettes and little chocolate doughnuts wondering what the heck you got yourself into.

Indicators that your organization is in this stage include:

- Reduced funding for the process.
- Mentioning the programs and processes less in various communications (out of sight, out of mind).
- A lack of participation and involvement of the management team.
- Constant shuffling of people involved in the process.
- Fewer requests for products and services around the accountability process.

TABLE 12–3

TRAINING AND WORKPLACE LEARNING TASKS AT STAGE TWO

WLP Role in this Stage: Catalyzer

Key Tasks
- Prod individuals and groups from inertia
- Activate initial goal setting and action planning
- Rejuvenate enthusiasm about the desired future state
- Openly address objections
- Give consistent, renewed messages about the vision, purpose, and value of change

- Postponing or eliminating review sessions aimed at keeping the process on track.
- Complaints about the time or cost of evaluation activities.
- A redirection to some other process that appears to be competing or eliminating the need for the accountability.
- Reduction in the dissemination of information and communication surrounding the progress of ROI and ROI studies—even in a streamline fashion. Table 12–3 shows the key tasks for WLP at this stage.

Stage Two: Key Tasks

Prod individuals and groups from inertia.

Do . . .	Don't . . .
Break implementation project tasks down into manageable, meaningful activities	Neglect to develop contingency plans for attrition of key people or players
Work from an implementation plan	Neglect to provide ROI implementation team members with a copy of the implementation plan
Invite project team members to contribute information, insights about reviving the effort	Neglect to ensure that the results sought are manageable in the time available

Activate initial goal setting and action planning.

Do . . .	Don't . . .
Translate the ROI change effort into job-level details	Neglect the need to establish specific accountabilities and responsibilities for implementation team members
Direct managers to link individual ROI implementation accomplishments to performance appraisals	Neglect to hold regular meetings with executives and stakeholders to inform and gather input
Identify the budget impact of implementation efforts	Neglect to involve financial experts when estimating the financial impact of the change to the organization

Rejuvenate enthusiasm about the desired future state.

Do ...	Don't ...
Publicize successes of other like organizations with the proposed training and workplace learning change	Hesitate to determine more appropriate ways of measuring progress if certain metrics are not working as well as intended
Hold contests for solving some quandary in the results-based training and workplace learning transformation effort	Neglect to continually assess conditions or change processes that falter
Publicize and celebrate progress towards goals	Declare victory too early when it seems that progress is being made

Openly address objections.

Do ...	Don't ...
Initiate a task force to address and remove inhibitors	Neglect to use stakeholders' influence to neutralize or remove blockages quickly
Debunk rumors and reconfigure systems or dynamics which foster negativity	Neglect to follow up relentlessly
Communicate any apprehensions about the implementation plan, scope, or schedule to appropriate executives or stakeholders	Neglect to develop clear milestones for focusing the ROI implementation plan

Give consistent, renewed messages about the vision, purpose, and value of change.

Do ...	Don't ...
Leverage personal alliances to communicate business drivers for the training and workplace learning change effort	Neglect to define specific accountabilities and responsibilities for the executive sponsor and key stakeholders
Model and communicate learning opportunities on a regular basis	Neglect to develop a communication plan or to stick to it

Stage Three: Renewal

In this stage, the organization starts to move past its inhibitors and explores how to renew its initial commitment to invest in expanded evaluation solutions. The need for integrated evaluation processes and solutions shows increased visibility and attention from internal staff, including senior management. Indicators that your organization is in this stage typically include:

- Initiated adjustments in evaluation progress and organizational course corrections toward desired state.
- Embracing ROI concepts, methodology, and value.

TABLE 12–4

TRAINING AND WORKPLACE LEARNING TASKS AT STAGE THREE

Training and Workplace Learning Role in this Stage: Process Helper

Key Tasks
- Recognize and define needs within the change process at each leverage point
- Encourage teamwork, interdependence
- Focus on priorities and short-term goals
- Recognize and reward "small wins"

- Renewed mechanisms for monitoring and addressing evaluation mind-sets, behaviors, and practices.
- Increased energy and potential chaos around identifying where further support is needed and how to get it.
- Increased conflict as multiple solutions are explored.

Table 12–4 identifies the key tasks for WLP at this stage.

Stage Three: Key Tasks

Recognize and define needs within the change process at each leverage point.

Do ...	Don't ...
Continue to monitor milestone achievements, needs, gaps	Hesitate to scale back plans as needed
Integrate training and workplace learning change efforts into existing management systems/cycles, such as:	Neglect to:
■ Business planning	■ link ROI accomplishments to individual performance appraisals
■ Budget development	■ include accomplishment of ROI implementation goals as criteria for team bonus plans
■ Corporate and departmental measurement planning	
■ Compensation planning	■ incorporate informal rewards such as congratulatory notes, special luncheons, equipment access, etc.
■ Succession planning	
■ Employee orientation and training and workplace learning	
Continuously ensure that results are related to business and strategic goals	Neglect to tailor targets and metrics to appropriate organizational life-cycles

Encourage teamwork, interdependence.

Do ...	Don't ...
Incorporate action-oriented project members into the implementation effort	Neglect to continually monitor the effectiveness of the implementation team
Identify tactics to build project team strengths and minimize weaknesses	Neglect to fill any skill gaps with education, training, and workplace learning, or recruitment
Develop a team charter for the ROI implementation team	Hesitate to recommend team changes to the executive sponsor.
	Don't let team issues fester.

Focus on priorities and short-term goals.

Do . . .	Don't . . .
Keep it simple	Make the metrics more complicated than necessary
Agree on data sources	Neglect to define where information for each metric is coming from, who will obtain the information, and in what manner results toward goals will be reported
Incorporate review of performance data into routine implementation meetings	Neglect to make performance data available to implementation members prior to meetings

Recognize and reward "small wins."

Do . . .	Don't . . .
Identify and communicate any "success" examples to signify that the ROI effort is taking hold	Neglect to establish executive metrics to routinely show management the status of the effort
Create communication vehicles to ensure that the organization is systematically updated on ROI implementation achievements	Neglect to address the milestones outlined in previous communication plans
Ensure that formal and informal rewards are specific to the ROI implementation effort	Forget that performers will generally achieve those things for which they are rewarded

Stage Four: Integration

In this stage, enabling strategies and infrastructures are clearly in place to ensure that the ROI process is firmly integrated in the "DNA" of WLP work. This may range from technology-based support processes to having standardized guidelines, policies, and procedures, which were introduced as recommended steps to transition planning during your Chapter 10 action-planning exercise. Here, too, the ROI process is universally and mutually understood by all who are involved.

Indicators:

- Increased focus on linking workplace learning and performance to strategic directions of the organization.
- A spirit of continuous improvement, innovation, and "out of the box" thinking around the management and measurement of workplace learning and performance.
- Training and workplace learning function as a key player in organizational change initiatives.
- A growing training and workplace learning budget.
- Strengthened collaborations between WLP and other key functional areas.

TABLE 12–5

TRAINING AND WORKPLACE LEARNING TASKS AT STAGE FOUR

WLP Role in this Stage: The Stabilizer

Key Tasks
- Build and maintain stable links for integration of the change effort within other organizational systems
- Build and maintain cohesiveness and interdependence on all sides of the change effort
- Ensure that the pace of organizational change does not compromise the integrity of the ROI process

- The training and workplace learning team viewed as internal experts in organizational performance evaluation.
- The training and workplace learning team able to routinely perform evaluation at "best of class" levels.
- Evaluation mentoring and support of increased internal capabilities.
- Identified and shared best practices.

Table 12–5 presents the key tasks for WLP at this stage.

Stage Four: Key Tasks

Build and maintain stable links for integration of the change effort within other organizational systems.

Do . . .	Don't . . .
Build organizational self-reliance by reinforcing new behaviors and systems	Neglect to position ROI implementation at the forefront of your organization's strategic plan
Establish accountability everywhere	Delegate accountability away from senior leadership
Follow up on established consequences if desired performance levels are not being met	Neglect to evaluate all environmental factors contributing to lack of progress

Build and maintain cohesiveness and interdependence on all sides of the change effort.

Do . . .	Don't . . .
Maintain strategic alliances with key stakeholder groups and individuals	Neglect to hold people accountable for their commitments
Emphasize that comprehensive integration and ROI implementation may take several years	Neglect to secure commitments for the long haul
Plan informal rewards and recognition to support milestone achievements	Forget that most team members must carry out implementation assignments without relief from daily job duties

Ensure that the pace of organizational change does not compromise integrity of the ROI Methodology.

Do . . .	Don't . . .
Challenge the implementation team to develop appropriate metrics	Neglect to continuously evaluate assigned metrics to ensure that they are measuring desired change outcomes in appropriate intervals
Balance organizational priorities to protect resources dedicated to ROI implementation efforts	Neglect to examine any negative impacts of ROI resource allocation on the organization's ability to perform in terms of critical business issues
Recognize, analyze, and respond to organizational threats to ROI implementation	Forget that senior management may not be close enough to the implementation effort to appraise its value to the organization and its level of accomplishment
Make necessary compromises or adjustments in the implementation schedule to meet organizational needs	

Share excitement about the process and its value to the organization.

Do . . .	Don't . . .
Schedule and conduct periodic, enthusiastic reviews from the implementation team to senior management	Neglect to include intangible benefit statements when reporting on progress with targeted metrics
Publicize success stories and identified best practices	Neglect to tailor benefit statements to reinforce business pay-offs from multiple stakeholder perspectives

Figure 12–2 illustrates key WLP roles during each of the stages identified.

It's important to note that these stages of implementation do not necessarily occur in a linear fashion, one after the other. However, the concerns and indicators of each stage are typical, in varying degrees, of most organizations as they begin to implement the process as standard practice. By understanding these stages, an evaluation practitioner or consultant can identify critical leverage points and assume roles that will accelerate organizational movement from one phase to the next. Exercise 12–2 will help you identify where your organization is now in its current stage of ROI implementation.

Enabling Strategies: Moving Toward Renewal and Integration

The key is to keep moving toward integration and avoid prolonged inertia. Specific actions that facilitate movement are called enabling strategies. Routine enabling actions that will increase the likelihood of reinforcing the program and the process to others include the following:

FIGURE 12–2

WLP ROLES DURING STAGES OF ROI PROCESS IMPLEMENTATION
™EVALUATION WORKS

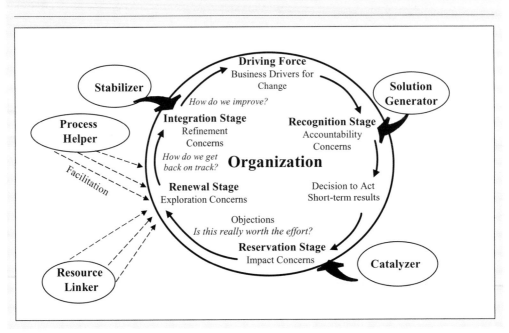

Case Studies

Applied, targeted, case studies foster internal capabilities in the methodology and build acceptance for the process. Regular attention to select impact studies is also important to show:

- Which programs have achieved success.
- What organizational enablers or barriers occurred in the process of achieving desired results.
- What new program expenditures are justified.

By now, you've applied the ROI process to a specific impact study and followed recommended guidelines for communicating the results.

The Annual Review

It's helpful to hold regular reviews to show how well the ROI process is working. This review is typically for the senior executive team and is designed

EXERCISE 12–2. IMPLEMENTATION PLANNING

1. Using the stages of implementation as a guide, identify what stage your current organization is in with respect to ROI implementation and list indicators that support your assessment. If you are not currently in an organization to which this applies, then identify the stage of implementation that you consider to be most challenging for you as a professional.

   Identified stage of implementation:

   _____

   _____

   _____

   Indicators:

   _____

   _____

   _____

2. Identify roles, tasks, and enabling strategies that will assist your organization (or you as a professional) in either: (a) moving successfully to a more integrated stage of implementation; or (b) sustaining its current progress with process integration.

Roles	Tasks	Enabling Strategies

to show how the process is working, what success has been enjoyed, what is planned for the near future, and what is needed to keep it going. A typical annual review agenda includes the following topics:

- Review of previous year's WLP programs.
- Methods/levels of evaluation.
- Results achieved from programs.
- Significant deviations from expected results.
- Basis for determining WLP needs for the coming year.
- Scheduled WLP initiatives/programs/services.
- Proposed methods of evaluation.
- Potential payoffs.
- Problem areas in the WLP process.
- Concerns from management (all levels).

These sessions should be framed as a continuous improvement mechanism so that you can systematically:

- Show the value derived from specific actions recommended in impact studies.
- Track targeted improvements.
- Track suggestions for continuous improvement.
- Establish and review policy and practice around communication mechanisms.
- Reinforce the role of management in building and sustaining a results-based culture.

ROI on the ROI

It is important to understand the payoff of this complete process. No management team is going to support something if they don't see the value. Individually, an impact study will show the value of a particular program. Managers will quickly realize that the resources required to develop these studies are very significant. Does the entire process have a payoff? In other words, many managers will ask for the ROI on the ROI. Significant payoffs associated with using the ROI process over time include the following:

- It transforms the role of WLP in the organization.
- It increases WLP alignment with business needs.
- It improves the efficiency of solution design, development, and delivery by:
  - reducing costs.
  - preventing a program from being implemented after the pilot process shows that it delivers no value.
  - expanding programs when other areas need the program.
  - discontinuing programs when they add no value.
- It enhances the value of learning and development in the organization.
- It builds respect, support, and commitment from internal groups, including senior executives and major program sponsors.

It is important to tackle this issue early. Evaluating these questions to ensure that the process delivers on its promised value could be the role of the task force created during transition planning activities.

Review Staff Roles

The internal WLP group must continue to ensure that policies are implemented, practices are adhered to, and the data are delivered in a timely manner. If the staff loses their enthusiasm for the process or fails to complete their part of the steps, it will be perceived as a lack of commitment. This can be very contagious and cause others to lose support and commitment as well.

The importance of staff's role as an advocate and champion for sustaining ROI over the long haul can be illustrated by the experience of one health care organization. In this case, 11 employees involved in the original ROI training, along with the senior executive team, were convinced and committed to adopting ROI as a standard policy practice. However, members of the group described initial frustration with their own inexperience with the process and the incorporation of ROI projects into busy schedules. To deal with these challenges and continue moving forward, group members learned to find support in each other and in their shared belief about the value of ROI to the business. As the team continued to develop ROI expertise and to see the successful measurement of workplace learning projects, their confidence and enthusiasm galvanized partnerships with managers and the senior executive team, which in turn helped sustain ROI implementation throughout the system. To continue ensuring organizational understanding, acceptance, and adoption of ROI as "routine," the team worked closely with senior executives across all levels to establish ROI as a systemwide philosophy in which accountability for adding value became the responsibility of everyone in the organization. In addition, they assisted department managers in conducting front-end needs assessments, provided learning opportunities on the ROI process, and partnered with them on subsequent ROI projects with the goal of having all agency managers comfortable with the ROI process.

Periodic reviews of staff roles and how they translate into day-to-day job descriptions are helpful to ensure that:

- Every person in the group understands his or her responsibilities to make the process work as a systemwide approach.
- Every person in the group understands what he or she is supposed to accomplish and how and when he or she should do it.
- Specific responsibilities are incorporated into job descriptions so they become a routine part of work.

This process can be integrated into midyear or annual performance appraisal processes or incorporated into individual developmental planning checkpoints and review dates. Any issues in managing evaluation outputs or work products associated with revised WLP roles and/or the broader results scope of the WLP function should also be a factor in annual budget planning.

Continuous Improvement Mechanisms

Implementing the ROI process and monitoring its progress within the realm of the WLP function may be a relatively simple task. But as the process becomes more visible and integrated in the organization, it becomes increasingly more critical to build continuous improvement mechanisms into the process so that it remains credible and flexible over time. Report on progress with recommendations in the annual reviews mentioned earlier. Publish success stories with improvement recommendations that were implemented. Establish routine meetings where lessons learned with solution implementations are reviewed and tracked. Many organizations use a "post-mortem" forum to review lessons learned from specific projects that entailed considerable time or expense. Figure 12–3 provides an example of a lessons-learned report used in a public-sector organization. In this case, the report mirrored an organizational template and was used (a) as a supplement to impact study reports with projects that did not achieve desired results, or (b) in lieu of an impact study report when the resources for an impact study were diverted and the impact study project was

FIGURE 12–3

LESSONS LEARNED REPORT

Version: Draft vo.2
Date:
Author:
Owner:

Table of Contents

About This Document

Who should use this document?

Related Documents

This document should be used in conjunction with:

Workplace Learning Evaluation Policy and Procedures
Impact Study "X" Communication Plan
Impact Study "X" Data Collection Plan

FIGURE 12–3—*Continued*

LESSONS LEARNED REPORT

Summary of Changes

This section records the history of changes to this document. Only the most significant changes are described here.

Version	Date	Author	Description of change

Where significant changes are made to this document, the version number will be incremented by 1.0. Where changes are made for clarity and reading ease only and no change is made to the meaning or intention of this document, the version number will be increased by 0.1

Reviews and Approvals

This document requires review and approval.

Approval

This document was approved by:

Name	Role	Date

Reviewers

This section lists persons or areas that have specific, formal roles in the project.

This document was reviewed by:

Name	Role	Date

Distribution

This section lists all the persons or areas that will receive a copy of this document after it has been finalized.

Name	Area	Date

Document control information

At the end of this document is a labeled box indicating the end of text.

Lessons Learned Report
END OF DOCUMENT

FIGURE 12–3—*Continued*

LESSONS LEARNED REPORT

Lessons Learned Report

1.1 Purpose of Document

Summarize the purpose of the Lessons Learned Report (i.e., to pass on any lessons that can be practically applied to other results-based evaluation projects).

1.2 Project Summary

1.2.1 Project Background

Summarize the business case for this results-based Workplace Learning project and identify its key objectives in terms of needs/gaps in the following areas:

- Reaction to the Workplace Learning project, including planned actions if appropriate
- Learning goals for project participants—desired knowledge and skills, as well as changes in perception
- Performance objectives—desired application and implementation of project learning
- Targeted business impact—metrics such as cost savings, productivity improvements, time reductions, increased sales, etc.
- As indicated, return on investment target—desired monetary benefits versus costs of the Workplace Learning project
- Desired intangible benefits, such as employee satisfaction and customer satisfaction

Include summary information about the project sponsor, key stakeholders or client groups, and expected deliverables from the Workplace Learning project.

1.2.2 Project Milestones and Metrics

Summarize the relevant milestones and metrics of the project. These may include the following components:

- Estimated Start Date
- Estimated End Date
- Actual Start Date
- Actual End Date
- Schedule Variance
- Team Size at Start Date
- Team Size at End Date
- Team Size Variance or Attrition (individuals)

FIGURE 12–3—*Continued*

LESSONS LEARNED REPORT

- Estimated Project Costs
- Actual Project Costs
- Cost Variance
- Estimated Project Cost Benefits
- Actual Project Cost Benefits
- Cost Variance
- Project's Return on Investment
- Number of Quality Assurance Reviews
- Number of Incidents

Project Components	Milestone or Metric
Estimated start date	
Estimated end date	
Actual start date	
Actual end date	
Schedule variance (days)	
Team size at start date	
Team size at end date	
Team size variance or attrition (individuals)	
Estimated project costs	$
Actual project costs	$
Cost variance (dollars)	$
Estimated project cost benefits	$
Actual project cost benefits	$
Cost variance	$
Project's return on investment	
Number of quality assurance reviews	
Number of incidents	

1.2.3 Project Deliverables

Deliverable	Due Date	Status/Comments

1.3 Lessons Learned

Summarize what went well or did not go well and what can be improved as it applies to this results-based Workplace Learning project.

FIGURE 12–3—*Continued*

LESSONS LEARNED REPORT

1.3.1 What Went Well

1.3.2 What Didn't

1.3.3 Enablers

1.3.4 Barriers

1.3.5 Suggestions for Improvement

1.4 Methodologies

1.4.1 Project Management

Include recommendations for enhancement/modification to the project management methodologies used by the Workplace Learning function to achieve desired results. Include strengths and opportunities for improvement with regard to the following project management components:

- Project Sponsorship
- Overall Project Planning
- Workplace Design
- Cost Estimates or Forecasts
- Managing/Deploying the Workplan
- Managing Resources
  - How Workplace Learning resources (including team members) were approved, allocated, diverted, constrained, and/or used during the project lifecycle
  - Recommendations for improving resource use for future results-based projects
- Managing Scope Change
- Status Report Communications
- Managing Stakeholder Expectations
- Managing Quality of Workplace Learning Services, Products, and Deliverables
- Managing Risk

Consider any recommendations to the project management tools used during the project.

1.4.2 Instructional System Design (ISD)

Include recommendations for enhancement/modification to the ISD methodology used, including the assessment and design phase; the develop, build and test phase; and the implementation and evaluation phase. Also, include recommendations related to any learning or performance testing tools used during the project.

FIGURE 12–3—*Continued*

LESSONS LEARNED REPORT

1.4.3 Evaluation Management

Include recommendations for enhancement/modification to the evaluation management methodology used by the Workplace Learning function to achieve desired results. Include recommendations to any of the following phases of evaluation management, such as evaluation planning, data collection, data analysis, and communication of results, including communication strengths/opportunities for improvement with key stakeholders. Include recommendations related to any data collection, survey, testing tools, or sampling groups used during the project.

Also include summary information on:

- Techniques used to isolate the effects of the Workplace Learning project from other influences
- Techniques used to convert data to monetary value
- Strategies used to communicate evaluation results

1.5 Summary of Findings

Provide a high level summary of your overall findings and conclusions with this project.

Describe results achieved in meeting desired business objectives, including:

- Reaction to the Workplace Learning project, including planned actions, if appropriate
- What the project participants learned—acquisition of knowledge and skills, as well as changes in perceptions
- Success with application and implementation of what participants learned
- Actual business impact linked to the Workplace Learning project, measured in cost savings, productivity improvements, time reductions, increased sales, etc.
- Return on investment, showing the monetary benefits versus costs of the project (as indicated)
- Intangible benefits, such as employee satisfaction and customer satisfaction

State how these results and lessons learned can be used for continuous improvement and action planning with results-based Workplace Learning projects going forward.

1.6 Appendix: Tables, Figures, Exhibits

Lessons Learned Report
END OF DOCUMENT

postponed or discontinued. This sample report can be found on the CD and customized to your specific project or business needs.

Finally, use the best practices outlined below as a framework for continuous improvement.

Identify and Share Best Practices

Over 1,000 organizations have taken the initiative to implement ROI, based on the number of organizations participating in a comprehensive certification process designed to help individuals and teams to implement the ROI Methodology. With the acceptance of ROI, much of the focus has now turned to best practices for ROI implementation. The following 11 best practices represent the state of the art with those organizations that have successfully implemented ROI.

Best Practice 1

The ROI Methodology is implemented as a process improvement tool and not a performance evaluation tool for the WLP staff. WLP staff acceptance is critical for the implementation of this process. No individual or group is willing to create a tool that will ultimately be used to evaluate his or her performance. Consequently, many organizations recognize that ROI is a process improvement tool and communicate this posture early.

Best Practice 2

The ROI Methodology generates a microlevel scorecard with six types of data. These data points reflect six distinct levels, each with a specific measurement focus:

Level One: Reaction and planned action—Measures participant satisfaction with the program and captures planned actions.
Level Two: Learning—Measures changes in knowledge, skills, and attitudes.
Level Three: Application—Measures changes in on-the-job behavior.
Level Four: Business impact—Measures changes in business impact variables.
Level Five: ROI—Compares program benefits to the costs.
Intangibles—Measures that are purposely not converted to monetary value.

As shown in the list above, the data represent a scorecard of performance, representing both qualitative and quantitative data, often taken at different time frames and from various sources.

Best Practice 3

ROI Methodology data are being integrated to create a macro scorecard for the learning and development function. As more and more studies are conducted, data are rolled up to create a macrolevel scorecard, showing the value of the function. As shown in Figure 12–4, the individual micro scorecard

FIGURE 12–4

INDIVIDUAL MICRO LEVEL DATA IS INTEGRATED INTO MACRO LEVEL SCORECARD

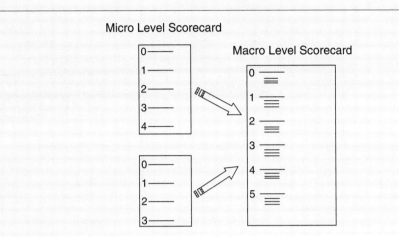

evaluation data are integrated into the overall macrolevel scorecard. This approach requires a few similar questions to be asked each time. These are then integrated, using technology to create the WLP macrolevel scorecard, as shown in Figure 12–4.

Best Practice 4

ROI impact studies are conducted very selectively, usually involving 5% to 10% of all programs and solutions. Programs that are usually targeted for Level 4 and 5 evaluations are those that are strategically focused, expensive, high profile, controversial, and reflective of management's interest. This does not mean that other programs are not evaluated. It is recommended that all programs be evaluated at Level 1 and the vast majority at Level 2, but only a few select programs are taken to Levels 3, 4, and 5. Most importantly, those programs that target a level 5 evaluation with an actual ROI calculation are, as best practice, evaluated across at all five levels, up to and including ROI.

Best Practice 5

ROI evaluation targets are developed, showing the percent of programs evaluated at each level. Target levels are developed reflecting the resources available and the feasibility of evaluation at each level. Targets usually begin at 100% of programs at Level 1 and conclude with 5% to 10% of programs at Level 5.

Best Practice 6

A variety of data collection methods are used in ROI analysis. ROI evaluation is not restricted to a particular type of data collection method, such as monitoring of business data. Instead, questionnaires, built-in action plans, focus groups, and observations are used in developing the complete profile of six types of data in the ROI Methodology.

Best Practice 7

For a specific ROI evaluation, the effects of WLP are isolated from other factors. Although a difficult issue, best practice organizations realize there must be some method in place to show the direct contribution of the L&D program to make a business linkage to a specific L&D effort. Many best practice organizations are currently using a variety of techniques discussed in this fieldbook, ranging from control-group analysis to expert estimation, to tackle this issue with each impact study. Some argue that this is too difficult or impossible. In reality, it must be done for executives to understand the relative contribution of WLP. Otherwise, there's a temptation to slash the budgets of major programs because there's no clear connection between the program and the business value.

Best Practice 8

Business impact data are converted to monetary values. These days, it may not be enough to report WLP program outcomes as expressed numbers in quality improvement, cycle time reduction, turnover reduction, or enhancement in customer loyalty or job satisfaction. The actual value in monetary terms is absolutely essential in developing ROI because an ROI calculation compares the monetary value with the cost of the program. Best practice organizations are using a full array of approaches to develop monetary values.

Best Practice 9

The ROI Methodology is being implemented for about 3% to 5% of the WLP budget. One of the common fears of ROI implementation is the excessive cost in both time and direct funds. Best practice firms report that they can implement the ROI Methodology for roughly 3% to 5% of the total budget, using appropriate evaluation targets discussed in number 5.

When implementing ROI, many organizations have migrated from a very low level of investment (around 1% or less) to the 3% to 5% level by a process of gradual budget enhancements. These enhancements sometimes come directly from the cost savings generated from the use of the ROI Methodology. Cost-savings approaches are also available for resource-constrained environments.

Best Practice 10

ROI forecasting is being implemented routinely. Senior executives are sometimes asking for a forecast of ROI before a project begins. Consequently, best practice organizations are routinely using ROI forecasting approaches to enhance the decision-making process. The credibility of the process is greatly increased by the use of conservative adjustments and built-in steps to secure input from the best experts.

Best Practice 11

The ROI Methodology is used as a tool to strengthen and improve the WLP process. A significant payoff for using the ROI process over time is that it transforms the role of L&D in the organization. Application of the process increases L&D alignment with business needs, improves the efficiency of design, development, and delivery, and enhances the value of learning and development in the organization. Furthermore, it builds respect, support, and commitment from internal groups, including senior executives and major program sponsors.

Collectively, these best practices are evolving as hundreds of organizations use ROI each year. The best practices underscore the progress in the evolution of ROI application and use.

PUTTING IT ALL TOGETHER

One of the best pieces of advice we can give any WLP professional seeking to standardize the ROI process as a way of doing business is this: Commit to the long haul. As with any change effort, constant attention and focus must be maintained to build and sustain the ROI process over time. Without this attention, any initiative will ultimately fade out and be labeled as a passing fad. Reinforcing this type of regular and constant attention is often one of the most difficult challenges you'll face as an evaluation leader.

After initial measurement changes are implemented, there's a natural tendency to lose the sense of urgency and drift back to old cultures, mind-sets, behaviors, and systems. Ultimately, the task of sustaining the process over time is not the sole responsibility of the training function. Subsequently, a key challenge is securing and fostering ongoing ROI support, cooperation, interaction, and dedication of individuals and groups across all organizational levels.

Focus on the following to assist you with these challenges:

- Remember that organizations go through predictable growth stages in the move from episodic implementation to long-term integration of the ROI process.
- Look for specific indicators that the ROI process may be off track.
- Identify key roles and actions that will help the organization move successfully from one stage to the next.
- Continually renew and refresh commitment to the process across individual, process, and organizational levels so that it remains consistent, reliable, and credible in the eyes of stakeholders.
- Develop best practices for capturing organizational responses and lessons learned in the entire cycle of your accountability journey.
- Continually seek best practice examples from professional associations, training literature, journals, case studies, colleagues, and the ASTD ROI Network.

EXERCISE 12–3. IMPLEMENTATION CHECKLIST

	Yes	No
Have stages of ROI implementation been identified?	❑	❑
Have appropriate training roles been deployed to assist with organizational movement towards the integration stage?	❑	❑
Are case studies implemented on a regular basis?	❑	❑
Are annual ROI review sessions held?	❑	❑
Has the "ROI on the ROI" been effectively and routinely communicated to stakeholders?	❑	❑
Are staff roles around ROI process implementation regularly reviewed, revised, and updated?	❑	❑
Are continuous improvement mechanisms in place for the ROI Methodology?	❑	❑
Are best practices routinely identified?	❑	❑
Are best practices routinely applied?	❑	❑
Are best practices routinely shared?	❑	❑

Exercise 12–3 presents a checklist you can use to help you sustain momentum for ROI process implementation in your workplace.

ACTION STEPS

Now that we've identified typical stages of ROI implementation, defined training and workplace learning roles in the implementation process, and outlined specific enabling strategies to assist in this effort, it's time to commit to action. Exercise 12–4 will help you plan the action steps you will take.

CHAPTER SUMMARY

This chapter focused on the actions needed to build, maintain, and sustain the ROI Methodology over time. Emphasizing the ROI Methodology as a long-term process-improvement tool adds tremendous value and keeps it from becoming a passing fad or short-term phenomenon. If ROI measurement is not an integral part of the way your function does business, then the accountability of training projects will ultimately suffer. Specifically, this chapter helped you

- Identify organizational stages of ROI implementation.
- Define training roles in facilitating movement from one stage to the next.
- Identify inhibitors and enablers to successful integration of the ROI methodology.
- Apply enabling strategies to sustain integration of the ROI Methodology over time.

EXERCISE 12–4. ENABLING STRATEGIES ACTION PLANNING

Commit to take action on one or more of the following enabling strategies defined in this chapter:

1. Implement specific impact or case studies.
2. Schedule and enthusiastically conduct periodic review sessions.
3. Show the payoff of the actual ROI process to show that it's worthwhile.
4. Build continuous improvement mechanisms to ensure that enhancements to the process are routinely explored.
5. Routinely review roles.
6. Publicize success stories and identified best practices.

Identify one enabling strategy or continuous improvement action on which you're willing to focus for the next 30 days. This can be an action that you've already taken that you want to keep doing as well as an action that you want to do more of in the future.

Enabling strategy or continuous improvement action you will take, by when:

_____

_____

_____

Identify a person with whom you will share your plan and select a review date where you both will review your progress (30 days from initiation)

Action plan partner: _____

Review date: _____

If you've read this fieldbook all the way through and have completed the exercises, congratulations. All the collective tips, tools, and strategies we've shared with you really work! Applying them will support you in implementing the ROI methodology as a value-added, mainstream activity in your own workplace. Refer to them often and use them as an ongoing guide.

Remember, though, that there are no shortcuts to building a results-based learning culture. It is an ongoing process that takes time, real effort, and a desire to make a difference. The alternative is to put this book on a shelf and carry on with old habits. But if you've taken the time to read this far, you obviously want to improve the role of workplace learning in your organization and/or your role as a workplace learning professional. So take what you've learned (or relearned) from these pages and put new evaluation and measurement habits into action.

- Work through each phase, principle, or strategy one at a time
- Set specific goals toward your personal vision
- Break your goals down into achievable action steps
- Transform your limiting beliefs or assumptions
- Enlist someone to be your accountability partner

Keep in mind that mastering any valuable discipline takes time, patience, and a willing spirit. Take up the challenge. Commit to making a little progress every day and keep moving forward. Finally, consider this—the more you help other people achieve the results they want, the more they will want to help you achieve yours. People naturally support those who have supported them. The same will be true for you. We guarantee it.

We wish you an abundance of joy and good fortune in your accountability journey. Please let us know how the fieldbook is working for you and send us your success stories.

REFERENCES

Mourier, Pierre, and Martin Smith. *Conquering Organizational Change.* Atlanta, GA: CEP Press, 2001.

Phillips, Jack J., series ed. *Implementing Evaluation Systems and Processes.* Alexandria, VA: ASTD, 1998.

Scott, Cynthia, and Dennis Jaffe. *Getting Your Organization to Change.* Menlo Park, CA: Crisp Publications, 1999.

CD 💿

Exercises	Tools and Templates
Exercise 12–1. Ineffective Implementation	Figure 12–1. Stages of ROI Implementation
Exercise 12–2. Implementation Planning	Figure 12–2. WLP Roles during ROI Process Implementation
Exercise 12–3. Implementation Checklist	Figure 12–3. Lessons Learned Report
Exercise 12–4. Enabling Strategies Action Planning	Figure 12–4. Individual Micro Level Data Is Integrated into Macro Level Scorecard
	Table 12–1. Reasons for Ineffective Implementation
	Table 12–2. Training and Workplace Learning Tasks at Stage One
	Table 12–3. Training and Workplace Learning Tasks at Stage Two
	Table 12–4. Training and Workplace Learning Tasks at Stage Three
	Table 12–5. Training and Workplace Learning Tasks at Stage Four

INDEX